INTERNATIONAL CHRISTIAN
GRADUATE UNIVERSITY

THE

FALL OF CONSTANTINOPLE

BEING THE

STORY OF THE FOURTH CRUSADE

BY

EDWIN PEARS, LL.B.

BARRISTER-AT-LAW

LATE PRESIDENT OF THE EUROPEAN BAR AT CONSTANTINOPLE, AND
KNIGHT OF THE GREEK ORDER OF THE SAVIOUR

'Der Geschichtschreiber ist ein umgekehrter Prophet'—HEGEL

NEW YORK
COOPER SQUARE PUBLISHERS, INC.
1975

Originally Published 1885
Published 1975 by Cooper Square Publishers, Inc.
59 Fourth Avenue, New York, N. Y. 10003

Printed in the United States of America

Library of Congress Cataloging in Publication Data

Pears, Sir Edwin, 1835-1919.
    The fall of Constantinople.
    Reprint of the 1885 ed. published by Longmans,
Green, London.
    1. Crusades—Fourth, 1202-1204. 2. Istanbul—
Siege, 1203-1204. 3. Byzantine Empire—History.
I. Title.
D164.P3   1975   949.5'03   74-11847
ISBN 0-8154-0493-X

PREFACE.

——◦⋄◦——

No historical subject has attracted more attention in France and Germany during the last twenty years than the Latin conquest of Constantinople. No other historical question has had devoted to it during the same period the labours of an equal number of illustrious historical students. A literary controversy has been waged, and is still waging, about several of the important questions which have arisen in connection with the subject.

The larger question of the history of Constantinople and of the Eastern Empire in the middle ages has likewise during the last quarter of a century occupied the attention of a considerable number of Continental scholars, whose labours have added much to our stock of knowledge on the subject. Among the most important of their contributions a few may be here noticed. Muralt's 'Chronography of Byzantine History,'[1] between 1057 and 1453, is an immense aid to all students of the period treated of. It is hardly possible to mention any statement respecting any event, however trifling, within the period dealt with for which all the authorities are not cited. Heyd's 'History of Trade in the Levant during the Middle Ages' is also a monument of careful research.[2] Hurter, though belonging to a some-

[1] *Essai de Chronographie Byzantine*, 1057 à 1453. Par Edouard Muralt. Bâle et Genève, 1871.

[2] *Geschichte des Levantehandels im Mittelalter*. Von Dr. William Heyd. Stuttgard, 1879.

what earlier period, has given a singularly vivid and impartial sketch of the dealings of Innocent the Third with the Eastern Empire, perhaps the more remarkable that he was himself a Protestant pastor.[1] The labours of Charles Hopf and of Tafel and Thomas have thrown light on much which was obscure in the dealings of Venice with the New Rome. Krause's examination of Byzantine manners, customs, court and domestic history, gives a useful and interesting account of the social life of Constantinople.[2] The valuable histories of Finlay were written before most of the works to which I allude in this Preface appeared, but still show considerable insight into Byzantine history. On the influence of the Saracens and the Turks invaluable suggestions are found in Professor Freeman's 'History and Conquest of the Saracens,' his 'History of the Ottoman Power in Europe,' and in his 'Historical Essays.'

The labours of a considerable number of other writers to whom I allude have been mainly occupied in elucidating the story of the Fourth Crusade, to which the second part of this volume is exclusively devoted. Contemporary authors have been carefully edited. The great work of Nicetas and those of other Greek authors have been diligently compared with the narratives of Villehardouin and others belonging to the West. Forgotten manuscripts have been brought to light. Incidental references in charters, bulls, and other documents, have been carefully collected to control, confirm, or condemn the statements in the usually accepted narratives of this portion of my subject. I am indebted for many valuable suggestions to Klimke's essay on the 'Sources of the History of the Fourth Crusade,'[3] to Krause's History,[4] and

[1] *Histoire du Pape Innocent III. et de ses Contemporains.* Par Frédéric Hurter. Paris, 1867.

[2] *Die Byzantiner des Mittelalters in ihrem Staats-, Hof- und Privatleben.* By Professor Dr. Johann Heinrich Krause. Halle, 1869.

[3] *Die Quellen zur Geschichte des Vierten Kreuzzuges.* Von Dr. C. Klimke. Breslau, 1875.

[4] *Die Eroberungen von Constantinopel im dreizehnten und fünfzehnten Jahrhundert.* By Professor Johann Heinrich Krause.

to Dr. Mordtmann's history of the two captures of Constantinople.[1] The latter work, as well as the 'Meletai' of Dr. Paspati, are especially useful for the topography of Constantinople during the Middle Ages. Dr. Paspati and Dr. Mordtmann, the son of the author of the work just quoted, the Rev. Canon Curtis, and a number of archæologists in Constantinople, have worked very successfully at the topography of the city, and by means of the excellent Greek Syllogos have brought to light much interesting information on the subject, and have especially produced a map of the ancient walls, embodying all the recent discoveries, which is extremely valuable.

Most of the writers I have named have occupied themselves more or less with the conduct of Venice. This is a subject of controversy as old as the crusade itself. A contemporary of the fourth crusade, a Franco-Syrian named Ernouil, was the first to charge Venice with treason to Christendom. Other contemporary authors are quoted in the following pages who took, speaking generally, the same side. Gunther, a Cistercian monk belonging to Pairis in Alsace, and who died about 1210, has given us in his ' Historia Constantinopolitana' many facts which are not to be found elsewhere, and was one of the few contemporaries of the crusade who appears to have understood that there was an understanding between the Sultan of Cairo and Venice.[2] Light has been thrown on the question by the ' Devastatio Constantinopolitana,' the discovery of which is due to recent research. This work was written, according to Charles Hopf,[3] by a clerk from Germany; according to Klimke, by one from what is now Austria; according to Tessier, by a Lombard, possibly writing under the orders of Boniface himself. Robert de Clari's valuable book, ' La Prise de Con-

---

[1] *Die Eroberungen von Constantinopel.*

[2] See both the text of Gunther and a notice of his life in *Exuviæ Sacræ.*

[3] *Chroniques Greco-Romanes inédites ou peu connues.* Par Charles Hopf. Berlin, 1873.

stantinople,' mentioned on page 244, is the most valuable contemporary account which modern research has brought to light on the Latin Conquest. Indications of great value upon the conduct of Venice, and upon various other points in the history of the event in question, are contained in many of the MSS. collected together in the 'Exuviæ Sacræ[1] of Count Riant, a writer who has done more than any other to elucidate the questions raised during the last few years regarding the Fourth Crusade. La Société de l'Orient Latin, the foundation of which was, I believe, due to Count Riant, is engaged in the publication of every scrap of evidence which bears on the Latin occupation of Constantinople and other places in the Levant.

Until within our own times the controversy as to the Fourth Crusade was allowed to sleep. The narrative of Villehardouin, clear, flattering to France, and singularly interesting, was taken from Gibbon to Finlay almost as a conclusive statement upon all which related to the conquest of the city. As his account coincided with others which are aptly classified by Dr. Klimke as official versions, those of more or less independent observers were forgotten or overlooked. M. de Mas-Latrie, in his 'History of Cyprus,' was probably the first to call attention to the untrustworthy character of Villehardouin's narrative, and to charge Dandolo with the failure of the Fourth Crusade.[2] His conclusion is that the Marshal of Champagne was insufficiently informed, and was not able to penetrate the designs of Venice. This position was attacked with great ability by M. de Wailly, Member of the Institut, the learned editor of Villehardouin, who maintains that there were no secret designs to penetrate. He insisted 'that the abandonment of the route for Syria by the crusading fleet was the unforeseen and accidental result of the journey of young Alexis to Venice,

---

[1] *Exuviæ Sacræ Constantinopolitanæ.* Par Comte Riant. Geneva, 1867.
[2] *Histoire de Chypre*, vol. i. pp. 161-4.

and that among the actors who took part in the conquest of Constantinople there were neither dupes nor traitors.'

Thereupon a controversy arose in which the last word has certainly not yet been uttered. This controversy has in the main taken the form of a discussion as to the authenticity of the narrative of Villehardouin. A great number of incidental questions have been raised which are now being hotly debated upon the Continent. On one side are M. de Wailly, M. Streit,[1] and M. Jules Tessier,[2] whose able examination of the causes which led to the diversion only came into my hands a few weeks ago, when the present work was already in the press. On the other side is Count Riant, whose papers on the Fourth Crusade[3] and whose ' Exuviæ Sacræ ' are models of careful research worthy of the study to which Du Cange devoted the exuberance of his energy and the deluge of his learning. M. Hanoteaux[4] writes on the same side. It will be seen that on the whole I agree with the conclusions of Count Riant.

Each of the following questions has been and is still the subject of controversy.

(1.) The conduct of Venice ; as to which the questions to be settled are :

    a. Was there a treaty with Malek-Adel like that described by Charles Hopf, by which, in return for benefits conferred on the republic, Venice undertook not to convey the Crusaders to Egypt ?

    b. Did Dandolo intentionally make difficulties while the Crusaders were on the island of Lido, in order to carry out his part in such treaty ?

---

[1] *Venedig und die Wendung des Vierten Kreuzzuges gegen Konstantinopel.* Von Ludwig Streit.

[2] *La Diversion sur Zara et Constantinople.* Paris, 1884.

[3] *Revue des Questions historiques*, vols. xvii, xviii, and xxiii.

[4] *Revue historique, Mai-Juin* 1877.

    c. Was the expedition to Zara part of Dandolo's design
for a diversion of the crusade, or was it due to accidental circumstances, without premeditation on the
part either of Dandolo or Boniface ?

Count Riant maintains that the treason of Venice was
premeditated even before the arrival of the Crusaders at the
Lido. Against this hypothesis M. Tessier has presented
what is undoubtedly an argument worth attention, derived
from a letter of Innocent, calling upon the Venetian clergy to
emulate the devotions of their own laymen to the cause of
the Holy Land. Hurter doubts whether there was premeditation.

    (2.) The design and conduct of the Crusaders :

    a. What was the destination desired by the Crusaders,
and were they agreed that this should be Egypt ?

    b. Were the Crusaders duped into violating their vows by
acquiescing in the diversion upon Zara, or did they
willingly accept the proposal as the best under the
circumstances ?

    c. Was Villehardouin cognisant of the treachery of Venice,
if there were treachery, and does he conceal facts
which were within his knowledge ?

According to Villehardouin and his adherents, the diversion of the expedition towards Zara was due to no foreign
interference, to no intrigue, to no treachery on the part of
Venice, but to the facts, first, that from the commencement the
Crusaders were unable to agree upon the destination to be
adopted, the leaders wishing to go to Egypt as undoubtedly
the best point of attack, the majority of the host obstinately
insisting upon going to Syria ; and second, that in consequence of the non-arrival of the stipulated number in Venice
the Crusaders were compelled to accept the proposal of the
Doge to take part in the expedition to Zara. Instead of being

due to design or treachery, the diversion was thus purely accidental.

(3.) The conduct of Boniface.

(4.) The conduct of Philip of Swabia.

(5.) The conduct of Innocent the Third.

In reference to these latter subjects, the principal questions under discussion are:

a. Was there an undertaking or an understanding between Philip, Boniface, and Dandolo, previous to the departure of the expedition from Venice, that it should be diverted from its purpose as a crusade into an expedition directed against Constantinople?

b. How far was Innocent cognisant of the designs of Philip and the leaders?

Upon this subject M. Winkelmann's[1] researches have thrown considerable light. He believes that there was an understanding between Philip and Boniface.

c. When did Philip first entertain the idea of an attack upon Constantinople for the benefit of young Alexis?

M. Tessier is of opinion that Philip interfered with the plan of the crusade not so much to further his own designs upon the New Rome, or to aid his brother-in-law, as to put Innocent in a dilemma and to secure his own position as Roman Emperor in the West. His argument is in brief the following: either Innocent would fall in with his plans or he would not. If he did, he must almost necessarily declare against Otho, the rival of Philip for the rule over the Western Empire. If he did not, and the Crusaders went to Constantinople, then the great object of Innocent's pontificate would be thwarted and his influence proportionately decreased.

In connection with the conduct of Innocent, the controversy of the last fifteen years has amply demonstrated that

---

[1] *Philip von Schwaben und Otto von Braunschweig.* Leipzig, 1873.

this great Pope condemned the expedition to Zara, and never authorised that to Constantinople. It will be seen that I believe that Innocent took an active part in endeavouring to prevent the expedition to Constantinople, but this view is still the subject of much controversy. The utmost that my own examination of the facts would allow me to concede is that, while Innocent was bitterly disappointed with the diversion of the expedition to Zara, and while he certainly assumed an attitude of opposition towards a possible attack on Constantinople, which his judgment condemned, there are yet certain passages in his correspondence which tend to show that he would not be dissatisfied if the heterodox capital were punished.

While I have to acknowledge my indebtedness to the various writers I have mentioned, as well as to authors to whom I refer in the body of this work, I may be allowed to point out that my own object is different from that of any of them. While occupied during my residence in Constantinople in the study of Byzantine history, I arrived at the conclusion that the diversion of the Fourth Crusade caused the introduction of the Turks into Europe, that the destruction of the Empire of the New Rome was then virtually accomplished, notwithstanding its struggle for existence after the recapture of the city by the Greeks in 1261, and that this great European calamity was only brought about by a series of circumstances which rendered the New Rome at the moment of the attack by the Crusaders exceptionally weak. I came to the conclusion that the fall of Constantinople in 1204 was the necessary prelude to the Ottoman Conquest in 1453, and that the political consequences of the Latin Conquest thus place it among the most important events in European history.

My object is to call attention to the political aspect of the conquest of Constantinople, to point out that the Empire had fought continuously and in the main successfully for one hundred and fifty years against the forces of Asia, and had spent its strength partly in this struggle and partly in educating the races which had flowed into the Empire, and that it was only when it was struck in the rear that the New Rome was unable to defend itself; that the conquest of the Empire was the final blow given after a long series of attacks by enemies on every side, and that the capture of Constantinople by the Crusaders was the cause which brought about the fall of the Roman Empire in the East, and rendered its ultimate capture by the Turks both certain and easy. The conquest of Constantinople was the first great blunder committed by the West in dealing with the Eastern Question. That question really means whether Asiatic influences and an Asiatic religion are to be tolerated in Europe. 'Europe for the Europeans,' might at all times have been its battle cry. Constantinople had been for centuries the strongest bulwark of defence against Asia. The men of the West had every interest to maintain and to strengthen it. Instead of doing so they virtually let loose Asia upon Europe.

EDWIN PEARS.

CONSTANTINOPLE : *August* 1885.

CONTENTS.

———◦◆◦———

CONTENTS.

THE STORY

OF

THE FOURTH CRUSADE

THE FALL

OF

CONSTANTINOPLE.

————◆◇◆————

CHAPTER I.

THE Greek-speaking Roman empire at the end of the twelfth century was very much smaller than it had once been. It is no part of my purpose to trace the history of its decline, further than to show what were the immediate causes which led to its weakness in 1203, when the Fourth Crusade effected what is generally known as the Latin Conquest of Constantinople. In the year 1200 the territory over which the Roman emperor in the East ruled no longer included any part of Italy or Sicily. Cyprus had been taken possession of by our Richard the Lion-hearted in 1190, and never again came under the sway of the emperors. The Saracens had captured some of the fairest Asiatic provinces which had owned allegiance to Constantinople. The successes of the Crusaders had for a time established a kingdom of Jerusalem, and had won a considerable number of important places from the enemy, but as the century closed nearly all of them had been lost. The principality of Antioch, together with Beyrout and two or three other strongholds of less importance, were still held by the Christians. But the progress made under Saladin had threatened to drive every western knight out of Syria, and the victories of the Third Crusade

Extent of empire.

had proved fruitless. Saladin, however, was now dead, and members of his family were quarrelling about the division of his territory. In Asia Minor the Seljukian Turks had firmly established themselves in the interior, with unbroken communication into Central Asia. But in 1200 a quarrel similar to that which was weakening the Saracens was dividing also the Turks. The ten sons of the famous Sultan Kilidji Arslan of Iconium had apportioned his empire among them, and were themselves quarrelling about the division. The Armenians and the Georgians, or Iberians, had again struggled into national life. Under Leo the Second the former had established themselves in Little Armenia around Marash, where they were destined to hold their own for centuries, and to play a part which recalls the struggle for independence of the Montenegrins down to our own time. The shores of Asia Minor on all its three sides, with the exception of a few isolated points, still acknowledged the rule of the New Rome. In the Balkan peninsula, at the close of the twelfth century, the empire, though still supreme, had many troublesome neighbours. The Normans had indeed been expelled from Durazzo and from Salonica. But on the north-west of the peninsula Dalmatia and Croatia had fallen under the rule of Venice, with the exception of two or three cities on the coast held by Hungary. Branitzova and Belgrade had been captured by Bela, king of Hungary, though Emeric, his successor, had not been able to extend his dominions further south. Volk, king of the Servians, held his own on the eastern frontier of Hungary, and was attempting to conquer territory from the Huns rather than from the empire. The Wallachs and the Bulgarians were unsettled, but were attempting, on the north of the Balkans, to shake off the imperial yoke. South of the Danube, as far westward as Belgrade, and thence westward still to the boundary of Dalmatia, the whole of the peninsula, with the exception of a territory pretty closely corresponding to the newly-established Bulgaria, remained loyal to the capital.

Empire
Roman.

Until the accession of the first of the Basils in 867, the empire is usually regarded as the eastern branch of the

Roman empire. With Basil, however, commences a period when its rulers had turned their attention almost exclusively eastward. Hence the empire is often spoken of as the Byzantine, rather than the Eastern empire. If the term Byzantine be used, it is important to recall that the empire was also Roman. The emperors and people called themselves Romans, and their country, even by Western writers, was usually spoken of as Romania. The latter writers sometimes indeed speak of the European portion of Romania as Greece, but no inhabitant of Constantinople would have used the term in this sense. The capital was called indifferently Constantinople and New Rome, to distinguish it from what its writers speak of by contrast as the Elder Rome. Throughout the East, Rome was the name which attached most completely to the city and Roman to the territory which it ruled. The Turks, the Arabs, and the Persians knew the capital by this name only. The people under the rule of the empire were known to them not as Greeks but as Romans. The descendants of these races still call the Greek-speaking population of the empire I-roum, or Romans. The language of the Greek-speaking population of the empire is still known as Romaic. The traces of the ancient name are widespread. The imperial city founded on the borders of Armenia is Erzeroum. The Turkish province to the north of Constantinople is Roumelia. The Patriarch of the Orthodox Church still commonly describes himself as Bishop of the New Rome.

The language of the capital and of the empire had become, in the time of Basil, Greek. Latin lingered on in certain official formulas, and had supplied many technical words to common speech, but, on the whole, the triumph of the language of the great mass of the people had been as great as that of English over the Norman-French introduced into England by William the Conqueror. *Language.*

Under the Basilian dynasty—that is, from 867 to 1057—the empire of the New Rome had attained its most perfect development. Everywhere it gave signs of good government and great prosperity. *Long-continued prosperity of empire.*

The impression left most deeply in the mind of the reader

of the native historians of the Byzantine empire, down to the middle of the twelfth century, is one of strength, of success, and of a government with singularly few changes in its uninterrupted prosperity.   The organisation of the government of the empire was built upon the solid foundations of Roman administration and of Greek municipal government.   From the selection of Byzantium as his capital by Constantine down to 1057, the machine of government had worked steadily and well.   There had been few violent changes.   There had been general accumulation of wealth.   There had been security for life and property, and a good administration of law under a system of jurisprudence brought, indeed, from Rome, but developed in Constantinople—a system the most complete which the human mind has ever formulated, a system which has been directly copied or adapted by the whole of modern Europe, and which is the foundation of every body of jurisprudence now administered throughout the civilised world. While the New Rome had thus given to the world a body of law which was far in advance not only of the civil law, but even of the law of the Prætor Peregrinus of the Elder· Rome, the same city had developed and formulated the religion of Christendom.   Christianity and law were the bonds which united the various parts of the empire together.   But there was, in at least the European portion of the empire, a spirit which made the inhabitants of the cities and provinces self-reliant, and to a great extent independent of the central government.   Once that the communities were protected from external enemies, they had hardly any need of other protection.   They formed their own police.   They wished only to be let alone, to be allowed to engage in commerce or cultivate their own lands without being harassed by government.   On the whole, they succeeded in their wish.   Under the influences of Orthodox Christianity, Roman law, and the Greek spirit of individualism as represented in municipal government, a steady progress had been made, which had met with but few interruptions.   No other government has ever existed in Europe which has secured for so long a period the like advantages to its people.

Under the rulers of the Basilian dynasty, a series of absolute monarchs who were men of genius gave the country
security and wealth at home and success abroad. The very
successes of these emperors had, however, tended to weaken
the empire. They had caused power to flow into the hands
of the rulers. Centralisation became the bane of the empire.
The spirit of municipal life was weakened. The attachment
to the city or province ceased to exist. When the attempt
was made to transfer local sentiment to the empire, it began
rapidly to disappear. The subjects of the New Rome dwelling in remote provinces acknowledged its rule, but were indifferent about its rulers so long as they had no heavier
burdens to bear than their fathers. Thus, while outwardly
the empire had become stronger under the Basilian dynasty,
it had been actually weakened by the diminution of municipal
and provincial spirit. The same system of centralisation continued as long as the empire existed. Perhaps it was inevitable that under the circumstances centralisation should be
preferred by the emperors to local government, and should
ultimately triumph. In the absence of the modern devices of
representative institutions, of rapid communication, or of a
press, the only government possible over a large extent of
territory was absolutism. This might have been checked by
local municipal government, but the tendency of the emperors
had been hostile to such governments. Municipalities were
imperia in imperio, and the independence they developed was
unfavourably regarded by absolute rulers. The employment
of foreigners as mercenary troops, and also very largely in the
administration of government, was due to a desire on the
part of the emperors to render themselves independent of
their troublesome subjects. Still, the municipal spirit never
altogether perished. The progress which the small Greek
communities had made was in great part the result of the
development of this spirit, which made the head of every
household anxious to obtain the goodwill of his fellow-
citizens, and jealous for the reputation of the community to
which he belonged. The great success of the Roman empire,
and the long duration of that branch of it with which we are

concerned, is due to the fact that the municipal spirit had lasted during many centuries after the towns and cities had been brought into subjection to the empire. In the capital itself the population always preserved the forms of its ancient municipality, and usually had a voice in the change of emperors. Indeed, until the empire fell, it was always necessary to satisfy the population of the capital. Although it had no official representation, or nothing better than that provided by the trade guilds or *esnafs*, the populace of the city could usually obtain its object by the dread of a riot. Absolutism had gradually undermined the municipal spirit, and was always tempered by fear of the masses of the capital. The soldier had been separated from the citizen. Byzantium preserved the bad tradition of the Elder Rome, which regarded with jealousy the attempt of the soldier to become a citizen. It was the duty of the latter to pay taxes and furnish conscripts, and the emperors had gradually found it more convenient to receive payment in substitution for military service, and to find soldiers elsewhere than among the agricultural or mercantile population of the empire. The Roman citizen had at length been forbidden to carry arms. He was placed in subjection to Slavonians, to Italians, to Warings, and to other foreigners, some of whom were merely mercenaries, while others had been invited to settle in Romania in order that they might furnish troops to keep the Roman citizen in subjection. But notwithstanding these changes, the opposition of the masses was a popular power which had to be taken into consideration.

Position of the emperor.   It is difficult to form a satisfactory idea of what was the popular conception of the position of the Roman emperor in the East during the tenth and two following centuries. But I would suggest that the Russia of to-day, with certain important reservations, offers a tolerably close analogy to the position under a Basilian emperor or a Comnenos.

The traditional sentiment which had regarded the emperor as divinity lingered on long after the teaching of Christianity had made the holding and avowal of such an opinion impossible. Though the coins of Constantine and his successors no longer proclaimed the emperor as a god, he still in the minds of his subjects retained many divine attributes. Before Constantine it was not merely that a divinity hedged in the ruler, but that the emperor himself was divinity. Although the adoption of Christianity by the State deprived him of the title, yet the popular idea would be likely to linger long. It became modified rather than completely changed, and had not altogether been forgotten even at the end of the twelfth century. In its new form it gave to the emperor the same position as a divine ruler which peasant opinion throughout Russia still attributes to the Czar. While, therefore, it is impossible for us to realise the attitude of mind which worshipped the emperor as divine, we may learn much from the curious analogy presented by the empire of the Czar. In Russia the Czar, in the popular conception, is a sacred person ruling by divine authority, if not, indeed, through divine inspiration. In Russia alone would the mass of people feel no surprise if the ruler were to be spoken of as divine. In Russia alone are the ruler's acts unquestioned and unquestionable by the bulk of the population. The halo of sanctity which still surrounded the Byzantine emperors was singularly like that with which the Russian peasant surrounds the Czar. Allowing for the presence in the nineteenth century of the newspaper press, of telegrams, and of railways, which compel a certain attention to political movements, not only in Russia but in other countries, we have in this respect a counterpart of the Byzantine empire during the Basilian epoch. All that the devout and ignorant Catholic attributes to the Pope, added to that which a country parson of the reign of Charles II., who was fully imbued with the principles of Filmer, attributed to the sovereign who was the Lord's anointed, the Emperor of Russia is to his subjects and the early emperors of the New Rome were to theirs.

The conception was not precisely the doctrine of the divine right of kings as such doctrine was developed in Western Europe after the Reformation, though there was much in common between the two ideas. The more recent doctrine was widely accepted, probably because the Reformation

Comparison with theory of divine right.

had, in England at least, attached to the person of the
sovereign the attribute of supremacy in spiritual things which
in the West had, before the Reformation, been conceded to
the Pope.   But in Constantinople, as at present in Russia,
the emperor had always been supreme in things temporal and
in things spiritual.   The advocates of divine right in England
based their argument on the assumption that certain families
had been divinely chosen, and retained a divine right in consequence of this choice.   In Eastern Europe the assumption
was rather that an inspiration was granted to them on their
appointment.   A divine right of succession, so far as I am
aware, never formed part of the popular belief.   The ruler
was the 'Lord's anointed,' and is so called by the Greek
writers [1] of the twelfth century, but he was only entitled to
be regarded as possessing this sacred character after he had
been anointed.   His selection was another matter, and the
people of Constantinople never lost sight of the fact that they
had a right to appoint an emperor when there was a vacancy.
With this exception the right of the emperor was theoretically
undisputed and indisputable.   The conception of government
was of an authority over the nation with which the people
had nothing to do but obey its decrees.   The duty of the
government was to protect the empire from external foes, to
provide security for life and property, and to give protection
at sea to the commerce of merchants ; but also to propound
the religious belief of the nation, and to be at once the
guardian of its faith, its morality, and its orthodoxy.   All
the attributes which in the West were possessed by the Roman
emperor as head of the State in things temporal, and by the
Pope in things spiritual, were in Constantinople possessed by
the Roman emperor alone.   In this respect, indeed, the
Russian Czar is the true successor of the emperor of the
Greek-speaking Roman empire.

Influence
of Greek
municipal
spirit.

But, as I have said, important reservations must be made.
The old municipal spirit had never become altogether extinct.
In so far as the empire consisted of men of the Greek race it
could never be wholly extinguished.   And a large proportion

---

[1] Χριστὸν ὄντα Κυρίου, Nicetas, p. 477.

of the subjects of the empire to the last were of the Greek race. The home of the Greek has always been the islands and shores of the Ægean and the neighbouring seas. The Greeks have always been rather a mercantile than an agricultural people. The islands of the Ægean have scarcely been influenced by the waves of invaders which have swept over the mainland on each side of it. The features of the race have by the genius of its artists been moulded into shape for all time in bronze or chiselled in marble, and the living counterparts are still to be found in abundance among the islanders of the Ægean and even on the mainland.[1] The spirit of the Greek was too much steeped in individualism to allow it to give the unquestioning obedience which is rendered by Slavs. Its traditions and its intelligence alike made it take an interest in the course of government, and thus to this extent made the condition of things in the Byzantine empire different from that which exists under the ruler of Russia.

Thus it happens that while, when we reach the twelfth century, we find ourselves with abundant traces of a traditional sentiment in favour of absolute right, we find also equally abundant evidence of the dawn of the modern idea that the ruler holds a trust for the benefit of the people, and is responsible to them. Trade and commerce had contributed largely to the introduction of this new view of government, though Christianity and ancient philosophy had also had a share in bringing about the change. The people of the capital were essentially a commercial people. The inhabitants of the leading cities of the empire were principally engaged in trade. Salonica, Smyrna, Nicomedia, Rodosto, and a host of other cities derived their prosperity from the fact that they were seaports frequented by merchants coming from far distant countries. The islands of the Archipelago and coasts of the Ægean have at all times supplied great numbers of sailors. The movement within the empire itself for the purpose of government over so wide a territory as that ruled from Con-

Influence of trade.

---

[1] This is, after all, the strongest argument against the conclusions of Fallmerayer and his school, that there can hardly be said to be any descendants of the ancient Greeks.

stantinople must also have been great. The result was a
population in which there was an unusually large number of
travellers.   Travel brought intelligence and the profits of
commerce brought independence.   The interests of the population required security for life and property, and the people
on many occasions showed that they were indisposed to
tolerate a ruler who neglected these first necessities of a good
government.   We shall see that the population of the capital
cared little for mere dynastic changes, but on many occasions
showed resentment against rulers who tampered with the
coinage, or who could not repress piracy and keep the peace
of the seas.

Power of
merchant
nobles.   In the twelfth century the government of the country was
in the hands of the emperor and the nobles.   Many of the
latter were merchant princes ; sometimes, indeed, men of
imperial blood, but still men who engaged in commerce.   In
the dynastic struggles of the last quarter of that century, men
belonging to the class of nobles were continually putting
themselves forward, or being put forward by others, as candidates for the imperial throne.   The frequency of such attempts,
together with the support they met with, points to the fact
that the monarchs were coming to be regarded merely as the
persons chosen as rulers from the class of nobles.   The nobles
had lessened the distance between themselves and the emperor, and as each generation passed had become possessed
of a larger share of the government of the country.   There
was, indeed, nothing like a caste of nobles.   One family
became impoverished and sank into obscurity, while another
family, like that of Angelos, rose from small beginnings, and
by prosperity and alliances with the nobles rose to power, and
ultimately furnished occupants of the throne.   The power of
the merchant princes had been continually increasing, while
that of the emperor had been growing less.   To such an
extent had this change gone, that the rule in the capital itself
had become not much unlike that which prevailed in Venice.
The government was nominally absolute ; actually in great
part oligarchical.   There was the lingering tradition of the
divine right of the emperor still strong in the provinces, and

not altogether forgotten in the capital, but there was also a control exercised by the merchants throughout the empire, and especially in the capital, which seriously modified the absolutism of the imperial rule. The actual government was, therefore, something between that which prevails in Russia now and that which prevailed during the fifteenth and sixteenth centuries in Venice.

If, indeed, the comparison were restricted to Constantinople, the condition of things in the New Rome during the later half of the twelfth century resembled far more closely that which existed in the most prosperous days of Venice than that which exists or has existed in Russia. If the latter empire is the successor and representative of the imperial rule of New Rome, Venice was in a still more striking manner the successor and representative of the greatness and also of the narrowness of the intellect and of the internal life of Constantinople. Each city was imperial in the sense that it domineered over the whole of the territory under its rule, and absorbed into itself the life, the intelligence, the wealth, the art, and the commerce of such territory. The palaces of the city of the Adriatic were built from the spoils of commerce and by merchant princes, as were most of those of the city on the Bosphorus. The Great Church of Venice was a small copy of the Great Church of the Divine Wisdom ; less beautiful, less shapely, less harmonious as to its interior, though with the advantage of having had its exterior finished, which the earlier and larger church never had. The domestic as well as the earliest ecclesiastical architecture of the city of the Adriatic were the development of that which the Venetians had seen in Constantinople. The joyous life of Venice and its love of art were the reproduction of Byzantine life. Like Constantinople, too, the source of all or nearly all its wealth was commerce. Trade was the life and soul of both cities. Their governments, indeed, differed, but the difference was rather in form than in reality. If Venice, in the language of Wordsworth, had once held ' the gorgeous East in fee and was the safeguard of the West,' she was so only as the continuator of the work of Constantinople, which, as we shall see,

Government tended to become like that of Venice at later periods.

was in a far truer sense the first bulwark of defence against the advance of the hordes of Asia. Under the rulers of the Basilian dynasty, Constantinople had not only resisted all foreign invasions, but had carried the development of trade to a very remarkable extent. Roads, bridges, and security had made access to the coasts easy. Harbours, a powerful fleet, and freedom from restrictions in trade had encouraged commerce.

Decline of empire.

With the end of the Basilian dynasty comes a time when, though very slowly, there begins a period of decline. This period I may place between 1057 and 1203, when the capital was captured by the Latins. By the latter event the long and prosperous history of the Byzantine empire was suddenly interrupted, and the European State which was by far the most advanced in civilisation was handed over to anarchy and subsequently to barbarism. At the beginning of this period of, speaking generally, one hundred and fifty years preceding the Latin conquest, the empire was still strong. In order to show how it had become weakened, it becomes necessary that I should describe at some length the events in which it took part during the period in question, and which were the cause of this weakening.

CHAPTER II.

WEAKENING OF THE EMPIRE BY ATTACKS OF THE SELJUKIAN TURKS.

CONSTANTINOPLE during the century and a half preceding its conquest was an island amid a sea of peoples. On every side peoples were in motion, new races coming in, old ones being pushed aside. The Normans, who were troubling our fathers at this very period, were likewise troubling the Byzantine empire. The great wave of population from Central Asia, which was rushing westward, spent its force in the Balkan peninsula and in Asia Minor. Constantinople was the strong barrier at once against Asia and Arabia. Since the time of Mahomet all Western Asia had been in motion, and had been hurling itself on Europe. The Byzantine empire had furnished the strongest line of defence, and had hitherto held its own with a consummate ability to which Western Europe has never yet done justice. Huns, Bulgarians, Patchinaks, Avars, Comans, Uzes had passed to the north of the Black Sea, and had maintained a hold, for a time at least, over some portions of the Balkan peninsula or neighbouring territories. The Wallachs, the Croats, and the Scythians had repeatedly given trouble. Men of our own race, the Warings, had come with Russians, and had at an early period tried and proved the strength of Micklegard, the imperial city. The great movement, however, from Central Asia was principally felt in Asia Minor. Again and again during the nine centuries from Constantine was the empire able to beat off its enemies, but again and again was the attack renewed. During the last one hundred and fifty years preceding her fall, Constantinople was almost continually fighting the battle of civilisation against barbarism, and during that period she was afflicted by almost every ill that can distress a nation. She had defeated external and internal foes. But these conquests, by their very success hardly less than by the expenditure of her force, were weakening her, and when, during the last quarter of a century which preceded the Latin conquest, she added to her other troubles those which arose from a series of dynastic revolutions among thoroughly incompetent men, she found herself too weak to resist the invader from the West.

Attacks
upon
empire

The troubles of the century and a half preceding her fall come respectively from the side of Asia and from that of Europe. Those from the former were the more serious, and arose from the attacks of the Turks—a race which had recently commenced to push its way southward and westward. The Asiatic hordes, known under the generic name of Turks, included various tribes spoken of sometimes as Comans, at other times as Turcomans, and more rarely at first as Turks. The Patchinaks, the Uzes, and other less known divisions, were also occasionally called

from Asia.

Turks. All who were called by this name were probably of the same stock as the ancient Scythians, who were famous as bowmen. The terms Scythian and Turk or Turcoman had come to be synonymous with each other and with barbarian ; and Turk bears the same signification among the Moslem subjects of the Sultan to this day.[1] The people so designated came from Central Asia, and especially from the country which still bears the name Turkestan. They belonged to the Turanian race, and were thus cut off from the traditions, the common stock of language, and the influences which have always formed a tie among peoples of Aryan origin. The central plains of Asia furnished during many centuries a constant supply of new emigrants of this race, who, from various causes—the commonest being probably the pressure of the Chinese—were constantly pushing their way to the West. The inhabitants of these plains were then as now mostly nomads. The rich pastures which have been the rearing grounds of innumerable horses have enabled the

---

[1] The Turks call themselves Osmanlis. This is of course a modern name, and ought only to distinguish them from other Turks as being the descendants of Osman or Othman, the leader of the tribes who finally captured Constantinople.

The King's Library

people, on the several occasions when they have had a
leader of military· genius, to descend like locusts upon the
countries to the West. The Tartar emperors are said to have
maintained in the field for many years at least half a million
of cavalry, and at all times the strength of the inhabitants of
these plains has consisted in their horses and flocks. The
early history of these races is involved in much obscurity. The
Byzantine and Arab writers speak of Turks, Tartars, Mongols,
Turcomans, and Scythians, and the Byzantines, sometimes
even of Persians, without caring to distinguish between them.
The Turks, however, are ethnographically distinguishable from
the Tartars,[1] though the two words are radically the same, and
call attention to the fact that they were roving hordes, confirmed wanderers, nomads, as the Bedouins and Turcomans
are to-day. These wandering emigrants from Turan,[2] during
the six centuries which preceded the final conquest of Constantinople by the division of the race known as. the Ottoman
Turks, caused a constant movement of the populations in the

[1] I write Tartar instead of Tatar because I agree with Dr. Koelle that the
first is the form which the Tartars themselves used until they came into contact
with foreigners, like the Chinese and Russians, who had changed the form of the
word. A like cause has induced the Arabs and Turks to use the word Mogul
instead of Mongol, a form which we curiously retain when speaking of the Great
Mogul. According to Dr. Koelle's view, Tartar is a duplication of a word signifying to move or to draw. Tartar therefore equals ' Move-move,' and thus accurately characterises the distinguishing peculiarity of the race, as it has always been
known, and as it is represented among the Turcomans of to-day. The derivation
of the word from Tartarus seems to have had its origin in an obvious pun made
by St. Louis of France. Writing to comfort his mother on the rapid advance of
the horde of Mongols in 1241, he says : ' We shall either thrust back those whom
we call Tartars into their own places in Tartarus, whence they come, or they will
send all of us to heaven.' The Greek writers use the form τάρταροι uniformly.
The late Mr. O'Donovan informed me that the accepted derivation in Merv of
the word Turcoman is from ' Tir,' signifying to draw, to shoot, to move, and
' coman,' an arrow, the latter being a word still well known. The name would
thus signify bowmen, and would not be contrary to the early reputation of the
race.
[2] I adopt the term Turan to designate the country north of Persia. The
Persians called their own country Iran, and the barbarous lands to the north
Turan, the names signifying respectively the land of light and the land of darkness. This derivation is on the supposition that they are of Aryan origin. Dr.
Koelle (' On Tartar and Turk,' *Journal of R. Asiatic Society*, XIV. Part 2),
however, suggests that Turan is of Tartar-Turk origin, from indeed the same root
as these words, and would therefore signify ' rising,' mountainous.

north and in the east of the empire. Two great routes were open to them in their progress westward. The first, a broad strip of country lying on the north shores of the Black Sea, and bounded on the north by Little Russia, was the way in which the Bulgarians, the Hungarians, and, at a later period, the Comans, the Patchinaks, and the Uzes had entered into Europe. The second was to the south of the Black Sea, and was the way by which the larger division of the Turks harassed the empire and ultimately reached Constantinople.

The Seljukian Turks Returning, however, to the Turks before their emigration had commenced, the most famous division among them at the end of the tenth century was that of the Seljuks. The traditional story of Seljuk, the founder of the tribe bearing his name, is that he was banished from Turkestan in consequence of his having forced his way into the harem of his father. Subsequently he and his followers, who travelled as easily as the inhabitants of the same region do now, went southwards. After crossing the Jaxartes they pitched their tents in the country around Samarcand. They were a nomad race, terrible as fighters, and but slightly advanced in civilisation. They had neither towns nor fortifications, and little knowledge of agriculture. They pitched their tents wherever they found a place convenient for their flocks and horses. When they moved they struck their tents, drove away their cattle, and settled down as their descendants of pure blood do to this day in Central Asia.[1] The fact of their emigrating probably indicates that the followers of Seljuk were the most enterprising men of their race. They brought with them from the north the energy of a cold climate, and found the task of conquest by no means difficult. They embraced Moslemism almost contemporaneously with their emigration southwards, and immediately commenced a religious war with all the zeal of newly-made Moslem converts.

embrace Moslem-ism.

I propose in this place to point out what were the influences of the religion of Mahomet upon this and similar

[1] The account given by William of Tyre, writing circa 1180 (*Recueil des Histor. Occidentaux*, p. 22) of the Turks whom he had seen in Asia Minor, would be singularly accurate as a description of the Turcomans of to-day.

barbarous nations who have accepted it. Such an examination is not out of place if we would understand the progress which was made by the Seljukian Turks, and how they inflicted a fatal blow upon the Roman empire in the East.

The history of the progress of Islam shows that wherever a nation which has been given over to idol worship or to any of the lower forms of paganism has adopted the simple creed of Mahomet, the immediate effect has been to produce a great advance in its national life. Religion usually forms a strong common bond among a people, but no religion has ever succeeded so completely as Moslemism in causing barbarians at once to sink their differences and to unite with fierce energy for the propagation of their faith. The success of Mahomet and his followers had been marvellous, and remains unexampled in history. The whole of Arabia had accepted Islam during the lifetime of the prophet. The Empire had lost Damascus and great part of Syria in the year after his death in 632. Five years later the Saracens captured Jerusalem. In 640 they took Alexandria. Persia and Egypt almost immediately afterwards fell under their sway. In 668 they made an obstinate attack upon Constantinople itself. Large conquests had been made in Central Asia. The Christian kingdoms of North Africa were rapidly wiped out, and the whole of Spain, with the exception of the north-western corner, had to accept the yoke of the Moors. It appeared as if Western Europe would have to share the lot of Christian Syria and Africa. The invaders passed the Pyrenees, and the fate of Europe trembled in the balance, when the decisive victory of Charles Martel at the great battle of Tours in 732, exactly a century after the death of Mahomet, turned the scale in favour of Christianity, and rescued Western Europe from the religion and law of Mahomet. A few years before, namely in 718, Europe had experienced a deliverance in the East of at least equal importance with that obtained at Tours. The strongest army which Arabia had ever furnished made an attack upon Constantinople, and 180,000 men and a great fleet were utterly defeated by the military skill of the Byzantine generals. The tide of Mahometan progress was, however, only momentarily

Immediate effect of Mahometanism beneficial.

Its early successes.

checked, and amid the conquests in the East as far as Sinde the failure before Constantinople was forgotten.

Among the causes which contributed to this amazing success were the enthusiasm with which Mahomet had inspired his followers, the peculiar character of his teaching, and the accidental circumstances of the time in Arabia and Syria. Much was no doubt due to the enthusiasm with which Mahomet by his personal influence inspired his followers. Every Caliph or pretender to authority over Moslems has claimed to reign in his name. Mahomet to-day rules over Moslemdom in a sense in which Jesus does not rule over Christendom. Mahomet only claimed that he was the Apostle of God, and distinctly repudiated any title to divinity, and his followers have never asserted the higher claim. The Christian Church, on the other hand, has almost universally affirmed that Jesus is God. Yet the authority of Mahomet is much more absolute over Islam than that of the Divine Founder over Christendom. While Christians, or, to speak correctly, some of them, claim that the Bible is the only safe guide in matters of religion, all Moslems admit that the Koran is all that any Christians admit the Bible to be, and is, moreover, the rule of daily life in things temporal as well as spiritual. The Christian Church, in its various forms of organisation, has taken possession of much of the power over the followers of Christ which belongs in Mahometan countries to the direct authority of the successors of Mahomet. The Prophet's acts and words constitute throughout Islam the standard of morality.

The explanation of his influence is to be found in various facts—in the strong individuality and power of attraction which Mahomet possessed, 'as one of the great governing and leavening minds of the world, one able to stamp his own image upon nations and generations;'[1] in the character of his teaching, which in the short and simple creed repeated at least three times daily associates the name of the Prophet with that of God, whose greatness and unity are for ever insisted on; but above all, I think, in the fact that the character of Mahomet is one which is much more likely to

---

[1] *Religions of the World*, F. D. Maurice, p. 18.

attract barbarous men than that of the meek and gentle
Jesus. The 'White Christ' of our forefathers, the beloved of
children and women, the Teacher who had not where to lay
His head, who bade His followers when struck on one cheek
to turn the other, who forbade His disciples to use force, who
was in sympathy with the poor in spirit and who prayed that
His murderers might be forgiven, whose religion demands
self-sacrifice as the first of duties, appeals to those who are
capable of a lofty ideal. The acceptance of Christianity has
a humanising effect, which becomes the stronger the more
thoroughly the people embracing it become imbued with the
teaching and the spirit of its Founder. The claim that
Christianity has done more than any other religion towards
diminishing the amount of cruelty and suffering in the world
is a just one. The Christian Churches, indeed, like most other
human institutions, have had a tendency to become crystallised, to become the apologists of abuses, as of slavery and
of others which they have found in existence. Progressive
spirits have, however, always found teaching in the Bible which
has enabled them to attack such abuses. Christianity has
thus always been better than the teaching of the Churches. Its
tendency is humanitarian, and at all times has supplied men
with encouragement who have longed to realise a loftier
ideal. It would be, perhaps, fair to say that the Christian
Churches or sects which have most directly aimed at living in
accordance with the teaching of Christ have been those which
have been foremost in aiding every kind of work which has
had for its object the benefit of humanity. Self-sacrifice for
the benefit of others is of the essence of Christianity, and may
yet, deriving its arguments from early Christian teaching, be
capable of advocating opinions and bringing about results,
the mere mention of which would shock the existing orthodoxy of the Churches. But the teaching of self-sacrifice,
meekness, and humility is repugnant to a barbarous and a
warlike people. A religious system which requires merely
the acceptance of a simple creed, the first part of which is
ennobling and the second a direct incentive to fighting, and
which is coupled in the believer's mind with the conferring of

the highest rewards in case he dies fighting against the unbeliever, is much more likely to be popular with a naturally
warlike horde than a religion of lowliness and self-denial. The
Moslem ideal during life and its heaven after death were in
every way as welcome to the barbaric mind as those of
Christianity were repugnant. Mahometanism and Christianity
are alike missionary religions, and, judged by their fruits, the
former has furnished equally as strong incentives towards the
propagation of its faith as the latter. But the missionary
spirit is widely different. Every Mahometan army was for
centuries, and to a considerable extent even now is, an army
engaged in Holy War. There have been Christian soldiers
in plenty, but it has been only at rare intervals that there
has been a Christian army which has believed itself engaged
in a Holy War. There is and has always been a lurking belief
among the followers of Jesus that fighting is an unchristian
occupation, and that the Christian soldier is Christian in spite
of his profession. Fighting the unbeliever is, to the Moslem,
the highest of duties, because a missionary duty, and death
in such a fight merits and obtains the highest reward. The
Moslem soldier is the minister of God's will and of His vengeance. His life may be impure, but he can atone for every
crime as a fighter against the unfaithful, and, dying, can
obtain the crown of the highest sensual felicity conceivable to
a barbarian. The religion thus appeals on the one side to
the highest, and on the other to the lowest side of human
nature. Hence it is that wherever Moslemism has been
received it has been followed by a remarkable access of fighting power. The central fact which Moslem teaching insists
upon in regard to God is His greatness. Christian teaching
calls attention rather to His goodness. The daily prayer of
the Moslem begins with the declaration ' God is great,' and
this declaration is repeated again and again in each recital of
the ordinary daily prayer. The daily prayer throughout
Christendom, common to all Christians as being that of their
Founder, begins with an assumption of the fatherhood of
God. The cry of the Muezzin, which is ringing in my ears
while writing these pages, is ' God is great, God is great,

God is great! There is only one God, and Mahomet is His apostle. Come to prayer, come to salvation : God is great!' The difference in the lives of the Founders of the two religions is like that which exists between the two creeds. Mahomet is the warrior, the apostle to drive men into the acceptance of his creed if need be. Jesus is the meek and lowly, whom His followers have represented as wishing to draw all men to Him with cords of love. To barbarian converts the oft-repeated creed gives the great conception of Monotheism. It meant, God exists ; there is but one God, a living and a great God ; all these pictures of the Christians, these images of the pagans, this fire of the Persians, are dead things. It meant the realisation that there is a God, whose greatness it is impossible to realise. God's prophet is Mahomet, and we are the servants of God, to accomplish His will, to put down His enemies, to kill pagans outright, and to subdue all nations who refuse to recognise the mission of Mahomet to carry out God's will. The teachings of the Koran are unknown to the mass of the followers of Mahomet, as those of any religion are for the most part unknown to ignorant masses ; but the two doctrines known to every Mahometan, proclaimed universally throughout Islam with the clarion-like clearness and constant reiteration necessary for a popular creed, are that God is great, and that His will, as revealed through Mahomet, is to subdue the enemies of God and Mahomet. To recognise these doctrines and to live up to them is to be faithful, to refuse to recognise them is to be an unbeliever.

The feeling of superiority which such a revelation supplies over races which have not acquired such knowledge gives compactness to the nation, all the members of which believe they are specially under the Divine protection. Translated into action, this portion of the creed means that it is the duty of those who have accepted Mahomet's teaching to regard as enemies those who have not so accepted it. The result was that an amount of fanaticism was created in fighting, which at various times in the history of Moslem states has carried on their armies irresistibly to victory. The Moslem faith, with its sure and certain hope of black-eyed houris, has

Islam makes believers fighters.

always supplied a certain amount of fanaticism ; but Moslem fanaticism has always been at its height when its non-sensual, its great positive side, the revelation to men, who had ceased to believe in their idolatry, of the existence of a God, has first dawned upon its votaries.

Final influence of Mahome-tanism is deadly,

I am speaking here of the influence of Moslemism when it is first embraced by a savage or barbarous race, and it is with this period that I am mainly and almost exclusively concerned.   There comes a time in the history of such a race, after its adoption of Islam, when. other teachings of the religious system come into play, and when the poison of Moslemism begins to work.   Family life is impossible where Islamism exists.   Sensuality has everywhere been increased under its rule—a sensuality which causes directly and surely a moral and physical decay of the race.   ' Mahomet,' says Sprengel, who has written an exhaustive life of the Prophet, ' became a licentious theocrat.'   Mahomet affirmed that his devotion was increased by the innocent pleasures of sen-suality and perfumes.   Wherever his religion has had full sway the consequent increase of sensuality has always been the means of weakening the race.   The modern Turks have diminished in numbers, have been incapable of advancing in civilisation, have lost ground, and have gradually become weaker through their sensuality, and especially through that form of it which is least known where Christianity prevails. The inevitable and invariable history of Moslem races after the first spurt has been spent which the adoption of Mono-theism had given them has been the same—decay in family life ; spasmodic attempts to bring about a revival of religious and political life ; steady but sure decay.[1]

especially in destroy-ing family life.

The fact that family life is impossible among a Moslem people, that to raise the position of woman is contrary to the teaching of the Koran, that in common belief women have no souls and are necessarily degraded, is the great and un-answerable indictment upon which Moslemism must be con-

---

[1] Or, as described by Mr. Palgrave, ' Convulsive fanaticism alternating with lethargic torpor, transient vigour followed by long and irremediable decay ; such is the general history of Mahomedan governments and races.'

demned as an enemy to civilisation. Weighed in the balance against the lowest and most degrading form of Christianity, it is found wanting. No matter how completely even an Abyssinian or Chaldean Christianity has forgotten the body of principles which Western Churches have treasured, it has yet never invented a theory by which it becomes degrading for a man to live as an equal with his wife and children. It has never tolerated polygamy or recognised the sinlessness of concubinage. It has never allowed marriages for a limited time,[1] or an almost unchecked power of divorce and exchange,[2] or allowed the husband to repudiate his wife without any reason being assigned and without warning. It has never made rules as to intercourse with slaves, which make the abolition of slavery impossible in Moslem states. Lastly, no form of Christianity or any other great religious system has ever offered as a reward to its followers a heaven where the enjoyments are purely sensual. The advance made under certain forms of Christianity has been often slow, but the fault cannot fairly be laid to the charge of Christianity itself. Mahometanism, however, by debasing the race and by presenting a base ideal, makes progress in morals or civilisation impossible. Whether Moslemism be examined by the lights of its sacred books, or historically, by the light of its practical working, it will be found to be baneful to the race which adopts it. I have suggested some of the teachings which make it a hindrance to progress, and which would lead an observer to condemn it *à priori.* I am willing to admit that thousands of Moslems are better than their creed. But, judging such creed historically, looking over the centuries and avoiding individual cases, if the practical rule, ' By their fruits shall ye know them,' be applied, the conclusion cannot be evaded that Moslemism is a mischievous creed, and, except on its first adoption, is a distinct hindrance to progress in a nation.[3]

---

[1] Hughes's *Notes on Mahommedanism,* p. 178. The Sunis are said to have abrogated this law, although the easiness of divorce virtually amounts to the same thing.   [2] *Sura,* iv. 18.

[3] What I have said on the sensuality of Moslemism results partly from my own observation during residence in Turkey and partly from the observations

It was in the early stage of their history that the Seljukian Turks embraced Moslemism. The fierce northern energy of these Asiatic warriors became at once fired with religious fanaticism, and their history continues to be for a considerable time an almost unbroken series of triumphs.

Seljuk was succeeded by his grandson, Togrul, who was filled with fervour for his faith. After the conquest of any city his first care was to build a mosque, and it was only after

of a crowd of writers on the subject. Sir William Muir has many remarks on the subject. He errs, in my opinion, in taking too charitable a view of Mahomet's personal character, as I trust that another great Oriental scholar, the Rev. Mr. Koelle, will shortly prove. But he says: 'Polygamy, with the barbarous institution of servile concubinage, is the worm at the root of Islam, the secret of its decadence. By it the purity and the virtue of the family tie are touched . . . the State itself too often crumbles to pieces.'—*Life of Mahommed*, p. 60. A very thoughtful paper in the *British Quarterly Review*, April, 1882, on 'Mahommedanism and the Ottoman Turks,' from the pen of one who has had exceptional opportunities of forming a right judgment on the practical working of Moslemism among the Turks, and who is known to me as a cool observer, calls special attention to the deadly effects of the sensual teaching upon the Ottoman Turks. He concludes that the Turks 'will become extinct as a race,' and adds that 'the most potent cause' of this extinction 'is the inherent corruption of the people themselves.' He believes that 'the sensual character of the Turks is derived from and nurtured to a very large extent by their religion. 'He (Mahomet) was a sensualist, and his religion is a sensual religion ;' and again, 'The antipathy of the Christians to the Turks is due more to the dread of their sensual passions than to mere religious animosity. No Christian likes his children to associate with the Turks ; especially is he careful to prevent his sons remaining alone with them.' This writer specially calls attention to the terrible prevalence of one form of sensuality. Dr. Hamlin, the founder of the American College on the Bos-phorus, says (*Among the Turks*, p. 349): 'The fourth and worst attribute of Moslemism is its sensualism. . . . The Mahommedan religion is found in the traditions more than in the Koran. The multitude know little of the Koran except through tradition : this is sensualistic in the extreme ; it is untranslatably vile.' It would be easy to multiply testimony to show how completely sensuality has saturated the Ottoman Turks. Their ordinary language in anger is sufficient evidence to those who hear it. The Hon. Mrs. Digby, who died recently in Damascus, and who had had better opportunities, perhaps, than any other English woman of knowing what harem life is, spoke to me of the sensuality among the more respectable classes as being indescribably great, though an even more striking feature of such life, according to her, was its utter imbecility and childish-ness. In *Harem Life in Egypt and Constantinople*, by Emmeline Lott (4th edition), the writer says: 'Their conversation (that is, of the ladies in a royal harem) invariably touched upon things which in Europe are regarded as criminal, abominably indecent, filthy, and disgusting.' Our own consular reports give abundant evidence that the Ottoman Turks are dying out rapidly from natural causes.

the sacred building was completed that he ventured to lay the foundations of a palace. He extended the dominion of the Seljuk Turks eastward, southward, and westward. He made himself ruler of Persia. He inflicted upon Christendom a serious blow in the conquest of Iberia, the modern Georgia, and in the partial destruction of Armenia, which had hitherto existed as the first barrier of Christendom against the inroads of Asiatic races. Armenia had been invaded by the Seljuks or by other Turks as early as 1016, and from that time was the object of a series of attacks. The invaders, though often defeated, were as continually reinforced by new emigrants, tempted by the rich rewards to be obtained by the sack of wealthy cities and the plunder of comparatively civilised provinces. The city of Arsen was the principal object of one of these attacks. It had long been the great city of Eastern Asia Minor, the centre of Asiatic trade, the depôt for merchandise transmitted overland from Persia and India to the Eastern empire and Europe generally. It was full of warehouses belonging to Armenians and Syrians, and is said to have contained 800 churches and 300,000 people. Having failed to capture the city, Togrul's general succeeded in burning it. The destruction of so much wealth struck a fatal blow at Armenian commerce, and was the first of a long series of acts of destruction by which the Turks have marked the whole course of their dealings with Indo-Germanic peoples, and have converted some of the richest and most populous cities and provinces in the world into comparative deserts. The Armenians fought bravely even after the destruction of Arsen. Togrul's army met them in great force in 1048, and a battle was fought, which, though indecisive, compelled the general to change his plan of attack upon Asia Minor. In the same year Togrul in person invaded the provinces of the Emperor of Constantinople. The independent principality of Kars was attacked by him and the Armenians were defeated, but in an attack upon Manzikert Togrul was compelled to retire into Persia. In 1052 he again invaded the Empire, but the Greeks with the aid of the Warings, or, as they are generally called by the

[margin note:] Togrul attacks Armenia.

Byzantine writers, the Varangians, marched to meet him in such force that the invaders did not venture to give battle. Eight years later he again attempted an invasion of the Empire on the frontier of Mesopotamia, but without any decisive result.

He becomes Caliph.

Togrul had, however, obtained a success which added greatly to his influence over his followers and over Mahometans generally. There were rival claimants for the Caliphate, one of whom resided at Bagdad, the other in Egypt. Togrul threw the weight of his influence in favour of the Bagdad claimant, defeated and executed the chief of a rebellion against him, and then contrived to have himself named as the temporal substitute of the Caliph.[1] He thus became the Commander of the Faithful and Protector of the Mussulmans.[2] Togrul died in 1063.

His successor was Alparslan, 'the Strong Lion,' who reigned from 1063 to 1073. It is unnecessary for my purpose to attempt to follow in detail the career of this Sultan—a career which was one long series of attacks upon the dominions of the Empire in Asia Minor and upon the neighbouring states of Georgia and Armenia. The latter had developed a large amount of industry, commerce, and civilisation. Ani, the capital of Armenia, was taken by storm in 1064. The Prince of Kars in consequence of its capture made a degrading submission, and was allowed to retain his principality as a vassal under the Sultan. Shortly afterwards he ceded his territories to the Emperor in exchange for the city of Tzamandos. The inhabitants of Kars, feeling that there was no security against the next Moslem invasion, fled westwards into Cappadocia or southwards to their brethren, who were yet to make a bold stand for independence under their native princes. In 1070 Alparslan besieged and captured Manzikert. Various small principalities were established, the rulers of which endeavoured unsuccessfully to stem the advance of the Seljuks.

---

[1] The title is 'Emiroloumera, Prince of the Princes of the Supreme Head of the Empire of the Caliphs.'—Von Hammer, p. 12.

[2] It is doubtful whether the investiture of Togrul was before or after the invasion of the Empire. Cedrunus and Zonaras place it before. Weil, *Geschichte der Chalifen*, iii. 87, places it after. Von Hammer avoids giving his opinion.

The barriers of the border states being thus broken down, the Turkish hordes began to pour into the dominions of the Emperor in an irresistible flood. The condition of Asia Minor offered a strong temptation to the invaders. We know it to-day as a country which does not contain a single city except Smyrna that would be considered as of third or fourth rank in England, France, or Germany. Smyrna is, indeed, rich and flourishing because of its irrepressible Greek population, and of its having had for centuries large colonies of Franks who, by means of the capitulations, are not under the curse of Turkish rule. Elsewhere the fertile districts of Asia Minor lie idle for want of roads to convey the produce to market. The absence of security for life and property makes the people careless about producing more than is necessary for the supply of their scanty needs. Famine, in some districts, recurs periodically, while there is abundance at no great distance. Everywhere the people are poverty-stricken and wretched. Large tracts of country which were once thickly inhabited are now so feverish that they have been altogether abandoned. Cities like Ephesus, which were populous and contained a highly-civilised community, are absolutely and literally abandoned, or, like Nicæa, contain only a hundredth part of their former population, while the yellow faces and hollow cheeks of the unfortunate inhabitants show the continual presence of the devastating fever which Nature imposes as the penalty for allowing a city to fall away from civilisation. But Asia Minor, at the time of the invasion of the Seljuk Turks, was a country full of cities and towns in the midst of flourishing provinces. Its mines, nearly all of which have gone to ruin, were producing large sums for the government and private individuals, and were making the byzants of the New Rome the most important medium of circulation even in Western Europe. Its rich soil brought forth a large supply of grain for export to the capital. Everywhere there were signs of a local life and local civilisation which had retained the features which Greek cultivation had stamped upon it. Asia Minor has, as yet, been hardly explored by the archæologist, but the hasty examination of a

number of travellers gives evidence of a wide-spread prosperity in times not very remote. Out of the usual tracks
taken by travellers in the interior of Asia Minor lie many
ruins of what have evidently been important cities, the former
names of which no traveller has yet been able to identify,
and this although the labours of several modern travellers,
from Millingen to Mr. Ramsay, have identified a great number
of almost forgotten cities.

Its former
condition.   So far as one can judge from the evidence of modern and
mediæval travellers and of Byzantine historians, Asia Minor,
at the time of the Seljuk invasion of Alparslan, was thickly
occupied by races who were industrious, intelligent, and
civilised—races with a certain mixture of Greek blood and
mostly Greek as to language. The numerous provincial
cities were the centres of civilisation. Their walls and am-
phitheatres, their works of art, aqueducts, and other public
buildings, give evidence of a long-continued sense of security,
of peaceful and progressive peoples, and of a healthy municipal life. Wealth was widely diffused. Given an industrious
and intelligent people like the Greeks and the races which
had inhabited Asia Minor within historic times, with a
government sufficiently strong to secure peaceful occupation,
and one which would not interfere to prevent the accumulation
of wealth, and it is imposible that Asia Minor should not be
wealthy.

Attacks
upon Asia
Minor.   It was against this prosperous portion of the Empire,
which had contributed largely to the wealth of the capital,
that Alparslan turned his attention when the border states
were no longer able to resist his progress. It is unnecessary
to describe how he swept through and through the country,
and how the efforts of Romanos Diogenes were ultimately
fruitless to arrest his progress. The Strong Lion of the Seljuks
devoured many cities and devastated the fairest provinces.
Cappadocia was laid waste ; the inhabitants of its capital,
Cæsarea, were massacred, and the great church of St. Basil
was stripped of the wealth with which many generations of
the devout had endowed it. Mesopotamia, Mitylene, Syria,
and Cilicia were plundered. While the Emperor, at the head

of his army, was pushing forward towards Akhlat, on Lake Van, in order to protect the Armenian frontier, a band of the Seljuks passed him, forced their way through Cappadocia and Lycaonia, and reached Iconium, and having plundered the latter city made a hasty retreat with a large quantity of spoil. The career of Alparslan was, however, cut short by assassination in 1073. He was buried at Merv, one of the many districts in Central Asia which, once densely populated, has gone backwards in the paths of civilisation under Turkish rule.

Alparslan was succeeded by his son, Malek Shah, in whose reign the power of the Seljukian Turks attained its greatest height. That power had been steadily increasing as new hordes of barbarians from the great central plains of Asia and from the surrounding countries, conquered in the name of Mahomet, were brought under its sway. Turkestan, the home of his race, including Bokhara and Samarcand, was annexed by Malek, and the rule of the shepherd Sultan was admitted at Cashgar. In addition to Persia and the countries just mentioned, his territory included at one time nearly the whole of what is now Turkey in Asia. Malek was a man of energy and ability, and a master of the art of keeping one part of his dominions in order by means of the inhabitants of another. The Arabs, who despised and hated the Turks as sheepskin-clad barbarians, were yet compelled to admit not only the power but the desire for knowledge and the appreciation of science which Malek showed. The country over which he ruled has long been in the most complete anarchy, and it is difficult to conceive that about the eleventh century the strongest power in the world had there its seat. The Seljukian empire, however, broke up on the death of Malek, which took place in 1092, and, after a period of civil war, was divided into four parts. During the half century which followed the death of Malek it again for a little time flashed into fame under Sandjian, who won renown in the East as the second Alexander; but though the Seljukians maintained themselves for some time longer in Syria, and gave trouble to the Crusaders, the steadfast and able opposition of the

Seljukian power at its height

Empire prevented any Sultan being able to reconstruct the empire of Malek.

Seljukian empire divided. The only one of the divisions into which the empire split up on the death of Malek with which I am concerned is that which was carved out of the dominions of the Roman empire, and of which the capital was, for the most part, at Iconium, a city which to-day, under the name of Konieh, retains somewhat of a sacred character among the Turks, because of its connection with the first Sultans who obtained the right to be Caliphs. Sultan Malek, eighteen years before his death, had prevented a quarrel with Suliman, his cousin, by consenting to allow him to be Sultan of the Seljuks in the lands of the Christian empire.

Sultans of Roum. With Suliman there begins the famous line of robber chiefs who are known as Seljukian Sultans of Rome or Roum, or as Sultans of Iconium. Suliman made himself entirely independent of the Grand Sultan, Malek Shah. Hitherto the policy of the Turks in their conquests of Asia Minor had been one of simple destruction. Finlay goes so far as to say that their object was to depopulate the country to such an extent as would admit the establishment of permanent nomad encampments in the midst of uncultivated plains far within the frontiers of the Empire.[1] The history of the dealings of the Turks with Asia Minor had, at any rate, been such as would have been compatible with the existence of this intention. A long series of raids had been made, which had resulted first in the depopulation of the border states, and then in the impoverishment of the imperial provinces. What the Turcomans and the Moslem Kurds have been doing in Armenia under the rule of the Ottoman Turks during the last fifty years, the Seljukian Turks did during the century between 1050 and 1150, but with this difference, that the latter were in greater numbers, and had an irresistible number of men behind them. The result of each raid was the weakening of the Empire, which was the representative to the Turk

---

[1] Finlay, ii. p. 33. My own impression is rather that the Turks were so entirely barbarous that their only conception of the use of land was as pasturage for cattle.

of Christian power.   The great inducement of those who took part in these raids was the large amount of plunder which could be obtained from the wealthy inhabitants while fighting the battles of Islam.   Either from the spirit of wanton destruction, or to make sure of their plunder and to prepare their way for subsequent raids, they burned or otherwise destroyed the first towns and villages which they captured.   As they progressed further into the interior of Asia Minor they began to rear their tents on the lands they had devastated. The Christian inhabitants were driven into the cities, or if they submitted were made rayahs and treated as serfs.[1]   They struggled manfully against their fate.   Over and over again the invaders were driven back ; but until the time of Suliman, although their inexhaustible numbers had always enabled the Turks to recover the ground which the rightful owners had been able for a time to re-occupy, yet the inhabitants of the Empire had never ceased to be united in regarding the invaders as the common enemy.   Under the first Sultan of Roum, however, a remarkable change of policy was adopted. Suliman saw that so long as the inhabitants of the cities were against him, and were in communication with the capital by the great Roman roads, so long as there was a hostile agricultural population which could not be absolutely destroyed, so long would it be impossible for his nomads to maintain possession of the territory which they had conquered.   He therefore determined to declare for the tenants of the lands against their lords.   The Byzantine nobles claimed rights over the village communities which cultivated the lands, as part proprietors with them.   Sometimes these nobles held their lands on a tenure which Englishmen would call fee simple, and had them cultivated by slaves or serfs, or by both. Oftener, probably, the village community was co-proprietor with the noble in much the same way that prevails in the Mir system in Russia and in our own Indian village communities. Suliman allowed these communities and the slaves or serfs to

They ally themselves with peasants.

---

[1] Rayah signifies literally ‘cattle kept or pastured for the Sultan, and upon which are his brands and marks.’   The word thus indicates the light in which they were regarded.

become or remain proprietors on their paying tribute to him. In other words, he allured them to his side by confiscating the share which had gone to the landlord, and by making the villagers exclusive proprietors of the soil. This policy was so far successful that an emigration began, which within a century grew to serious proportions, of Christians who flocked to obtain protection under the Seljuk Sultans from the troubles which, as we shall see, were pouring in upon the Empire.

Settlement of Seljuks.

Up to the time of Suliman, though Asia Minor had been devastated by the Turks, as at an earlier period it had been subject to invasions by the Arabs, no serious attempt had been made to conquer and annex it. Circumstances, however, favoured Suliman in his design to establish his followers permanently in the Roman empire. During the reign of Michael the Seventh, 1071 to 1077, a Norman soldier of fortune whose name is connected with Scotch history, Russell Balliol, had undertaken to assist the Emperor in Asia Minor. He seems to have conceived the idea of carving out a principality for himself, and took possession of Sebaste, the modern Sivas, in Pontus. An imperial army was sent against him, and was defeated near the source of the river Sangarius. The imperial generals were taken prisoners, and the victorious Norman marched to Chrysopolis, the modern Scutari, and announced his presence to the imperial city, a mile distant, by burning some of the houses on the shores of the Bosphorus. Balliol, however, was well aware that as a foreigner he would be unable to obtain the imperial crown for himself, and he therefore determined to have an emperor of his own choosing. His choice fell upon one of the imperial generals whom he had captured, the Cæsar John Ducas, uncle of the Emperor. In presence of a victorious army only a mile from his capital, with a defeated army in Asia Minor and rebels threatening him in Europe, Michael made an arrangement which was suicidal. He concluded a treaty with Suliman by which the latter was appointed governor of the provinces of which the Seljuk Turks were already in possession. In return Suliman undertook to furnish an army to support the Emperor. By this treaty the Turks were enabled to fix themselves in the country with such success that their rule over Asia Minor was never shaken off. Balliol was given up to the Emperor Michael by the Turks, but after having been whipped and shut up in a cage like a wild beast, the Emperor was obliged, three years afterwards, to request his aid against Briennias, who hâd rebelled. The Emperor in vain appealed to the Turks. Balliol gave his assistance, and, with the aid of the trusty Warings, defeated the rebel.

Another claimant to the throne, Botaniates, almost immediately afterwards—in 1077—was proclaimed Emperor under the title of Nicephorus III. The Turkish mercenaries joined him, and with their aid he took possession of Nicæa, which from this time became for a hundred years a great centre of the struggle between the Turks and the Empire. His troops pushed on to Chrysopolis and Chalcedon, or, as they are now called, Scutari and Kadikeui, immediately opposite Constantinople. For a time the aid of the Turks appeared to render him invincible, but he was captured in 1078, and his eyes were put out, the Warings again being the means of saving the reigning Emperor.

It would be useless to attempt to follow in detail the history of the struggle which went on between the Empire and the Turks during the next century. The essential fact to be noted is that the Seljukian Turks were able to establish themselves firmly in Asia Minor. They already held several outposts on the Marmora, and were at times almost in sight of the Bosphorus. Eastern and Western contemporary writers agree that nearly the whole of the south and west of Asia Minor had been conquered from the Empire by the end of the eleventh century.[1] Their strongest position was at Nicæa, the ancient capital of the Empire, a city which was well fortified, and was only about seventy miles from Constantinople.

The Turks had thus, in the course of a century, pushed their conquests to within sight of the New Rome. Their progress had been steady, in spite of a series of defeats. At the same time the Saracens in Syria had placed the whole of

Seljuks reach the Marmora.

[1] Will. of Tyre, III. I. *Recueil*, vol. i. pp. 112, 113.

the Christian population in subjection. The Empire had lost
almost as much territory in Asia as it possessed in Europe.
The statesmen of the capital were fully alive to the necessity
of using their utmost efforts to arrest the progress of their
countless enemies. Unfortunately, at the time when Suliman
was gaining his greatest success the Empire had other
enemies to meet. Robert Wiscard, the Norman, was attacking it on the south-west at Durazzo, and had succeeded in
destroying the Italian exarchate over the two Sicilies, while
another branch of the Turks was making war in Europe on
the north-eastern frontier. Still, as we shall see, the New Rome
was yet to make a stout resistance against its Asiatic foe.

Turkish
successes
attract at-
tention in
West.

While the Byzantine armies had been defending Europe
on the East, the more intelligent of the statesmen in the West
had not failed to observe the danger to Christendom from the
continual attacks of the Turks and the Saracens. Among
such statesmen the Popes were pre-eminent. They had their
own quarrel with the Byzantine empire, a quarrel which was
all the more bitter because it was founded mainly on the
rejection of the claim of supremacy advanced by the elder
Rome, but they nevertheless saw that the Empire was fighting
the battle of Christianity against Mahometanism, and that it
was the interest of the West to help. Hence, as early as
1074, Pope Gregory the Seventh summoned all Christian
rulers to unite their forces in favour of the Eastern Emperor
against the Turks. A few months later he again called upon
all the faithful to go to the aid of the Empire against the
miscreants. Four years after the Pope's summons the Turks
had become more formidable than ever. On the one hand,
they had received new strength from an irruption of fresh
hordes from the East, who knew no other occupation than
war, no other wealth than plunder, and, on the other, their
power was strengthened by the appearance of another pretender to the imperial throne, who had applied for and
obtained their assistance, and who, in return, delivered
several fortified cities to them. An Armenian writer of the
period [1] describes the kingdom of Roum under Suliman as

_____
[1] Haiton.

extending from the Euphrates to Constantinople, and from the Black Sea to Syria. Anna Comnena, the daughter of the Emperor Alexis, says that every part of the Empire was at this period attacked with mortal convulsions, that the Turks overran and ravaged the East, whilst Robert Wiscard lighted up the fire of war in the West, and that the Empire had never been reduced to such a pitiable weakness.[1]

Suliman, who took the title of Ghazi on account of his successes over the Christians, made Nicæa the base of operations against the Christian population all round him as far as the Bosphorus, and levied taxes within sight of the imperial city itself.[2]

Alexis, the first emperor of the great house of Comnenos, did his best to drive away the invader; fought him and defeated him, and might possibly, as his daughter thinks, have recovered the Asiatic provinces, if the attack of Robert in the west of the empire had not compelled him to make peace. As it was, he succeeded in obtaining a treaty by which Suliman promised that he would not pass the river Drakon.[3] A little later the difficulties in the western portion of his empire compelled Alexis to ask assistance from the Turks, and 7,000 men were sent[4] to his aid. When the Emperor had defeated his western invaders he attempted again to check the inroads of the Turks. The governor of Nicæa, Aboul Cassim, had violated the treaty, and the Turks were again on the shores of the Marmora. Their ruler was Kilidji Arslan, the son of Suliman, who became Sultan in 1095, and is often spoken of by Latin writers under the same name as his father.

Alexis the First.

But now new actors appear on the scene. The same month in which Kilidji Arslan became Sultan witnessed the departure of Peter the Hermit from Jerusalem to preach a crusade. In the autumn of the next year, Godfrey de Bouillon had started for the East with ten thousand cavalry and

Crusades commence.

---

[1] Ann. Com. III. chap. vi.   [2] Will. of Tyre, 112, 113.
[3] Ann. Com. III. c. 7. This was in 1081. The Drakon runs into the Gulf of Ismidt opposite the modern Gibseh. Helenopolis, the modern Yalova, was near its mouth.
[4] Ann. Com. V. c. 4.

seventy thousand foot. The history of the early Crusades does not concern directly the purpose I have in view. It is sufficient at present to note that though the Crusades delivered many blows against the Turks as well as against the Saracens, they greatly disorganised the Empire. In many instances they grossly disregarded the rights of the subjects of the Greek empire. They regarded the latter as schismatics and insulted them on account of their religion. Wrangling as to the price of provisions was inevitable when a large army was suddenly thrown into a thinly populated district. According to the illustration of Gibbon, the shepherd had prayed for water, and the Ganges was turned from its channel into his grounds and swept away his flock and cottage. Alexis had asked for help, but a devouring host had forced its way through his dominions. There were reputed to be half a million of Crusaders who left their homes and who marched in more or less disorderly fashion to the Holy Land. Anna Comnena describes the army as like the sand of the sea or the leaves of the trees—as Europe loosened from its foundations and hurled against Asia.

But it was in Asia Minor that the First Crusade met with its chief difficulties, and the obstacles which the Crusaders found it impossible to surmount gives us a fair gauge of the difficulties with which the Empire had had to contend. Once more Nicæa became the centre of interest. The ancient city which had in great part formulated and had given its name to the creed which is common to all Christians was, as we have seen, in the occupation of the Turks. The Church of the Divine Wisdom, where probably the second General Council was held, had become a mosque.[1] Kilidji Arslan had

Crusaders before Nicæa.

---

[1] Gibbon says, in speaking of the appearance of the Crusaders before Nicæa (vol. vi. Bohn's edition, p. 386) : ' The divinity of Christ was denied and derided in the same temple in which it had been pronounced by the first General Synod of the Catholics.' This is a mistake. The temple which Gibbon had in view was the ancient church of Hagia Sophia. This was converted into a mosque, which is now in ruins, but still bears traces in its form, and in the remains of fresco painting and mosaics on its walls, of its Christian origin. I visited and made a careful examination of it in April 1882, and have no doubt whatever that it is of Byzantine origin, and that it belongs to the middle period of Byzantine architecture. It is built, like most of the Byzantine churches, on the model of the Church of the

done all that he could to make the city impregnable. Its walls, built partly under the rule of the Roman emperors immediately after the commencement of the Christian era, but mainly by the Byzantine emperors, were strengthened, and the city was prepared to offer a terrible obstacle to the progress of the Crusaders. In May 1097, Godfrey de Bouillon and a host, variously estimated, and no doubt exaggerated, at from 300,000 to 700,000 men, arrived before Nicæa and laid seige to it. A more imposing army had rarely appeared even in Asia Minor. Its leaders would have been glad to push forward without delay to the Holy Land, but it was impossible that they should leave the capital of the Turkish kingdom in their rear. The ancient city stands at the eastern end of the beautiful lake Ascanius, which is about thirty miles long. It has no navigable outlet to the Marmora, or rather to the Gulf of Moudania, though there exists a small stream by which it might be connected with the gulf. The lake supplied it with abundant fish, and as the Crusaders were without boats it was almost impossible to deprive it of its supplies from the southern end of the lake.

The Crusaders found among the hills near the city the remains of the first band which had pushed forward in the vain hope of taking Nicæa by a rush. This band had been led by a certain Reynard, and with them had been Peter the Hermit, who seems to have sunk into oblivion after the crusade got fairly under way. The sufferings of these Crusaders had been terrible. The few survivors were covered with rags or were entirely naked, and were dying of starvation. They had been utterly crushed by Kilidji Arslan. The great body of Crusaders under Godfrey, when they encamped to resist the attacks of their enemy, used the countless bones of their brethren to aid in constructing the fortifications which they hurriedly threw up for their defence.

Kilidji Arslan had left his family within the besieged city. The Sultan himself had remained outside to harass the

Divine Wisdom at Constantinople, and is therefore long subsequent to the meeting of the first General Synod in 325. It may, however, have been the meeting place of the second General Council held in Nicæa.

besiegers. The neighbouring hills enabled him to do this with
safety to himself, but with terrible loss to the besiegers. After
a siege of six or seven weeks it became evident that the
numbers of Crusaders were overwhelming. The city was
attacked on three sides. The enthusiasm of the besiegers
was fired by the renown of Nicæa, the birthplace of their
creed. The Sultan soon found that he had an enemy to deal
with far different from the undisciplined hordes which Peter
the Hermit had accompanied. The religious zeal of the
Crusaders was at its best. Priests went daily through the
host, urging the warriors to obedience, to prayer, and to
courage. 'This mass of warriors,' says Baudri,[1] 'was the
image of the Church of God, and Solomon could have said on
seeing them, " How beautiful art thou, O my well beloved !
how like to a tabernacle of cedar ! " ' 'The two armies,' says
Matthew of Edessa, 'attacked with equal fury ; the horses
shrank from the clash of arms, from the whizzing of arrows ;
the plain was covered with javelins and the *débris* of war.'
As the siege progressed both parties became more bitter in
their hostility. The Crusaders imitated the Moslems in barbarism. Christian knights cut off the heads of their enemies,
and tied them to their saddles. A thousand of these heads
were hurled by the besieging machinery of the Crusaders into
the city. Another thousand were sent as a trophy to Alexis
in Constantinople. On the other side, the besieged threw
down boiling oil on the besiegers, and defeated many attempts made to destroy the walls. The breaches made during
the day were repaired during the night. To prevent the
Turks from receiving provisions by the lake, the Crusaders,
in the seventh week of the siege, transported a considerable
number of boats overland from Civitot, the modern Guemlik,
into the lake. The besieged were at once astonished and
discouraged by this manœuvre, while the besiegers pressed
on the siege with renewed vigour. No part of the walls was
left unassailed. A breach was at length effected, and one of
the strongest towers was undermined and fell. The day
after, the wife of the Sultan, with her two children, in en-

Siege and
capture of
Nicæa.

---

[1] *Bibliothèque des Croisades*, t. i.

deavouring to escape by the lake, fell into the hands of the Christians. On every side were indications that the city must shortly surrender. The surprise of the Crusaders was therefore great when, one morning at dawn, they saw the standard of Alexis, the Emperor of Rome, flying triumphantly above the walls.

The first thought among the soldiers of the Cross was that they had been betrayed ; but the better informed among them were aware that Alexis had come upon the invitation of their own leaders. He had been asked to send his own troops to take possession of the city, in order that the Crusaders might be left free to pursue their march towards the Holy Land, and might not be exposed to the delay and demoralisation of plundering a hostile city. They were not there to plunder imperial cities, but to fight the infidel. Alexis had reached the city on its water side by taking his boats overland from the Gulf of Moudania into the lake.[1]

The loss of the Crusaders is put down as 13,000 men, that of the Turks at 200,000. When the victorious army began its advance into the country its troubles recommenced, and the men of the West learned by experience with what an obstinate enemy the Empire had had to contend. Stragglers from the army were cut off, and before it advanced one-tenth of the distance to Antioch it was met by the Sultan at Doryleon. After a battle obstinately fought on both sides, the Crusaders were again victorious, and the Sultan had to beat a hasty retreat, in order to seek the aid of his fellow-countrymen in the east of the kingdom of Roum. Had the Emperor been in a position to have followed up the victory of the Crusaders, Asia Minor might again, with the aid of this great army from the West, have been replaced under the rule of Constantinople. There was even a disposition on the part of other Moslems to abandon the Turks. The Arabs then, as now, expressed contempt for their ignorance and barbarism. The Sultan of Bagdad requested the Crusaders to drive them out of Jerusalem. The Crusaders replied to the Sultan of Egypt, who had represented that Syria belonged to the

---

[1] Will. of Tyre, p. 127, *Recueil* 655.

Saracens, that the Turks had only acquired the rights of robbers.   In June 1098 the Crusaders took Antioch ; but the conquest almost proved fatal.   Before they could provision the town which they had taken, 360,000 Turks surrounded it ; when, at the last extremity, the Crusaders were encouraged by the fraudulent discovery of the holy lance, or, according to other accounts, one of the nails, which pierced our Lord, and obtained a great victory.   A hundred thousand Turks are said to have been slain.   The enemy's camp and baggage was captured, and the Turkish general himself was killed.   A year afterwards—namely, in 1099 —Jerusalem was taken by assault.

Thus by the army of the First Crusade, as well as by the troops of the Eastern empire, the Turks had been seriously defeated.   Victories had been gained over them which, under ordinary circumstances, would have been decisive.   Three large armies had been destroyed ; but every defeat was followed by a new advance of the enemy.   Central Asia was always pouring in a new supply of recruits ready to fight for Islam and the plunder of the New Rome.   As it was in the eleventh century so also it continued to be during the twelfth. The first eighty years of the century was an almost uninterrupted period of war between the Empire and the Turks. The superior discipline and civilisation of the Empire gave them on many occasions the advantage.   The Greek accounts of victories may fairly be looked on with suspicion ; but Armenian and Moslem historians relate many defeats inflicted on the Mahometans.

Meantime the lands in Asia Minor were falling out of cultivation or were being occupied by the invaders.   That which had been a mere conquest in the eleventh century became a devastation or a settlement in the twelfth.   Cities which at the beginning of the century had been populous, well built, and prosperous, were in numberless instances falling into ruins, while the inhabitants had been ruthlessly slaughtered.[1]   The war, like most religious wars, even when religious fanaticism is only present on one side, had become one of great cruelty.   Quarter was rarely asked or given.   The

Turkish numbers recruited after every defeat by new immigrants.

[1] Nicetas, XIV.   Alexis, ch. i.

imperial armies were fighting for their homes and lives, the Turks for Islam and plunder.

Scarcely a year had passed between the opening of the century (when the first Kilidji Arslan, Sultan of Iconium, was reigning), and 1192, when the second of the same name died without a battle being fought between the Greeks [1] and the Turks. In 1105 the latter had again obtained possession of Nicæa. In 1108 the Greeks destroyed an army of 24,000 men which had pillaged the country around Philadelphia.[2] Four years later the Emperor Alexis found that a new band of Turks from Khorasan [3] had arrived and was ravaging Bithynia. These were attacked, and with such success that, according to one writer,[4] these Khorasan Turks were never again seen ; according to another,[5] they vanished like smoke. While the Empire was obtaining these successes over the Turks, the Crusaders, who had established themselves in the north of Syria, were continually struggling against them. Still their numbers enabled them to hold their own against the soldiers of the West as well as against those of the Emperor. In 1111 the province of Gihon was taken from the Franks, and the next year Baldwin, the Count of Edessa, a principality which the Crusaders had established around the city of that name to the north-east of Aleppo, found an innumerable army of Turks marching towards his territory.[6]

Two years later, in 1114, Alexis is again fighting the Turks in the neighbourhood of Nicæa and Nicomedia, the modern Ismidt, under the leadership of Saison or Malekshah, Sultan of Iconium, the son of Kilidji Arslan.[7] Following up the victories he obtained, the Emperor pushed on to Iconium, where he found what is again described as an innumerable horde of Turks ravaging the country, and captured the city of Philomelium, near Iconium. Saison, utterly defeated, had to sue for peace, and obtained it on condition that the Turks

---

[1] It is difficult to avoid the use of the term. The people called themselves Romans, though the Byzantine writers themselves occasionally called them Greeks.

[2] Ann. Com. XIV.   [3] Ann. Com. XIV.

[4] Zonaras, XVIII. 27.   [5] Michael Elycas, II. 624.

[6] Matthew of Edessa, 212.   [7] Ann. Com. XV.

should remain content with the territory occupied by them before the defeat of Romanos Diogenes.[1]

New incursions under Tanisman. In 1126 another division of the Turks appeared in the north of Asia Minor under the leadership of Tanisman, an Armenian renegade, who had with him also a considerable band of Persians. The family of Tanisman contained the fiercest and most redoubtable enemies, says Nicetas, which the Empire had seen in that age. Tanisman had captured Castamouni. The Emperor, John Comnenos, allied himself with the Sultan of Iconium against him and his successor, Mahomet. Such alliances were, however, always risky, and Mahomet was able to induce the Sultan to break faith. The Emperor laid siege to the city of Gangra, south of Sinope, and took it.[2] But his triumph was of short duration. The Moslems returned after the departure of John Comnenos in great numbers and recaptured Gangra. Thenceforward for the next ten years the war was of a desultory character, the Turks being opposed by the Armenians and the Crusaders in the east and by the troops of the Emperor in the west. The nearest approach to a peace with the Empire since the Turkish hordes had left Central Asia was during this period.

In 1139 the Turks gathered in force on the Sangarius, a river running northwards into the Black Sea, and flowing in one part of its course about twenty miles to the east of Nicomedia. The Emperor attacked them, and continued the war until the enemy had again been driven back as far as Neo-Cæsarea.

In 1144 the Turks were once more upon the shores of the Marmora in great numbers. They were chased back as far as Iconium. The country occupied by them around that capital was plundered, and a desultory war was carried on, in which the balance of advantage was always with the Greeks. Wherever the Turks could be fairly met they were defeated by the superior discipline of their enemy ; and the enemy, knowing this, employed his strategy principally in endeavouring to avoid a pitched battle.

The Emperor John Comnenos died in 1143, and was

[1] Zon. XVIII. 27 ; Ann. Com. XV. 377.

[2] Nicetas, c. vi. This author often speaks of Persians and Turks indiscriminately when his intention is to signify Moslems simply.

succeeded by Manuel, a prince of great ability. To add to the new Emperor's difficulties, the preparation for a second crusade, which was to pass through the whole extent of his dominions, divided his attention and required all his efforts lest the very deluge of men which was to pass through his territory should utterly overwhelm it.

In 1147 the German division under King Conrad was the first to enter the Empire. 900,000 [1] men are said to have crossed the Danube. Another division of Crusaders, under Roger of Sicily, was pillaging Thebes and Corinth, in the south of the peninsula, while the King of France and 70,000 horsemen had entered and were devouring the produce of a wide track from the Danube towards Adrianople. While the attention of the Emperor was directed towards the task of lessening the mischief done to his territory by the passage of Christian armies, the Turks were pouring into the fertile province of Lydia, occupying the country on both sides of the Meander, and making their way to the shores of the Ægean, where the inhabitants then as now were almost exclusively Greek in race. Before the year 1147 was over, Conrad had encountered and defeated them on the Meander. The battle was a severe one. The Turks refused to allow the Germans to cross, and they were in sufficient force to justify them in making a stand. But they were unable to resist the attack of the Crusaders, and were utterly defeated. The battlefield was covered with the dead. Nicetas says that one might judge of the extent of the slaughter by the great hills of bones which were there, and which he himself had seen and marvelled at.[2] The battle, however, had been so severe that Conrad's march was for a time arrested. He retreated, with his army greatly reduced in strength, owing to this battle and to disease, and fixed his head-quarters at Nicæa, in order to await the arrival of Louis. The French king was not far

[1] Here and elsewhere I give the numbers as they are recorded in the chronicles. I have very little doubt that they are always largely exaggerated, but no means exist of checking them.

[2] *Recueil*, Nicetas, p. 264. The notes of the learned editor in vol. ii. of the same, p. 277, throw doubt on the assertion that the battle was so severe as Nicetas thought.

behind, and on New Year's Day, 1148, had his first encounter
with the Turks, likewise on the shores of the Meander. Again
the common enemy of Christendom was defeated. Before the
year was over, Mahsoud, the new Sultan of Iconium, had
raised an army sufficiently strong to capture Marash, which
was then, as it is now, the centre of a large Armenian population. His victory was followed by the usual devastation of
the neighbouring country. Within a year he had succeeded in
taking possession of the whole of the Crusaders' principality
of Antioch, with the exception of the city of Antioch itself.

The war was continued against the Turks by the Emperor
Manuel and the Crusaders until 1155. The former were
again beaten and compelled to surrender the territory they
had recently recovered. The death of Sultan Mahsoud in
1156 did not interrupt the war. His empire was divided
among his three sons.[1] Kilidji Arslan, to whose share
Iconium had fallen, was the most powerful. Another son,
the Sultan of Cappadocia, quarrelled with Kilidji Arslan.
The Emperor Manuel sided with the former and marched
to assist him. Apparently before his arrival, the Sultan of
Iconium deemed it best to lay down his arms and submit
himself to the Emperor. Kilidji Arslan was taken to Constantinople, and a triumph was ordered to do honour to the
occasion. He was well treated—received, indeed, with too
much honour, according to the opinion of the inhabitants—
and promised to assist the Emperor in future.[2] No sooner
had he quitted Constantinople than he broke his promise,
and commenced a series of attacks on the cities which the
Emperor had recently recovered in Asia Minor.

Within the next five years two other Moslem nations
gave trouble to the Empire—the Persians and a new detach-

---

[1] Nicetas, *Man.* III. 6.

[2] Nicetas, III. chaps. v. and vi. The presence of a Turkish Sultan was
evidently a great shock to the Constantinopolitans. 'God hindered the triumph,'
says Nicetas, ' by an earthquake, which shook down the finest houses, and by
various other signs of His displeasure.' The priests said, and the Emperor was
not far from agreeing with them, that God would not permit an infidel to be
spectator of a triumph in which the relics of the saints and the standard of the
Cross were to have been the chief ornaments.

ment of Turks from Khelat. George, King of Georgia, which had struggled into life again, attacked the Lord of Khelat, who had come with 80,000 men, and succeeded in defeating him. The war which he conducted on the frontier went on with varying success until 1166, when George was defeated, and the city of Ani was abandoned to Kilidji Arslan the Second. During the whole of these later years Manuel had been fighting the Turks, and had been steadily gaining upon them, and in 1167 we find him endeavouring to rebuild or repair Pergamos, Adramyttium, and other cities of Asia Minor.

The war, however, broke out again in the year 1175. The immediate cause of the renewal of hostilities was the reconstruction by the Sultan of the fortifications of Doryleon, a strong position on the river Sangarius. The neighbouring district had been found peculiarly convenient for the pasturage of the flocks of his nomad hordes. These hordes ravaged the country, burned the villages of the Greeks, and were doing their best to complete the devastation most natural to Turkish rule.

The Emperor collected a large army, consisting in part of Servians and Hungarians, upon the river Rhyndacus. The Sultan's army was reinforced by a body of Turks from Mesopotamia, and probably also from Armenia. Unwilling, however, to risk a battle, he sent to beg for peace on any terms. The Emperor replied that he would treat only at Iconium, and continued his march towards that city. Summer had already arrived. The Greeks suffered greatly from the heat. The Turks attacked them while wearied with hot marching and inflicted a severe defeat. Many of the best soldiers of the Empire perished. The Emperor himself escaped covered with wounds. The next day the Turks continued the attack and the Greeks retired. The whole country about the Meander was ravaged, and the Emperor received the most serious check he had yet had from the Turks. Again, however, he rallied, and in 1179 the Sultan was compelled to cede the city of Iconium to Manuel. The Turks, on their side, were soon able to reopen the war and to recapture several cities.

The Emperor Manuel defeated.

In 1180 the Emperor Manuel died, and there commenced a series of dynastic struggles in which pretenders for the throne of Constantinople sought the aid of the Turks. His successor, Alexis, was a boy who reigned less than three years, and who was bowstrung at the age of fifteen. His murderer became Emperor under the title of Andronicos. On his accession to the throne a considerable party refused to recognise his authority, and his enemies declined to surrender Nicæa and Broussa. Both cities, however, were captured under circumstances which I shall have subsequently to narrate. In 1185 Andronicos was deposed. His successor, Isaac Angelos, found himself surrounded with difficulties which were all but insuperable. There were invaders from without ; there were pretenders to the throne within the Empire. In the first year of his reign he was compelled to promise an annual tribute to the Sultan of Iconium. Andronicos had made a treaty with Saladin, the Saracen leader, by which he had promised to aid the latter against the Sicilians and in conquering Palestine, on condition that Saladin should assist him in taking Iconium, and providing that Palestine should be held as a fief of the Empire. This treaty was renewed by Isaac Angelos, notwithstanding his promise to pay tribute to the Sultan of Iconium. Probably no treaty could have better shown to what straits the Emperor was reduced. Saladin proceeded at once to the conquest of Palestine, and captured in 1187 the cities of Acre, Cæsarea, Jaffa, Nablous, Ramleh, and a number of others,[1] finishing his campaign by the capture of Ascalon and Jerusalem itself.

The taking of Jerusalem was followed by an appeal of Gregory the Eighth to Germany to join in a new crusade. Saladin meanwhile observed his part of the treaty made with Isaac. He sent to Constantinople the Greek captives whom he had released and valuable presents. His envoys were received in the capital with great respect. On his side the Emperor renewed the treaty with Saladin, and returned presents even more valuable than those which had been sent by the Moslem.

Meantime the Turks were active in hostilities. The

---

[1] Michaud, iv. 201.

dynastic struggles which had commenced in the capital had weakened the Empire. During a hundred and twenty years a series of victories had been obtained over the Turks, who had been perpetually harassed and constantly defeated. Now, however, that in consequence of these dynastic struggles the efforts of the New Rome were relaxed, they began at once to make headway. They plundered Laodicea, and struck wherever they found the Roman garrisons weak. Finding that the new army of the Cross would give trouble to the Emperor, the Sultan of Iconium sent to Frederic Barbarossa, offering him every assistance in his passage through Asia Minor to the Holy Land. The Crusaders were raising the hopes of the Sultan of Iconium, while the Emperor was receiving the ambassadors of Saladin. A game of cross purposes continued for some time, the representative of the Roman empire in the East allying himself with the Arabs against the Turks, the representative of the Roman empire in the West allying himself with the Turks. While it is impossible to avoid regretting such a division in Christendom, it must be admitted that the Greeks were right in concentrating their efforts against the Turks. Peace with the Turks was virtually impossible ; all alliances with them by the Crusaders came to nought. When the Crusaders had passed over into Asia Minor the Turks continued for a time to be friendly and furnished them with provisions. Soon, however, their friendliness ceased. It was, in fact, impossible that the passage of an enormous army, certainly not short of a hundred thousand men, should not arouse the hostility of the inhabitants of the country through which they were passing. Troubles soon arose which broke up the unnatural alliance.

Differences between the Empire and the Crusaders.

In 1188 Kilidji Arslan had divided his empire among his ten sons.[1] The division shows how entirely the Turks had come to recognise Asia Minor as their own. There can be little doubt that this division diminished their strength. Before a year had passed there were wars between them, with which, however, we are not concerned, except in so far as they facilitated the task of the Crusaders in pushing their way to

Division of Seljukian Empire.

[1] Von Hammer, i. 29, and note xix.

the Holy Land.   In the spring of 1190 Koutbeddin, to whose
share Siwas had fallen, attacked the army of Frederic.   During
a month's hard fighting, in which, according to some accounts,
300,000 Turks were beaten,[1] Frederic was entirely successful.
In one battle 5,000 Turks were slain.   After Iconium had
been captured, amid a slaughter in which 27,000 of the enemy
perished, Frederic continued his march.   When he neared
Alexandretta he received offers of assistance from Leo of
Armenia, who was engaged in attacking the Turks.   The
incident is interesting as showing the vitality which remained
in the Armenian kingdom, and suggests that under a very
slight change of circumstances a strong Christian kingdom
might have been re-established from Alexandretta to the
Caspian, which might have been maintained as the first line
for the defence of Christendom.   Leo continued to give aid
to the Crusaders, and at length, in 1200, during the internal
divisions among the sons of Kilidji Arslan, he received Kai
Khosroe, the Sultan of Iconium, as a fugitive seeking his
protection.   In truth, the Seljukian Turks had become so
completely weakened by the continual attacks of the Empire,
and by the partial damming of the stream of emigrants by
the re-establishment of Armenia and Georgia, that after the
severe losses suffered at the hands of the German Crusaders,
they are scarcely heard of until after the fall of Constantinople.

Struggle
had ex-
hausted
Empire.

The long struggle against this brave, fanatical, and persistent enemy had, however, wearied out the inhabitants of
Asia Minor.   The exactions of the Empire, in order to meet
the invaders, made the population ready to accept any conditions which gave a reasonable hope of peace.   Many of the
Christian subjects of the Emperor took advantage of the
inducements which the leaders of the Turks began to hold
out to them, and emigrated from the imperial territories into
those of a sultan who governed better than usual.

The sketch that I have here given of the struggle with
the Seljukian Turks shows how formidable was the difficulty
which they constituted for the Empire.   They were defeated

[1] Tageno of Passau.

in a long series of battles, and yet they continually renewed
the struggle. Great armies were slaughtered, and yet new ones
shortly after took the field. The victory of the Empire was
on several occasions so decisive, and the number of Turks
slain so great, that the Romans might well think themselves
justified in believing that they had annihilated the foe. The
Crusaders, too, inflicted what they thought to be crushing,
and what were really very serious, blows. But the constant
flow of a stream of immigrants from Central Asia recruited
the strength of the invaders, and Romans and Crusaders were
alike powerless to put an end to their progress. The Empire
had, as we shall see, other and powerful enemies to contend
against. The struggle it had maintained for a century and
a half against the Turks, and the loss of revenue from so
wealthy a territory as that which it had lost, had greatly
weakened it. The cost in men and money had drained the
imperial treasury, and compelled the Emperors to inflict a
burden of taxation upon their subjects greater than they could
bear. No fact could show more conclusively to what despe-
rate straits Asia Minor had come than that Christian populations should have voluntarily exchanged the rule of the
Empire for that of the Turk. Whole districts had been
allowed to go out of cultivation. Villages had disappeared.
Cities of ancient renown were rapidly dwindling down to
insignificant villages, or were becoming altogether forgotten.
Asia Minor, instead of being a source of strength to the
Empire, had become one of weakness. The increasing
attacks of a barbarous horde, whose losses were immediately
supplied by the stream of barbarians whom the hope of
plunder and religious fanaticism attracted, had lessened the
strength of the Empire, largely exhausted its resources, and
diminished its reputation,

CHAPTER III.

WEAKENING OF THE EMPIRE BY ATTACKS FROM THE NORTH.

IN order to understand how it came to pass that during the last century and a half before the Latin Conquest the Empire was almost continually receiving attacks from the North, it is necessary to recall what was the position of the capital in regard to the populations of the Balkan peninsula. As the frontier guard of Europe, Constantinople had had constantly to fight frontier battles against the races of Asia in their march westward. During many centuries a great forward movement of these races had been going on along the north shores of the Black Sea, and when the twelfth century closed this movement had not altogether ceased.

Remains of many races in Balkan peninsula. Constantinople, as I have already said, during the rule of the Byzantine emperors, had been like an island amid a sea of peoples. On its north, its west, and its south, hardly a generation had passed without some great change in the masses of people who had been submitted to its rule. Neither the people of Constantinople nor the bulk of the inhabitants of the Balkan peninsula were of Greek origin. The efforts of comparative philologists have not yet conclusively decided how to classify the Epirots, the Thracians, and even the inhabitants of Macedonia. What is certain is that to this day the Balkan peninsula is strewn with wrecks of races which represent successive waves of population that have flowed into Europe from Asia. The shores and the islands of the Ægean were inhabited in Byzantine times, as they are now, by people of Greek origin. The Illyrians, whose descendants are the present Northern Albanians, occupied parts of Dalmatia,

Bosnia, and Herzegovina, as well as the country now held by. their descendants. Between the Balkans and the Carpathians were great settlements of Slavs, who had held their position from a time preceding the Christian era ; and, so far as the north of the peninsula is concerned, this fact may be taken as the starting point in any examination of the settlement of the peoples who subsequently swarmed into the Empire. That position, before the time with which I am concerned, had been successively disturbed by the inroads of various races. In view, however, of the importance which has always attached to the Slav element in the Balkan peninsula, and of the influence of its members upon the various populations with which they came in contact, it is necessary to remember that they were among the first and most widespread of the races which inhabited that great district within historical times. It has been contended that the Slavs had even settled so far south as the Peloponnesus itself, and the evidence in support of this theory has been the statement of the Byzantine writers that in the west of that peninsula there were people, called Slavs by these writers, who were of a different race and who spoke a different language from the Greeks. It has, however, I think, been clearly shown that while in the capital these settlers were regarded as hostile, their Greek neighbours of the same period looked upon them as brothers and as liberators. In all probability they were Albanians—a people who in the Middle Ages were regarded as the descendants of the Macedonian race to which Alexander the Great belonged.[1]

The Huns, a Turanian people, had in the fifth century The Huns. invaded the territory of the Slavs, devastating whole provinces and creating wastes for their cattle. They formed part of the great Asiatic race which was destined to give so much trouble to the Empire and finally to overthrow it. The Byzantine writers correctly called them Turks.[2] Like all of their race, they were a nomadic people. During the ninth and tenth centuries they overran Illyria and Macedonia, and had

[1] See preface to *Documents inédits relatifs à l'Histoire de la Grèce au Moyen Age*, by C. N. Sathas (Paris, 1880), where the authorities are collected.
[1] Leo Grammat, p. 458, ed. Paris.

devastated Attica. After the many incursions of these and
other similar races, we continually find that, while they are
compelled to abandon most of the territory they have
plundered, they leave in it isolated settlements which remain
permanently, usually keeping distinct for many generations,
but generally becoming merged after a time in the surrounding populations. Thus Anna Comnena mentions a colony of
Huns at Orchrida in the eleventh century, although when she
wrote the boundaries of the kingdom of Hungary were fairly
well established, and very far to the north of that town. At
an early period a number of them were converted to Christianity. Such portion sought the protection of the Emperors
and usually received it, being planted in isolated colonies in
various parts of the Empire. Many of these colonies retained
their language until quite recent times.[1] Ultimately the
whole of the Huns became Christian, and at the close of the
twelfth century constituted an important Christian state.
They were always a turbulent people, and gave constant
occupation to the imperial forces. In 1182 they were un-

They attack the Empire.

usually troublesome. During the dynastic struggles in Constantinople, Maria, the dowager empress and widow of Manuel,
was accused of having urged her brother-in-law, Bela, King
of Hungary, to invade the Empire and to attack Branitzova
and Belgrade, and this while she had been acting as regent
for the boy-emperor, Alexis the Second. She was tried, found
guilty, and executed. Thereupon Bela, her brother-in-law,
entered the Empire and devastated the neighbouring provinces.
He was successfully opposed, but he continued hostile as long
as he lived. In the Crusade of 1189 he gave all the assistance
he could to Frederic Barbarossa. The great army of that
prince, intended to attack the Saracens, was hardly less
troublesome to the Emperor of the East, and was greatly
aided by the Huns, the Servians, and the Bulgarians. The
latter devastated the country around Sophia. Frederic himself pushed on to Philippopolis, destroyed it, and then, wasting
the country as he continued his march, went on to Adrianople.
The news of his conduct had preceded him, and he found the

[1] Pouqueville, *Voyage de la Grèce*, iii. p. 74.

city deserted. At Adrianople he received hostages from the Emperor, and left for Gallipoli, on the Hellespont, where barges had been prepared for his crossing. His march through the Empire had left a broad tract of wasted territory and of burnt villages. Bela kept the field against the Empire after Frederic had passed into Asia, and until 1196, when he died, treated it always as hostile. The history of the Huns is, generally speaking, that of the various other races which entered the Empire. At first they came on with a rush which appeared almost irresistible. They were defeated, were too numerous to be expelled, and were allowed to settle in the Empire ; became troublesome subjects, and, as the Empire became weak, acquired independence, while always retaining an attitude of hostility towards the Empire.

Shortly after, or almost contemporaneously with, the arrival of the Huns, a first detachment of the Bulgarians moved westward from the Dniester, and, passing the Danube, established themselves in the country which now bears their name. In the sixth century a band of Slavic origin had pushed on to within sight of the Marmora, committing every kind of horror. As, however, they failed in obtaining a permanent settlement in the Empire they need not be further mentioned. In the same century the Lombards had swept across the peninsula, and bands of Visigoths had in their passage left colonies which settled around Salonica. The Avars had crossed the Danube, and had been permitted to settle in the Empire after their king had passed like a scourge through the peninsula and had been defeated by Belisarius. The Avar invasion had destroyed nearly every trace of civilisation in Bosnia, Servia, Bulgaria, and Albania. The devastation caused by these enemies was complete. They had swept away the Bulgarians. They had destroyed all the buildings in the districts through which they passed. Ruins of well-constructed temples, churches, aqueducts, and other buildings are to be found at every step south of the Rhodope ; north of it the Avars have destroyed every such sign of civilisation.

The Slàvs who are now found in Dalmatia and in Lower

First appearance of Bulgarians in Empire.

Of Avars.

Illyria are the descendants of men who were driven forward by the Avars. The number of Slav emigrants had been so great that a process of absorption commenced in these countries, by which the earlier inhabitants had become by the end of the twelfth century as much Slavic as they are now. William of Tyre says that in 1097, when the Crusaders passed through Dalmatia, the inhabitants of the coasts spoke Latin. Behind them, however, the people were Slav-speaking, and at the end of the twelfth century Slav had superseded Latin everywhere except at a few points on the coasts.

The forward movement of the Slav population extended throughout the Balkan peninsula. The Servians soon held possession on the Dalmatian coasts at Ragusa and Cattaro, and in the north have always been able to maintain their position. The isolated settlements of the Slavs in Macedonia, some of which had formed at one time an autonomous state,[1] either totally disappeared or were absorbed by the Greeks or the Bulgarians.

A new detachment of Bulgarians in the seventh century appeared and took possession of the delta of the Danube, pushing on as far as Varna. They came from Black Bulgaria, a half-civilised state on the Volga, which disappeared in the thirteenth century during the Mongol invasion. They were probably a Uralian people allied to the Finns. On their re-entry into the peninsula, they had to contend with the Slav population between the Danube and the Balkans, and soon became firmly established in the country they have ever since inhabited. The country north of the Danube, now called Roumania, and formed out of Wallachia and Moldavia, was often called Bulgaria by the Byzantine writers. There is, however, no reason to believe that the Bulgarians ever, in any considerable numbers, occupied it. Their extension was rather southward and westward at the expense of the Slavs, the Greeks, and other inhabitants of the Empire. At the

The Slavs.

Second irruption of Bulgarians.

---

[1] The Drugubites occupied the plain of Macedonia. Sprüner, in his map of the Byzantine empire at the time of the Crusades, makes this Slav people occupy the centre of Macedonia from the Balkans to Edessa. It was probably never so extensive in either direction.

opening of the ninth century military colonies had been established along the whole length of the Balkans on the Bulgarian frontier. During that century the Empire was engaged in a continual struggle against the Bulgarians, but, while any great advance southward was prevented, they pushed across the peninsula as far as Durazzo. When they had thus won their position they had not yet become Slavicised, though Slavic names begin to appear at a very early period, and ultimately their own language was entirely forgotten. During the tenth century they were attacked on all sides, but held their own. In the eleventh century the Byzantine emperors tried something like a policy of extermination, and Basil the Bulgaroctone, or Bulgarian slayer, commenced the execution of this policy by making a broad belt of waste country across the peninsula to Durazzo. In the twelfth century we find the Bulgarians settled in isolated colonies in the neighbourhood of the capital itself, just as they are to-day. In like manner there were Slav colonies in various parts of the southern portion of the peninsula. In the neighbourhood of Mount Olympus, which is now principally occupied by Wallachians, there was also a Slav people. Indeed, the peninsula was dotted over with small settlements of the races which had invaded the Empire. At one time the interior of the Balkan peninsula was constantly spoken of as Slavinia. The Bulgarians, however, were a numerous and powerful people, the boundaries of whose territory, though continually shifting, were always wide ; and, up to the moment of the Latin Conquest, were always a source of weakness to the Empire.

Another stream of people which had passed into the Empire along the broad tract to the north of the Black Sea were the Patchinaks. Like the Huns, they, too, were of Turkish origin. They had occupied Wallachia and Moldavia, which for centuries was the battle-ground of the races coming from Asia, of those who had already arrived, and of the Empire. They had on one side of them the Huns or Magyars from whom they had conquered their territory, while on the other they were pressed by a new division of Turkish origin, namely, the Uzes.   The latter came in such numbers that, in the eleventh century, the Patchinaks were defeated, and had to seek refuge in the Empire.   Protection was afforded them, but they were always unruly subjects.   Some of them had embraced Mahometanism, while others were pagans ; all were barbarian nomads.   Towards the end of the same century the Uzes swept over Moldavia and Wallachia, crossed the Danube, and devastated the country as far south as Macedonia.[1]   The imperial troops, with the aid of the Bulgarians and the newly protected Patchinaks, succeeded in driving them across the Danube.   Even in this case, however, permission was given to some of them to establish settlements in Macedonia.

As, we approach 1200 we find the Patchinaks a constant source of trouble.   In 1148 a division of them crossed the Danube and invaded the Empire.   Under the vigorous rule of Manuel they were driven back, but they returned again and again, and in 1186 and 1187 united themselves with the Bulgarians to pillage Thrace.   Their hostilities were encouraged during the last years of the Empire, when the dynastic struggles helped to weaken it.   In 1200 they laid waste Macedonia.   Their race, however, was almost run. Another division of the great Turkish horde was already attacking their rear.   These were called simply Comans, the second half of the word Turcomans.[2]   Like so many of their predecessors, they had come from Central Asia by the great tract of country between Russia and the Black Sea.   Their struggle was at first confined to the territory which forms the modern kingdom of Roumania.   They are described, like other Turks, as of nomadic habits, armed with bows and arrows, lances and shields, and drinking mares' milk.   In 1200, while the Empire was troubled with a host of other enemies, the Comans ravaged Thrace, but were compelled to withdraw to meet an attack on their rear by the Russians. Yet again they returned with the Wallachs in 1201.

[1] Zonaras estimates their number at 60,000.

[2] The Byzantine writers are always loose in their geography, and sometimes confound the Comans with the Polofzes, a Finnish people which still inhabited what is now South Russia.

Another race, with more vitality than most of those I have
mentioned, gave great trouble to the Empire, and assisted largely
in weakening it. These were the Wallachs. Whether they
were of Slavic origin or of Gaelic or Welsh origin, whether
they were the aboriginal inhabitants of the country who had
come under the influence of the elder Rome, and had acquired
so many Latin words as to overlay their language and to
retain little more than the grammatical forms and mould of
their own language, or whether they were the descendants of
the Latin colonists of Dacia with a large mixture of other
peoples, are all questions which have been much controverted.
It is remarkable that while no people living on the south of the
Balkans appear to be mentioned as Wallachs until the tenth
century, when Anna Comnena mentions a village called
Ezeban, near Mount Kissavo, occupied by them,[1] almost sud-
denly we hear of them as a great nation to the south of the
Balkans. They spoke a language which differed little from
Latin. Thessaly during the twelfth century is usually called
Great Wallachia. The French chroniclers speak of it as
Blaquie la Grant. In this they followed the Byzantine
writers, who call it Μεγάλη Βλαχία. Besides the Wallachs in
Thessaly, whose descendants are now called Kutzo-Wallachs,
there were the Wallachs in Dacia, the ancestors of the present
Roumanians, and Mavro-Wallachs in Dalmatia. Indeed, according to the Hungarian and Byzantine writers, there were
during the twelfth century a series of Wallachian peoples,
extending from the Theiss to the Dniester. Whether the
Wallachs in Thessaly were relations of the Wallachs to the
north of the Danube may be doubted. The word Wallach is
used by the Byzantine writers as equivalent to shepherd, and
it may be that the common use of a dialect of Latin by all
the Wallachs is the only bond of union among the peoples
bearing that name. They were all occasionally spoken of
by the Byzantine writers as descendants of the Romans.
As the districts which they usually occupied were the mountains or the least accessible of the plains, there is reason
to believe that they were the descendants of a people

The Wal-
lachs in
Mace-
donia.

[1] Anna Comnena, p. 245, ed. Bonn.

which had been settled in the peninsula subsequent only to that which had seen the settlement of the Greeks and Albanians. They were possibly an offshoot of that division of the Aryan race which passed across into Italy, and to which the Romans belonged. What is certain is that they had settled in the Balkan peninsula before the entry of most of the various other peoples I have mentioned, and that they had come under Roman influence. In any case, their numbers to the north of the Danube had been added to by the descendants of the Roman colonists who had settled in Dacia.[1]

Whoever the Wallachians were, they contributed not a little to the weakening of the Empire, and especially during the last years of the twelfth century, when all sorts of troubles were crowding thick upon it. In 1186, Isaac attacked them in the Balkans. They were aided by the Bulgarians. The troops of the Emperor succeeded in driving them across the Danube. Then and there they sought the aid of the Patchinaks and returned to meet the imperial troops. Cantacuzenos, the general acting for Isaac, was defeated. His successor, Branas, was more fortunate, but, after harassing the rebels, he himself revolted against his sovereign and marched towards the capital. Thereupon the Wallachs, Patchinaks, and Bulgarians made a destructive raid, in 1189, upon Thrace, where for a considerable time they held their own against the imperial troops. In 1193 they ravaged Thrace, and the imperial troops were beaten. The war continued without interruption during the next two years, during which the Emperor Isaac left Constantinople to take the field himself against them. In 1196, while the new Emperor, Alexis the Third, was chasing a pretender to the throne, the imperial troops were decisively beaten and their general captured. The Wallachs and Bulgarians advanced as far as Rodosto, where, after they had pillaged all the country round, they were met by the imperial troops and defeated. The two peoples

Attacks by the Wallachs on the Empire.

[1] At an early period the Wallachs of Dacia were believed to be of Latin descent. Leo, about 890, being at war with Hungary, ordered a levy from them. '*Vlaquos, qui quondam fuisse colonia Italorum memorantur, ex locis Ponto-Euxino vicinis irrumpere Hunnicam jubet.*'

formally established a Wallach-Bulgarian state under a king named John. Two years afterwards a Wallach, whom the Byzantine writers call Chrysos, made an attempt to carve out for himself a Wallachian principality in Macedonia. He was able to hold his own against the imperial troops. Strumnitza and Rosak were ceded to him, and he ended by marrying a princess of the imperial blood.

In 1202, John of Bulgaria, wishing to throw off all connection with the emperors of the New Rome, sent to Pope Innocent the Third in order that he might receive the crown from him as the representative of the elder Rome. I shall have further occasion to mention that the Popes contributed not a little towards disturbing the loyalty of the nascent North Balkan states. The hostility towards the Orthodox Church always urged them to try and weaken the patriarchal authority by detaching these states from their allegiance towards Constantinople. In 1202 Innocent sent a legate to Servia to endeavour to persuade its church to place itself under his rule.

Servia, a state formed out of the Slav peoples already mentioned, had now become of considerable importance, and towards the close of the century frequently attacked the Empire. The Serbs are usually called Triballes by the Byzantine writers, and were regarded by them as barbarous mountaineers and robbers. For upwards of a century they had been turbulent and little disposed to submit to the rule of the Empire. In 1124 they rose in insurrection, were defeated by the Emperor, and, in accordance with a plan very usually followed, a body of them was detached from the race and was settled in Asia Minor, this time near Nicomedia, the modern Ismidt. Under Manuel, a few years later, the Serbs again revolted, and after a desultory war were only reduced to subjection in 1170. Two years afterwards, aided by the Venetians, they again rebelled and were again defeated. In 1192 they had so far been able to hold their own under Nemania, or Neeman, and Morava that the Emperor treated with them for peace, and Servia was recognised as an independent state.

We have thus seen that during centuries the capital had

The Servians attack the Empire.

had to contend with a stream of Asiatic barbarians pouring into Europe as well as into Asia, and with uncivilised races which were already established in the Balkan peninsula.

Progress of subject races under Empire. At the end of the twelfth century, the Wallachs and the Servian division of the Slavs, the two races which had been placed under Roman rule at the time when Constantine chose Byzantium as his capital, had so far progressed as to have adopted Christianity and to have won national independence ; the Huns, the first of the Asiatic races who had obtained a permanent settlement in the Empire, and the Bulgarians had similarly progressed, and had likewise become independent ; the more barbarian of the invaders had either been totally destroyed or, like the Patchinaks, the Uzes, and the Comans, still retained their nomadic habits and were still either Mahometans or pagans, and had not come under the civilising influence of the New Rome.   Though we read of Hungarian, Wallachian, and Bulgarian kingdoms, of Servian or other principalities, yet it must be remembered that these were all rather states in the making than countries under established rule and settled governments.   Their boundaries changed continually.   One year they acknowledged the suzerainty of the New Rome and the next they claimed to be independent.   New claimants for power were constantly rising in their midst.   They were continually at war with their neighbours, while behind each and all of them was always, until later than the twelfth century, the constant stream of Asiatic immigrants, fresh from barbarism and hostile alike to all who had adopted Christianity or who had ceased to be nomads.

The history, in truth, of the Byzantine empire is in great part the history of the education of barbarous races.   The population of the capital and the Greeks of the south of the peninsula and of the islands still retained the traditions of art, of science, and of philosophy.   The student of theology and of Roman law, as developed under Justinian and his successors, does not require to be reminded how acute was the intellect which dealt with these two great subjects, how great was the power of generalisation, how subtle the power of distinction, which was brought to bear on theological and legal questions. During long centuries the masses of people who appeared in the Empire were being leavened with the Greek spirit. In time all the races of the Empire would have to come within its influence. Huns and Bulgarians had been converted from cruel savages and nomadic hordes into nations which had entered upon the path of civilisation. The conversion of Russia to Christianity, the great glory of the Orthodox Church, had placed the Slavic race upon the same road. Patchinaks, Comans, and Uzes would have also felt the influence of the New Rome, which might, indeed, have been powerful enough to recover Asia Minor had its existence not been brought to an end. The warfare of the Empire in Asia Minor during the century and a half preceding 1200 was hardly more severe or constant than was that which she had to wage against the hordes still pressing into the Balkan peninsula from the north-east and against their predecessors, whom she was succeeding gradually in reducing to the habits of civilised life. The imperial city stood firm as a rock amid the moving masses of people about her, the centre and source of good government ; the teacher by means of commerce, of law, and of civilisation ; subduing one horde only to find others coming to the front ; reducing finally all to subjection, only to begin again with new immigrants. Much of her wealth and of her strength was spent in this work, for it was long and continuous. While security and peace remained in the capital, while all the efforts of Arabs and others had failed before her walls, while in the Ægean and the Marmora she had preserved a security for life and property which enabled her nobles to live in their splendid villas in security and her merchants to pass un-molested, and made all men in the east of Europe and the west of Asia look to her walls as the one absolutely safe deposit for their wealth, the Empire itself had, during long centuries, never known peace. While the Teutonic and the Latin races behind her were developing their strength, form-ing themselves into nations, making progress in civilisation, she was fighting their battles against Asiatic barbarians. Her armies had been for long centuries thus continually employed.

Races whose very names have been forgotten were crowding into Europe, and, but for her, might have overwhelmed the peoples of the West.   From the time when Charles Martel won his victory at Tours—a victory all modern writers have justly glorified as having saved Western Europe from a Mahometan invasion from Africa, the Byzantine emperors had been waging a much more serious, because a permanent, warfare for the same purpose.   The great defeat of the Arabs before Constantinople almost contemporaneously with that at Tours was itself as great a victory for civilisation.   But while, in the West, one strong and crushing blow to an isolated body of Mahometans had been decisive, in the east of Europe this blow had to be repeated again and again, and generations of men had to be expended in saving European civilisation. These efforts, however, were rapidly exhausting the strength of the Empire.   Step by step the enemy was gaining ground. The Turks in Asia Minor, the Bulgarians, the Slavs, the Huns, the Patchinaks, the Uzes, and the Comans, in Europe, had largely contributed, and especially during the century and a half preceding 1200, to that weakening of the Empire which was preparing the way for the great catastrophe of the Latin Conquest.

CHAPTER IV.

WEAKENING OF THE EMPIRE FROM DYNASTIC TROUBLES.

AT the time when the Byzantine empire had need of all her strength, when half-civilised hordes were pouring into the Balkan peninsula from the North, when she had been almost overwhelmed by the wave of Turkish invasion in Asia Minor, when Sicilians, Venetians, and Crusaders were alike hostile to her, a series of dynastic troubles commenced in the capital itself, which greatly diminished the reputation of the New Rome and lessened its strength. These troubles were for the most part what we may call accidental. They did not arise, directly at least, in consequence of the struggles of the Empire with foreign enemies, though undoubtedly these troubles increased their importance. Under ordinary circumstances and in other times—say, for example, a century earlier—they would have settled themselves, and the Empire would have presented a united front to the various enemies who were attacking it. The earlier of these dynastic struggles weakened the Empire. The later contributed largely to its destruction.

The Emperor Manuel, who reigned from 1143 to 1180, had ruled with ability and energy. But he had become unpopular with his subjects on account of his fondness for the Latins and of his extravagance. The citizens of Constantinople complained that their own merchants were ruined by the favours which were heaped on the Italians. Manuel's leaning towards the West was due, in part at least, to his personal character. He had been influenced deeply by the spirit of Western chivalry. He was tall, of quite exceptional

strength,[1] and of great skill in all military exercises. The
wonderful stories of his strength and his love of warlike
display made him a favourite with his troops.   His own
desire seems to have led him to seek the reputation of a
Western knight rather than of a Roman emperor. Few
sovereigns of Constantinople were ever more completely
absolute than he, but he on several occasions used his wealth,
strength, and ability rather for personal display than for the
benefit of the Empire.   Had he shown the spirit and the
statesmanlike energy of John Zimiskes or of Basil, the Bulgarian Slayer, the future of the Empire might have been
otherwise than it was.   The enormous wealth gathered by
his predecessors was recklessly expended in foolish ostenta-
tion, in donatives to the soldiers, and in tournaments in which
the Emperor found his satisfaction in using a heavier spear
and shield than any Western knight.   His own subjects cared
nothing for these displays, and noted them only as further
illustrations of the sovereign's fondness for everything Latin.
They noted, too, that each time that he had married it had
been to a Latin princess, and that his daughter Maria had
been married in 1178 to Reynier, the Marquis of Montferrat—
a marriage which bore bitter fruit, since the Western writers
pretended that Manuel had made him King of Salonica.[2]
The wasteful expenditure of Manuel caused him to commit
the tremendous blunder, for an Emperor of Constantinople, of
neglecting the maintenance of the fleet, an act which more
than any other facilitated the capture of the capital.   Making
allowances for his extravagances and overlooking the neglect
of the fleet, which might have been remedied by his successors,
the reign of Manuel had, however, not been unsuccessful.
His death, at the age of fifty-eight, was contributed to by
grief at the progress of the Turks in Asia Minor.   He had
fought them bravely, had resisted them steadily, and in the
main successfully.   Six years before his death he had made
a great effort to recover Iconium, but his army had suffered
a serious defeat.   The Turks attacked the imperial army

His Latin
tendencies.

---

[1] Cinnamus, pp. 72, 140.
[2] No Greek writer mentions such promise.

near Doryleon, which commanded an important mountain-pass about thirty miles south-east of Nicæa. The imperial army had been weakened by sickness, and its leaders advised Manuel to postpone the intended attack upon the enemy. Manuel, however, refused. The army entered a defile, was attacked near Myriokephalon, and a considerable portion of it was cut to pieces. The Emperor gained a small table-land, and tried desperately, against a superior force which had surrounded him, to break his way through.[1] He succeeded, though with thirty arrows in his buckler. Thence to the end of his reign there was a series of troubles with the Turks, who were continually advancing. The Sultan, as Nicetas states, was persuaded that nothing was so much against his interest as peace. Like the Soudan Mahdi in our own times, and like all Turkish rulers, his strength began to diminish as soon as his armies ceased to advance.

The troubles with the Turks were not the only ones with which Manuel had to contend. He was attacked by the Sicilians, by the Servians, by the Hungarians, and by the Venetians, and defeated or made honourable terms with all. His greatest effort against the Sultan of Iconium had been rendered fruitless by the attack of Roger of Sicily. The necessity of watching the great armies of the Second Crusade had driven him to the necessity of concluding a treaty of peace with the Sultan. Manuel had led his own troops, and had been for a considerable time absent from the capital ; and to this cause, in part at least, must be attributed the weak hold which he had over the court and populace of Constantinople. We shall have occasion to see how he had encouraged foreigners to settle in the capital, and that the population believed that this was the reason why the Italians had become possessed of a large part of the foreign trade. Hence, on his death in 1180, the citizens of Constantinople were willing to support anyone who was the enemy of his policy in regard to the treatment of foreigners.

Manuel had left a son who was only twelve years old, and

Manuel's successes.

---

[1] Manuel wrote an account of this battle to Henry II. of England, there being English soldiers in his army.

Accession
of Alexis
the
Second.
who now became emperor under the style of Alexis II.
He was a weak boy, and of an age when it is absurd to
charge him, as Nicetas does, with vanity, love of pleasure,
and incapacity. On the death of his father there was at
once a scramble for the office of chief minister. His mother,
Maria of Antioch, who had retired in her grief to a monastery,
was compelled in the interest of her son to return to the
world, and assume the rule of the capital. Her power was
unfortunately shared with the protosebastos Alexis. The
latter, who was soon regarded as her paramour, was a member
of the imperial family and grandson of the Emperor John.

Court
intrigues.
Maria and Alexis, in order to gain to their side as many
of the nobles as possible, allowed the courtiers to plunder the
treasury, and for some time Constantinople was witness of
wild scenes of disorder and riot. During eighteen months
the court was full of intrigues, but at length the influence of
the protosebastos became supreme. His design was apparently to make himself emperor. He took the government
entirely into his own hands. He disregarded alike the orders
of the Empress and of the Emperor her son. He obtained an
edict, by which it was declared that any grants made by the
Emperor were null until they were countersigned by him. The
late Emperor's sister, also named Maria, who was the wife of
the Cæsar John, entered into an arrangement with a natural
son of Manuel and others in order to free her brother, the
young Emperor, from the control of his mother and the protosebastos, or possibly in order to depose the boy-emperor
and place John on the throne. Whatever may have been her
motive, the first step to success was to get rid of the protosebastos. A plot was formed to assassinate the latter, but
failed, and the conspirators were arrested. The Cæsar and
his wife, however, had the sympathy of the people. They
took sanctuary in Hagia Sophia. An attempt to arrest them
by force in the church was defeated. A band of Italian
gladiators and of Georgians defended them, and they were
protected by the patriarch and had the support of a large
portion of the inhabitants, who were indignant at the treatment of the late Emperor's sister and at the arrogance of the

protosebastos. The mob, led by the priests, paraded the streets, declaring for the Emperor and against the Empress and her lover, and pillaging the houses of the partisans of the latter. Meantime, the Emperor and the protosebastos determined to tear Maria out of Hagia Sophia. An army was collected in the grand palace of Bucoleon, which adjoined the Great Church, and a point of attack was chosen. Maria Porphyrogenita was, on her side, no less active. By her advice a house was pulled down in order to give an advantage to her defenders, and a strong barrier for defence was hastily constructed. At the third hour of the day the attack commenced. A great number of the soldiers of Maria were wounded. The people outside had flocked to her assistance. New troops, however, came up and took possession of the streets leading to the cathedral. The fight continued to rage in and about it all the day, but at sunset the discipline of the soldiers had gained an advantage for the protosebastos. The troops of Maria quitted the Augusteon and the other buildings where they had fortified themselves, and took possession of the porch of Hagia Sophia, over which stood the famous figure of Michael the Archangel. There they were safe, for the access to the building was up narrow streets, in which the Emperor's troops fought at a great disadvantage. At this moment the patriarch, holding the Gospels in his hands, descended and came between the combatants. The Cæsar, on behalf of himself, his wife, and their following, claimed asylum, and declared that all that he and they were doing was in defence of the church. The patriarch undertook to negotiate with the protosebastos, and warned him of the dangers of violating sanctuary. Several persons were named to arrange terms, and it was agreed next day that Maria Porphyrogenita, her husband, and her followers should lay down their arms and an amnesty be granted.

The struggle had shown that the populace was divided in its allegiance but strongly disinclined to favour the protosebastos. The latter seems to have attributed a large portion of the blame to the patriarch, and he accordingly ordered him to withdraw to a monastery which he had built in the small

island of Terebinth, now called Anderovithos, about ten miles
from Constantinople.   This design was checked by Maria,
who had now returned to the palace, and although for a short
time the patriarch was sent to the monastery of Pantepoptis,
by her influence also he was soon restored to power.   His
return was a scene of triumph for him and of humiliation for
Alexis.   He was accompanied by an enormous crowd, which
included all that was most honourable among the priests and
magistrates.   Indian woods were burnt to give incense as he
passed, perfumes were sprinkled along his path, and every
mark of respect was shown to him.   The crowd was so dense
that all the day was spent in making the journey from the
monastery, in the west of the city, to the Great Church, which
is in the east.

People
look to
Andronicos
for deliver-
ance. Meantime the people were looking to Andronicos Comnenos as their deliverer.   His claims to the throne were by
no means slight.   The Emperor Manuel himself had not
succeeded by hereditary right.   He was the youngest of the
four sons of John Comnenos ; two of these had died in their
father's lifetime.   A few days before the death of John that
Emperor had called a council of his family and of the nobles
who were near him, and had pointed out that in the troubled
condition of the Empire it was expedient to place the ablest
man upon the throne, without regard to priority of birth.   Of
his two sons, Isaac and Manuel, the former had not shown the
qualities which recommended him as a strong ruler, and John
urged that the council should recognise as his successor
Manuel, who in various expeditions had already given evidence of the ability which subsequently characterised his
reign.   Isaac, the eldest surviving brother of Manuel, was
absent when this council was held, but the members present
admitted the wisdom of John's choice.   Manuel was accepted
by them as heir to the throne, was solemnly crowned, was
clothed in the imperial purple, and on the death of his father
a few days afterwards was everywhere hailed as his successor.   Isaac, the elder brother, was for a time imprisoned,
and Manuel reigned with the free consent of the people of the
Empire.

Andronicos, to whom, on the outbreak of the troubles during the reign of the boy-successor of Manuel, the people looked for relief from the rule of the Empress and her lover, was a cousin of Manuel, being the son of Isaac, the younger brother of John. During the reign of Manuel he had been a troublesome subject. At the commencement of his reign Manuel and Andronicos had been boon companions. They were of about the same age. But a quarrel broke out between them as early as 1151, in consequence of the nomination of John Comnenos to the dignity of protosebastos. Andronicos at once intrigued against Manuel, and treated with the King of Jerusalem, the Sultan of the Suljukian Turks, and the King of Hungary.[1] The attempt of Andronicos was discovered. He was deprived of his duchies of Branitzova and Belgrade,[2] and was imprisoned in a palace. His freedom of manners, his high spirit, and his handsome person and great strength had made him popular with the people of the capital. He grew in favour with them in consequence of a series of adventures, which recall those of the young Pretender to the throne of England. It would be difficult to name a prince who could boast of more escapes, or who had succeeded in making himself more popular alike with men and women. His noble presence, and, above all, his wonderful powers of persuasion, won him admirers everywhere. Yet he was a worthless hypocrite. He was heartless, sensual, and cruel. Skilled in military exercises, he was destitute of courage, and as a general was a failure. Capable of attaching men and women to him, he sacrificed them whenever his interest no longer required their services.

His adventures began early in the reign of Manuel. He was captured by the Sultan Mahsoud. On his return from captivity his cousin Isaac and he had an altercation in presence of the Emperor, in which the first drew his sword and attempted to kill Andronicos, and was only saved by the personal intervention of Manuel, who himself received a wound, the marks of which he bore till his dying day. The most note-

Previous history and character of Andronicos.

His adventures.

---

[1] Cinn. iii. 124.
[2] Nicetas, p. 133. δουκικῆς ἀρχῆς βρανιτζόβης.

worthy amours of Andronicos were carried on with members
of the imperial family. Eudocia, his second cousin, was his
first mistress. As a marriage between the two was regarded
by the Church as incestuous, her brother and other relations
did their utmost to separate the offenders. When their
efforts failed, her brother John with others plotted to assassinate Andronicos. The members of the imperial family had
encamped in luxurious tents at Pelagonia. Eudocia was
known to be in the habit of receiving her lover at unseasonable
hours, and a number of men were employed to kill him as
he left her tent. Her spies, however, gave warning of the
danger, and while her attendants were noisily engaged in
bringing lights, Andronicos escaped by cutting a slit in the
tent and creeping between the sentries. Shortly afterwards
he was imprisoned by Manuel in consequence of his political
intrigues with the King of Hungary, but under pretext of
his conduct with Eudocia. He was loaded with chains and
confined in a tower built of brick. There he found a passage
partly walled up. He enlarged the hole, laid up a stock of
provisions, entered the passage, and from within walled up
the entrance. The guards, finding the tower empty, in great
alarm reported the escape of Andronicos to the Emperor.
Eudocia, who was suspected of having aided in the escape,
was captured and sent to the same tower, and when the
guards had withdrawn was surprised to see her lover break
through the wall covered with lime and dust. He subsequently escaped, but was soon afterwards recaptured and
again loaded with chains and imprisoned. A second time he
escaped. He had succeeded in obtaining an impression of
the keys of his prison in wax. From this his son had new
keys made, which he conveyed to his father together with a
coil of rope in an amphora of wine. Choosing a dark and
stormy night, he let himself out and reached a boat which a
confederate had ready. In order to elude the guards he
pretended to be unable to understand Greek, and passed
himself off as the slave of the boatman. He reached his
house, made himself known to a servant, and escaped to the
frontier. There, however, he was captured by the Wallachs

and sent back to the Emperor. Although at the time he was
friendless, he escaped from his guards during their journey
towards the capital. While passing through a forest he
pretended on several occasions that it was necessary for him
to dismount in consequence of severe diarrhœa, and on one
of these occasions he disappeared into the forest and was lost,
leaving, however, behind him a cloak and hat, fixed on the
stick with which he had apparently with difficulty supported
himself. Subsequently he reached Jaroslaf, the Russian
prince of Galitza.[1] His attendant, who had aided him in his
house, was a faithful Turk. He was arrested, and, after being
beaten, was led through the streets with a cord round his
neck, preceded by a herald who cried aloud, ' Thus will he be
punished who aids the enemies of the Emperor.' The brave
fellow replied, ' I am willing to be accused of the crime so
long as I am not charged with having betrayed my benefactor
or being ungrateful to him.'

Andronicos was welcomed by the governor of Galitza,
and made himself so popular that the Emperor, fearing that
he would ally himself with the Russians, gave him assurances
that he would not be molested, and invited him to return to
the capital.

Manuel's first wife was now dead, and though the Emperor had again married he had no son. On setting out on
a war against Desa, prince of Servia, the Emperor exacted an
oath from his nobles that on his death they would recognise
Alexis, king of Hungary, and his wife Maria, who was
Manuel's daughter, as Emperor and Empress. The only
person who refused to accept this oath was Andronicos.
There can be little doubt that as he regarded himself as
having as much right to the throne as Manuel, he was unwilling to encumber himself with a promise which would have
lessened his chances of succession. He alleged, however, that
as the Emperor had married again he might still have a son,
and that in such case the oath would be valueless. The
Emperor, finding he could not obtain his consent, made him
governor of Cilicia, and thus virtually sent him into banish-

[1] Nicetas, 168.

ment at Tarsus. As a governor he was a failure. He suffered
a severe defeat in battle at the hands of the Armenian prince
Thoros. Finding himself beaten, he made a wild, reckless,
and altogether foolhardy attempt upon the life of Thoros.
Though this attempt failed, it probably helped to maintain
his popularity.

He escapes from the Empire.

It now became necessary for him to escape out of the
Empire, in order to avoid dismissal or more severe punishment.
Collecting all the money from Cilicia which he could obtain,
he went with a large retinue to Raymond, prince of Antioch.
He was always a favourite with women, and soon after his
arrival fell in love with Philippa, daughter of Raymond and
sister of the Empress Maria. The Emperor did his utmost to
separate them, and found a candidate for Philippa's hand ;
but that lady, in the only interview she would grant the imperial nominee, asked him if he thought any woman after
having looked on him and on Andronicos would hesitate
about her choice. Persuasion and threats by her family and
the Emperor were in vain. Andronicos, however, was afraid
of being captured and surrendered by Raymond to his
suzerain, and therefore escaped to Jerusalem. Once more he
found an imperial princess willing to abandon herself to him.
Theodora, daughter of his cousin Isaac, the sebastocrator,
and widow of Baldwin, king of Jerusalem, succeeded to the
place of Philippa. The looseness of morality among the
crusading knights in the holy city of Christendom was so
great that Andronicos and Theodora hardly made a pretence
of secrecy in regard to their relations. The Emperor again
did his utmost to gain possession of his unruly subject, and
gave orders that his eyes should be put out if he could be
caught—the commonest punishment for political offences,
and one inflicted with a frightful frequency. The command
was conveyed in an imperial bull, but the document fell into
the hands of Theodora. When it was shown to the intended
victim he felt it necessary once more to fly, and accordingly
took refuge among the Turks, finally settling down under the
sultan who then ruled in Chaldæa,[1] whither Theodora accom-

[1] Nicetas, 185.

panied him. Thus once more he escaped ; for, as Nicetas remarks, whatever were the traps laid for him, he was always able to avoid them by his cunning. The outlaw occupied himself in assisting the Turks to plunder the Empire. With the permission of his host he collected a band of renegades and adventurers, and made a series of incursions into his cousin's territory in order to carry off Christians and sell them into slavery. After many attempts made by the imperial troops to capture him, all of which, however, failed, Theodora was taken prisoner, and Andronicos succeeded in making peace with Manuel and obtained pardon and permission to return to the capital.

It was in 1169, while Andronicos was living with the Turks, that Manuel's son, Alexis, who was now occupying the throne, was born. Andronicos Comnenos, during the considerable period he had remained in voluntary exile, had lived with Theodora, by whom he had two children. He now came boldly to Constantinople, and sought to flatter Manuel. He presented himself at court with a chain round his neck, which he hid under his cloak. When he was brought into the presence of the Emperor he fell on his face, showed his chain attached to a collar around his neck, wept, and asked for pardon like the humblest suppliant. Manuel, amongst whose faults ill-nature did not exist, ordered him to rise. Andronicos refused unless he were dragged by his chain to the foot of the throne. He was pardoned, but was ordered to reside at Oenæum in Pontus, where he was living at the time of Manuel's death.

He returns to the capital.

Amidst the follies of the Empress and her lover, it was natural that the inhabitants of the capital should turn their thoughts to this adventurer. His very vices had been those which, among a people whose political education is but slightly advanced, help to make a prince popular. He was believed to be fearless and resolute. He was known ostentatiously to despise luxury. He disregarded the ordinary pleasures of the table, was sober and abstemious. His rule could hardly be expected to be worse than that of a child-emperor and his foolish if not profligate mother. His foolhardiness and his

wild adventures were regarded as the faults of youth, which
by this time had probably passed away.

As soon as Andronicos heard of the divisions in the court
he saw that his chance was come. Apparently on his last
submission he had taken the oath which he had refused on a
former occasion. The terms of this oath bound him to oppose
with all his power anything which tended to the dishonour or
against the interest of the Emperor.

He in-
trigues for
the throne.

He was careful to keep the letter of his oath and scrupu-
lously anxious to seem to regard it, but he was also crafty
enough to avail himself of its terms to compass his own
purpose. He wrote to the young Emperor, to the patriarch,
and to others in authority, that in honour of the memory of
Manuel he wished to put an end to the open profligacy of
the court and to get rid of the protosebastos. Nicetas says
that as his letters were full of quotations from St. Paul,
and gave the impression that he was sincere, they produced a
very marked effect, and caused many to believe that he was
anxious mainly for the salvation of the State and the welfare
of the young prince. On his journey to Constantinople he
everywhere made the same professions, and was in consequence welcomed by the people, was received with imperial
honours, and increased the number of his followers. Few
were found to resist the patriotic professions of one who
seemed to burn with zeal for the public weal, and who professed to have no other design than that of setting the child-
Emperor free. His first check was at Nicæa, a city which is
about seventy miles from the capital. The governor, John
Comnenos, a brother of the protosebastos, was so convinced
of his powers of persuasion that he refused to see him and
shut his gates against him. Andronicos thereupon crossed
over to Nicomedia, the modern Ismidt. Andronicos Angelos,
two of whose sons subsequently came to the throne, was sent
against him, but was defeated. Andronicos then pushed
boldly on to Constantinople, and on the hills opposite
Prinkipo lit a great number of fires, in order to make the
people of the capital believe that he was accompanied by a
large army.

The protosebastos was greatly alarmed at his approach, and the more so that he had no confidence in the army. The inhabitants were known to be friendly to Andronicos, and, although he counted on the fleet and on the foreign colonists in the capital, he was by no means assured of the loyalty of either. He at once collected every available ship and manned them in part with Romans and in part with Italians, distributing amongst them large sums of money. Contostephanos claimed the command of the fleet as a right, and although Alexis distrusted him he was obliged to give way and content himself with surrounding him with friends in whom he had confidence. Having thus barred the passage of the Bosphorus, he sent an embassy to Andronicos, with a letter in which he promised many dignities, favours, and rewards, if he would consent to disband his army. The embassy failed, possibly, as Nicetas thinks, because the ambassador himself urged the rejection of the proposals which he carried. Andronicos returned answer that he would retire into private life if the protosebastos and his friends were dismissed, if the Empress cut short her hair and re-entered a monastery, and if the Emperor alone assumed the government.

Attempts to resist him.

The suspicion of the protosebatos against Contostephanos was soon shown to be well founded, for, a few days after the answer of Andronicos, the admiral passed over with the whole of his ships to the side of the enemy. The protosebastos was in despair while his enemies took courage, held meetings, and publicly declared for Andronicos. Great numbers of citizens crossed over to Chalcedon, and brought back reports which increased the reputation of the deliverer. Instead of the young man whom a former generation had known as the captivator of the hearts of a hundred dames, and as the hero of numberless escapes and adventures, they spoke of a stately and venerable old man who charmed them with words which flowed from his mouth like honey, or like the dew of Mount Hermon, a man who quoted Scripture largely and impressed his hearers with his patriotic and disinterested character. The city was ready to declare for Andronicos ; his sons and others of his friends who had been imprisoned were released ; the

favourites of the court were put in their place.   The protosebastos, with some of his chief followers, was arrested in the
palace by the Waring guard, and at midnight was removed
secretly for greater safety into the church of the palace.   The
Warings treated him with harshness, their cruelty taking the
form of preventing him from sleeping.   The patriarch inter-
ceded with the guards, but in vain.   A few days later the
prisoner was brought forth, placed on a pony, carried in mock
procession down to the seaside, and sent across the mouth of
the Bosphorus to Andronicos, who at once ordered him to be
deprived of his sight.

He suc-
ceeds.

The only force which now opposed the popular favourite
was that of the foreign colonists.   They took the part of
Maria, probably because she was a Latin princess.   Andronicos
being possessed of the fleet, sent an army to attack the city.
The Greeks, or Romans as the inhabitants still called themselves, rose in his favour, and the colonists, who occupied a
large part of the slope towards the Golden Horn, were
attacked in front and rear and fled.   Many, however, found
safety in the palaces of the nobles.   All who were taken were
killed.   Others took ship and sought refuge in Prinkipo and
other of the Princes' Islands, where in revenge for their own
losses they burnt the monasteries and plundered the inhabitants.   The attacks which the Latin colonists drew on themselves, by taking sides in this struggle, were the beginning of
the alienation which culminated in the capture of the city.

By this time almost every one of importance had crossed
the Bosphorus to welcome Andronicos.   Among the last to
do so were the patriarch and the leading ecclesiastics.   A few
days afterwards, the pretender entered a trireme, and, leaving
Damalis or Scutari, passed over to the capital.   Manuel had
built two towers, one off Damalis where the present Maiden's
Tower stands, and the other near the present Seraglio Point,
and called the tower of Manganes, from the name of an
adjacent palace.[1]   To this palace the young Emperor and his

---

[1] A chain connected these two towers, and probably floated on wooden buoys,
and thus protected the entrance to the Bosphorus.   Another chain passed from
the tower of Manganes to a tower on the Galata side, probably on the site of the

mother had been brought at the request of Andronicos. The latter visited them, professed his wish to serve them in every way, and then returned to his tent and the army. A few days later he again visited Constantinople in order to see the tomb of Manuel, and took every opportunity of impressing upon the populace the unselfishness of his designs and his desire to strengthen the Empire. Meantime he was making every preparation with his friends for the furtherance of his designs. He encouraged the boy-Emperor to amuse himself. He dispersed those on whose aid he could not count, surrounded himself and Alexis with those whom he could trust, and rewarded those who had been favourable to his own designs. He imprisoned many ; he put out the eyes of others, and this, as the populace noted with surprise, without trial. The city was divided. Civil war was already within its walls. Brothers were informing against brothers, fathers against their children. Members of the imperial family fared no better before the ruthless cruelty of Andronicos than those of a lower class. John Cantacuzenos was blinded because he had saluted his brother Constantine Angelos, who had already been thrown into prison. Andronicos was relentless in the execution of his designs and cunning in his means of getting rid of his enemies. To receive favours from him came soon to be regarded as a sign of his hate and the beginning of ruin. In proportion as he obtained power his real nature showed itself. One of his first victims was Maria, the sister of Manuel, who had been with her husband, the Cæsar, the chief of the party which had intrigued and finally declared for him. She was found poisoned, and, as it was believed, by Andronicos. Her husband shortly afterwards died, under circumstances which led to the belief that his death was not natural.

It was for some time doubted whether Andronicos had determined to become Emperor. He was an old man, was infirm, and apparently would have been content to have had

His cruel-
ties.

modern Custom House. The reader will remember that Mahomet the Conqueror constructed a tramway from the Bosphorus to the Golden Horn, in order to take his ships into the harbour, and thus avoid the barrier which the latter chain formed to the entrance.

the government of the Empire in his own hands while leaving the young Emperor on the throne. In order, however, to make his position the stronger, he ardently desired the marriage of Alexis to his own daughter Irene. As, however, they were second cousins, such a marriage was against the laws of the Church. He called a council and submitted to it the question whether a marriage, which would do much to the reconciliation of the East and the West, and would produce other public benefits, could be celebrated, although it was, as he suggested, to some extent against the law of the Church. The patriarch and other ecclesiastics opposed but were out-voted, and the patriarch retired to the small island of Tere-binth, opposite Prinkipo. Though authorisation was obtained from a new patriarch, the marriage was never celebrated, Andronicos probably having already decided to make himself emperor.

The Turks attack the Empire.

It was during this time, as we have already seen, that the Turks took advantage of the troubles in the capital to renew their attacks. Manuel had kept them fairly quiet even up to the time of his death, but the instant the capital was divided against itself, the Sultan of Iconium recommenced war. On the borders of his territory John Comnenos had declared against Andronicos. A well-tried soldier was sent against him, but John, from the bed where he was dying, directed his two sons how to order the battle and won it. A few days after his death the people of Philadelphia, near which the contest had taken place, surrendered, and the two sons of John sought refuge with the sultan. Shortly after, however, in attempting to reach Sicily, they were captured, and by order of Andronicos their eyes were put out.

The ex-Empress brought to to trial

After having removed from the court all the persons whom he distrusted, Andronicos caused Alexis to be crowned for the second time in the Great Church. Once more the pretender shed tears and made professions of his affection for his cousin. Immediately afterwards it became evident that Andronicos was playing for his own hand. He lost no occasion of bringing charges against the Empress. The mob clamoured for her banishment. But the forms of law were still too powerful in the city of Justinian to be lightly set aside. The judges were sounded. Three of them answered that, before replying, they must know whether they were asked to give an opinion on a question which would afterwards come before them judicially. Andronicos endeavoured to arrest these judges, and the mob joined in an attack upon them and tore their robes from their backs. The judges, however, escaped. Shortly afterwards, Andronicos having found more pliable instruments, a charge was brought against the Empress of having urged Bela of Hungary, her brother-in-law, to take possession of Branitzova and Belgrade. She was arrested and treated with the utmost ignominy in prison. Andronicos again took the opinion of the judges upon a case stated, and, having secured that it should be favourable to his wishes, he had her condemnation pronounced, and compelled the boy-Emperor to sign his own mother's death warrant. *and executed.* Two near relatives were charged with her execution, but refused the task. Andronicos, however, found others ready to carry out his orders, and another victim was added to those whom he had slain.

While the Empress was in prison a conspiracy, headed by several nobles, had been formed against Andronicos. Upon its discovery some of the leaders escaped. Others, however, were arrested. Contostephanos and his four sons and a host of others were blinded, while others again were exiled.

Andronicos now took bolder measures. His partisans had everything to gain by advancing his interests, and he had not yet lost the popular voice. The cry was raised wherever he *Andronicos is crowned Emperor.* appeared of 'Long life to Alexis and Andronicos.' A demonstration was made in front of the palace at Blachern when the nominal and the real rulers respectively were present, and the young Emperor went through the form of requesting Andronicos to share the imperial throne. The request was no sooner made than some of the partisans of the elder carried him to the throne, while others took off his brown pyramid-shaped hat, replaced it by one of imperial scarlet, and clothed him with an imperial stole. Next day Andronicos was crowned in the Great Church, but it was noted that the

order of the names was now reversed ; the herald proclaimed
Andronicos, son of Comnenos, and Alexis, emperors and
princes of the Romans. Once more, and for the last time,
Andronicos protested that he sought only the welfare of
Alexis, and added that he only accepted the crown with that
object. Hardly, however, were the coronation festivities at
an end when a council, which he had formed of his supporters,
deprived the co-Emperor of all his dignities, and before this
sentence was well published condemned the unhappy lad to
death. The following night Alexis was bow-strung. His
body was carried to his murderer, who, giving it a kick, remarked that the boy's father had been a perjurer, his mother
a prostitute, and the boy himself a fool. The corpse was
then thrown into the sea.

The boy-Emperor murdered.

Andronicos had now attained the object of his ambition,
and could throw off all disguise. Though an old man, he
insisted upon going through the form of marriage with Anne,
aged eleven years, a daughter of the King of France, to
whom Alexis had been affianced.

The remainder of his short reign was occupied in endeavouring to impose his rule upon the whole of the empire,
in suppressing revolts, and in the exercise of the most relentless cruelty. One of his generals, Lapardas, had been
occupied in fighting against the King of Hungary, who had
invaded the Empire as soon as he found that Alexis was to
be set aside. Lapardas endeavoured to join those in Nicæa,
Broussa, or elsewhere, who had not yet acknowledged the
rule of the usurper. He was captured at Adramyttium,
and by the imperial order had his eyes put out. The two
cities first mentioned had walls, the ruins of which still remain
in wonderful preservation, which made them very strong.
The Emperor himself set out to reduce Nicæa. His efforts at
first met with little success. The city was well provisioned,
and, as one side is situated on the lake of Ascanius, the
inhabitants had the country open to them unless the Emperor
could command the lake, which apparently he was unable to
do. The besieged, confident in their strength, insulted the
Emperor and his troops, and made a sortie in which they

Andronicos lays siege to Nicæa.

destroyed his battering-rams and other machines directed against their walls. The army within was commanded by Theodore Cantacuzenos and Isaac Angelos, who subsequently came to the throne. Seeing his want of success, Andronicos had recourse to a stratagem which appears to have shocked even the soldiers of what was undoubtedly a cruel period, He sent to the capital and had brought to Nicæa, Euphrosyne, the mother of Isaac Angelos, and tied her on the top of one of the battering-rams, so that it would be impossible or difficult to shoot at those working the ram without endangering her life. The occupants of the city, however, placed their most skilled archers opposite the machine and continued to shoot, killing a great many without injuring her. At night the troops made a sortie, destroyed the ram, and rescued Euphrosyne. Many sorties were afterwards made, in one of which Theodore was killed. The command was then offered to Isaac, who probably, because he believed that the city could not hold out, refused it. The bishop then urged that the inhabitants should make terms with the enemy, and, after he had brought over a majority to his way of thinking, headed a procession to Andronicos to propose a surrender upon terms. The Emperor was only too glad to accept their submission and to promise them safety, a promise which was in great measure disregarded; for many of the leaders were thrown from the walls, while yet more were hung or banished.

Andronicos passed from Nicæa to Broussa. For a time the city resisted bravely, but, a portion of the wall having fallen, the inhabitants believed that their enemies had already entered, and in the panic they succeeded in doing so. The city was sacked and the inhabitants massacred. Theodore Angelos had his eyes put out, was tied upon an ass and sent out into the open country, where he would probably have perished had he not fallen in with some Turks who rescued him. Forty of the leaders were hung. Others had a foot or a hand cut off, or an eye put out. After reducing Ulubat, where he blinded the bishop, he returned in triumph to Constantinople.

The nephew of Andronicos, Isaac Sebastocrator, the son

He attacks Broussa.

of the Emperor's sister, seeing the unpopularity of his uncle,

Isaac seizes Cyprus.

made an effort to obtain the crown. He made his way to Cyprus, assumed the government of the island, and seemed to believe that a policy of cruelty and severe punishment towards all who opposed him was the likeliest to insure his safety. The Emperor, being unable to seize and punish Isaac, vented his spite on two of his relations who had become sureties for his good behaviour. One of these had been a violent partisan of Andronicos : neither of them had been in a position where he could control the movements or influence the conduct of Isaac. According to custom, all the nobility attended the Emperor on the feast of the Ascension. The two nobles in question were present, and were in fact taken to court against their will. One of the wretched instruments of the tyrant, a certain Hagiochristophorides, whom the people not inappropriately called Antichristophorides, took up a large stone in presence of the nobles, invited the bystanders to follow his example, and threatened those who neglected to do

His sureties are murdered.

so that they themselves would be stoned. The two sureties were stoned to death ; one of them was buried in the Jewish cemetery and the other thrown into the Golden Horn.

Reaction against Andronicos.

The tide of popular sentiment had now begun to turn. Andronicos was recognised in his true character as a brutal and selfish tyrant. It was observed that he was now as anxious to get rid of those who had helped him to obtain the throne as he had formerly been to remove the partisans of the boy-Emperor. In spite of the tears of the old hypocrite, his regret that the laws should be so severe—for in most cases his victims were duly condemned according to regular process of law—his protests that the decisions of the judges had overridden his own desires, the people justly attributed the unusual cruelties to him alone. These cruelties marked almost every day of his reign, and were the sole cause of the growing disaffection. He had begun his reign amid a popular welcome. His splendid physique and his stately appearance had always done much to recommend him. The people would have pardoned the looseness of conduct which caused him always to have one or

two mistresses at the same table with his wife, if he had
restrained his savage cruelty. He had begun several reforms His reforms.
which justly tended to make him popular. He had repressed
the rapacity of the nobles, though he plundered them himself
unmercifully. He was the terror of the tax-farmers, from the
severity with which he punished any exactions. He made
unjust judges tremble. He chose able governors for the provinces, and insisted upon order being kept. He increased
the imperial revenue without levying new taxes. He punished
wreckers with a severity which was greatly applauded in a
seafaring community. He commenced a new aqueduct in
the capital, was easy of access, and, in the words of Nicetas,
had only one balance, in which he weighed alike great and
small, the strong and the weak. But these benefits were forgotten in presence of the madness which had come over him,
and which made him a monster of cruelty. The day on
which he left his palace on the Marmora to visit his capital,
some six or seven miles away, was looked on as a fatal day,
because experience had shown that some one was certain to
fall a victim to his insensate fury. The desire of bloodshed
had become his strongest passion, and he counted that as a
lost day on which some one had not been killed.

It is worth noting some of the principal acts of his cruelty. Instances of his cruelty.
Alexis, a natural son of Manuel, had been married to a
natural daughter of Andronicos. He was charged with being
concerned in an attempt on the life of the Emperor. His eyes
were put out ; he was banished and sentenced to perpetual
imprisonment. The tyrant forbade his own daughter to come
to court, because she wept for her husband and put on
mourning against his orders. Most of the servants of Alexis
were blinded. His secretary was burned alive in the hippodrome, a punishment which was altogether unusual, and
appears greatly to have shocked the people. The eyes of
Tripsycos, one of his chief ministers, were put out, though,
with the exception of Antichristophorides, he had been the
chief instrument of the Emperor's cruelty. The prisons were
filled with victims, most of whom had been blinded.

The troubles which were crowding upon the Empire by

the forward movement of the Turks in Asia Minor, and
especially by the conquest of Salonica and the subsequent
advance of the Sicilians, enraged the Emperor. He called
a meeting of the judges, and, taking care that Hagiochristophorides was present to intimidate them by the
roar of his voice, he submitted to them the question
whether—in presence of the facts that there were various
pretenders to the throne, that there were many rebels who
had been banished or had escaped, that there were conspirators in prison who were not only hostile to the State but gave
encouragement to its enemies, and that so long as it was
known that they did not meet with the most severe punishment, there would be no safety—all political prisoners had
not forfeited their lives, and whether death was not the sole
remedy against traitors thus incurably hostile ? They had
taken the sword and ought to perish by the sword.[1] He had
taken care that the decision should be as he wished. The
sentence was not carried out, in consequence of the interference of the Emperor's son Manuel, who took the legal
objections that the authority of the judges was not sufficient,
that the death warrant ought to be signed by the Emperor
himself, and that the condemnation was too general and
included far too many persons ;—an answer imbued with the
spirit of Justinian law.

Attack
upon Isaac.

The old tyrant became daily more anxious for his own
safety, and for this purpose sent Hagiochristophorides to
learn from a soothsayer, who during the reign of Manuel had
been imprisoned and blinded for the practice of witchcraft,
the name of his successor to the throne. The soothsayer
produced in the dregs of a cup a *sigma* and an *iota*, which
were taken to indicate Isaac. The Emperor judged this indication to point to Isaac, the Isaurian, whom he had for some
time distrusted as a claimant to the throne. Hagiochristophorides determined to obtain possession of another Isaac to
whom he believed the prediction to refer, and, in order to
prevent its fulfilment, went with a sufficient following to his
house to arrest him. This was Isaac Angelos, who appears

[1] Nicetas.   Andronicos Comnenos II. gives the commencement of the decree.

to have been regarded by the Emperor as a man not worth troubling about. Isaac refused to go with Hagiochristophorides, and when the minister attempted to arrest him, rushed at him, sword in hand, and struck off his head. Immediately afterwards he galloped at full speed to the Great Church to seek sanctuary, crying, as he entered, that he had killed Hagiochristophorides. As the news spread throughout the city a great crowd sympathising with Isaac rushed to the church. Those who had given bail for the good conduct of the fugitive and all his friends were in the utmost alarm, and in their despair appealed to the people to hide them or to fight for them. Isaac remained all night in the church, accompanied by some of his friends. On the following morning many of the inhabitants returned to the church and vowed to do all that they could to save him and to ruin Andronicos.

On the day of the death of Hagiochristophorides, the Emperor was absent at his summer palace, probably at Maltepe on the Marmora.[1] When the news reached him he appears to have recognised that the sympathy of the city was with the slayer, and to have believed that his safest policy was to make no fuss about the death. He wrote at once to warn the people against sedition, but he commenced his warning with the declaration : ' Let bygones be bygones. There will be no inquiry into what is past.' . His friends endeavoured to quiet the people, and the Emperor returned to the capital for the same purpose. It was indeed high time to act, for the populace was furious. There was scarcely a man who had not some friend or acquaintance who had fallen a victim to the tyrant's cruelty, and by this time all the halo of his youth and early reputation had been dispelled. The mob broke open the prisons. All who had arms brought them out. Isaac was proclaimed Emperor. One of the guardians of Hagia Sophia, which continued to be the centre of the agitation, reached down the famous crown

Revolt of Isaac.

---

[1] At Meludion, says Nicetas. Constantius says that this was at Hunkiar Scalessi, near Beicos on the Bosphorus. But this is inconsistent with the description given of the locality by Nicetas.

of Constantine, which usually hung over the high altar, and endeavoured to place it on his head. Isaac at first refused. John Ducas, an old man, one of his sureties and uncle of Isaac, offered to accept. The people, however, cried out that they would have no other old Emperor with white hair and forked beard.[1] They had had enough of such men with Andronicos, and clamoured for Isaac. The patriarch was pressed into service by the crowd, and in this way Isaac Angelos was proclaimed Emperor and compelled to receive the crown.

The Emperor returns to the city. Andronicos on his arrival in the city went at once to the Great Palace which adjoined Hagia Sophia. From its windows he could see much that passed. His first idea was to attack the populace in and around the Great Church, and his orders were given to this effect, but the imperial troops had no heart for the fight. They could see that all sections of the people were animated with but one object, to replace their old ruler by Isaac. Among their own number there were many who sympathised with the people against the white-bearded monster whose crown was now hanging in the balance. When the tyrant saw that his orders were not obeyed, he himself took a bow, went up into one of the balconies of the palace, and drew upon those who were below. The people saw him, and cared nothing for his arrows or for anything he could do. He then endeavoured to treat. Speaking probably still from the balcony overlooking the precincts of the Great Church, where the surging populace which had rallied round Isaac Angelos was closely packed together, he proposed to abdicate in favour of his son Manuel. The proposal was treated with scorn. The mob answered that they would have neither him nor his son. Every kind of opprobrious epithet was hurled at him. His appearance had only added to the popular fury. The populace, no longer content with declaring for Isaac, determined to revenge itself upon their enemy. An attack was made upon the palace. A small gate called Karea was broken open, and the mob rushed through in pursuit of their victim.

---

[1] The coins of Andronicos represent him with a forked beard.

Andronicos saw that resistance was useless, and that the only chance of saving his life lay in flight. Hastily throwing aside a cross which he usually wore, and by which he might have been recognised, taking off his purple buskins, and exchanging the imperial hat for a common Russian cap, he re-entered the galley which had brought him from his summer palace, and, taking his young wife and a concubine with him, he fled the capital with all speed, in order if possible to take refuge among the Russians.

Meantime the populace was pouring into the palace with Isaac at its head. All resistance seems to have been at an end with the flight of the Emperor, and in a short time Isaac had obtained entire possession of the imperial dwelling. The mob was wild with excitement. Discipline there was none. Isaac was again hastily proclaimed Emperor, and immediately gave orders for the pursuit of his enemy. The mob meantime swept through the various rooms of the palace, and helped itself to a large amount of treasure. According to Nicetas, it carried off not only all the coins which were there, but twelve hundred pounds weight of gold, three thousand pounds of silver, two hundred pounds weight of copper, and indeed almost everything else that was portable. Even the chapel, perhaps with the exception of that in the other palace at Blachern, the richest in the world, was not spared, and among other objects pillaged on the occasion was the reliquary, which was said to contain the letters written by Jesus Christ to King Abgarus.[1]

Isaac proclaimed Emperor.

After some days, when order was restored, the news arrived that Andronicos had been captured. He had gone through the Bosphorus, but had stopped a few miles from the Black Sea entrance at Kilia. The inhabitants did not recognise the Emperor, though from his appearance and that of his party they suspected him to be a fugitive of high rank. They even prepared a vessel with the object of capturing him, but

Capture of Andronicos.

[1] In the Greek Church the reliquaries are usually of very great value. At Mount Athos, where the Virgin's girdle and a great number of other relics are preserved, the caskets in which they are contained are composed of silver and gold set with precious stones, and are often, as I can testify from a visit made there in 1883, of great beauty and value.

neglected to make the attempt until he left their village.
The sea, however, drove the imperial party back, and the
villagers taking courage seized him and the two ladies, bound
him, and placed all three in one of their vessels. Then the
old man disclosed who was their captive, and used his utmost
eloquence to persuade his captors to allow him to escape.
All his efforts were in vain. He was carried back to Constantinople, some thirty miles distant, and was surrendered
to Isaac. The latter had now taken up his residence in the
palace of Blachern, and ordered Andronicos to be imprisoned
within its precincts in the tower of Anema, a tower which
with its prisons still exists. He was brought before Isaac
with a chain around his neck and his feet also in irons. The
mob which had assembled on the occasion claimed the
prisoner as justly their victim. He had been the public
enemy, and he ought to be punished by the populace. He
was kicked ; he was struck with fists ; his teeth were knocked
out ; his white hair was pulled out. The women were more
violent than the men. The tyrant who had murdered or
blinded their husbands, who had cut off their hands or their
feet, was now in their power. He was hastily condemned to
have his hand cut off, and was sent back to the prison of
Anema, where he was left for a time without even bread or
water. Some days after he was again exposed to the fury of
the mob he had outraged. He was deprived of an eye, and
then, bareheaded and with no clothing except a common shirt,
was placed upon a camel and led through the streets. There
he was given up to the popular fury, and amid mad excitement and a burning desire to make an end of the man who
had done so much wrong, he was led to the hippodrome, was
hung up by his feet between two columns, and perished
miserably at the hands of the mob.

Isaac
Angelos.

Isaac Angelos, the new Emperor, was the child of the
revolution. He had not been anxious to become Emperor,
but had accepted the throne almost in self-defence. He was
a weak sovereign, and little fitted to cope with the difficulties
which the dynastic struggles since the death of Manuel had
created. He was the grandson of Constantine Angelos, who

had married Theodora, the youngest daughter of Alexis the First. Constantine had given no evidence of ability. His son, Andronicos Angelos, had in 1178 shown himself so great a coward that Manuel had threatened to send him around the streets of Constantinople dressed in women's clothes. Isaac, the new Emperor, and his successor, Alexis the Third, were the sons of this coward. By the laws of succession Isaac had no right to the throne. But there was no strict law as to hereditary succession, and inasmuch as Isaac reigned by the consent of the capital, his title was as good as that of his predecessors. In theory the Emperors still reigned by the will of the people, but the machinery by which that will was expressed had long since become useless. Usually, when there had been an able son ready to succeed his father, he had mounted the throne without opposition. When, as in the case of Manuel, there was only a boy, the want of a well-understood and generally-accepted law of succession made itself felt. Soon after Isaac ascended the throne, he declared that he would never consent to put any one to death, a sentimental declaration which has been made in our own times by a sovereign in the same city, and has been equally well kept.

The position of affairs when Isaac succeeded was worse than it had ever been in the Empire at any earlier time. The Sicilians, who had invaded the Empire, nominally in order to support Alexis, a nephew of Manuel, against the tyrant Andronicos, had crossed the Balkan peninsula, had taken possession of Salonica, had sacked it, and were steadily and successfully working their way northwards with the design even of attacking the capital itself. The Turks in Asia Minor were everywhere on the watch, and were soon to make their first serious expedition into the European territories of the Empire. Isaac Comnenos was still in possession of Cyprus, which he refused to deliver up to Isaac as obstinately as he had refused to surrender it to Andronicos. The Bulgarians and the Wallachs, seeing the troubles in the capital, were preparing for revolt, and were dreaming of placing the descendants of their ancient kings upon independent thrones. Members of the imperial family were at different places meditating revolt and awaiting favourable opportunities to proclaim themselves emperors. The ten years between 1185 and 1195, during which Alexis Angelos reigned, were full of troubles, not the least of which arose directly from the dispute among the members of the imperial family itself.

The first and most pressing difficulty which Isaac had to encounter arose from the presence of the Normans in Salonica. His general's efforts against them were crowned with success. Mosynopolis was recaptured and the enemy was again defeated on the plains of Demetriza. Salonica was recaptured. Alexis Comnenos, who had urged the Sicilians to undertake the expedition and had accompanied them, was taken prisoner and blinded. Those who could took ship and endeavoured to escape. A storm destroyed many and drove others back, who were slaughtered by the people whom they had grievously wronged.

In the engagement of Demetriza the two leaders, Count Baldwin or Aldwin, and Richard, the brother-in-law of Tancred, were made prisoners. They were sent to the capital, and when brought into the presence of the Emperor behaved themselves with characteristic insolence. The Emperor, clothed in imperial purple set with pearls, seated on his throne of gold, and surrounded by his guard, ordered his distinguished prisoners to be brought before him. He asked Baldwin why he had written in reply to the Anointed of the Lord[1] letters which were full of insolence. Baldwin answered by expressing his contempt for the Emperor, remarked that the imperial sword was good enough against effeminate and unarmoured bodies, alluding to the death of Hagiochristophorides, and told him that instead of being used to wear a helmet and armour, and to sleep in the open air under his shield, he had been brought up tenderly, had feared to be whipped by his tutor, and was a stranger to the noise of war or the call of the trumpet to battle.[2]

He volunteered the advice that the best thing the Emperor could do would be to lay aside his crown, and give it and the other imperial insignia to a prince who could win

[1] Nicetas, 477.   [2] Ib. 478.

battles, and to be careful to keep in the good graces of such a prince. The Emperor appears to have taken the insolence good-naturedly, and on Baldwin afterwards endeavouring to explain away his offensive language, and on his flattering the Emperor, he and Richard were sent back to prison. Shortly afterwards Baldwin was set at liberty, on his consenting never again to give aid to those who were fighting against Isaac.

Isaac's enemies, however, were pressing upon him from every side. The aged Sultan of Iconium, when he heard of the revolution in Constantinople which had placed Isaac on the throne, and that the imperial army was engaged against the Sicilians, passed over into Thrace and made a great raid, in which he captured many flocks, much other booty, and a great number of prisoners. Nicetas hints that he only retired on receiving large presents and a promise of an annual payment.

With the Turks.

Isaac escaped invasion from the King of Hungary by asking the hand of a daughter of Bela, king of that country, who was only ten years old. The expenses of the marriage led him into new difficulties. To meet these expenses he levied heavy tribute upon the Wallachs of the Balkans.[1] Thereupon they revolted. They were led by two brothers, Peter and Asan, who came to the capital to represent their grievances, were treated as barbarians and otherwise insulted, returned to the mountains, and were soon at the head of a formidable movement. Peter was crowned and assumed the purple buskins, and captured a considerable number of prisoners and of booty. Isaac put himself at the head of his troops and chased him beyond the Danube. No sooner had the victor commenced his march home than Asan recrossed the river, accompanied by a large band of Patchinaks. Instead of returning, Isaac sent his uncle John Sebastrocator to attack the enemy. But the imperial family was full of suspicion and distrust, and before any engagement had taken place Isaac recalled him, under the belief that he would use the imperial army to obtain possession of the throne. He was replaced by John Cantacuzenos, the Emperor's brother-

With the Wallachs.

[1] Nicetas says, 'on the Mysians, who are now called Wallachs.'

in-law, a man whose eyes had been put out by Andronicos. The blind general soon came to grief. The enemy retired before him into the mountains, whither the imperial troops followed him. A battle took place, where Asan had the advantage of the ground, and in spite of an attempt at a rally, in which John leaped on a horse and called on his men to follow him, without knowing whither he was going, the imperial troops were cut to pieces.

Revolt of
Branas.

John was succeeded by Alexis Branas, a careful soldier, but a man who had already made an attempt to obtain the imperial throne. He had tried to bring about a revolution in the capital, like that which had placed Isaac himself on the throne. He had entered the Great Church, had spoken of his services against the Sicilians, and had claimed the help of those present against Isaac. The latter, however, had pardoned him, and now placed him in command of the army. After he had defeated the enemy, he once more proclaimed himself Emperor at Adrianople, and set out for the capital. The best portion of the imperial troops was with him. On arriving before the walls he endeavoured to persuade the people and the troops to open the gates and to receive him as emperor. This attempt having failed, he drew up his troops and prepared to attack the city. The Emperor had already sent out men belonging to the city-guard to harass his movements. On the day following his arrival, these troops fought with the rebellious army from dawn to midday, the latter having the advantage in consequence of their better discipline, of the number of Sicilians who were in their ranks, and of their being better armed. The city-guard, therefore, had to retreat within the walls. Branas gave his troops five days' rest, and prepared for a general attack. He sent a detachment of soldiers round to the north side of the Golden Horn, and collected a great number of fishermen and sailors from the Marmora, who were ready to assist in the siege. A severe fight took place at the junction of the Bosphorus [1] and

---

[1] Ἥτις πόρος βοὸς κικλήσκεται, Nicetas, 494. The name Bosphorus, so far as I can find, was never applied by the Byzantine writers to the whole of the Straits, but only to the part between the city and Chrysopolis or Scutari. At the latter

the Golden Horn, between the fleet of small caïques, probably little different in their graceful shape from those which still dot the Marmora, aided by the detachment already mentioned from the army and the imperial fleet. The caïques were well handled, and gave great trouble to the heavy vessels of the fleet ; and though the victory was claimed by the latter, the caïques were, in most cases, able to reach the shore when hard pressed, and were there protected by the troops of Branas.

The rebel general now made preparations to take the city by famine. He forbade the entry of any provisions by land, and prepared a fleet to cut off the supply by sea after it had defeated that of the Emperor. Isaac was not unpopular in the city, and the people were disposed to stand by him, but he was wanting in energy, and might have lost his throne had there not been present one who was ready to lend his services in the defence. Conrad, the son of the Marquis of Montferrat,[1] had come to Constantinople to marry Theodora, the Emperor's sister, and it was while he was there that Branas appeared before the walls. Conrad found that the preparations for resistance were feeble, that the palace was filled with monks, whom Isaac had invited in order that they might pray for the cessation of civil war, and for his continuance in authority as Emperor. Conrad pointed out that other arms than spiritual ones were necessary, and that the Emperor must be ready at once to sacrifice money and men if he would meet a rebellion, where nearly the whole of his soldiers were fighting in revolt.

Isaac is aided by Conrad.

The Emperor, aroused by Conrad's remonstrances, prepared vigorously for resistance. His efforts were seconded by the inhabitants. Conrad himself set to work to organise the defence. He raised two hundred horsemen and five hundred foot, principally from the Italians. He found Georgians

city there is still a wharf or scala known as the Ox-scala, and I would suggest that the myth which has gathered around the name Bosporos has its foundation in the fact that, from the earliest existence of Byzantium, the ox-ferry would be in the place to which the term is applied by the Byzantine writers.

[1] This Conrad was an elder brother of Boniface, the leader of the expedition to Constantinople in 1203. See tables in Du Cange's *Observations on Villehardouin*.

and Saracens in the city, who were there for the purposes of
commerce, and enlisted them also in the imperial service, and
from the court he enrolled a thousand men of good condition.
The spirit of Conrad seemed to have passed into the Emperor. He collected the inhabitants in the precincts of Blachern, and urged them to do their utmost for the defence.
He begged those who might be hostile to him—in this having
specially in view John Sebastrocator, whose son had recently
been married to the daughter of Branas—to remain quiet
and await the issue of the combat, or to pass openly to the
enemy.

Defeat of
Branas.

Meantime the besiegers had drawn up their troops for the
attack. Conrad advised that the newly-raised forces should
make a sortie and fight them on the outside of the walls. The
gates were accordingly opened. Conrad took command of
the foreign troops, Isaac of the right wing, and Manuel the
Protostrator of the left. After some hours spent in skirmish-
ing, the infantry joined their bucklers, raised their lances, and
charged, while at the same time the cavalry struck at the
flank of the rebels In spite of the exertions of Branas, who
urged his troops to remain firm, reminding them that they
were far more numerous than their adversaries, the rebellious
army could not withstand the charge, and Branas was unable
to stop their flight. He himself rushed at Conrad, who was
fighting without helmet and with his body bound round with
eighteen folds of linen instead of a buckler. Branas, as he
came close to Conrad, threw a dart at him, which wounded
him slightly in the shoulder. At once Conrad charged him
with his lance and sent its head into his cheek. The rebel
fell from his horse, received other wounds, and died on the
field. The day was already won ; but, to the credit of the
citizens, when once it was clear that the army had been dispersed very little blood was shed. Isaac pardoned those who
had taken part in the revolt and were willing to swear fidelity
for the future. So far all was well. Then, however, there
followed an incident which showed how completely demoralised the capital had become in consequence of these various
struggles for the throne, and of the disputes between the

natives and foreigners. The citizens had been on the side of the Emperor. The Italians and other foreigners in the city had helped him to defeat Branas. When the victory was gained, permission was given to, or taken by, the troops under Conrad to plunder the villas and the houses in the neighbourhood of Constantinople belonging to those who had fought on the side of the rebel. As we have seen, the fishermen and others outside Constantinople had assisted Branas, and the sack also of their houses and churches was the result. But these people had many friends within the city, and, indeed, it is probable that many of the houses plundered belonged to the inhabitants of the capital. More-over, as the plunderers had a large admixture of foreigners among them, the sack was resented by the population of the capital as due especially to foreign influence. The resentment of the mob naturally fell upon the foreigners. The whole city was in commotion. The Italian quarter was attacked. The nobles and the Emperor did their best to prevent a fight, as, indeed, they had done to prevent the plunder of the houses and churches on the Marmora. But their influence over the mob was for a time fruitless. The wine-shops had been visited, and a portion of the mob was half drunk. The Italians raised barricades in the streets leading to their quarter, fought bravely behind them, and killed a considerable number of the mob before the troops sent by the Emperor could disperse it and restore tranquillity. The riot had continued all night.

While the Emperor Isaac Angelos was contending with Wallachs and Bulgarians, with Sicilians and with the Pretender Branas, Isaac Comnenos still retained the possession over Cyprus which he had seized during the reign of Andronicos. He imitated the latter in one respect—that of cruelty—with great success. The Emperor endeavoured to buy his sub-mission, and suggested that, as he had been justified in resisting Andronicos, he had come fairly into the possession of the island, but that, now the tyrant was dead, he should give it up to the lawful Emperor; if he did so he would be rewarded. Isaac, however, refused, and there followed im-

Attack upon the Latin colonists.

Isaac of Cyprus.

perial decrees, which were as fruitless as the offers of reward. The Emperor accordingly prepared a fleet of seventy vessels for the conquest of the island. The command was given to John Contostephanos, who was an old man, and to Alexis, the nephew of the Emperor, who had been blinded by Andronicos. The expedition was a failure. It arrived safely, the troops landed, but a storm dispersed the ships, which were in great part taken possession of by Sicilian vessels.[1] The troops were defeated, the leaders captured and sent prisoners to Sicily. Isaac of Cyprus offered service in his army to some of the rank and file of his captives. Those who refused were subjected to horrible cruelties. This defeat was in 1186. In 1190 our

Richard of England seizes Cyprus.

English Richard the Lion-hearted left Sicily with a hundred and fifty ships and fifty galleys, landed in Cyprus, defeated the force which opposed him, and on the following day surprised the rest of Isaac's army and utterly routed it. The inhabitants hastened at once to throw off the rule of their tyrant and to accept that of an English king. Richard took possession of all the island, captured Isaac, loaded him with chains, and sent him to Palestine. The captor drew his stores from Cyprus as long as he remained in the Holy Land.

Revolt of Wallachs and Bulgarians.

Meantime, the Wallachs and Bulgarians, although defeated by Branas in the Balkans, had been dispersed but not crushed. They had again mustered their forces, and were in rebellion. While Branas had been making his attempt before Constantinople in 1186, their preparations for a second war were being completed. The Emperor determined in the spring of the following year to march against them himself. He invited Conrad to accompany him, but the crusader, who was dissatisfied with the empty title of Cæsar, and apparently with his wife, preferred rather to sail for Palestine, where, after obtaining several victories over the Saracens, he was assassinated by an emissary of Khasis, the Old Man of the Mountain. Isaac went to Adrianople, and thence to Basterna, near to which place he came up with the enemy. Nicetas accompanied him in this expedition as his secretary, and

---

[1] Nicetas. *Isaac*, i. 5. *Annales Reicherspergenses*, quoted by Muralt, 225.

relates in detail what he saw ; how the Wallachs first threw their darts, then charged with their lances, but fled before the steady march of the Romans in order to induce the latter to break their line ; how, as soon as the imperial troops ceased to advance, they returned to the charge with the utmost fury, and would have succeeded if the Emperor had not brought up his reserve. The enemy was defeated, but Asan continually harassed the imperial troops, marched hither and thither, kept them occupied during the whole of the summer, until at length the Emperor returned to the capital, and placed his troops in winter quarters near Philippopolis, and postponed operations until the spring of 1188. When spring came three months were spent in the siege of Lovtcha, without being able to capture it, and Isaac returned to the capital. During the next three years the Wallachs and Bulgarians continued in revolt. They were joined by a band of Comans, and held possession of a large portion of the open country to the north of the Balkans. In 1191 Isaac himself again took the field against them, but with the result that he was surprised and narrowly escaped capture. This success encouraged the enemy to make further attempts against the Empire. The rebels were no longer content to ravage the open country and to plunder villages, but they boldly attacked the fortified towns. They pillaged Achialos, the port of the Gulf of Bourgas ; they captured Varna, and burnt or otherwise injured Triaditza and Nyssa. Isaac acted with vigour, recaptured Varna and Achialos, but found that the whole of the country between the Danube and the Balkans was in revolt. Even the Servians had now broken out into insurrection. Isaac marched against the latter, met the enemy on the banks of the Morava, and defeated him. Thence, after a journey beyond Nisch to visit Bela, king of Hungary, he returned to Constantinople.

Constantine Angelos, his cousin, who had been appointed governor of Philippopolis, was more successful against the Wallachs than the Emperor had been. Peter and Asan were defeated. Constantine seems to have thought that his successes supplied the opportunity he wanted to assume the *Attempts upon the throne.*

imperial robe. He accordingly wrote to his brother-in-law, Basil, who was then at Adrianople, asking his aid in an attempt upon the throne. He set out from Philippopolis to meet Basil, but was arrested by some of his own followers, who sought safety in this act and in delivering Constantine to the Emperor. He was sentenced to lose his eyes, and gave no further trouble to the Emperor.

The struggles with the Wallachs, Bulgarians, and Comans, and the pretenders in Europe, had encouraged a Theodore Mankaphas to revolt. He had raised a party in his favour in 1189 in the city of Philadelphia, had taken the title of king, and had coined money in his own name. Isaac hastened to oppose him, but the city was too strong to be taken by assault, and the Emperor had to be content to treat. The pretender consented to abandon his claims to a crown, and the city gave hostages for good behaviour. Shortly after, however, when an imperial general was sent against it, Mankaphas fled to the young Sultan of Iconium, who gave him assistance for a while, but who ultimately considered it safer to surrender him to Isaac.

Other pretenders of less importance were continually cropping up during the whole of Isaac's reign. A certain Alexis gave himself out to be a son of the Emperor Manuel, and bore to the real Alexis a resemblance which made many believe in his tale. He alleged that his father had ordered him to be thrown into the sea, but that he had been saved by his intended executioners. He made his way to Iconium, told his tale to the Sultan, who professed to believe that he was the person he represented himself to be, and received from him promises of aid. These promises were so far kept that he was allowed to raise volunteers, with whom he devastated the country round the Meander. The leaders sent against him feared to attack, because of the belief which existed among their own followers that Alexis was what he claimed to be. Even the Emperor's brother shared this fear, and the pretender might have given much more serious trouble than he did if he had not been murdered in a private quarrel. Hardly was his death known than another impostor took the same name, pretended to the same origin, and obtained a following in Paphlagonia. His career, however, was soon cut short by the imperial troops. There were many other pretenders in the provinces. Even the capital was not free from such attempts. A nephew of Andronicos, named Isaac, who had escaped from prison, took refuge in Hagia Sophia, endeavoured to raise the people, was captured and died under torture. Andronicos, a son of Alexis Comnenos, who was governor of Salonica, was accused of an attempt to make himself Emperor, was brought to the capital to answer the charge, and was condemned to lose his eyes. Nicetas mentions other pretenders both in the provinces and in the capital, whose attempts similarly failed, and justly attributes these revolts mainly to the weakness with which Isaac governed. It must be added also that the attacks which had been made during a generation past upon the throne and upon the Empire had destroyed the reputation which had surrounded the sovereign authority. For centuries after the Emperors had lost the attributes of divinity, they had yet been regarded as sacred personages. Though the doctrine of the divine right of kings, as known in England two centuries ago, had not yet been invented, there had yet been a sanction hedging in a king in the sense that rebellion had been regarded as a sin of the deepest die, as well as the greatest of crimes. Moreover, the growth of the commercial spirit was rapidly changing the form of government from an absolute monarchy to an oligarchy of nobles and merchant princes. The will of the people of the capital, when led by a popular noble and expressed by popular riot, and not even in a regularly constituted fashion, had come to be regarded as the sole source of authority, and the Emperor thus easily appointed could be as easily deposed. When, as in the case of Isaac, the sovereign had little to recommend him to the favour of the populace, it is not surprising that many attempts should have been made to supplant him. The old machinery for learning the popular will through a college of senators and a representation of the artisans only existed in form. The modern devices of representative government were unknown. At a time when even

in the New Rome the soldier readily became a peaceful
citizen, and the peaceful citizen a soldier, a popular tumult
was sufficient to change the ruler.

Isaac himself was idle, or rather was willing that the labour
of government should be on his ministers. We may see how
diminished the authority of the Emperor had become in the
fact that one of these ministers, Theodore Castamonites,
allowed himself to be called lord and emperor [1] by the flat-
terers who hung about his court. So long as Isaac could be
free to visit his palace on the shores of the Marmora and his
houses in the islands, could be attended with his mistresses
and his buffoons, could be dressed in what his subjects regarded as the magnificence of Solomon and have everywhere
and always a luxurious table, he was content that his favourite
of the hour should bear the burden of government. His
laziness and extravagance, his meanness and rapacity, had
already alienated the sympathy of the populace, while his
misgovernment contrasted unfavourably with the rule even of
the cruel Andronicos. It began now to be remembered that
the tyrant had reformed the judiciary, had punished judges
with severity for the taking of bribes, had sent the best men
to be governors and judges at his own charge, and had given
them salaries instead of allowing them to buy their offices and
sell their judgments. Isaac sent officers into the country after
the fashion of the apostles, says Nicetas, without purse or
scrip, although he knew that it was their duty to do justice
indifferently, and to pay into the treasury what they had levied
from the people. Andronicos had encouraged traders, and had
been especially anxious to increase the commerce of the
country and to allow ships to pass to and fro in safety. Isaac
debased the coinage, increased taxation, spent what he raised
in building palaces or on his own luxuries, and was believed

---

[1] Nicetas, p. 575. δεσπότης καὶ βασιλεύς. *Despot* had formerly been a title exclusively belonging to the Emperor. At a later period it was conferred on other
members of the imperial family. *Sebastocrator* was a title which during the
twelfth century seems to have been the highest given to a minister. *Cæsar* was
in that century the title next in rank below the sebastocrator, but it had been
given to several persons at the same time. *Protosebastos* indicated a rank below
each of these.

to share the bribes which his ministers exacted. Even Nicetas, monk though he was, complained of his selfish superstition, of the money he had wasted on churches, chapels, and monasteries. The Emperor went into ecstasies when he saw a picture of the Virgin, endowed several of her shrines, and exposed pictures at street corners to excite the devotion of the people. He scattered money with profusion among the populace, but had to sell the magistracies and other public appointments in order to obtain it. His conduct had made him deservedly unpopular with the people, since his misgovernment in tampering with the coin, in selling monopolies, in debasing the justiciary, in harassing commerce, and in diminishing the security of property seriously injured the trade of the country, which I must repeat was by far the most important interest. A new trouble with his old enemies the Bulgarians and Wallachs brought his reign to an end.

In 1195 these peoples were again troubling the Empire, and as the experience of Isaac had shown him the danger of entrusting the command of the imperial army to his generals, he determined himself once more to take the field against them. He had collected a large army and had asked for the aid of the King of Hungary. In the month of March he left Constantinople. He had been warned that it would be unsafe to leave the capital without taking precautions against his brother Alexis, and had accused those who warned him of wishing to destroy the fraternal understanding which had always existed between them. Isaac went to Rodosto on the Marmora, about seventy miles from Constantinople, and there celebrated Easter. Thence he went on to Cypsella, the modern Ipsala, on the Hebrus or Maritza, and while waiting for the arrival of a portion of his troops went out hunting and invited his brother Alexis to accompany him. Alexis excused himself on the pretence that he was about to be bled on account of illness. Isaac therefore went alone. His brother remained at home to carry out a plot in which he was the principal figure. A conspiracy, the secret of which had been well kept, had been formed among the nobles for deposing Isaac and placing Alexis on the throne. During the absence of the

Conspiracy headed by his brother to depose Isaac.

Emperor the pretender was proclaimed. As Isaac returned
he was met by a few of his servants who remained faithful,
and informed of what had taken place. He stopped, crossed
himself, took out the miniature of the Virgin which he always
carried, kissed it, and, seeing that the friends of Alexis were
galloping towards him, turned and fled. He was, however,
intercepted, given up to the rebels, and was sent as a prisoner
to a monastery in Pera. From thence he, together with his
son Alexis, was transferred to a prison in the palace and afterwards to one in the Taurus, where his eyes were put out and
where he was treated like an ordinary criminal. At the time
of his deposition he was in his fortieth year. He remained
in prison, as we shall see, until the Crusaders who effected the
conquest of Constantinople set him free.

Accession
of Alexis.
    The accession of Alexis Angelos to the throne of his
brother was followed by a distribution of money, including
that which had been collected for the pressing necessities of
the Wallach-Bulgarian war, of public honours, titles and
dignities, of the crown lands, and of almost every available
species of wealth. He granted every concession that he was
asked for, and would have given the privilege, says Nicetas,
if he had been asked for it, to cultivate the sea, to sail over
land, or to pile Mount Athos on Olympus.[1] His sole object
was to render his position secure, and he had reason to believe
that all his efforts were necessary if that end were to be
attained. His first measure was to disband the army. Then
he set out by easy stages for Constantinople, where his wife
was preparing for him a triumphal entry. The senate was
content with his accession, although there were some dissentients, and the people of the capital did not oppose or show
any indignation or resentment, notwithstanding, says Nicetas,
that it had been deprived by the army of the privilege which
belonged to it of electing the Emperor.[2] The only opposition,
indeed, which was made was by a knot of workmen and rabble,
who when Euphrosyne, the wife of Alexis, went to take possession of the Great Palace adjoining the Great Church, proclaimed
an astrologer named Alexis Contostephanos. Her partizans,

---

[1] Nicetas, p. 600.   [2] *Ib.* 600.

however, attacked the mob, declared that they were tired of the family of Comnenos, to which the pretender belonged, and would have no more of them, caught the would-be Emperor and imprisoned him. The ecclesiastics, seeing how the popular feeling went, declared in favour of Alexis. Some of the nobles and a priest, with a few of the judges, though without the consent of the patriarch, proclaimed him.

Alexis Angelos, who arrived a few days afterwards in the capital, was crowned with the usual ceremonies in Hagia Sophia, and discarding the name of Angelos assumed that of Comnenos. We have already seen that among at least a portion of the populace the name Comnenos had been unpopular, but, remembering the able rulers of that house, this sentiment can hardly have been general. Nicetas suggests that the new Emperor made the change in order to divert attention from the fact that the deposed Emperor was his own brother, and the suggestion is plausible. Alexis took quiet possession of the throne. There was, however, a strong party in the city which was dissatisfied with the events of the last few days. The treachery of one brother to another, the abandonment of the enterprise against the enemies who had taken possession of the Balkans, the panderings to the mob and the soldiery, and the lavish way in which the imperial treasures had been distributed, disgusted men of sense and especially the well-to-do classes. This disgust was increased when it was seen that the new Emperor cared for nothing but his own pleasures, that the interests of commerce were disregarded, that the government was left in the hands of his favourites, and that his lavish profusion in squandering what should have been employed for the use of the State forced him to levy new taxes.

Takes the name of Comnenos.

The ease with which Alexis had obtained the throne increased the supply of pretenders. Three months after his accession the news arrived that another Alexis had arisen in Cilicia, who claimed to be the son of Manuel; that the Sultan of Angora had received him favourably, and professed to believe him to be the boy-emperor Alexis, who had been strangled by Andronicos. The Emperor took the field against him, but after two months of unsuccessful warfare he returned

to Constantinople. The pretender, however, was shortly afterwards killed.

While the Emperor had been in pursuit of the false Alexis,
the Wallachs, still under Asan and Peter, had attacked the
imperial troops, had cut them to pieces, and had captured their
leader. The Emperor sent a new army to repel their attacks,
but the imperial troops were again beaten and their leader
captured. Alexis then sent his son-in-law Isaac, who fought
valiantly, but was likewise defeated and captured, and brought
before Asan. Shortly afterwards, however, this leader was
himself assassinated by his nephew John, who then found it
necessary to ask the assistance of the Emperor against Peter.
The war dragged on with little credit to the imperial troops.
Their leader died in captivity, the troops were unwilling to
continue a mountain warfare where the enemy had a great
advantage in his knowledge of the country and was gaining
ground every day. In the midst of it Peter himself was killed
by one of his own followers. The leadership of the Wallachs
then fell to Ivan, a younger brother of Peter, who came to
Constantinople and thus gave peace to the Empire for upwards
of a year. But until the fall of Constantinople there was no
rest to the Empire either on the north or in Asia Minor. In
1198 another Wallach leader who had been always opposed
to Peter and Asan took possession of Strumnitza, and made
incursions into Thrace, principally for pillage. He held his
own against the feeble attacks of the Emperor, who was
harassed not only by the Turks but by dynastic conspiracies in
the capital. Alexis made terms, ceded Strumnitza and other
places, and promised the rebel a member of the imperial
family in marriage.

Two years later, in 1200, the Patchinaks made an incur-
sion into Macedonia, while about the same time Ivan, who had
taken the name of Alexis when he had married the niece of
the Emperor, and who had been appointed to command the
troops stationed at Philippopolis to check the Wallachs and
Bulgarians, headed a revolt. The two sons-in-law of the
Emperor were sent against the rebel, but he succeeded in
capturing one of them, and in defeating the imperial army.

The Emperor now took the field himself against the rebels, but his troops were so demoralised that he found it necessary to treat with Ivan. The latter refused to listen to any proposals, except upon the basis of his retaining possession of the places he already held. These terms were accepted. A treaty was signed, and then the Emperor, having lured Ivan to the capital by the most solemn assurances of safety, imprisoned him, attacked the towns which he had taken, and recaptured them without difficulty.

A year afterwards, in 1201, the Comans followed the example of the Patchinaks, and made an irruption into Thrace, whence, after having plundered it, they returned unmolested. They would probably have marched to Constantinople if the Russians, 'a most Christian people,' had not opposed their progress, and had not come to the defence of the Romans, partly from their own good-will, partly on the prayers of their bishop, who could not see without indignation that every year a number of Christians were taken into captivity by these infidels.[1] Romanos, the Russian leader, entered upon the territory of the Comans while its army was invading the Empire, and forced them to retire. Romanos was regarded in Constantinople, says the great contemporary historian of the age, as a divinely-sent protector for the defence of religion. from the Comans;

During Lent in 1202, Ivan of Bulgaria was again at the head of a large army devastating territory in the Rhodope, whence, passing eastward, he laid siege on Good Friday to Varna. It was defended by a body of Italians in the pay of the Emperor; but no one appears to have believed that he would attempt an assault at a time so generally observed in both churches as a holy season. They were disappointed, however. The city was attacked and taken, the walls were destroyed, and the enemy returned in triumph to Bulgaria. Manuel Camyzes, the captured leader of the imperial troops, who had remained prisoner in Bulgaria, had begged the Emperor to pay the ransom demanded by his captors from the property which the Emperor was supposed to be guarding in from the Bulgarians.

[1] Nicetas, 691.

trust. When Alexis refused, Manuel joined the Bulgarians, assisted them in sacking Prosacus, passed down through Macedonia into Thessaly as far as the vale of Tempe, and plundered even the Morea. Alexis sent one of his sons-in-law, who succeeded in compelling him to leave Thessaly, and in forcing him and Ivan to come to terms.

Numerous
pretenders
to the
throne.
The short reign of Alexis, like that of his predecessors, was troubled with a host of pretenders to the throne, and while he was continually engaged with external enemies, his most constant foes were those of his own household. He had no son. Many candidates for the imperial succession were suggested, and were supported by those who believed that in their election they saw a means of furthering their own interests. Among those best qualified for the dignity was Manuel Camyzes Protostrator. He, however, was strongly opposed by John Sebastocrator, his uncle. Each of the three brothers of the Emperor, as well as his brother-in-law, had a son. Each of the four fathers, all of whom it may be mentioned had been blinded by Andronicos, was desirous of seeing his own son upon the throne, and plotted to attain that end. Apparently these rival candidates, or their protectors, were willing to wait until the death of Alexis, or at least to be content if they could succeed in obtaining from the Emperor a recommendation or nomination which should come into effect upon his death. Other aspirants, however, outside the near relatives of the Emperor, attempted to deprive Alexis of the throne. A certain John Comnenos, who was nicknamed the Fat, entered the Great Church with his followers, who were mostly of the nobility, and taking down a small crown which hung suspended over the altar, put it upon his head, and was proclaimed Emperor. He took possession without difficulty of the Great Palace, took his seat upon the throne, and proceeded at once to make a distribution of the great offices of state. His followers proclaimed him throughout the city, and a mob seemed to think itself entitled to the reward for having shouted for him of pillaging the houses of the wealthy. John apparently thought his position secure, for at night he took no precautions for

guarding the palace. The Emperor, who had probably been absent at the palace of Blachern, assembled his friends, who made a night attack by sea, joined the guards who had remained faithful or indifferent, surprised the followers of John near the hippodrome, entered the palace and beheaded the pretender.

About the same time Michael, a natural son of John Sebastocrator, who had been sent to levy the taxes due by the province of Mylassa, in Caria, made an attempt to obtain the throne. Troops were sent against him, and he was defeated. Like so many other pretenders and enemies of the Empire, he sought and found refuge among the Turks. From the Sultan he received troops with which he pillaged the cities and country round the Meander. The Emperor set out in November to attack him. In returning to Constantinople he stopped to take the hot baths at Pythia, near the modern Yalova, on the Gulf of Ismidt. A violent storm, however, forced his party to take shelter on Prinkipo, whence they returned to Chalcedon and the capital.

At the time when Manuel Camyzes had given his assistance to the Bulgarians, and had been ravaging Thessaly and the Morea, another rebel gave trouble. This was John Spyridonaces, a man of low origin, who had raised himself to be the treasurer of the Empire. The troops, however, who were sent against him under Alexis, the son-in-law of the Emperor, made short work of the rebellion, and the Emperor had the satisfaction of seeing about the same time the suppression of this revolt, the expulsion of Manuel Camyzes, and the recapture of several towns.

To the list of rebels must be added also, though belonging Isaac of to the early part of the reign, the name of that Isaac Cyprus. Comnenos whom we have already seen as the captor of Cyprus and the defeated of Richard the Lion-hearted. Nicetas states that the captor gave him as a slave to an Englishman, that Isaac broke his chains, declared himself emperor, and made a bold attempt to attain the sovereign authority. The Emperor, acting on the suggestion of his wife, invited him to come to court, but Isaac haughtily refused, replying that he was a sovereign, and not a subject, and that he had learned to command and not to obey. As usual amongst these pretenders, he applied for assistance to the Turks, promising them in return a great number of concessions. Even the Turks would have nothing to do with a man whose cruelty had alienated his own subjects and made his name universally detested, and who was likely, therefore, to stand no chance of success. He died before he was able to cause serious trouble to the Empire, but under circumstances which gave rise to the suspicion that he had been poisoned by his cup-bearer on the instigation of the Emperor.

Troubles with the Turks.

While the reign of Alexis was troubled with these various pretenders to the throne, while Bulgarians and Wallachs gave him no rest on the north, while the foreign colonies and the states to which they belonged were making almost continual attacks upon other portions of the Empire in Europe, the Turks were still a constant source of trouble. We have seen that on the death of Kiliji-Arslan, Sultan of Iconium, a division had taken place of the Seljukian empire among his sons. Shortly after Alexis came to the throne, Mahsud, Sultan of Angora, one of the most important of these divisions, laid siege to Dadybra in Paphlagonia. The Emperor had himself gone into Asia Minor to put down the revolt of Alexis, the Cilician pretender, who had sought and obtained aid from this Sultan of Angora. He urged the inhabitants of Dadybra to hold out, and they maintained the defence of their city bravely during four months, but, as no succour was forthcoming, they made terms with the besiegers. They surrendered the city on condition of being allowed to leave with their women, children, and goods. The Emperor, finding that his safety required him to return to the capital, was obliged to confirm the surrender.

A little later, in 1198, Alexis was at war with the Sultan of Iconium, named Kaikhosro. The war arose out of a slight matter, which, but that the Emperor and Sultan were always ready to contend with each other, might easily have been arranged. Two Arab horses having been sent as a present to the Emperor by the Sultan of Alexandria, were stopped by Kaikhosro, and one of them had its leg broken while in his possession. Kaikhosro expressed his regret and offered to send others, but the Emperor, either enraged at the insult, or wanting a pretext for war against a prince who had so often given aid to his enemies, imprisoned all the merchants in Constantinople who were the subjects of the Sultan of Iconium, and allowed their houses to be pillaged. Thereupon the Sultan immediately declared war, ravaged all the imperial territory around the Meander, and captured a great number of prisoners. Worse than this, he energetically carried out a policy which inflicted a severe blow on the Empire. The subjects of Alexis in Asia Minor, who had been heavily taxed, were by no means well affected towards the Emperor personally, and were weary of the various demands upon them. The Sultan collected his prisoners, gave them lands according to their social rank, provided them houses at Philomelium, near Iconium ; distributed seed-corn and provisions among them, promised that he would make their peace with the Emperor, and that if the latter refused they should become his subjects, with the right of exemption from all taxes for five years, and of a light taxation afterwards. The treatment of these prisoners had the effect which the Sultan desired. It drew from the Asiatic provinces of the Empire a considerable number of emigrants, and made further conquests easier. In the words of Nicetas, the cities of Greece were depopulated to make colonies in the territory of the barbarians.[1] The opposition which Alexis made was of a very feeble character, partly because the presence of other enemies required his return to the capital, and partly because he himself was suffering from gout.

As the century closed, the history of the Seljukian Turks entered upon a phase which at another time might, as we have seen, have enabled the Empire to recover lost ground. The division of the Sultanate of Iconium was itself an advantage to the Empire, but a further gain was shortly obtained

---

[1] Nicetas usually and correctly speaks of the subjects of the Greek-speaking Roman empire as Romans. The inhabitants—to this day almost purely Greek— of the western provinces of Asia Minor he calls Greeks.

by the jealousies of the sons of Kiliji-Arslan.   On the death
of one of these, two out of the others who had divided their
father's empire among them contended for the succession of
their dead brother.   The victor then attacked Kaikhosro,
Sultan of Iconium, who was the son of a Christian mother,
and was hated on that account.[1]   Kaikhosro thereupon made
a truce with the Empire.   He subsequently asked the aid of
Leo, king of Armenia, but was nevertheless defeated and
came to Constantinople, where he was allowed to live as a
private citizen.   The further quarrels among the sons of
Kiliji-Arslan contributed to make the end of the century
a favourable opportunity in the eyes of the Pope, and of
other Western statesmen, for striking an effective blow at
Moslemism.

Demoralisation of the Empire.   The troubles of the Empire were now crowding upon it,
and Alexis was not the man to meet them with success.   He
had begun his reign amid a considerable amount of popularity.
He had promised to maintain that which was good in the
policy of his predecessor, to remove the restrictions in the
way of trade, and especially to appoint the most capable men
to govern instead of selling public offices.   But he was surrounded by creatures who had placed him upon the throne,
and who intended to be rewarded for their trouble.   These
men acquired immense wealth by selling their influence and
the favour of the sovereign.   We have already seen how they
induced him to grant monopolies.   They publicly sold the
highest dignities and the governorships of the provinces.
Not only nobles but money-lenders and changers, Scythians
and Syrians, were able to buy the title of Cæsar.   The
Empress herself was at the head of the avaricious gang which

[1] That the Turkish sultans were often the sons of Christian slaves has had a
very important effect upon Turkish history.   This is a point which the late Mr.
Scudamore carefully examined.   The undoubtedly able sultans who carried the
Turkish arms successfully, first to Constantinople and then to the gates of
Vienna, were almost in every case the sons of Christian mothers, and were
therefore after a few generations of almost purely European descent.   The
decline in ability amongst the Ottoman sultans dates from the destruction in the
last century of the corsairs who ravaged the coasts of Italy, France, Spain,
and, in the previous century, even the south coast of England, for the capture of
slaves.

traded on the weakness of the Emperor. Her brother-in-law, Michael Stryphnos, the admiral of the imperial fleet, used his office solely to enrich himself, and sold the stores from the arsenal, confident that his influence with the Empress would save him from punishment. The Emperor made a feeble protest against her conduct, and was supported by some of the nobles, who openly charged her with unfaithfulness. Notwithstanding that she claimed a public trial she was shut up in a monastery, and remained thus banished from the court for six months, after which she returned again to the palace to become a centre of evil influence. An incident is mentioned by Nicetas which is strikingly like what has happened in Constantinople in our time, and what is happening continually throughout the Turkish empire at the present day. From the manner, however, in which Nicetas makes mention of the fact, it was evidently of rare and exceptional occurrence even among the worst days of the Byzantine empire. A jailer who had probably bought his appointment allowed his prisoners to leave the jail at night, and shared with them the proceeds of their plunder. He was accused of the offence, and, although the Emperor promised to punish him, was set at liberty. Popular feeling, however, was much more healthy at Constantinople then than now. A workman having been beaten by this jailer, the companions of his guild came together, attempted to seize the offender, and to lynch him for his misdeeds. When they found that he had fled, they hastened to the Great Church to proclaim a new emperor. The guards, however, opposed their entrance. A tumult was raised, and the news was conveyed to Alexis, who was at Chrysopolis. He sent orders to attack the people, but the mob fought with stones, scattered the troops, broke open the prisons, set free the prisoners, and destroyed a Saracen mosque. The son-in-law of the Emperor appeared with a fresh detachment of troops, but even then the mob, consisting of unarmed and unarmoured men, fought valiantly against well-clad troops. Some of them threw down the tiles from the houses, others attacked with stones. The fight was kept up till night, during which the mob dispersed. The

populace on other occasions made demonstrations against
the attempts of the court to extort money by unlawful means
from private citizens, and numerous instances are recorded
which show that the people of the capital would not tolerate
anything like general or unusual oppression.

Nicetas himself charges the Emperor with having been in
league with a pirate. He states that Alexis sent a certain
Francopolous with six galleys to the Black Sea, on pretext of
collecting the salvage of a ship which had been wrecked near
Kerasund, but in reality to plunder the merchants who lived
at Aminsos, a town on the coast near Kerasund. Francopolous plundered all the ships he could find, whether going to
or from Constantinople. Some of the merchants escaped,
came to Constantinople, and entered the Great Church with
candles in their hands as suppliants demanding justice. The
Emperor threw all the blame upon the pirate. His subjects
obtained no redress. Those of the Sultan of Aminsos who
had been similarly plundered were more fortunate, and the
Emperor was compelled to give as an indemnity fifty of the
silver lead mines with which the north shore of the coast of
Asia Minor abounds. In this instance, as in so many others,
the necessity of money to meet his personal expenditure and
that of the creatures around him was the motive which led to
his infamous conduct. The excessive amount of taxation
which he had levied upon his own subjects had made him
unpopular, while the restrictions upon trade made with the
same object, and in violation of the capitulations, had contributed to alienate the Venetians and Pisans, as well as his own
merchants. To maintain himself upon the throne he was compelled to bribe the nobles and the populace ; to raise money for
maintaining the defence against Turks, Wallachs, and Italians,
his exactions had become intolerable. The trading classes
were crushed down under taxation. The capital, instead of
being the city which gathered through the government an
immense income, which was in great part distributed among
the citizens, had become the city where the inhabitants felt
most heavily the exactions of their ruler. These exactions
made the people anxious for any change, hopeful that any

new Emperor would be less exacting than the actual occupant of the throne. The inhabitants of the provinces were not less dissatisfied. They had lost the sense of protection and security with which during long centuries the New Rome had surrounded them. They, moreover, had lost their respect for the imperial city, which had seen within a generation so many changes and attempted changes of rulers. The revenues of the Empire had been squandered by the last three occupants of the throne, partly in useless gratification of their own love of luxury, partly in maintaining themselves upon the throne. The whole population had lost patriotism under the belief that the existing order of things was not worth defending. The machinery of government had been strained to the utmost during the period when Constantinople had been occupied with dynastic struggles. Roads were neglected ; bridges, harbours, aqueducts, and fortifications were allowed to fall into ruins. Governors were too frequently changed. The organisation of the army was allowed to get out of order. The navy had been sacrificed. People even lost confidence in the administration of justice. The dynastic struggles had produced anarchy and national demoralisation. Contemporaneously with these struggles there was no side of the Empire which was not repeatedly attacked, and these attacks were often, as in the case of Tancred's expedition, and as in the case of the Turkish attack following the accession of Andronicos, due directly to the dynastic troubles ; while in other cases, where it is inexact to say that they were the direct cause, the attacks were invited by the disturbed state of the Empire. The opposition of pretenders to the throne, the struggles and differences in the imperial family within the city, and the attacks from without upon the Empire contributed tremendously to the weakening of the Empire.

CHAPTER V.

WEAKENING OF THE EMPIRE BY THE CRUSADES.

THE Crusades, and especially the third, contributed not a little to the weakening of the Empire. When the continual inroads of the Saracens, and, at a later date, of the Turks, had begun to tell upon the strength of the Empire, Western Europe grew alarmed at Mahometan progress. Although the Pope had summoned Christian princes to take up the cross, yet the movement of which he made himself the head, and which resulted in the first crusade, was in great part spontaneous. The first crusade, which was also the most successful, was the one with the least careful organisation, and is in this sense correctly described by Michaud, the historian of the Crusades, as a republican movement. Its members were inspired by a religious fervour which formed an excellent basis for discipline.

Difficulties in way of co-operation between Crusaders and Empire.

At an early period the Emperors of the East were glad to take advantage of the religious movement in the West, in order to inflict a defeat upon the common enemy of Christendom. I have already traced the history of the first and second crusades in so far as they affected the Empire, and have shown that the soldiers of the West found the Seljukian Turks of Asia Minor the most formidable enemies they had to encounter. In 1137 the Emperor, John Comnenos, took an active part in the crusade and captured several cities. His intention was to make Antioch his base of operations against the Mahometans. But the old spirit of jealousy between the members of the Eastern and Western Churches soon displayed itself. John considered that as the cities and countries taken from the Saracens had been captured by them from the Empire, they ought to be placed under his rule.

This interfered with the plan of forming an independent Christian state under the suzerainty of the Pope. Hence the soldiers of the East and the West respectively looked with jealousy on each other's conquests. The Pope naturally took the side of the Latin soldiers, and in 1137 ordered all who recognised his authority to leave Constantiople if John persisted in his design of taking possession of Antioch and of the places captured by the Crusaders.

The Empire continued, however, to be desirous of obtaining the aid of the Crusaders, and in the reign of Manuel we find the churches of the East seeking the aid of the Pope and of the Christians of the West. The favour shown by Manuel during the whole of his reign towards the Latin colonies in Constantinople, and which was the most unpopular part of his policy, the constant attempts which he made, and especially in 1166, to bring about a union of the churches even at the expense of the recognition of the supremacy of the Bishop of the Elder Rome, are all indications of that able Emperor's desire to make as much use as possible of the great religious movement of the West. But the feeling of hostility between the two churches was too strong to allow of a harmonious working together of their respective forces. The great breach in the Christian Church had been during several centuries continually widening. The Eastern Church, which was the more educated, had occupied itself with philosophical and theological questions with which the churchmen of the West gave themselves little trouble. The West had been more engaged with the spread of Christianity than with the accuracy of its teaching. The Eastern called itself Orthodox. The Western claimed rather to be Catholic ; and the difference in the names by which each chose to be called gives an indication of the difference of the leading tendency of each church respectively. 'The East,' says Dean Milman, 'enacted creeds, the West discipline.' [1] The East was occupied with

---

[1] Dean Stanley points out that the Orthodox Church has a special celebration of orthodoxy, and that at the beginning of Lent the anathemas against heresy take the place of the curses on crimes, which in the English Church are pronounced on Ash Wednesday.—*Eastern Church*, p. 22.

speculation, the West with practice. The want of harmony
between the two churches continually displayed itself, and in
the twelfth century, with which we are most concerned, there
took place the definite, formal separation between the Catholic
and the Orthodox Churches.

Decline of
the reli-
gious spirit
among the
Crusaders.

Meantime in the West, and in the latter half of the twelfth
century, the spirit of chivalry and the religious enthusiasm
which had been the chief motive forces of the first and second
crusades were rapidly disappearing. The nobles of Western
Europe were beginning to find occupation at home. A
movement had begun amongst them which spread to England, and in the time of John produced lasting benefits at
Runnymead. The barons of the West were beginning to
make common cause with the people against incompetent
sovereigns. The noble and lofty ideal which the early Crusaders had tried to realise, which a few years later was revived
in Saint Louis, was in great part forgotten. These men, from
Godfrey downwards, had dreamed of establishing Christ's
kingdom, of trying to execute an almost impossible task,
because it was that which God had given them.[1] The
Crusader affixed the cross to his shoulder in order that he
might 'offer to God cross for cross, passion for passion, and
that by mortifying his desires and making himself like unto
Christ he might share with Him in the resurrection.'[2] To us
Jerusalem is an ancient city with more or less sacred or
archæological associations, to be reached easily by steam
from Marseilles and shortly by rail from Jaffa. To the
Christian of the twelfth century it was very far distant, the
marvel of the earth, and so filled with relics and other
memorials of the Divine Life that it was readily confounded
with the heavenly Jerusalem. The crusades, in their practical
effect, helped the young nations of the West to shake off their
provinciality, to absorb a part of the civilisation of the East,

---

[1] The work of the crusades is repeatedly called *opus Dei, e.g.* Anon. Suessionensis, p. 5, *Exuviæ Sacræ*, and in many other places. The records of their
work are *Gesta Dei*. The Crusaders themselves are *Dei populus*. (*Recueil*, i.
256, and elsewhere.) They fought bravely *pour le party de Dieu. Lect. Long.
Exuv.* ii. 14.

[2] *Lectiones Longiprat. Exuv. Sac.* ii. 11.

and to think of something better than family or feudal quarrels. They prevented the civilisation of the West from becoming crystallised. They kept alive the great ideal of a kingdom presided over by the King of Righteousness, the Prince of Peace, under whose rule the continual state of warfare, the bloodshed, the treachery, the cruelty, that the Crusaders found among their own people, as among all half-civilised races, should cease. They breathed throughout the Western nations the breath of a common life, furnished them with a high ideal, and gave a great impetus to poetry in Western literature.

As we reach the end of the twelfth century we come to the end of this noble dream. The nations of the West were preparing to reap the harvest of results which had sprung from their efforts, by themselves developing national life, national art, and national literature. The crusading spirit, though it still existed, had lost much of its freshness, and each successive effort made by the forces of Christendom upon the Saracens was made with less fervour, less religious spirit, and less spontaneity than the effort which had preceded it.

During the crusades the men of the West were continually brought into contact with the inhabitants of the New Rome, and with other subjects of the Byzantine Emperor. The characteristic differences between them come out with great clearness in the pages of Anna Comnena, and at a later date in those of Nicetas, of William of Tyre, of Villehardouin, and a host of other contemporary historians. While it is clear that the men of the West were comparatively a horde of barbarians, who entered and finally destroyed a refined and civilised capital, the virtues and vices of the two races stand out with equal distinctness. The Crusaders felt, spoke, and acted in presence of the civilisation, but also of the unmanly luxury, the lying and treachery of the Byzantine court, as Englishmen have so often done in presence of some of the courts of farther Asia. They were rough and rude, drunken and licentious, and at times could be false and cruel. But their falseness and cruelty, compared with that of the

The Crusaders and the Romans.

Byzantines, were those of an average English private soldier in comparison with the craftiness and falseness, the ingenuity and persistence in cruelty of an Eastern sovereign of the worst type.   In their way and according to their lights they were religious, by which I mean that they were actuated, not only with a profound belief that they were doing a duty which God had appointed them, but that they hated lying, and cowardice, and cruelty because they believed them to be sinful.   The religion of the West, though allied with number-less superstitions, existed side by side with a sense of duty. The religion of the East was not only involved in an almost equal number of superstitions, but seemed to the Crusaders to be divorced from morality.   The great defect of the Eastern Churches then, as now, was the very slight effect which they exercised upon the conduct of life.   Comparatively indifferent to morality, they were jealously watchful of the last iota of what they chose to consider orthodoxy.   The Byzantines were ready to spend their time in discussing the attributes of the Unknowable, in arguing upon some shade of meaning to be attached to a phrase in the Creed or to the performance of a ceremony.   All the intellectual ability of the race seemed at times to be spent in subtle hair-splitting.   The Western Crusaders could no more hold their own in argument with the Greeks than an English private in presence of a Bengalee. But they could get to the root of the matter, could recognise, in spite of the shower of words with which the Byzantines sought to deceive them, what was right and what was wrong. They lost patience occasionally, and when they saw that their opponents were endeavouring to entangle them in words, boldly told them that they were not to be thus deceived.   Man for man, they felt themselves stronger than the Byzantines, and with the contempt of ignorance despised them on account of their wealth and learning.   On the other hand, the Byzantines wrote and spoke of them as bar-barians, recognised their superiority in strength and energy, but thought of them in return as ignorant men and as fanatics.

The disastrous failures of the second and third crusades

were attributed, for the most part unjustly, to the intrigues
and hostility of the Emperor of the New Rome. In the
second crusade, which commenced in 1147, the armies of the Difficulties
Cross were led, respectively, by Conrad, the first Swabian with the
king, and founder of the line of Swabian emperors of the crusade.
western division of the Roman Empire, and by Louis VII.
of France. Conrad's army was the first to reach the dominions under the rule of Constantinople. There was fair
reason to believe that the Crusaders would be well received.
The Eastern Empire, even more than the West, was at this
time interested in resisting and driving back the various
Moslem races that had already swamped so considerable a
part of its territory, and had invited the Crusaders to share
in this task. Moreover, Conrad and Manuel, the reigning
Byzantine emperor, had married sisters, and family affection
might have aided the two to work harmoniously together.
But the brothers-in-law were jealous of each other, and family
quarrels added fuel to the unfriendly feeling which soon
displayed itself. It must be noticed, in fairness to the Empire,
that it was hardly possible that the Western army should
march across the Balkan peninsula without giving cause for
dissatisfaction. The messengers sent by Manuel estimated
the number of men who had crossed the Danube at ninety
thousand. The army was at once attended by another of
Byzantine troops, intended to see that the Crusaders complied
with the conditions on which they had been allowed to enter
Manuel's territory. But the army, as indeed all armies at
that time, was much less under discipline than are those of
modern states. The crusading armies in particular had so
much of a volunteer character about them that great licence
had to be allowed. Conrad's was attended by an unusual
number of pilgrims, over whom it was difficult to exercise
control. Pilgrimages in the East are in our own day, usually
at least, occasions for the widest licence. The pilgrims among
the Crusaders were ready to plunder the inhabitants of the
districts through which they passed on every occasion. As
great numbers of them were without money, plunder was
indeed necessary if they were to live. The inhabitants

naturally demanded high prices, and perhaps as naturally cheated the Crusaders as much as possible. Conrad seems to have done his best to preserve order, but neither his precautions nor those of Manuel were sufficient to prevent continual attacks with the object of plunder on the inhabitants of the country through which the army was passing. Before long the provinces were ransacked by pilgrims and troops alike for provisions—as if they formed part of an enemy's country. The Bulgarians and other subjects of the Empire retaliated. A relation of Conrad was plundered and murdered in a monastery at Adrianople by Byzantine soldiers. Conrad, who had advanced two days' journey beyond that city, sent back a body of troops under his nephew, the celebrated Frederic Barbarossa, to punish the offenders. The monastery was burnt. The Byzantine troops were attacked, and it was not until after several men had been killed that the commander of the imperial troops succeeded in preventing a general engagement. The incident served to increase the ill-feeling that existed between the two armies. At length the Crusaders reached Constantinople, and behaved in its vicinity as if they were in an enemy's country. The beautiful villas of the Byzantine nobles and merchants existing in the neighbourhood of the capital were ruthlessly plundered and destroyed. After passing the Bosphorus the army began to encounter more serious difficulties and met with a series of disasters. The latter were due partly to bad management and partly to the difficulties inherent to the enterprise itself. The difficulty of finding provisions in a country which was already thinly inhabited and the inhabitants of which were treated as enemies was the first cause of these disasters. The fact that the journey was made in summer through a country which was even then largely troubled with malarial fever added much to the difficulties. All their misfortunes were attributed by the Crusaders to the Greeks, and a disposition began to develop itself very early among the former to conquer Christian people when they were unable to subdue the Mahometans.

The division of Crusaders under Louis VII. met that under

the leadership of Conrad at Nicæa. The feeling of hostility created among the French division was not less than that which had been aroused among the Teutons. Louis found the subjects of the Emperor Manuel not less exacting than had Conrad. It must be said to his credit that he put down disorder in his camp with a stronger hand. Soldiers found plundering were severely punished. Some were sentenced to the loss of their hands and feet. Both king and nobles had about them much more of the religious spirit of the Crusaders than was to be found in the division under Conrad. Louis seems also to have prevented his army being encumbered by so large a crowd of camp followers and pilgrims as accompanied Conrad. In spite, however, of the more complete organisation of his army, it was with difficulty that he made his way to Constantinople.[1] On his arrival an incident occurred which showed the bitter feeling of hostility towards the Greeks which had sprung up, and the intensity of the sentiment which had led the Crusaders to take up arms. While the army was encamped before the capital they learned that Manuel had concluded the treaty with the Sultan of Iconium, of which I have already spoken. The shock to the Christians of the West was severe. The alliance was treason to the cause of Christianity. If we assume that the sole cause in dispute between the northern and the seceding states of America was that of slavery, that the North fought with the sole object of setting the slaves free, and that England had made an alliance with the South, we may judge what the feelings of the French Crusaders were from what the feelings of every honest and righteous man would have been in our times. A council was held in the French camp. Indignation was loudly expressed, and the Bishop of Langres proposed that before attempting the deliverance of Christ's sepulchre they should punish Christ's enemies in Constantinople. Better counsels prevailed. All the invective, the indignation, and the eloquence of the bishop and his party

---

[1] Heyd (*Geschichte des Levantehandels*, p. 243) observes with justice that it is remarkable, considering the annoyance Manuel had received from the Latins, that he allowed the Crusaders to pass through the Empire.

were in vain. The French nobles declared that they had taken the cross to fight against infidels and to defend Jerusalem. It was not their business to punish heretics or destroy Christian cities.

The army crossed the Bosphorus and pushed forward toward the Turkish dominions in Asia Minor. But fever, the necessity of finding forage, and the difficulty of making progress over a country where the roads had been destroyed, greatly reduced the numbers of the army. Many of the sick had to be abandoned. Louis embarked with the bulk of his army at Adalia for Antioch. Seven thousand men were left behind. These attempted to force their way along the coast to Antioch, but with disastrous results. Most of them perished in the attempt, though a few saved their lives by embracing Mahometanism.

Failure of crusade attributed to Empire.

The attempt upon Damascus under the combined efforts of Louis, Conrad, and Baldwin of Jerusalem completely failed. Much had been expected of this crusade ; preparations had been made on a gigantic scale by both the great nations of the West ; and when at length the tidings reached Europe of terrible disasters and general failure men's hearts sank within them. In the West fault was largely attributed to the schismatic Christians of the East. They had betrayed Christ ; they had assisted His enemies ; they had united themselves now with the Turks and now with the Saracens in order to defeat the cause of the Cross. The disorder, the jealousies among the Western soldiers, the want of discipline, were for a while forgotten. The news of the apostasy of the Emperor of the New Rome, in allying himself with the infidel, deepened the prejudice against what was called the treachery of the Greeks. In the months and years during which the evil tidings came pouring into the West every fresh calamity was attributed to the heretical schismatics of the East.

The third crusade.

The failure of the next, that is, of the third, crusade, which was undertaken in 1187, still further increased the animosity of the people of the West towards the subjects of the New Rome.

Saladin had succeeded in again bringing Egypt under the

spiritual rule of the Caliph of Bagdad. In 1187 he had captured Jerusalem, and nearly all Palestine was again under Moslem rule. William, Archbishop of Tyre, the chronicler who has left us the most complete account of this crusade, was, with others, commissioned by the Pope to preach a Holy War. He went to France, met Henry II. of England and Philip Augustus of France, who laid down their arms on his invitation to join in a nobler warfare. He pointed out to them that the Christian states of the East, whose duty it was to protect the West from the invasions of the Saracens, were reduced to the cities of Tyre, Antioch, and Tripoli ; that the people of forty Christian cities had been chased from their homes, spoiled of their goods, and were wandering among the miscreants of Asia without finding a stone whereon to lay their heads. According to the Monk of Peterborough, he preached so successfully that both kings determined to take up the cross, and from enemies became friends. A tax for the purpose of the crusade was levied both in England and France upon those who should not take part in the expedition, and was known as the Saladin tithe. The friendship of the two kings was of short duration ; but on the death of Henry his son Richard entered heartily into the preparations for the crusade. The kings and the Pope, warned by the disorders of the previous expedition, made stringent rules for the preservation of discipline. Gambling was forbidden. As the presence of women in the first crusade had given rise to much trouble, orders were given that they should not be allowed to join the new expedition.

Frederic Barbarossa, the nephew of Conrad, whom he had already accompanied into the Holy Land, took charge of the great German division of the Crusaders. It was this division of the army which passed through the dominions of the new Emperor, Isaac Angelos. Frederic had not only experience but great natural ability. He was able to prevent some of the worst evils which had attended the march of the German army under Conrad. No pilgrim was allowed to accompany the army unless he could show that he possessed sufficient money to maintain him for two years. Discipline was fairly maintained. Careful dispositions were taken for the supply

of food, and the Emperor was himself anxious to avoid anything like hostility between his army and the Byzantine
troops. Frederic sent an embassy to Saladin requesting him
to surrender Jerusalem. The answer was a declaration of
war. He sent another embassy to Kilidji Arslan, the Sultan
of Iconium, which apparently met with greater success. The
Turkish Sultan was accused by the Moslem writers of belonging to the sect of philosophers, and was indeed believed by
Pope Alexander III. to have secretly embraced Christianity,
or to be ready to do so. The 'Sultan of the Turks, the
Armenians, and the Syrians,' as he styled himself, promised
help of various kinds to Frederic, and Europe was astonished
at the novel sight of fifty Moslem knights who came to bring
these promises of aid. Frederic sent to Manuel to ask permission to pass through the Byzantine dominions, promising
at the same time to prevent any disorder and to pay for all
that was supplied them. A treaty according such permission
was solemnly entered into. Frederic's progress, until he
entered the Empire, met with no obstacles. Bela, king of
Hungary, received him with magnificence at the famous river
fortress of Gran. As soon, however, as he had reached the
imperial territories troubles began. The Wallachs, Bulgarians, and Greeks, who remembered but too well what they
had suffered from the former crusade a generation earlier,
impeded his progress. The Servians asked the aid of Frederic
against Isaac. Nicetas himself, the historian of Isaac Angelos, and who was at this time governor of Philippopolis,
admits that the Greeks gave trouble and broke the treaty.
Convoys of provisions on their way to Frederic were sent
back. The passes were impeded by trunks of trees, which
were placed there, as he alleges, by Isaac's orders.[1] The
Germans, however, managed to reach Philippopolis by an unexpected route in August 1189, and occupied the city. They
found that the bulk of the inhabitants, alarmed at the approach of what they regarded as a hostile army, had fled, and
that the only occupants belonged to an Armenian colony

---

[1] Nicetas is always bitterly hostile towards Isaac, and his statement, therefore,
can hardly be taken as altogether trustworthy.

which had long been settled there.[1] A little later the Protostrator, acting under the orders of Isaac, endeavoured to
surprise the Germans while making a raid for provisions.
But the Armenians had given notice of the ambuscade to
Frederic. The Germans met Isaac's troops and utterly defeated them. They attaked Adrianople and Didymotica and
made raids into Macedonia and Thrace. Isaac was now only
too anxious to get rid of the Crusaders, and therefore renewed his treaty with Frederic, agreed that his army should
cross into Asia Minor by the Dardanelles, sent him nine
hundred hostages, and prepared a flotilla of fifteen hundred
ships and twenty-six galleys, on which the army passed out
of the European dominions of the Empire. Isaac, according to
the Arab writers, still maintained the show of friendship with
Saladin, and was, in fact, playing the double game of a weak
man, professing to be friendly with Frederic while he was
writing to Saladin that the German army was so weak that it
would accomplish nothing. When Frederic reached the dominions of the Sultan of Iconium, the Turks endeavoured to
delay his progress. From them, however, he would brook no
delay. He defeated the Sultan's army in a pitched battle,
stormed Iconium and captured it. The Turks, as usual, Its diffi-
offered a continued resistance. 'The more,' says a report culties with the Turks.
written by a pilgrim to the Pope, 'the more we killed, the
more they multiplied. During many days we fought from
morning till night.' The army was in the greatest distress
for want of food and forage, and was decimated by disease.
All this time the Turks, or rather their ruler, Kilidji Arslan,
professed to desire the friendship of the Germans, so that the
Western chronicler remarks that the Turks were greater dis-
semblers than even the Greeks. In this crusade it was noted
that the Christian populations, which had on previous occasions flocked to the Christian armies for support and to give
aid, fled before it, a fact affording striking evidence that the

---

[1] Nicetas, Book II. c. iv., is careful to point out that there was a great resemblance between the religious opinions of the Germans and those of the Armenians.
They used unleavened bread, and had other customs which had been 'improved
upon' by the Orthodox.

subjects of the Empire had lost all hope of relief against the Mahometans from the soldiers of the West.

Complete failure of the expedition.

As the army of Frederic advanced its sufferings became more intense. The Turks harassed them daily, and yet were always defeated. The straits to which the Crusaders were reduced were terrible. Horses were killed in order that their blood might be drunk. The foul, fever-impregnated water of the marshes became sweet to the soldiers in their extremity. Some even deserted the faith and went over to the infidels. Yet the discipline preserved by Frederic was worthy of the race which he led. The Armenian patriarch, writing to Saladin, describes the Germans as extraordinary men, of inextinguishable courage—an army submitted to the severest discipline and in which no crime remained unpunished. Passing from Asia Minor through the territory of the Armenians in Cilicia, Frederic proceeded to Antioch, and the conquest of Palestine appeared within his grasp. There, however, his progress was checked. He died in June 1190, according to one account, from cold caught while bathing in the Calycadnus, near Seleucia. Nicetas, however, affirms that he was drowned in that river. The Greek historian, like the Western writers, does justice to his ability, his burning zeal for Christianity, his bravery, and his disinterestedness.

Death of Frederic.

After his death his son, also named Frederic, became the leader of the German Crusaders. Their success was, however, slight, and six months after his father's death the son perished with a good many of his followers.

A hundred thousand Crusaders had left Europe. Only five thousand arrived in Palestine. Battle and disease had worked havoc among them. In all the country of North Syria, says an Arab writer, there was not a family which had not three or four German slaves. The German army, in the words of Michaud, overcame every enemy which it met, and disappeared at the moment when its obstacles and its dangers had been overcome. Saladin was for a time everywhere successful.

Conrad in Jerusalem.

While Richard of England was on his way to Palestine, Conrad, the son of the Marquis of Montferrat, who, as we have seen, after the defence of Isaac Angelos in Constantinople had refused to follow the Emperor to Adrianople, had gone to the Holy Land. In the year 1191 he was at Tyre, which he saved from an attack of the Saracens. His aged father had surrendered on his parole, and was prisoner in the hands of the Saracens at Damascus. Saladin promised to release him and to give him rich possessions in Syria if Conrad would open to him the gates of Tyre. If the son refused, Saladin threatened to place the old man in the fore-front of the battle. Conrad replied that he despised the gifts which Saladin offered, that the life of his father was less dear to him than the cause for which the Christians were fighting, and that if the Sultan was sufficiently barbarous to kill an old man who had given himself up on parole, he would glory in being the son of a martyr. The city was saved.

Conrad, like most of the members of his house, was full of ambition, and conceived the idea of making himself king of Jerusalem. On the death of Sybilla, the wife of Guy de Lusignan, the heir to the sacred throne was her sister Isabella, who was wife of Humphrey of Thoron. Conrad determined to marry her, but there were two obstacles in the way : each party was already married. Conrad persuaded Isabella to apply for a divorce on the ground that she had married Humphrey against her will. Conrad possessed, says Geoffrey de Vinsauf, the eloquence of Ulysses. He bribed the court and corrupted the clergy. In vain did the Archbishop of Canterbury protest against the divorce as a bigamous or, as Geoffrey says, a trigamous marriage, and threaten the thunders of the Church. A council of churchmen declared Isabella's marriage null, and Conrad, who had already been married in Constantinople, where his wife was still living, took to himself a second wife.[1]

---

[1] Conrad, who succeeded to the title of Marquis of Montferrat, is said to have been thrice married. Of his first wife nothing is known. His second was Theodora, sister of the Emperor Isaac Angelos, whom he married in 1186, at the time when he was present in Constantinople and gave aid in suppressing the rebellion of Branas. The story of the marriage, as told by Nicetas, is that Isaac had sent to propose marriage between his sister and Boniface of Montferrat, that when the messengers found that Boniface was already married and that Conrad was a widower, they considered that the proposal might be made to the latter, and that

The archbishop excommunicated those who had contracted and those who had agreed to the marriage. The
scandal increased the discord which already existed among
the Crusaders. Guy de Lusignan still claimed that the
throne of Jerusalem was his. After considerable difficulty
the Crusaders agreed to leave the choice to Richard and
Philip. The two kings, however, were themselves at enmity.
Each accused the other of treason, and their subjects naturally
took the part of their sovereigns.

England
contributes
to weaken-
ing the
Empire.

In April Richard of England left Messina, in Sicily, with
a hundred and fifty galleys for the Holy Land. It was in
connection with this enterprise that England contributed her
share towards the weakening of the Byzantine empire. Isaac
Comnenos had seized Cyprus and declared himself emperor
of the island. He might have continued to reign had he not
attacked Englishmen. Richard's fleet was scattered in a
storm. Three ships belonging to it were wrecked on the
coast of Cyprus. The Englishmen who escaped from the
wreck were imprisoned, put in irons, and their property con-
fiscated. The act was done probably to convince Saladin
that Isaac was his friend. Not content with this outrage, he
ventured on an insult which a high-spirited man like Richard

---

it would be more advantageous since he was the elder brother. Their promises
were large. Conrad accepted, and came to Constantinople and married Theodora.
After defeating Branas he refused to follow the Emperor to Adrianople, alleging
that he had not received sufficient honours, that the privilege of being Cæsar only
conferred upon him the doubtful honour of wearing different coloured buskins
from ordinary mortals, and that he had married Theodora incidentally and attached no importance to the marriage (πάρεργον ὁδοῦ, Nicetas, p. 516; 'obiter
imperatoris sororem duxerat'). The account of Nicetas is in conformity with that
of other historians. Robert de Clari, however (p. 24-6), states that Conrad
escaped because he learned that Isaac had meditated treachery against him, that
he had sent him out to fight Branas and had shut the gate of the city behind him,
and that after his success he was warned that it was not safe for him to remain.

The question whether Conrad's wife was living when he married Theodora is
doubtful. Geoffrey is contradicted by Nicetas (p. 498) in saying that his *first*
wife was alive. The subject is examined in the *Recueil des Historiens Grecs*, vol.
ii. p. 421. It appears to me that the balance of evidence is in favour of the
opinion that Theodora was living at the time of the second marriage. See the
Itinerary of Richard I., Bohn's Translation, p. 141. The part played by the
family of Montferrat in connection with the fall of Constantinople was more important than that played by any other family.

was not likely to forgive. Richard's sister and Berengaria of Navarre, to whom he was betrothed, sought shelter from a storm in the port of Limasol. The rebel Emperor refused to allow them to remain in his dominions. The ship proceeded to Rhodes, where Richard was then residing. He sailed at once for Cyprus, demanded the surrender of the English prisoners, and when Isaac refused, landed his army. His attacks upon the Emperor ended with the conquest of the whole island and the capture of Isaac himself. He carried the usurper with him to Palestine, and gave him as a slave to one of his followers. He ruled the island in Western fashion, established the feudal system, and soon changed a rich into a poor province. Subsequently he gave Cyprus to the knights of the Temple.

In the year 1192 Conrad, while still at Tyre, was assassinated, as I have already mentioned, by an emissary of Khasis, the Old Man of the Mountain. There were suspicions at the time that the murder was done on the instigation of Richard, but according to the Arab writers the suspicions were unfounded. The leadership of the Crusaders was now in Richard's hands, but his hasty temper, and the same want of statesmanship which characterised his reign in England, caused the victories which he gained by his valour to be fruitless. In the beginning of 1193 the Pope wrote to the English clergy that on account of the dissensions of its leaders the crusade had not answered his expectations, and almost immediately after Richard left Palestine.

With the truce signed between Saladin and Richard, the third crusade came to an end. The united forces of England, France, and Germany had been completely defeated. No expedition so numerous or so well equipped had either before or has since left Europe, and none has more signally failed. The Germans had lost a magnificent army and their Emperor. The French and English had lost the flower of their chivalry. The disasters which had befallen the armies of the West had been of a crushing character. Germans, Frenchmen, and Englishmen alike had learned, by a terrible experience, with what a persistent, unrelenting, and dangerous enemy the

Failure of the third crusade,

Byzantine Empire had to deal. It is, in fact, in reading the history of so gigantic a failure, that we realise what the strength of that Empire had been which had been able to hold its own against the Turks. The Crusaders in their dealings with the same enemy had had a similar experience. The imperial troops had also won almost every battle, had inflicted crushing defeats upon the Turks, had reconquered the country again and again, but new hordes, ever pressing into Asia Minor from Central Asia, had enabled the enemy to fight successfully for Islam and to drain away the strength of the Empire by ever-renewed struggles.

Two years after the departure of Richard, namely, in 1195, the truce which he had concluded was broken. Saladin died suddenly in 1195, and his empire was at once divided. One of his sons named Aziz took Egypt, the eldest named Afdal became possessed of Palestine and Damascus, and a third, Dahir, of Aleppo. Saladin's brother Malek-Adel seized Mesopotamia. When Aziz and Afdal quarrelled, Malek-Adel took advantage of their differences to make himself sultan and became master of Egypt, where as we shall see he played an important part in the outrage of the fourth crusade.

and of supplementary expedition. At the end of 1196, Henry the Sixth, the Swabian successor of Frederic, determined to undertake a crusade, and for this purpose sent an embassy to Constantinople to make exorbitant demands on the new Emperor Alexis. This crusade, which may be regarded as supplementary to the third, lasted but a few months and was a miserable failure. The Emperor of the New Rome dreaded the passage of the Crusaders through his territory, and for the first time in Byzantine history, says Nicetas, the Emperor determined to buy peace. Five thousand pounds of gold were promised to Henry as an annual contribution towards the crusade. The Emperor levied a 'German tax' on the people in order to raise this sum, and for this purpose assembled what we may describe as the three estates of the realm, the senate, the clergy, and the guilds which represented the artizans. The people, however, refused to pay the new tax, and the Emperor was reduced to the necessity of raising what he could from the treasures of the churches. In 1197, Henry died at Messina, much to the relief of the population of the Two Sicilies and of Constantinople, and before the money which had been collected was remitted.

The failure of the third crusade and of the supplementary expedition increased the bitter feeling in the West towards the Empire of the East. Again was the cry raised that the heterodox Empire had betrayed Christendom. Instead of assisting the soldiers of the West, Alexis was accused of giving aid and support to the Saracens and the Turks. The failures which were due to the division of the Crusaders themselves, to the quarrels between Philip and Richard, and later on to those between Richard and Conrad, and to the opposition of the Turks and Saracens, were set down to the intrigues of the Byzantine emperors. Even the dreadful mortality among the Army of the Cross in Asia Minor and in Syria was charged to the same account. The Greeks had poisoned the wells, had infected the provisions, had diverted the water-courses. No crime was too monstrous to attribute to those who had for the most part been passive spectators of the sufferings of the Cross. 'Those who were not with us were against us,' says one of the chroniclers. *Increase of ill-feeling towards the Empire*

It must not be forgotten that during the whole period of the crusades, and to the last, this sentiment of hostility was increased by the great importance which the popes attached to the schism of the Orthodox Church. The history of the century had been one long effort to endeavour to persuade or to frighten the rulers of Constantinople into acknowledging the supremacy of the Bishop of Rome. As these failed many attempts were made, and especially during the last twenty years of the twelfth century, to detach from Constantinople the various churches which had hitherto acknowledged the authority of its patriarch. Considerable success had rewarded these efforts so far as the Armenians were concerned. Innocent the Third continued them with the energy which he threw into everything which he undertook. In 1199 he had induced a provincial council in Dalmatia to accept the Roman rite by promising aid against the King of Hungary. In the same *added to by ecclesiastical differences.*

year he had sent a legate to Constantinople and an agent
to John of Bulgaria, to negotiate the establishment of a
patriarchate, and to give that pretender the crown which the
Emperor denied.   Two years later he sent an embassy to
Servia to detach the Servians from Constantinople.   Like his
predecessors, he too made many attempts at Constantinople
to persuade its rulers to accept the authority of the Elder
Rome.   All these various attempts show how great was the
importance attached to this question by the popes.   The
feeling of irritation at their non-success found expression
among the Crusaders in bitter hatred for the schismatics.
It would be easy to give illustrations of this bitterness.   No
acts done by Protestants against Roman Catholics, or *vice
versâ*, exceed in barbarity the treatment of the Greek priests
and their worship as described by Eustathius of Salonica,
and these acts can only be attributed to religious hatred.
Thus it came about that having in the third crusade begun by
cordially hating the members of a heretical church, they
ended by attributing their own blunders, failures, and crimes
to the interference of those whom they thus hated.   This
feeling bore bitter fruit when almost immediately afterwards
the fourth crusade was organised, and was undoubtedly one
of the principal causes which, as we shall see, enabled its
leaders to divert the expedition from its lawful and intended
purpose into an attack upon a Christian city.

In another manner the crusades contributed directly to
the capture of Constantinople.   They had shown to the West
how greatly the power of the Byzantine Empire had been
lessened.   Constantinople was still a city which had never
been captured, but the weakness of its emperors, the ease
with which dynastic changes had been made, and the
continual troubles which existed within the city, led the
military leaders of the West to believe that she would be
unable to resist a combined attack by land and sea.   The
crusades   had   thus   not   only   largely   contributed   to   the
weakening of the Empire, but they had shown that weakness
to the West in a way which directly invited invasion.

133

CHAPTER VI.

WEAKENING OF THE EMPIRE BY ATTACKS FROM THE WEST.

1. *From Normans of Sicily.*

AMONG the troubles of the last century and a half preceding the capture of Constantinople which came from the side of Europe, the most serious were those which were caused by the inhabitants of Italy. At the very time that our fathers were feeling the heavy hand of the Normans from France, the Byzantine Empire was being weakened by their kinsmen in Italy, and that at the moment when it had need of all its strength to resist the Asiatic hordes who were pouring into it.

The population of the Two Sicilies was during the eleventh century still mainly Greek. The language, except among the Arab-speaking Mahometans, was not Italian but Greek. Several cities in Southern Italy still admitted the rule of the New Rome. The Normans had, however, conquered and settled many portions of Southern Italy, and in 1062 had won the island of Sicily from its Saracen conquerors. Robert Wiscard, and under him his son Bohemund, led the Normans into Epirus and Thessaly, and waged war upon the Emperor Alexis with considerable success until 1085, when, with the death of Robert, the Norman projects of conquest in the Byzantine empire came, for a time, to an end. The war had been costly to the Empire. Durazzo had been captured by the Sicilian Normans after a long siege, in which the enemy had been once severely defeated by the Greek commander. After its capture, owing to the jealousy of Alexis of his own general, Robert had pushed across to Larissa, and the Empire had been hard pressed to recapture that city. Alexis had been in such straits that he had obtained 7,000 light cavalry

Progress of Normans in Sicily.

from Suliman, Sultan of Nicæa, to assist him. In 1107, Bohemund again invaded the Empire. His army, as Finlay [1]
remarks, resembled that with which William the Norman
conquered England.   It was composed of experienced military
adventurers who joined Bohemund in the hope of plunder.
The Adriatic was crossed nearly at its narrowest part, and
siege was again laid to Dyrrachium, the modern Durazzo·
Alexis concluded a treaty with Faliero, the Doge of Venice,
by which the republic was to aid in the war against Bohemund.
By the energy of Alexis and the assistance of the Waring
guard, the enemy was worn out, and Bohemund had, in 1108,
to sue for peace and to accept it on humiliating terms.   In
the treaty [2] the invader declares that he repents him of
what he has done ; that he wishes to become for the future
the liegeman, the servant, and the subject of the Empire ; that
he will fight all enemies of the Emperor ; that, in regard to
cities which the Emperor may choose to give him, he will
receive the oath of fidelity from no one, and will take it to no
one but the Emperor.   All these promises he swears to observe
by the passion of Christ who is now passionless, by the cross
which is invincible, by the gospels which have conquered the
world, and by the crown of thorns, the nails, and the holy
lance.

In 1130, when Roger the Norman became king of the Two
Sicilies, his investiture was made by a legate of the Pope.
This was in itself a denial of the suzerainty of, and a formal
and successful attempt to detach the kingdoms from, the New
Rome, and was so regarded on both sides.   The power and
title of the Roman emperor was in the West held at this time
by a German king.   Roger made an alliance with Conrad
against the Roman Emperor in the East.   A desultory war
followed, which was continued by William, the son of Roger,
who conducted it with an energy and thoroughness which
would have done credit to his namesake in England.   William
captured Corfu, sent his fleets into the Ægean, pillaged
Corinth and several islands of the Archipelago.   In 1156 a

[1] Finlay, ii. 145. *Byzantine and Greek Empires.*
[2] Given in full by Anna Comnena, Book xl.

fleet of forty vessels sailed ostentatiously to Constantinople itself, to proclaim William, lord of Sicily, Aquila, Capua, Calabria, and the neighbouring isles. The vessels, or some of them, worked their way up to the Bosphorus and into the Golden Horn as far as the imperial palace of Blachern. The crews discharged gilded arrows against the palace walls, and pompously proclaimed the praises of their sovereign to the assembled inhabitants.

During the next twenty years the Sicilians gave little trouble to the Empire. When Andronicos seized the throne in 1180, Alexis, a nephew of Manuel, who had been attached to that emperor as cup-bearer, was banished by the usurper. He fled to Sicily, and, in the language of Nicetas, discharged upon his country the venom he had amassed against Andronicos. He succeeded, probably without difficulty, in persuading the Norman king, William the Second, to turn his arms once more against the Empire. Roger had done his best to plunder the southern portion of the Balkan peninsula, which lay immediately across the Adriatic. The subjects of his successors still looked in the same direction with envious eyes to the prosperous lands under the rule of Constantinople. They would probably in no case have been troubled to find excuses to justify them in their own sight in allying themselves with Alexis and in invading the country of the schismatics, who had cut themselves off from the rule of the Pope and the real Emperor. But they had now a fair pretext for the invasion. The Emperor Manuel had long been accused by his subjects of sacrificing their interests to benefit the Latin colonists. The Amalfians, Venetians, Pisans, and Genoese had all been the objects of his favour. They were accounted rich and were naturally believed to have enriched themselves at the expense of the Greeks. The Emperor himself had been twice married, and each time to a Frank wife. His son Alexis had espoused a daughter of Philip of France, and his daughter a Marquis of Montferrat. During the crusading troubles he had asked the Pope to send a legate with the army, and had expressed a wish to Alexander the Third, the reigning Pope, that Greeks and Latins might be

William attacks the Empire

united as one flock under one shepherd. All this leaning towards the West tended to make the Latin colonists, as I have already pointed out, unpopular with the other inhabitants of Constantinople. On the other hand, Manuel was a favourite with the Latins, and, on the whole, deservedly so.[1] The Latins were, however, regarded by his subjects as intruders, as professors of a hostile faith, as countrymen of the enemies of Romania and as court favourites. They were accused of having monopolised nearly all the wharves on the Golden Horn, and of having persuaded the Emperor to dispossess the Greeks of the best business quarters in the city. On the death of Manuel in 1180, the struggle took place which I have already described. On the approach of Andronicos the party of the protosebastos—which was largely increased from the Latin colonists—melted quickly away. The leader was arrested by the Waring guard, armed, as Nicetas is careful to tell us, with their double-edged axes, and imprisoned.[2] A few days afterwards his eyes were put out. His death was the signal for a massacre of the Latins, who numbered at this time no less than 60,000.[3] They had committed the blunder of taking sides in the quarrel between the two rival claimants for the throne, and, unfortunately for them, the candidate whom they favoured had lost. They were attacked on the one side by the fleet sent across the Bosphorus by Andronicos under the command of Contostephanos, and on the other by the mob of the capital. The Greek historian tells us only that the Latins, being unable to resist, abandoned their houses, full of silver and wealth, to pillage ; that some escaped by sea, but that those who were taken were killed. The Latin historian adds details which show the attack to have been much more serious in character than the account of Nicetas would lead us to believe. Hatred of rich foreigners and favourites ; hostility to those who had been alternately

on pretext of mas-sacres of 1182.

---

[1] ' *Il avoit esté li plus bons prince del monde.*' ' Defuncto enim domino Manuele, inclytæ recordationis imperatore felicissimo,' says William of Tyre, *Western Historians. Recueil*, vol. ii. p. 1079.

[2] Nicetas, 323, ed. Bonn.

[3] So says Eustathius of Thessalonica, who speaks of the Sicilian expedition as war of vengeance for the massacre of 1182.

threatening and coaxing them to betray their religion, by acknowledging the supremacy of the bishop of the Elder Rome, led to savage and brutal outrages. The Latins expected or feared an attack as soon as they learned that the protosebastos had been captured. Some knew, says William of Tyre, that there was a plot. But it is unnecessary to assume the existence of any organised scheme for plunder. They belonged to a defeated party, at a time when 'the spoils to the victors' was the universally recognised rule. Most tried to escape from the capital. A band of Latins seized forty-four galleys which they found in the harbour, while another took possession of ships, of which there were a great number in the Golden Horn, and fled. The sick, the aged, and those who did not believe that a massacre was likely, remained behind. Of these, some fought in the defence of their property but were soon overpowered. Four thousand of both sexes, says William of Tyre, were sold by the Greeks to the Turks and to other infidel peoples.[1] Few were spared. Women and children fell victims to an indiscriminate and reckless fury. The forces of Andronicos joined the mob and took part in a general pillage of the Latin quarter. The priests were struck down in the churches which Manuel had allowed them to build. The sick in the hospital of St. John were dragged from their beds or were burnt in the building. The Latin quarters after being pillaged were destroyed. Cardinal John, who had been sent to negotiate for the union of the churches, was beheaded. His head was tied to a dog's tail and sent spinning about the streets. The reports of the Western writers are doubtless exaggerated, but it is evident that the massacre was an insensate outbreak of mob violence, and caused a great amount of just anger in Italy and Sicily, and it was natural that the countrymen of the sufferers should be ready to avenge their death.

Tancred, the cousin of King William, was appointed leader of an expedition against the Empire, having among its objects that of avenging the outrages of 1182. In 1185 he seized

Tancred appointed leader.

---

[1] William of Tyre, xxii. c. 12, p. 1083 ; *Recueil*, vol. ii. ; and Eust. ch. 28-30, ed. Migne.

Durazzo, which we have already seen attacked by the grand-fathers of the present invaders.   More successful than Bohemund, he captured it, and then pushed boldly across the peninsula to Salonica.   Aided by his fleet he took the city by assault after a siege of nine days.   The slaughter of the Greeks was great, while the loss of the Sicilians was not more than 3,000.   The city was sacked in the fashion for which the Normans had obtained an unenviable renown.   Great numbers of the inhabitants were put to the sword.   The churches were robbed and defiled with every indignity that a brutal soldiery could devise against a people of a different religion.   The sacred vessels were used by the soldiers for the ordinary purposes of life, or destroyed for the sake of their metal.   The wealth of the city and the neighbouring country made them regard the occasion, says a contemporary, as Paradise open for them to loot.   Every form of insult and torture was used to compel the inhabitants to discover their wealth, and the most gross and wanton cruelties were inflicted upon the Romans simply for the sake of insult.   The soldiers polluted the wells, and in pure wantonness mixed filth with the food of those whom they met.   When the Greek priests intoned the liturgy of their church, the Sicilian soldiers howled in mockery.   The hymns of the church were sung down by indecent songs.   The impression created by the account of the two Greek historians of these events is, that the barbarous soldiers took a malicious pleasure in outraging a people whom they felt to be superior to themselves in civilisation and inferior in physique.   The sack was followed by the ravaging of Macedonia and Thrace.   Andronicos, driven to his wits' end to meet the attacks just then made upon the Empire from all sides, entered into an arrangement with Saladin, by which the latter was to be allowed to conquer Palestine on condition that the Saracen should hold it as a fief of the Empire.   Saladin, on the other hand, was to aid the Emperor in capturing Iconium from the Turks. Meantime the Emperor had prepared a fleet of one hundred vessels to send against the Sicilians.   But his brief reign was nearly at an end.   He was succeeded by Isaac.   The war was continued under the

Sack of
Salonica.

new sovereign with fresh vigour. The Sicilians were attacked at Mosynopolis and on the plains of Demetriza and were defeated. Salonica was retaken and the fleet in the Ægean nearly destroyed. Durazzo itself was abandoned by the King of Sicily, and the Norman fleet in the Adriatic was shattered by a tempest. In the short space of a few months the Sicilian expedition was thus utterly defeated. The rough vigour and genius for war possessed by the Normans had failed as completely before the disciplined troops of the New Rome as the Turks had always done when they had been met on anything like equal terms. The expedition, however, had weakened the hold of Constantinople over the southern portion of the peninsula, and had shown the Italians that the Empire was not invulnerable. The Sicilians continued to hanker after possessions in Romania, and in 1194, in the midst of the dynastic struggles of the Empire and towards the end of the weak reign of Isaac, Henry, king of Sicily, claimed from the Empire the restitution of all the country between Durazzo and Salonica. Irene, daughter of Isaac, was detained in Sicily as a hostage for the satisfaction of this claim. Isaac, fully occupied with other troubles, entered into negotiation with Henry, with the object of putting an end to the difficulty by paying an imdemnity. The death of the Sicilian king, however, in 1197, before the conclusion of these negotiations, relieved Isaac of the Sicilian claims.

The Normans of Sicily had thus been for more than a century a thorn in the side of the Empire. The troubles which they gave arose partly out of the desire for adventure, partly out of the desire to acquire new territory, and in the most important expedition from the wish to punish the authors of the massacre of 1182. The Norsemen were tempted to invade Romania much as their fathers had been tempted into Normandy and their brethren into England. They had succeeded in diverting a considerable amount of force from the Empire which would otherwise have been employed in fighting the Turks. Hitherto the south of the Balkan peninsula had been regarded as the portion of the Empire which was least open to attack. From the moment of the appearance of the Normans in Sicily, a considerable body of troops had to be continually on the spot to prevent new invasions. In this way the Normans contributed their part to the weakening of the Empire.

In Constantinople were many Italian colonies, whose rivalries during the last years of the twelfth century contributed not a little to the same result. Before, however, speaking of these colonies and of the troubles of which they were the cause, I propose to call attention to the conditions under which foreigners lived in the Empire. The subject is one which I venture to think has been overlooked, notwithstanding the fact that in its main features the system under which Italians and others lived during the middle ages has survived down to the present day.

2. *The Foreign Colonies in Constantinople and the Conditions under which Foreigners in the Empire Lived.*

The population of the New Rome, at almost every period of its history, has been composed of people of widely different races, religions, and tongues. Its geographical position causes it even now to have the most diversified population in the world. It is still the meeting-place of the East and West. It contains an English colony with its own courts and its own judges who administer English law. German and French colonies in Constantinople similarly under their own rulers aim at reproducing the institutions of their respective countries. No nation in Europe is unrepresented. But there is also a colony of Persians with its own laws, its Shiah observances, and its national government transplanted on the Bosphorus. A Bokhariot bey rules over Bokhariot subjects in Stamboul. Mervians and Kurds, Cabulese and Hindoos jostle against Montenegrins, Epirots, and Albanians. In no other city do the people of the various races which inhabit it keep so distinct from each other as they do in Constantinople. In no other European city is the foreign element, taken altogether, so alien and so incapable of entering into the feelings of the governing race as in the Constantinople of to-day.

(margin note) Diverse elements among population of Constantinople.

Yet in no other city has the foreign element played—and the remark is true of modern Constantinople—so important a part in its history.

Constantinople, indeed, can hardly be said ever to have had a population belonging almost exclusively to one race. It is a seaport and has derived its importance from that fact, and from its having been chosen on account of its command-ing position to be the seat of government. Like all large seaports, it attracted foreigners, but unlike other cities some-what similarly circumstanced, it attracted them in greater numbers than it was able to absorb. Modern observers who note how readily the United States and our own colonies convert English, Irish, German, and other immigrants into American citizens or English subjects, may require to be re-minded how long it was before the colonies of Huguenots who were received into England became merged into the general population, and that the Welsh still retain their ancient lan-guage. The Greek-speaking races, like the English and the French, possess through their language and religion a great power of absorbing peoples who come within their influence. But while they succeeded in the south of the Balkan penin-sula in making races, who, according to Fallmerayer and his school, were alien in race, religion, and language, more Greek than the Greeks themselves, the capital was unable to assimi-late the masses of people who poured into it during each century after it had been chosen by Constantine. The marvel is, not that the people of the capital failed, but that they succeeded to the extent they did during the eleventh and twelfth centuries. The people of Byzantium were not Greek in race, or exclusively Greek-speaking at any time. The transfer of the Imperial Government to the New Rome made it appear likely for a while that Latin might become the dominant language. The immigrants from Italy spoke Latin. Those from the north of the Balkan peninsula spoke a language more akin to Latin than to Greek. Latin was the language of the court. Greek ultimately triumphed, but it was only after a struggle analogous to that which took place in England after the conquest in 1066 between Norman-

French and English. During such time the Italian, or, to use the older and more appropriate term, the Latin, element in Constantinople was continually being recruited by settlers and merchants from Italy. Asiatic Greeks, that is, Greek-speaking inhabitants from Syria and Asia Minor, likewise flocked in large numbers into the capital. Armenians always constituted an important element in its population. Many of them rose to high office in the Empire. From the time of Nerses, the famous successor of Belisarius, to our own day, when another of the same name has been the patriarch of his church, and, as the Armenians express it, chief of his nation, there is no time in Constantinopolitan history when they have not had a considerable share in its making. Waring or Russians and other races from the North or from Central Asia have never been, during many centuries, without colonies on the shores of the Bosphorus.

So long as the Empire remained strong the existence of these various colonies was completely overshadowed by the rule of the Emperor. When, however, the Empire became weak, and especially when during the twelfth century the drain of men and money necessary to fight the Seljukian Turks and the other enemies who were attacking the Empire increased, the part played by foreigners became more important. The proportion of foreigners to the subjects of the Empire became larger. Their power from various causes increased even more than their numerical proportion would lead one to suppose. Towards the latter part of the twelfth century they formed a more important element in the population of the capital than they had ever done before. Against the 60,000 Latins of whom Eustathius speaks in 1182, there might be put perhaps in our own day at the outside 25,000.

How foreigners were ruled under Rome. Foreigners had been admitted to settle in Constantinople from a very early period. Let me attempt to trace how they were ruled. The laws of the Elder Rome had at first made a great distinction between the *jus civile*, or law applicable to those who had the privileges of Roman citizenship, and the *jus gentium*, which was the product of the law of the market evolved by finding what observances and elements of law

were common to all nations.   But the *jus gentium* applied
mainly to matters in dispute between Romans and foreigners,
and not to questions between foreigners themselves.   The
Roman was unwilling to give the privilege of his law to a
foreigner except where it was to the interest of the Roman
so to do.   The law of the New Rome, however, which is what
jurists usually think of when the term Roman law is used,
had, from the time of Justinian, two centuries after Constantine, merged the two systems of law into one in much the
same way that our own Judicature Acts have merged the
systems of common law and equity.   There was no time, however, either in the history of Rome or Constantinople, when
foreigners had the full rights possessed by Roman citizens.
Privileges were conceded to them for the purpose of trade.
Commercial treaties were made with the nations to which
they belonged.   Strangers were invited and inducements
held out to them to settle in the country.   In every case,
however, they were to be under their own government, and
they were never permitted to have all or most of the benefits
conferred on subjects of the Empire.   They might come to
the country and trade with its inhabitants, and would be protected in so doing, but they must govern themselves and
expect nothing but protection and the right to trade on certain
conditions imposed by the State.

This condition of things existed only to a modified extent
in the case of nations which had been brought into subjection
to the Empire.   The Emperors had to take in hand the
administration of law to people of widely different customs,
religions, races, and countries.   Ultimately the rights and
obligations imposed by a portion of Roman law were conferred and imposed upon all subjects of the Empire, though of
course not upon resident foreigners.   Caracalla for the sake
of increasing the revenue had made all subjects of the Empire
into Roman citizens.   But the most convenient way of
administering Roman law even to Roman citizens was, in the
words of Cassiodorus, the secretary of Theodoric the Great,
to allow the Roman to be a judge for the Roman, the Goth

*Rule as to
subject
races.*

for the Goth, and thus under a diversity of judges to have equal justice administered to all.[1]

Each subject of the Empire under such a system had the benefit or the burden of the laws of the people to which he belonged. He was bound by the laws which were common to all Roman subjects, but in addition the courts took notice of the law and customs of the race of which he was a member. The foreigner was in a different position. Roman law afforded him protection. For the rest, foreigners might settle their own disputes and regulate their own affairs as they liked. The Armenian in Constantinople had as an occupant of Roman territory to obey the laws which had been imposed for the preservation of public order, and to pay certain taxes. But questions of marriage, succession to property, of personal status generally, were left to be settled either by the Armenians themselves or by a magistrate named by the Emperor to administer Armenian law.[2]

Treaties or capitulations respecting foreign residents.

This condition of things was known to other cities, but received its largest development in Constantinople, where the system which created it has always existed, and still exists, under the treaties or capitulations with the Porte ; a system which is a striking illustration of the continuity of history. In other words, the system of capitulations under which foreigners to-day reside in Turkey is the one under which they have always resided there. As no writer with whom I am acquainted has called attention to this fact, I may be excused for sketching briefly the history of the capitulations. The

[1] 'Romanis Romanus judex erat, Gothis Gothus, et sub diversitate judicum una justitia complectebatur.'

[2] Justinian granted the occupants of the Armenian regio or quarter the benefit of the same laws on certain subjects as those by which his own subjects were ruled. This was 'a grant, or concession, or capitulation,' to use the words of our own Foreign Jurisdiction Acts. Such a concession was no doubt of value to the Armenians. Without it they remained subject to their own laws. Of course concessions from the Sublime Porte to Europeans in order to be of value are the reverse of the one mentioned, that is, the stranger has to be permitted to retain his own laws. But this simply arises from the fact that the Europeans are more advanced in civilisation than the Turks, and thus cannot see any benefit in being under Turkish law. The capitulation granted by Justinian was to grant the foreigner a right which he could not possess without such permission. *Novella Constit.* xxi. ; Just. *Corpus Juris : De Armeniis.*

first treaty granting the right of exterritoriality which I have been able to find was made with the Warings, a people who have left their name in England, and of whom I shall have more to say later on. In 905 and 945, when these treaties were made, the Warings were more usually called Russians, though one has only to read in Leo the Deacon and other Greek authors the accounts of their appearance, to recognise them as relations. From that date we have an unbroken series of capitulations down to the time of the Moslem conquest in 1453. The Venetians obtained such concessions early in the eleventh century. The Amalfians followed in 1056. The Genoese were not far behind, and obtained the rights of exterritoriality in 1098.[1] The Pisans, if they had not previously had such rights, gained them in 1110. Henceforward capitulations became so general, and granted so many exclusive rights to territory, that during the last quarter of the twelfth century the long shore of Constantinople on the Golden Horn was so occupied by foreigners that the Greeks complained that there were no wharves left to them. For our purpose we may pass at a bound to the Moslem conquest in 1453, when the Genoese had obtained capitulations which allowed them to occupy the fortified town of Galata, and thus enabled them to become a dangerous ally of the invader. On the conquest the capitulations of the Genoese were confirmed by Mahomet the Conqueror. During the next century the Venetians succeeded in obtaining perhaps the clearest definition which had yet been made of the privileges and exterritoriality granted by capitulations. These expressly included the right of having disputes with their fellow Venetians decided only by their own authorities, the right to have questions between Venetians and Ottoman subjects decided only in presence of a Venetian dragoman or interpreter, exemption from harach, the tax imposed on

Their history.

---

[1] I have serious doubts whether the right of exterritoriality was regarded at this time as a privilege. The impression I have gathered from reading many of the earlier treaties with the Italian states is that their rulers were quite content to submit questions in dispute to the imperial courts. See, for example, the treaties in Sauli's *Colonia di Genovese* and Gatteschi's *Manuale di Diritto Publico et Privato Ottomano*.

Christians in lieu of military service, and the right of the
Republic to name its own baily or magistrate in Constantinople.

Their
modern
form. These privileges were embodied in the capitulations with
France in 1536, and though this treaty has been often re-
drawn and embodied in many treaties with each European
Power, its provisions still remain the essential articles of the
capitulations under which foreigners now live in the Ottoman
empire. The system which was thus formulated in the
French capitulations has not materially changed from that
day to this. Each nation has now its treaty with the Porte.
But as each treaty contains a most favoured nation clause,
the whole of the treaties or capitulations form a body of law
which constitutes the capitulations under which foreigners
live, and under which their governments exercise jurisdiction
in the Ottoman Empire.[1]

Reasons
why they
have lasted
in Turkey. In the best days of the Byzantine Empire something
approaching a fusion or welding together of the various races
into one people had taken place. But the influx of newcomers into the Empire during the century immediately
preceding the Latin conquest formed a population of so
many different races, languages, and manners, that the
process of fusion stopped. As soon as the city came under
Moslem rule, fusion became impossible and has been so ever
since. The Mahometan is forbidden by his religion to grant
equality to unbelievers. Christian subjects are rayahs or
sheep. Hence, as might have been expected, there has never
been a serious attempt to weld the various races under the
rule of the Sultan into one people. But if it be impossible
for the Moslem to grant equal rights to Christian and Moslem
subjects, it is none the less impossible to extend similar rights
to Christian foreigners. On the other hand, foreigners could
not consent to live in a country where by law the Christian

[1] The treaties under which foreigners reside in the Turkish empire are usually
called capitulations, because their contents are arranged under heads. They
assume sometimes the form of letters patent or concessions, by which the sovereign
has granted certain rights to the subjects of another Power. At other times, and
more usually, they are in the form of treaties by which the sovereign of each
country grants certain privileges to the subjects of the other.

can hardly be said to have legal rights against a Mahometan. Hence the preservation of the system of capitulations became a necessity, if Christian foreigners were to be induced to remain or to settle in the Empire. The Turks were compelled to recognise this, and as they found capitulations in full vigour—Galata being, as we have seen, a fortified city in the hands of foreigners at the time of the capture of the city in 1453—they continued the system. The history of the last four and a half centuries in Constantinople has been the history of the development of the system of capitulations.

Such a juridical anomaly is only now possible or tolerable in a country where foreigners have, and are entitled to have, no confidence in the administration of the government as the protector of life and property. Other nations have outgrown this system. The Turks have not done so ; but though other European nations have progressed beyond the legal conception of a former time, there are many traces of the old system in their laws. The exterritoriality of ambassadors and the privileges of their retainers is a survival of this system. In Turkey also all the rights of jurisdiction enjoyed by foreigners are grouped round and closely connected with the rights conferred on ambassadors. But it is to be noted that in Constantinople the existing system is the direct lineal representative in unbroken succession of a wider exterritoriality which existed during the middle ages and had been continued from Roman times. Englishmen residing in France or other European states are properly left to seek redress in the courts of the country where they are dwelling. It is worth remembering, however, that Englishmen have had to fall back upon the early type of a colony in a strange country in several instances. The factories of India, of Lisbon, and of St. Petersburg during the last century, and the consular courts of China and Japan, all owed their judicial system to a conception of law resembling that which led to the establishment of the capitulations in Constantinople, and all ultimately develop the legal fiction that the territory in the foreign country is a portion of the Empire from whose shores they have been planted.

I have said that the idea in Constantinople was that foreigners should not be entitled to the privileges of the citizen, but should be allowed the advantages of their own laws. Mahometans have never advanced sufficiently far to outgrow this conception. All Christians are in a sense foreigners to Mahometans, and cannot have the advantages of Moslem law. Still, neither in the case of the foreign colonies under the Byzantine empire, nor in those which were found by the Turks, nor in those actually existing in Constantinople, was there any considerable sense of hardship. The colonists had their own predilections in favour of their own laws. The native was equally convinced that his system was the best.

They are a survival, and not an invention.
I repeat that there has existed no period in the history of Constantinople in which foreigners have not enjoyed the advantages, and been subject to the disabilities, of exterritoriality. The existing system of capitulations is a survival rather than, as it is generally represented, a new invention specially adapted to Turkey. Still less is it a system, as it is often said to be, of magnanimous concessions made by far-sighted sultans of Turkey in order to encourage foreigners to trade with and reside in the Empire. The capitulations were neither badges of inferiority imposed on foreigners, as they have often been described, nor proofs of exceptional wisdom peculiar to the sultans. As a fact, foreigners have never held so important a position in the capital under Ottoman rule as under that of the Christian emperors, and especially at the close of the twelfth century. While the native population has probably remained stationary during the last six centuries, the foreign population was probably never so large as at that period.

I now propose to point out what were the principal colonies of foreigners which existed in Constantinople, and in other of the important cities of the Empire, at the time immediately preceding the Latin conquest.

3. *The Warings.*

Among the foreigners who had been longest established in Constantinople in 1204 were the Warings, or Varangians.

They were kinsmen of our own, and on this account may be allowed a fuller description than the immediate object in hand would justify. Tacitus speaks of 'Angli et Varini,'[1] the English and the Warings. Both were in his time the inhabitants of the country south of the Baltic, or, as it came to be called at a later period, the Waring Sea. When the great movement began which caused the English to emigrate to Britain, some of the Warings took part in it. With them also were others whom Bede speaks of as Rugians or Russians.[2] At a later period the name Waring and Russian appears to have been applied indifferently to the same people, the truth possibly being, as the Russian monk Nestor says, that some of the Warings were called Russians. Many traces of Waring emigration into England exist, of which the names of Warwick or Waeringwick, Warnford and Warington, are examples. The record of their history shows them to be closely akin to the English, though whether through the Teutonic or the Norse element of our people may be open to doubt.[3] Their appearance was like that of Englishmen or Danes. Their language was virtually the same. Their exploits at sea, their legends, their habits, their very names, all convey the irresistible impression that we are reading of the kinsmen of our ancestors.

While the English went westward, the Warings spread themselves along the eastern shores of the Baltic, or went southward. They levied tribute from the neighbouring tribes, and especially from the Slavs. The Dwina and the Dniester were the great highways for their commerce, and for their plundering expeditions. Historians have in their case, as in so many others, occupied themselves so much with the latter expeditions as to leave the impression—altogether false—that plunder rather than commerce was the business of their lives. Slaves formed one of their principal articles of export to Constantinople, while they carried back into Waringia silk, spices, and other Eastern produce and Byzantine gold. The

Warings related to English.

Their progress from the Baltic.

---

[1] *Germania*, vii. ch. xl.　　　[2] *Hist. Eccles.* ii. 9.

[3] Professor Rafn, in his *Antiquités Russes et Orientales*, maintains that they were Norsemen. Royal Society of Northern Antiquaries, vols. 1850–1852.

Slavs at Kiev and Novgorod came at an early period under
their rule, and the process began by which they were to be
gradually absorbed into the conquered race, as the Normans
were at a subsequent period in England.   Between 863 and
869 they were engaged in plundering the remote provinces
of the Eastern empire.   Within a century they made four
attempts upon Constantinople, and in the boldness of these
undertakings showed a spirit akin to that of their countrymen,
with whose exploits as emigrants, explorers, and sea-rovers
the world is familiar.   It was the Waring Olaf who hung his
shield either on the topmost turret of one of the chief gates
of Constantinople, or, as the Russians assert, on the dome of
Hagia Sophia itself.   In 904 Olaf, or Oleg, made an attempt
against the imperial city, at the head of a band of Warings,
Englishmen, Norsemen, and Slavs, and proceeded to the city
in 2,000 boats.   A treaty of peace was concluded between
the Emperor and the invaders, which I have already mentioned as an example of the capitulations which have so long
existed in Constantinople, and under which foreigners are
still allowed to enjoy the benefit of their own laws, and to be
exempt under certain restrictions from the jurisdiction of the
rulers of the land.   This treaty, made in 907, was followed by
another in 912, and a third in 945.   All are given in the
chronicle of Nestor.[1]   Among those signing on behalf of the
Warings are Sigiborn, Adun, Adolf, Antiwald, Furst, Brum-
wald, Ingeld, Alden, and Swain, names which sufficiently
indicate their origin.   One of the signers is named as a
merchant.   The Warings were to have free trade throughout
the Empire, but were to take passports ; subject to this provision the Grand Prince of Russia and his boyards were to
be allowed to send as many ships and cargoes, as many
deputies and guests, as they liked.   The Waring merchants
were to receive a monthly allowance.   Waring offenders were
to be punished by Waring law.   Waring officers were to be
named to take possession of testamentary and intestate suc-
cessions.   The treaties were duly ratified by Christian oaths on

---

[1] *La Chronique de Nestor, traduite en Français par Louis Paris,* 1834, vol. i.
pp. 36-44 and 57-64.   See also Zonaras, ii. 173.

the part of the Greeks and on the part of those of the Russians who had become Christian, and by placing on the ground their swords, shields, and other arms on the part of those Russians who had not yet been baptized.

An interesting account is given of the Warings a little later by Leo the Deacon, a contemporary of the events he describes. The description he gives clearly shows that the Warings are meant, though he calls them Russians.[1] He does justice to their valour, but also to their cruelty. Like all the Greek writers, he makes mention of the fact that their distinctive weapon was the battle-axe. They never, says Leo, surrendered in battle, and rather than be taken prisoners would kill themselves. They had flaxen or reddish hair, and blue eyes. One of the most striking incidents of the Waring war, which he describes, relates to a leader named Swendoslav. He had led a host into the Empire on a plundering expedition, and had occupied Dorystolon or Silistria, which commands the Derwend pass through the Balkans. He had fought bravely, and held his own against great numbers, but found himself at length unequal to the task of breaking through the lines which the imperial troops, under the Emperor John Zemiskes (969–976), had drawn round Dorystolon. Eight thousand of his followers had been killed and he was compelled to accept terms. He stipulated that he should be allowed to leave the Empire, and bound himself to send back the captives he had taken. On the other hand, the Romans promised to give the Russians safe conducts for the purpose of trade in Constantinople as they had had before. After the Waring chief who had led his sea-rovers across the Black Sea into the Danube had signed peace with the Emperor, he expressed his wish to see his great and brave enemy. The interview took place on the banks of the Danube. Few more picturesque and characteristic scenes are recorded by the Byzantine historians. Each of the

Swendo-slav's expedition.

[1] 'Ρώς. The Septuagint quoted by Leo used the same word, Ezekiel xxxix. 1 and 2, which there reads : 'Prophecy against Gog, and say, Thus saith th Lord God. Behold I am against thee, O Gog, chief prince of the Russians, Meshech and Tubal. Leo, *Dia.* p. 93, ed. Reg.

leaders appeared in a manner characteristic of the nation to which he belonged. The Emperor, clothed in magnificent armour decked with gold and jewels, rode down to the river-side at the head of a body of mounted guards glittering in gold and arms, but evidently well-disciplined and capable of rendering splendid service. On the other hand, Swendoslav came to the meeting-place in a boat propelled by his soldiers, he himself rowing like one of the crew. His dress was a simple white garment, and in no way different from that of the rest except that it was cleaner. The two brave leaders and their followers represented respectively the spirit of the old time and the new : on the one side the stern imperial discipline, the sacrifice of the many for the glory of the few, and the machine-like order and regularity which was pro-duced at the bidding of one man and had made Rome the mistress of the world ; on the other, the equality and the self-reliance which recognises that all citizens have an interest in the well-being of the State, and which was especially destined to characterise the great modern nations descended from their kinsmen. The imperial leader saw a man of middle height, with thick eyebrows, light blue eyes, thick nose, thin beard, but with long and heavy moustache. His hair was cut short, except that two long locks hung down on each side of his face, declaring him to belong to the Varangian nobility. His neck was firm, his chest broad, his expression stern and fierce. From each ear there hung an earring ornamented with two pearls and a carbuncle between them. A few words passed between the two leaders, the Emperor sitting on horse-back, the Varangian seated on one of the thwarts of his boat. Swendoslav looked long and carefully at the great Emperor, and the interview finished with mutual respect.

They take military service.

Many of the Warings and probably of the English also had taken military service at an early period under the Byzantine emperors.[1] They formed a body-guard for the

---

[1] Two Arab writers, Mahsoudi and Abul-feda, assert that Russians, as the Warings had come to be called, had also enlisted in the service of the Mussulman rulers of the East. They were highly prized everywhere as soldiers. Muratori quotes two edicts, by different Lombard kings, which confer rights upon them and

Emperor, and soon gained for themselves a renown greater than that possessed by the earlier imperial guard of the Immortals. The Byzantine writers usually speak of them as the barbarian guard, or as the axe-bearers. Their weapon was the Danish battle-axe, or rather bill, and seems not to have had two blades turning different ways like those of a halberd, but to have had one with a sharp steel spike projecting so that the weapon could be used either to strike or to thrust.[1] Anna, the daughter of Alexis the First, calls them Warings or Varangians.[2] Nicetas speaks of them as Germans.[3] The Western writers call them usually Danes, or 'English and Danes.'[4]

The conquest of England by William the Norman caused many of the English to emigrate to Russia and so to Constantinople, where they joined the Waring guard.[5]

allow them to settle in their territory. The whole subject of the Warings is well worth examination. Mr. Hyde Clarke has collected a great many interesting and important facts relating to them.

[1] οἱ κατωμαδὸν τοὺς ἑτεροστόμους πελέκεις ἀνέχουσιν. Nic. 323, ed. Bonn. Dr. Mordtmann has given an illustration from the seal of the chief interpreter of the Waring guard, which shows an axe with only one blade. The bayonet is curved somewhat less than a reaping-hook, with the edge turned in the opposite direction from that of the axe. Dr. Mordtmann says it is not *bipennis*, as the Warings' axes are always described. I am inclined to think, however, that the curved bayonet, which was intended for cutting as well as thrusting, may have given it its ordinary name of double-edged. See *Archives de l'Orient Latin* (1881), vol. i. p. 698.

[2] ἐκ τῆς Θούλης βαράγγους. *Ann.* i. 120, ed. Bonn.

[3] Nicetas, 323.

[4] 'Les Anglois et Danois mult bien combattaient avec leurs haches.' Villehard.

[5] Ordericus Vitalis says : ' When therefore the English had lost their liberty, they turned themselves with zeal to discover the means of throwing off the unaccustomed yoke. Some fled to Sueno, king of the Danes, to excite him to the recovery of the inheritance of his grandfather Canute. Not a few fled into exile in other regions, either from the mere desire of escaping from under the Norman rule, or in the hope of acquiring wealth, and so being one day in a condition to renew the struggle at home. Some of these in the bloom of youth penetrated into a far distant land, and offered themselves to the military service of the Constantinopolitan emperor, that wise prince against whom Robert Wiscard, Duke of Apulia, had then raised all his forces. The English exiles were favourably received, and opposed in battle to the Normans, for whose encounter the Greeks themselves were too weak.' The Greek writers believed them to be of English origin. Du Cange collects the authorities (see vol. ii. Anna Com., p. 462 of his notes), and concludes that English and Danes is a correct description of the Warings (*Observa-*

Influence of Norman conquest.

While there can be no doubt that there was a large accession to the guard in consequence of the Norman conquest, it is also clear that there was a Waring guard in Constantinople before that event. In 1034 and 1035 this guard wintered in the western part of Asia Minor.[1] Romanos Diogenes, Emperor between 1068 and 1071, reorganised the Waring troops, and formed them into the body-guard of the Emperor. That they retained amid their Eastern surroundings their respect for women as well as their valour is shown by many circumstances, and is illustrated by a story told by Cedrenus.

Waring respect for women.

A peasant woman had resisted the violence of one of their number, and had stabbed him with his own sword. His companions, when they had learned the truth of the matter, not only pardoned her but presented her with his property, and left his body without burial, as if he had committed suicide.[2] The Warings, who had been converted to Christianity by the Greek priests, belonged to the Orthodox Church. The English who joined them acknowledged the spiritual rule of Rome, and had their church in the New Rome dedicated to St. Augustine of Canterbury.[3] Warings and English, while occupants of the Greek palace, still spoke their own language, had their own laws, and chose, with certain exceptions, their own officers.[4] The one in command

---

tions on Villehardouin). The same conclusion is adopted by the learned editor of the *Recueil des Croisades* (p. 518, vol. iv.), who seems disposed to believe that they were almost exclusively fugitives from England, who had fled either on the accession of Edward the Confessor or at the Norman conquest.

[1] Professor Rafn thinks that Harold, king of Norway, defeated at Stamford Brig, was chief of the Varangian guard when he left Constantinople in 1043.

[2] Cedrenus, p. 735.

[3] Their church was dedicated to SS. Nicolas and Augustine of Canterbury, and is said by Gotselinus to have been built by an English exile who arrived in Constantinople after the battle of Hastings. It was converted into a mosque after 1453, and was situated between the palace and the Adrianople Gate. Dr. Paspati found upon one of the towers near this gate many funeral inscriptions relating to Warings. The English ambassador about 1865 endeavoured to have them removed to the English cemetery at Scutari, but unfortunately without success. The stones were used by the Turkish government for building. Still more unfortunately, the only two copies which were taken were burnt in the great fire of Pera in 1870. See *Histoire de l'Eglise Latine de Constantinople*, par M. Belin, pp. 4 and 20. Also *Constantinop. Christ.* p. 130. Also Dr. Paspati's *Meletai*, 308.

[4] Cedrenus. Readers will remember that Sir Walter Scott has given a vivid

was called the acolyth,¹ or follower, because his place was immediately behind the Emperor. No body-guard in any Deserving
of trust.
country was ever more completely trusted than the Varangians. None more completely deserved such trust. They
retained their sturdy northern independence in the midst of
a corrupt court.

They were barbarous in the eyes of Anna
Comnena and of her father and the effeminate creatures
about him ; but they were barbarians as English soldiers at
a native court in India may be regarded now by the de-
generate representatives of a warlike race. They did their
duty as soldiers, despised the men on whose side they had to
fight, and the English at least among their number kept their
resentment for the Normans, against whom they were shortly
destined to fight on imperial territory. In the fourth crusade,
as we shall see, they did their best to resist the attack on the
royal city.²

We may well feel satisfied that the Greek writers repeatedly point out that the Emperors found their greatest
safety in the spotless loyalty of those among oͤur kinsmen
who guarded them, and among whom were so many who had
left England rather than accept a foreign rule.³

picture of the Waring guard in Constantinople in *Count Robert of Paris*. His
local colour and a considerable part of his plot are taken from Anna Comnena.
His descriptions of the prisons in the Blachern, as well as of the life in Constantinople, are singularly exact, though occasionally he falls into error, as when he
makes the Crusaders wait before crossing a bay on the Bosphorus until the tide has
ebbed. There is no tide in either the Bosphorus or the Marmora.

¹ Anna Comnena, however, calls him πελεκυφόρων ἐξάρχων. Codinus gives
the following description of the acolyth : Ὁ ἀκόλουθος εὑρίσκεται μὲν ἔνοχος τῶν
βαράγγων, ἀκολουθεῖ δὲ τῷ βασιλεῖ ἔμπροσθεν αὐτῶν. διά τοι τοῦτο καὶ ἀκόλουθος
λέγεται.

² After the conquest there are several traces of the Warings in the Empire.
Nikephorus Greg., pp. 187 and 243, ed. Reg. There is a curious mention in Busbeck
of what was probably an isolated Waring tribe in the Crimea. Busbeck gives a
list of words spoken by these men which are nearly all English, or as he considered them German. This was in 1557. The English or Waring guard was
probably kept up by constant emigration from Northern Europe. The question of
the national weapon, with which the Waring guard was armed, is discussed, vol.
iv. p. 518, *Recueil*. The Western writers generally speak of it as a Danish battle-
aᴋe.

³ Page 120, Anna Com., ed. Bonn. ἐκεῖσε δὲ τοὺς ἐκ τῆς Θούλης βαράγγους
(τούτους δὴ λέγω τοὺς πελεκυφόρους βαρβάρους) . . . . οἱ μὲν γὰρ αὐτόχθονες ὄντες
τῷ βασιλεῖ, πολλὴν τὴν εἰς αὐτὸν ἐξ ἀνάγκης ἔχοντες εὔνοιαν, θᾶττον ἂν τὰς ψυχὰς

It is difficult to determine whether Waring, English, or Russian traders continued to settle in Constantinople. It is, however, certain that they soon ceased to be of importance in comparison with the colonists belonging to other races who had found their way to the New Rome.

4. *Italian Colonies in Constantinople.*

The most important of these colonies consisted of Italians. There had probably always been a large Italian element in Constantinople. Latin had never ceased to be understood by some portion of the population of the capital and other sea-port towns. The *Lingua Franca* which the Crusaders were able to understand was closely allied to the dialect of Latin spoken in Italy, and was probably a compound of the Latin imported with Constantine and his successors, of the Italian introduced by the colonists, and of a kindred dialect more nearly related to Latin than to Greek, which had been spoken in the Balkan peninsula long before the time of Constantine. The people of Romania continue to our own time the dialect of Latin, which I believe to have been the language of a portion of the wider Romania which was under the rule of New Rome. Whether the modern language is a corruption of the Latin of Dacian colonists, or, as I have already suggested and as there seems more reason to conclude, an independent branch from the common Aryan stem, closely related to that which was developed in Rome, the readiness with which a Latin dialect could be understood throughout at least the littoral of the Empire, as well as in isolated communities in the interior of the Balkan peninsula, can be satisfactorily established, and greatly facilitated trade.

Latin always understood in seaports.

During the latter half of the twelfth century the Latins had obtained possession of a large part of the commerce of the Empire. They had important colonies in most of the great towns. Many Venetians were settled at Sardis, and at other places along the west coast of Asia Minor, as far north

Latin settlements

παραδοῖεν ἢ πονηρόν τι κατ' αὐτοῦ μελετῆσαι πεισθήσονται. Bryennios agrees with all in praising their fidelity. William of Malmesbury, Book ii. ch. 13, *De Gest. Angl.*, calls them English. Saxo Grammaticus and many others call them Danes.

as the Dardanelles, where at Abydos their colonists were found. Others were at Rodosto, on the north coast of the Marmora. During Isaac's reign they had settled at Adrianople, while an older colony of Latins was established at Philippopolis.

The chief city and natural port of Macedonia then as now was Salonica. It was the terminus of many roads, which immediately before and after the great fair of St. Demetrius were crowded with traders. The furs and salt-fish of Russia for winter supply were exchanged for the grain of the country, for the silks of the Peloponnesus, or the embroidered cloths of Spain. Syrian, Egyptian, Italian, and even Spanish merchants attended this famous fair, and met Russians, Bulgarians, Greeks, and Arabs. Venetians, Pisans, and other Franks had a large and wealthy quarter in the city. *at Salonica,*

A little to the south of Salonica, Volo possessed also a large settlement of Latin colonists, mostly Venetians, who had occupied a considerable number of towns in the Greek peninsula to the south of Volo. At Almyro and at Corinth the Latins had settled, the Arab merchants bringing their goods to one side of the isthmus, the Latins to the other. The islands of Euboea, Andros (which produced silk), and Lemnos had permanent settlements of Venetians. Rhodes, Chios, and Crete had also admitted Latins to the benefit of their commerce. In all the great trading cities the native population found serious rivals in men who had now become hostile to the Empire. *in the islands,*

It was, however, to the capital that most foreign merchants flocked. There each Italian state had its own khans, known to the population as *emboloi*, buildings looking like fortifications, and each surrounding a square courtyard upon which the shops fronted. These *emboloi*, as well as many of the streets in the city, were provided with arcades for protection alike from sun and rain. *in Constantinople.*

The Genoese occupied a position near the present Seraglio Point. To the west of them and around the former arsenal gate or Neorion were the Pisans. Still further west, and adjoining the site of the Stamboul end of the present bridge, around the Porta Peramaris, then as for centuries afterwards the principal place of entrance and exit to the city from Galata, were the favoured Venetians. Between them and the Pisans the colony of Amalfians still retained possession of their *emboloi*.[1] There were probably both Genoese and Venetians already settled at Galata. We have already seen that the people of Constantinople complained that the Latins had become possessed of the best business sites in the city, and those who know the localities I have mentioned will recognise that this complaint was not made without reason. Besides the Latin colonies already named, there was one of Anconians sufficiently numerous to possess its own church. Another consisting of Ragusans, who were probably mostly Slavs, had acquired the privileges of citizenship in Constantinople in return for aid which they had rendered against Venice.

We have already seen how these foreign colonies were governed. I may add here that the ambassador was usually the ruler of the colony from the State which he represented, that he took counsel on all important matters with the *prudentes viri* of the community, and that when the century closed each such community had, in addition to its political minister, officers who acted under various names as judges and governors. Each colony was regarded as so far prosperous that it had to send revenues home to the parent state, the Amalfians sending also tribute to St. Mark's at Venice.

Jealousy among the colonies ;   Italian commerce in Constantinople had during the twelfth century become of great importance both to the Italian states, to the Empire, and to Europe. But during the second half of that century there existed a considerable amount of jealousy between the Empire and the rising commercial states of Italy. Constantinople during many years was the battle ground of the vigorous Italian states, much as India was

---

[1] The topography of Constantinople at the period of the fourth crusade has been carefully studied by Dr. A. Paspati (see *Meletai*), and also by Dr. Mordtmann. I may mention here that I am greatly indebted to Dr. Paspati for many hints on the topography of the city. Heyd's *Geschichte des Levante-Handels im Mittelalter*, 1879, is the great authority on trade during the period with which I am concerned.

between the English and other European peoples during the last century. These states were now nearly independent of all external control, and made war and treaties with each other like the cities of old Greece. The traders of Constantinople were naturally impatient of commercial rivals who were rapidly depriving them of business which had been exclusively in their own hands, and were not careful to inquire to what particular Italian state their rivals belonged. The jealousy of the Greeks was increased by many causes. There was a traditional sentiment against the Eastern emperors, which was fully returned by the rulers of the New Rome against the portion of the Roman empire not under their control. These rulers were suffering the smart of recent losses inflicted by upstart states, the Norman kingdom in the south of Italy, the powerful republic in the north. The Roman Emperor in the West claimed to be the only living successor of the Roman Cæsars in things temporal. The Pope claimed even more positively to be the ruler of the world in things spiritual. Both claims were denied in the East.

The Latin colonists were always united in condemning the Greeks because they refused to recognise the supremacy of the Pope of Rome. Although divided at home, they were generally united against the Byzantines. The common bond of religion, race, and language, tended to make them live together as neighbours on a foreign soil. But the Latin colonists, while generally united by their common interests against the Byzantines, were jealous of each other's influence. The Venetians resented any grant of privileges to the Pisans or Amalfians. The Genoese were usually ready to intrigue against the Venetians. These internal quarrels continually brought trouble to the Empire. A concession granted to one Italian state made the others at once hostile to the grantor unless they also obtained like advantages. *but usually united against Empire.*

The first of the Italian states which obtained privileges from the Empire was the republic of Venice, though the city of Amalfi had sent traders to the capital at an earlier date. The policy of Venice had long been one of friendliness to the New Rome. She had obtained the largest share of the *Venice and the Empire.*

commerce of the Eastern capital, and had in turn been more influenced by its civilisation than any other Italian city.   As she was the first of the Italian states to exercise considerable influence in Constantinople, so also her influence survived that of all others.   As her people did more to bring about the ruin of the New Rome than those of any other city or state, so also she remains the one city of Europe where the impress of the New Rome's civilisation has left deep traces.

From the time that the lagoons had become the seat of the Venetian government, the trade with Constantinople had been one of her greatest interests.   The amount of commerce between the two cities was very great.   The Bosphorus was the chief highway between Persia, Central Asia, Russia, and Eastern Europe to the West.   The good government and the security for life and property which existed under the rule of Constantinople was an additional inducement for the trader to try his ventures with the imperial city.   The islands of the Archipelago were charged with the furnishing and equipment of ships for keeping order on the seas and preventing piracy. The arrangements made by treaties with the Venetians for the administration of justice show the existence of a higher degree of civilisation than prevailed elsewhere in Europe.   The standard of gold coinage created by the Empire remained the same until the capture of the city, and its fixedness of value gave great confidence to merchants.   Though two or three emperors, notably Nicephoras (963–976), were guilty of tampering with the money in circulation throughout the Empire, yet so long as the gold coinage remained undebased the Venetians, in common with other foreigners, were no more affected by the change than foreign merchants have been by the issue of paper money, and the many similar forms of public robbery by which the Turkish government in our own time has deprived its own subjects of many millions of pounds.   Moreover, the outcry which was made when the Emperors tampered with the coinage shows the importance which was attached by the people to a measure so injurious to trade, and is in favourable contrast with the acquiescence which was made in similar attempts at public robbery in the

West and in subsequent times. These advantages made the Venetians estimate at a high value their connection with Constantinople, and had caused them even as early as the time of Charles the Great, and in spite of his threats, to remain faithful to the Emperor of the New Rome.

They had obtained a treaty of commerce as early as 1056.[1] Henceforward, until near the end of the twelfth century, they had made common cause with the Byzantine Empire. The enemies of New Rome were the enemies of Venice. The Saracen pirates from Spain and Africa who had invaded Sicily were attacked alike by the imperial and republican fleets. But it was in the time of Alexis the First, who reigned between 1081 and 1118, that the ties between the Venetians and the Emperor became the closest. When Robert Wiscard, the leader of the Normans, who had obtained possession of the Two Sicilies, invaded the Empire, the Venetians became at once alarmed lest their trade should be placed at the mercy of these daring pirates. If the attack upon Durazzo had been successful the Normans would have commanded the narrowest part of the Adriatic. Hence they readily made the treaty, which has already been mentioned, by which they pledged themselves to oppose Robert.

The Norman fleet under Bohemund was defeated, and the communications of the army which was besieging Durazzo were cut off. While Bohemund was harassing the imperial army on the mainland, capturing Durazzo, ravaging Epirus and Thessaly, and taking Larissa, his father Robert had driven the Western Emperor out of Rome and had plundered the city. This done, he again turned his attention to the Empire of the New Rome. Again the Venetians were found aiding the Greeks. A fleet belonging to the two states besieged Corfu. Robert succeeded in defeating both. The Venetians, however, soon recovered and attacked Robert at Butrotis, where he was entirely beaten.[2] He died shortly after at Cephalonia. The Venetians were so disgusted with their Doge who had commanded in the naval action at Corfu that he was replaced by another, on whom the Emperor

[1] Mur. 81.   [2] Anna Com.

conferred the title of *Protosebastos,* accompanying it with a
pension. On the same occasion he recognised the title of
the Republic to the sovereignty of Dalmatia and Croatia.
The Emperor ordered the Amalfian colonists in Constantinople to pay an annual revenue to the church of St. Mark in
Venice, and gave the Venetians a quarter with shops and
bazaars in Constantinople in the choicest part of the Golden
Horn, with considerable land both in Constantinople and
Durazzo. But these presents, though of great value, were
not to be compared, says Anna Comnena, and rightly, with
the privilege he conceded to them of free trade in all kinds of
merchandise throughout the Empire, with the exception of the
Black Sea, without any payment whatever.[1] The concession
was so great that it was soon resented both by the merchants
of Constantinople and by the other Italian states. Venice
was sufficiently strong at sea to afford safer convoy to her
merchant ships than any other state. To allow her merchandise to enter duty free and her ships to export what they
liked without payment of duty was to give her almost a
monopoly of trade. Hence on the death of Alexis it is not
surprising to find that his son, John Comnenos (1118 to
1143), refused to confirm what was virtually the Venetian
monopoly.[2] Other influences, however, were at work, which
caused the Venetians to be less anxious to preserve friendship with Constantinople than they had been. The Holy
War against the infidels had been proclaimed by Pope Urban
in 1095. Jerusalem had been captured in 1099, and Godfrey proclaimed King. The trade with Syria had become of
great importance, and already commerce was beginning to
take the direction of its ancient route through Egypt rather
than through the Bosphorus. In 1124 John expelled the
Venetians from the Empire. In revenge they attacked Chios,
Samos, and Rhodes,[3] plundered them and captured many
youths and maidens, whom they sold into slavery. A desultory war continued during two years, in the course of which

---

[1] Anna Com. 287, Bonn.   [2] Dandolo, 269.
[3] Cimn. vi. 10 ; Fulcher, p. 470, *Recueil.* Fulcher is inclined to blame the
Venetians, though he preaches against both the Emperor and the Venetians.

each of the combatants inflicted serious injury on the other. In 1126 the war was brought to an end. The Emperor declared himself willing to forget the wrongs which the Republic had inflicted upon him in return for the promise given to aid in the defence of the Empire. The Doge was formally confirmed in his title of Protosebastos. The Amalfian colonists in Constantinople were compelled to contribute three pounds weight of gold annually to the church of St. Mark at Venice, and free trade was to be permitted to the Venetians in the capital and in all the important ports of the Empire south of the Black Sea, which was here, as in every other treaty, exempted from access to foreigners. With the reign of Manuel (1143–1180) there was a distinct change of policy. The Venetians had obtained a position in the Empire far superior to that possessed by any other foreign colony; they had exclusive rights of trade in some cities; they had less taxes to pay than any other foreigners in others; they had the best position in Constantinople and the best wharves; but they had shown that they were not in all cases to be depended upon as the friends of the Empire. Moreover, the other Italian states were becoming formidable rivals in spite of the privileges which had been granted to the rulers of the Adriatic. Manuel probably thought that it was in the interest of the Empire to encourage all foreigners to trade with Constantinople; that such a policy would enable him to obtain better terms from the Venetians, would allow him to play off one foreign colony against another, and had the additional advantage of increasing the imperial revenue, which had already become seriously reduced through the wars with the Turks and Sicilians.

The Pisans and the Genoese came next in importance to the Venetians, and Manuel directed his attention towards obtaining their good-will. The Pisans had obtained an important treaty in 1111, after and in spite of the assistance they had given to Bohemund.[1] They were, however, always troublesome colonists. The Genoese, who had likewise opposed the Greeks at the time of the struggle with Bohemund,

---

[1] Buchon, *Nouvelles Recherches*.

do not appear to have obtained a treaty until the reign of
Manuel.   Seeing, however, the great benefits obtained by
Venice, they consented to appear as the liegemen and vassals
of that Emperor in order to obtain similar privileges.   In 1154
Manuel granted them a golden bull, which set out the concessions that had been granted to them.   The Genoese were
to pay an export and import duty of four per cent. instead
of ten, which was the rate paid by other traders, except, of
course, the favoured Venetians.[1]   They were to have a khan
assigned them in the city of Constantinople and a quarter on
the opposite shore, where afterwards arose their important
city of Galata.   In 1157, however, they complained that the
khan and the wharf had not been given them.[2]   During the
next four or five years the friendly relations between the
Empire and the Genoese and Pisans alike were several times
disturbed.   The Genoese had allied themselves with Frederic
Barbarossa, while the Venetians and the Pisans supported
Manuel.

Partial
failure of
Manuel's
policy.

Henceforward the history of the Latin colonists in Constantinople is the story of a series of quarrels and rivalries
among themselves and of combined hostility towards the
Empire.   The Emperor's wish was probably to keep at peace
with all the Latin colonies.   Nicetas tells us that he sought to
bind them to him in friendship.   He aided Pope Alexander
the Third and the Italian cities against Frederic Barbarossa.
He invited Italian settlers and promised to protect their
commerce.   But the citizens of the rival Italian states could
not keep from quarrelling together in Constantinople, and
hence Manuel's policy met with imperfect success.

In 1169 we find Manuel making a new alliance with the
Genoese.   They obtained another treaty with Manuel in 1178,
which gave them liberty to trade with all parts of the Empire
except Russia.[3]

On the death of Manuel in 1180, Genoa, Venice, and
Pisa were all at peace with the Empire.   Manuel's policy had

---

[1] Sauli, *Storia della Colonia dei Genovesi in Galata.*
[2] ' Pro exigendis scalis et embolo promissis.'—Caffarus, *Annales Januenses.*
[3] Sauli, *Documenti,* ii. p. 192.

been so far successful that, according to the statement of
Eustathius already referred to, there were upwards of 60,000
Latins living in Constantinople in 1180, of whom by far the
greater number were Venetians, Pisans, and Genoese. It was
on the death of this Emperor that the dynastic struggles commenced which so greatly weakened the Empire. The mutual
jealousies of the Latin colonists soon broke out. The colonists, as we have seen, joined the Protosebastos Alexis, who
opposed the usurper Andronicos. Indeed, the army of
Alexis was largely composed of Latins. In the words of
Nicetas, which sound familiar, Alexis had the ships, the men,
and money too. The treasury of the Empire was in his hands.
He had galleys and Latin soldiers clad in mail. It was in
1182, on the triumph of Andronicos, that the inhabitants of
Constantinople rose against the Latins, murdered a great
number, and committed the outrages already described.

Three years later, the Latins had apparently fallen upon
better times. The new Emperor, the weak Isaac Angelos,
had been raised to the purple by a popular revolution. We
have seen that Branas, after he had suppressed the Wallach
and Bulgarian rising, took the opportunity, seeing the unpopularity of the sovereign, of declaring himself Emperor,
and that, being an able man, he would probably have succeeded if Conrad, Marquis of Montferrat, had not happened
to be in Constantinople.

With the assistance of a hundred and fifty Latin knights
and a body of Latin adventurers, mostly Pisans, found in
Constantinople, Conrad put the army of Branas to flight. As
the country immediately round Constantinople had been
generally on the side of the rebel, the Emperor gave the
Latins and those who had been on his side permission to
pillage and plunder it, as well as the houses of Greek nobles
whose loyalty was suspected. But these nobles were naturally
not without supporters. The Latins, who boasted they had
saved the Emperor, were attacked by the Greeks. Many
were killed, and the Latin quarters were attacked and plundered. Isaac was probably glad to be able to make his
peace with Venice, and confirm the former privileges of the

Venetians on condition that they should come to his aid
with a hundred galleys. Before the year was out similar
privileges were granted to the Genoese. They were to have
their own quarter of the city, their own wharves, churches,
and freedom of trade.

The obtention of privileges was, however, by no means
prized as it had been a generation previously. The commerce of the capital had already fallen off. The dynastic
rebellions had weakened the Empire, and had injured it still
more by showing how greatly it had been weakened by its
struggles with the Turks and other enemies. During the
last twenty years of the century the members of each Italian
colony had had troubles with the Empire, had been expelled,
and had then been allowed to return. A spirit of distrust
had arisen on both sides. Merchants and citizens had alike
taken in hand the redress of their own wrongs even in Constantinople, while the low condition of the Byzantine marine
enabled the Latins to ravage the coasts and the islands whenever they were at war with the Empire. During the last few
years of the century they were nearly always at war. In
1192 the Pisans and the Genoese were confirmed in their old
privileges, or had new ones granted them, although at the
very time Pisan and Genoese pirates were ravaging the Ægean
Sea. These pirates, in ships belonging respectively to the two
states, captured a Venetian vessel on its way to Constantinople. There was on board it an ambassador from Isaac
who was returning from Egypt, and another from Saladin
who was bringing gifts of horses, wild animals, amber, and
other valuable presents to the Emperor. The ambassadors
were murdered. Isaac resented their murder and the theft
of the presents intended for him. He made complaints to
Genoa and Pisa, seized merchant ships, and asked for indemnity. After some time the Genoese consented to give it,
but the Pisans gave no satisfaction. The Government of
Pisa was either unable or unwilling to control its citizens,
who took to piracy with impunity. In 1194 a fleet of
vessels belonging to similar freebooters virtually blockaded the
Dardanelles and plundered imperial vessels. The Emperor

Attacks
upon the
Empire by
Italian
pirates.

was powerless to capture them. The council of Pisa took no step to oppose them. One of these pirates in 1198 defeated the imperial admiral with thirty ships. The Emperor only succeeded in putting an end to his ravages by proposing terms to him through the Genoese, and then setting the Pisans to attack him.

The Genoese had, however, become equally troublesome. A Genoese pirate, named Caffario, had after great difficulty been captured and killed. On his death the Emperor requested Genoa to send an ambassador to his court with a view to negotiations. This was done, and arrangements were made for the restoration of the buildings and wharves that the Genoese had possessed in Constantinople, but the negotiations can hardly be said to have been concluded when the city was captured by the Crusaders.

The weakness of the Empire, and particularly at sea, from the accession of Isaac the Second, had become clear to every Italian state. The imperial shores had become the prey of every pirate who chose to attack them. Pisans and Venetians, though during the last fifteen years of the century almost constantly fighting against each other, occasionally united in piratical attacks upon the Empire, while they regarded Constantinople as neutral ground.

But while the hostility which had been growing between the Empire and the Italian states generally greatly weakened the former, that displayed by Venice was the strongest, and contributed most largely to the capture of Constantinople. The ill-feeling between the Greeks and Venetians had gained great strength with the grant of concessions to Pisans and other Italian states in the time of Manuel. It had been increased by several events in the same reign, until in 1171, in a moment of irritation, all the Venetians in the Empire were arrested and their property placed under sequester. A War with short but hotly contested war followed. In the following year Venice. the Republic sent a fleet of a hundred vessels to attack the imperial forces in Dalmatia. Ragusa surrendered on the second day of the siege. Dalmatia was conquered. Negropont, Chios, Scyros, and other places were pillaged. For a

while everything seemed to be going in favour of the
Republic. Everywhere, however, the Venetians were opposed
by the inhabitants. A portion of the Venetian fleet was
destroyed by that of the Empire, but the rest occupied itself
during the next three years in piratical attacks on the islands
of the Ægean. Aid was given on every hand to the enemies
of the Empire. The Serbians were subsidised. The Archbishop of Mayence, who on behalf of Frederic Barbarossa was
besieging Ancona, which was occupied by Manuel's troops,
received a detachment of men to aid him, and the city was
blockaded by a Venetian fleet. An alliance was concluded
with William of Sicily. Yet in spite of all its efforts the
Republic was unsuccessful. Weakened by sickness, which
they attributed to drinking water which had been poisoned
by the Greeks, and opposed everywhere, the Venetians were
driven to sue for peace. Manuel rejected their proposals.
The imperial fleet, which had made an unsuccessful attack
upon Egypt in 1170, was yet able to provide a hundred and
fifty galleys. The fleet of the Republic had to retire before it,
and of the one hundred and twenty ships which had left Venice
only seventeen returned, the rest having been either captured,
abandoned, or destroyed. The Venetians, in their rage at his
failure, assassinated the Doge, Vitali Michieli, who had conducted the expedition. Before leaving the Archipelago a
second embassy had been sent to Constantinople to sue for
peace.

On this mission Henry Dandolo went to the capital, and
during this period he lost his eyesight. Whether such loss
was partial or total ; whether it was due to the terrible epi-
demic which in the first year of the war had carried off
three or four thousand of the Venetians in the islands of
the Ægean ; whether, as Villehardouin asserts, he was blind
from a wound in the head ; or whether he was blinded in Constantinople with a burning glass at the command of the
Emperor, as his descendant affirms, it is certain that from
this time until his death Dandolo was filled with a passionate
desire for vengeance against the Empire. His mission, like
that of his predecessors, proved a failure.

Venice is
defeated.

Henry
Dandolo.

In 1175 the Venetians found that success had eluded
them everywhere except in Dalmatia. Ancona had been relieved. The Serbians had been driven back. Their own fleet
had been shattered. They accordingly sued once more for
peace. Manuel, who was being hard pressed by the Turks,
was on his side willing to make terms. He agreed to restore
the Republic to its privileges as they existed in 1171, and to pay
fifteen hundred pounds weight of gold as compensation for
the Venetian property which he had seized. It is doubtful
whether any considerable portion of this sum was ever paid.
Certain buildings in Constantinople were delivered to the
Venetians in 1189, probably in part payment.

As the century closed the relations of the Republic with
Constantinople appeared to have improved. In 1198 an
alliance was concluded by two envoys, sent for that purpose
by Henry Dandolo, now become Doge, and was followed by
an imperial bull promising an indemnity to the Venetians
and binding them on their side not to assist Alexis, the son of
the deposed Emperor Isaac. The old soreness, however, still
remained. The jealousy of the favours heaped on the Pisans,
the non-payment of the indemnity for the property seized in
1171, and, above all perhaps, the bitterness of Dandolo, which
had increased with his age, all tended to make Venice hostile.
She had, indeed, recovered the territory which had been taken
from her by the Empire, and her citizens had now as many
commercial privileges as were possessed by the subjects of the
Empire themselves. She recognised, however, that she held
these privileges on a precarious tenure, and that the Empire
no longer cared to give to the Republic exclusive rights ; and
the recollection of these facts and of her grievances, joined
with the knowledge of her own strength and of the imperial
weakness, combined to make her hostile. The very closeness
of the alliance which had existed between the Empire and
Venice had weakened the former where she had the most
need of strength. Constantinople had had such powerful opponents against her in the east, the north, and the south-west,
that most of her attention had been concentrated on her
armies. She had never altogether neglected her fleet, as the

Relations
between
Venice and
Constanti-
nople.

Venetians themselves had learned to their cost in the war between 1171 and 1175. But she had acquired the habit of looking for the aid of Venice in every struggle which had to be fought out at sea, and the result was that the strength of the imperial navy had been gradually lessening, until, when the hour of supreme trial came, her fleet was powerless to resist the invader who had been her hired ally. The rivalries of the naval states of Italy kept the Empire in nearly perpetual naval war with one or other of them ; but the navy which was strengthened by this warfare was that of Venice, and not of the New Rome.

During the last half of the century preceding the great expedition which Venice carried to Constantinople, her hostility and jealousy had been continually increasing. The tradition of her alliance with Constantinople was forgotten. Her later conquests had been won by her own strength alone. The alliance of the New Rome was no longer needful to her, and as that alliance had been withdrawn there was substituted for it the strongest desire to wound the Empire, to destroy its influence, and to take possession of its trade. Her intimate relations with the New Rome made her understand better than any other state how valuable was her commerce, and probably also how much her resources had been diminished by the attacks on land and sea ; and the tenacious hostility which she showed during the generation preceding her final blow contributed more to the weakening of the Empire than the opposition of all the other Italian states.

Summary of the causes which had weakened theEmpire. Its position in 1200.

I have endeavoured to show that during the century and a half preceding the Latin Conquest the New Rome and the Empire over which it ruled had been attacked as surely no state had ever been attacked before. The long contest of the Elder Rome with the states of Italy, the five centuries of warfare waged by the remnant of Spaniards who had never given in to the Moor, have each of them features which separate them distinctly from the contest waged by Constantinople. The Romans of the earlier time and the Spaniards who expelled the Moors were welded together by community of interest and of origin. Intercourse between the various citizens of each race was easy.   Sympathy between them was natural ; for their numbers were small, and each citizen felt that the welfare of the state was also his private interest.   The Empire had no such advantages.   It was composed of peoples widely different in origin, in history, and in sympathy.   The Greeks of the south had never altogether forgotten .their ancient civilisation, and were a race in intellectual decay. The fierce Bulgars and the Slavs of the north of the peninsula had not yet emerged from barbarism.   The various colonies of Wallachs, of Huns, and of other races which were settled in the Empire and were compelled to obey its rule, had little or no sympathy with the people by whom they were sur-rounded.   All the peoples, races, and tongues of the Empire regarded Constantinople, with its prosperity, its immense trade, and its luxury, with a certain rivalry or jealousy often amounting to hostility.   The community of feeling arising either from patriotism or religion, which has always been present in the great protracted struggles of nations, hardly existed in the Byzantine Empire.   Its territory was too wide-spread in an age when communication was slow for any such common sentiment to exert a powerful influence over the mass of the population.   The isolation of peoples of various races and languages was never under its rule so complete as it is now under that of the Ottoman Turks, where Greek, Turk, and Bulgarian live side by side without intermarriage and almost without intercourse.   On the contrary, the Empire had shown a wonderful capacity for assimilating the various races which had flowed into it ; but these races had come in such numbers and were of such widely different composition that the process was far from complete during the period we have been considering, when it was necessary for the nation to put forth all her strength.   A large portion of her army was con-tinually engaged in keeping order among the diverse peoples and the discordant elements of which her population was formed.

We have seen that the attacks made upon her from without were of a formidable nature.   While those from the Normans of Sicily and from the Italian states were of a kind

which have fallen to the ordinary lot of nations, those from
the East were of an altogether extraordinary and exceptional
character. Two broad streams of Asiatic barbarians, one to
the north and the other to the south of the Black Sea, were
flowing in upon Europe during the century and a half preceding 1200, and the Eastern Empire alone had to resist on
behalf of Europe. Every inducement which the accumulation
of wealth could offer to such barbarians was held out to them ;
but I cannot too frequently insist that the greatest incentive
to their attacks was furnished by religious fanaticism. Our
small war in the Soudan has reminded us how powerful
a motive the religious zeal of Mahometanism can supply to
its newly made converts. The hordes of Asia which hurled
themselves on the imperial armies of New Rome were filled
with the like new-born zeal for their faith ; but they had the
advantage of an almost boundless reserve of men behind
them, and the richest spoils of the world open for them to
plunder in case of success. As the magnificent German army
of the third crusade fought and defeated every attack of the
Turks between the Marmora and Syria, with the result only
that it had itself melted away by the time it reached its
destination, so the imperial armies had again and again by
virtue of their superior discipline defeated the armies of the
same enemy, only to find that after a few months another
army had come into existence, and that new battles had
again to be fought. The stories of these battles and of these
victories alike of Crusaders and of the armies of the Empire,
as told by the Western and by the Byzantine writers, are
confirmed by the Moslem historians. The history of the
contest between Christendom and Islam in the west of Europe
is, with the single exception of the centuries of struggle in
Spain, that of two or three great battles. We glorify Charles
Martel and the heroism of John Sobieski. But the story of
the same struggle against the New Rome is that of a long
series of battles, of a ceaseless contest, and of the steady
gaining ground by the enemy during centuries. I have
already said that the Arab siege of Constantinople may take
rank with the contemporary battle of Tours. But there is

nothing in Western history which, for its tenacity and its continuity, can be compared with the struggle made by the Empire against the Seljukian Turks. To compare small things with great, just as the Philistines were repeatedly defeated by the Judges in Bible story, but very shortly had again to be met, so the New Rome during a century and a half inflicted all but crushing defeats upon the hordes of Asia, only to find that after a few months other hordes had taken their place and had again to be fought.

The Empire during this period of almost constant warfare in Asia Minor, around the Balkans, and on the west coast of the Balkan peninsula, had made a long, and in the main a successful, resistance to the attacks of her foes. We have seen that when her strength had been sorely spent, five-and-twenty years of dynastic struggles, occasioned in part by the fact that she was passing through a transition period from absolute to oligarchical rule, still further weakened her. Scarcely three months passed during the last quarter of the twelfth century in which a new claimant for the throne did not make his appearance. Unfortunately during that period the actual occupants of the throne were imbecile and incompetent men. The Empire had held together in spite of these rulers. All attacks directed against the city itself had failed. All attacks by land would probably have continued to fail but for the remarkable combination of circumstances which led to her destruction. She had encouraged trade with Italy, and had treated foreign merchants with generous indulgence. Each of the flourishing states of the Italian peninsula had shared in her prosperity and had prospered by her adversity. They found their opportunity to obtain the trade of the East while Constantinople was fighting the battles of Europe. Venice had been peculiarly the favoured city of the New Rome. Her fleets had been the naval arm of the Empire until, under the demoralisation of the later occupants of the imperial throne, when court favourites had plundered the stores intended for the navy and had allowed the fleet to fall into decay, the Empire had virtually ceased to have a navy. The resistance which had been offered to the attacks made on land

commands our admiration.   Her huge blunder was neglect of
her fleet.   This neglect left her open to attack by sea, and
although such an attack was useless unless it could be
combined with a simultaneous attack by an army—although,
too, there was but one state in the world which could equip
a fleet adequate for the purpose in view, the peculiar position
of Constantinople ought to have taught her rulers that she
could never be safe unless she could effectually bar the passage
of the Dardanelles.   When at last the moment came in which
her old ally was to lead the attack against the imperial city, it
was by means of the Venetian fleet that the vulnerable point
was reached.

CHAPTER VII.

IN 1200 Constantinople was the chief city of the Western world. Many circumstances had contributed to give her this pre-eminence. Much was due to her geographical position. No city at that time or for many centuries previous was so well situated for commanding influence at once over Europe and Asia. Her situation seemed pre-eminently fitted for the seat of the universal empire to which Roman ambition aspired. All the trade between Western Europe and the countries bordering on the Black Sea, and those to which that sea was the highway, must pass her gates. The Sea of Marmora and the Bosphorus, called oftener the Straits of St. George, afforded the easiest of paths for the commerce of the neighbouring countries. The Golden Horn, the natural harbour of Constantinople, is protected from every wind, and is so deep throughout half its length that even large vessels can be moored quite close to the shores, while throughout the other half it shoals off so as to afford ample accommodation for the smallest vessels. The triangular peninsula upon which the city is situated slopes upward gently from the sea on the two long sides to a ridge at right angles to the base, and thus affords an easy natural drainage. The Bosphorus, which flows past the apex of the triangle, has always a strong current running either northwards or southwards according to the prevailing wind. With rare exceptions there is always a corresponding wind blowing across the city. These winds have at all times done much to keep the city healthy, and at the present day contribute more than any other cause to remedy the mischief to which the want of simple sanitary precautions would give rise. The site, excellent for strength

Advantages of its situation.

in defence, salubrious, and convenient for commerce, had indeed been admirably chosen by Constantine for the establishment of the New Rome, and nearly nine centuries of prosperity had added to the wealth with which its great founder had endowed it. The two chief sources of this wealth had been its political pre-eminence and its commerce.

Advan-
tages de-
rived from
its being
the capital, As the capital city of the eastern division of the Roman Empire and the residence of its Emperor and nobility, Constantinople drew together a large population. It had gradually attracted all that was most noteworthy throughout the Empire in art and science. The records of the Christian Church bear witness to the acuteness of intellect with which the great theological questions of the time were, in and about Constantinople, discussed and settled for centuries. The student of law recognises that the body of jurisprudence which was developed in the New Rome, and which is known as Roman law, owes to the labours of jurists in Constantinople most of its precision, its subtlety, its grasp of principles, and its wonderful generalisations. The modern world still retains the powerful impressions made upon it by Constantinople. The leading dogmas established by its famous divines and its councils are recognised throughout Christendom. Roman law, which never ceased to be practised throughout Western Europe, has, since its reformation under Napoleon, become the law of the whole civilised world with the exception of the English-speaking peoples, and even our law has been largely added to by doctrines taken, sometimes avowedly, sometimes without recognition, from the same storehouse of legal principles. All that Paris and Berlin have done towards attracting the ablest professors and specialists in the countries of which they are the capitals had been done by Constantinople. The sculptor, the painter, and the architect found the best market for their talents in the capital ; the poet or the divine, the wrestler or the actor, his most appreciative audiences.

from com-
merce. Commerce, however, had contributed still more largely to the wealth of the capital. The highway of the Bosphorus and the Dardanelles is one of the most important in the

world. No city which exists, or has ever existed, has so
completely commanded an open road leading to, and having
on each side of it, so many fruitful countries. From Batoum,
which is the most direct outlet from Central Asia, the best
available route to Europe was by the Bosphorus. This
channel, varying from half a mile to a mile wide, could be
easily defended. After a passage of eighteen miles these
noble straits lead to Constantinople, which commands on one
side of it the Marmora, a beautiful and convenient lake under
the entire control of Constantinople. Its outlet is at the
Dardanelles, where the facilities for its defence are equal to
those on the Bosphorus. Thence, through the Ægean, all
Europe, Africa, and Asia Minor was open to the trading
vessels of the capital. The imports for the supply of the
wants of Constantinople and the export of her own products
were themselves considerable. We have seen that the rulers
of Constantinople had conceded many privileges in favour
of trade to foreign subjects. But while these concessions
doubtless increased her wealth, she had reserved to her
own merchants the exclusive privilege of the Black Sea trade
and of the import of provisions. But she was then, as she
has continued to be till quite recently, and will be again
under a good government, a great mart for the collection and
distribution of goods. A large amount of the trade between
Asia and Europe passed through the Bosphorus. Persian
and Armenian merchants brought their merchandise to Constantinople, to be distributed from thence throughout Western
Europe. The city had occupied the first rank among the
great marts of commerce for so long a period that at the end
of the twelfth century she had supplied not only the Empire
of which she was the capital, but also Western Europe,
Central Asia, and even India, with gold coin.

At present all foreign merchants without exception live
outside the walls of Constantinople.[1] The aim of the Latin

[1] It must be remembered that the Constantinople of 1200 was only that
portion which is now called Stamboul or Istamboul, a word which is probably
the Turkish abbreviation of Constantinople, just as Skenderoun is the abbreviation of Alexandretta, Skender bey for Alexander bey, Isnik for Nicæa,
Ismidt for Nicomedia, &c. Another and more popular derivation traces Stamboul

colonists in the twelfth century was to obtain quarters inside the city.[1] These quarters, as they are usually called by the Western writers, consisted of what are known in the East as khans, and what were called ἔμβολοι by the Greeks.[2] All the Latin quarters, with the exception of two small settlements which were destined to grow into the city of Galata, were, as we have seen, inside the city walls, though it is known that inferior houses were built between the walls and the waters of the Golden Horn. All the Latin quarters were on the side of the city which slopes towards this great harbour. The great struggle between the rival colonies, and indeed with the Byzantines, was for the *scalas* or wharves. Across the harbour, on the slopes of Pera, and in what is now called Galata,[3] were the settlements of Jews who had been banished from the city, and probably the dwellings of a few Venetians and Genoese.

Policy of Emperors had encouraged trade.

The political economy of a succession of Emperors had encouraged trade. They rarely sought to place restriction upon commerce. Monopolies were discountenanced. Merchants were invited to trade, and their rights were strictly guarded. The imperial government left traders very much to themselves, and did not harass them by useless restrictions or by those attempts to protect the public which have so often prevented trade. The taking of interest was allowed, and hence a great deal of the capital which had belonged to

to εἰς τὴν πόλιν, but I think the evidence is in favour of the Turkish origin. The *Itinerario* of Clavigo states that before the Moslem occupation the inhabitants themselves called the city Escomboli. The Turks allow a few foreigners to have their warehouses in Stamboul, but will not permit them to reside there. All the embassies and legations are in Pera, that is, *across* the water (πέραν = on the other side); or at Galata, which is a part of what was originally called Pera.

[1] Dr. Paspati, the learned archæologist of Constantinople, has worked out very successfully the topography of Constantinople during the twelfth century. I may say that I am greatly indebted to his labours for a good many hints on this part of my subject.

[2] Several still exist in Constantinople; one in particular, well worth visiting, is inhabited by Persian merchants.

[3] There are two versions of the derivation of the name Galata. Dr. Paspati derives it from γάλα, milk, and would thus make it the town of the milk-sellers, like some other towns of a similar name. I am myself inclined to believe that it is rather the Italian *calle* or *galle*, which in Genoa is a slope, and in Venice an enclosed place.

the Mahometans on their eastern frontier, by whom the taking of interest was strictly forbidden, flowed into the Empire. Luxury was permitted. Few attempts were made to fix the prices of the merchandise sold. Duties on goods imported and exported were light in comparison with what they have been in other countries. Even as early as the time of Theophilus it had been formally declared that, as commerce was a benefit to the public, any interference with it was an offence against the public as well as against the person injured.

The great commerce which entered the capital brought with it much of the liberality which is due to the intercourse with foreign nations. Arab traders were allowed to live within the city, and foreigners from the West were scandalised to see that the Saracens were permitted to build a new mosque and to practise in a Christian city the rites of Mahometanism. ' It would have been even right to have razed the city to the ground,' says a chronicler of the Latin Conquest, ' for, if we believe report, it was polluted by new mosques, which its perfidious Emperor allowed to be built that he might strengthen the league with the Turks.'[1]

Commerce produced liberality of practice.

Manuel wished to remove an anathema from the Catechism against the Mahometan conception of God.[2] Italian merchants, Armenians, Chaldeans, and others not in union with the Orthodox Church were yet allowed the exercise of their religion. Not only had the Italian colonists their own churches, but the chief of their communities had official seats allotted to them in the Great Church. Even the Jews, who have always in the East been the object of the aversion of the orthodox Christians, were on the whole fairly well treated. When we remember that we are dealing with the period of the massacre of Jews in York, Lincoln, and elsewhere in England, it is satisfactory to find that Benjamin of Tudela finds, among the greatest hardships his countrymen had to bear, that they were not allowed to ride on horseback, and that they were defiled, according to their law, because the tanners who lived near their quarters were permitted to pour out their polluted

[1] Geoffrey of Vinsauf, *Chron. of Crusades*, p. 94.
[2] Nicetas, *Man.* Book VII.

water in the streets. This writer has to admit that the Jews were comfortably off, that many were manufacturers, many merchants, and several extremely rich.

In addition to the riches which had flowed into the capital from the fact that it was the seat of government and the greatest emporium of trade, Constantinople had in the twelfth century amassed wealth because during many centuries it had been the treasure-house of the Lower Empire. Men who had gathered wealth elsewhere flocked to Constantinople to spend, to invest, or to hoard it. Amid an insecurity which had been increasing since the Turkish invasion of Asia Minor, those who had movable property flocked to the one city which they believed to be invulnerable. During many centuries the New Rome had been pre-eminently the city of Christendom in which wealth had been largely and steadily accumulating. The riches of Asia Minor, which had contained many cities and states whose wealth had become proverbial, had been continually draining away towards Constantinople. The Spanish Jew, Benjamin of Tudela, already cited, who visited Constantinople in 1161, found it resorted to by merchants who came by land and sea from Babylon and Mesopotamia, from Egypt and Palestine, from Russia, Hungary, Lombardy, and Spain. No city, except Bagdad, the metropolis of the Mahometans, as he calls it, equalled it for business and bustle. The tribute brought to it every year in silks, gold, and purple cloth filled many towers. Its wealth and buildings were equalled in no other city of the world. The inhabitants were especially rich in silks, gold, and precious stones. They dressed in garments ornamented with gold, rode upon horses, and looked like princes. Benjamin seems to have been specially struck with the display of gold. The new palace of Blachern, built by the reigning Emperor, Manuel Comnenos, had its walls and columns covered with pure gold. The throne in this palace was of gold and ornamented with precious stones. A crown of gold was suspended over it, set with stones of inestimable value and unusual lustre. All other places of worship in the world did not equal in riches, says Benjamin, the church of the Divine Wisdom. It was ornamented with pillars of gold and

City was treasure-house of the East.

silver and with innumerable lamps of the same materials, and its riches were countless. Between the time of Benjamin and 1204 this wealth had but slightly diminished. The imperial territory through which he travelled was rich, and produced all manner of delicacies and abundance of bread, meat, and wine. The inhabitants lived comfortably, every man under his own vine and fig-tree. The neighbouring country, always fertile, and which four centuries of Ottoman misrule have not succeeded in altogether impoverishing, was able to furnish annually a large tribute to the capital.

The wealth of the capital was absolutely and exception- *Wealth in comparison with Western cities.* ally great. But in relation to the cities of the West it was enormous. The Crusaders, under the Marquis of Montferrat and Count Baldwin of Flanders, when they gained their first view of Constantinople, gazing at its walls and towers from the same hills whence, in 1878, the Russian troops wondered why they were not marched into the city, were struck with an amazement which Villehardouin can hardly find words sufficiently strong to express. The wealth, size, strength, and magnitude of the capital profoundly impressed them. There was not a man, says Villehardouin, who did not tremble at the thought that so strong and rich a city was about to be attacked. When ultimately they entered their first impressions were more than realised. The palaces were richer and the churches larger than any they had previously seen. The city was well enclosed with high walls and lofty towers. Each stone tower, no matter how lofty, had its height increased by two or three stories of wood. Never, in the opinion of this Western Crusader, was a city so well fortified. He gives us a more definite idea of the wealth of the city by a remarkable comparison. Speaking of a fire which broke out while his companions were besieging the city, he says that, though it was the third fire which had occurred in the city since the Franks had come into the country, more houses were destroyed by it than there were in the three largest cities belonging to the kingdom of France. The treasure in the imperial palace of Bucoleon was enormous, 'sans fin ni mesure.' The palace of Blachern was found equally well

supplied. 'There was gold and silver for all, vessels of
precious metal, satins and silk cloth, furs of various kinds,
and every sort of goods which have ever been found on
earth.'

Constantinople at the end of the twelfth century impressed the Western traveller with its wealth and magnificence
much more than any city in Europe would now be likely to
impress any inhabitant of any of the Western countries who
was tolerably familiar with the towns of his own province.
The picturesqueness and stateliness of Constantinople is that
which strikes every modern traveller when he gains his first
view of the ancient city. Imperial dignity, magnificence,
opulence, and prosperity were the characteristics which impressed themselves most deeply on the traveller at the end of
the twelfth century. The Crusader who arrived by sea caught
sight first of a group of domes and towers belonging to the
churches and great public buildings, most prominent of which
were Hagia Sophia, the Great Church, dedicated to the Divine
Wisdom, the churches of the Divine Peace, Hagia Irene, and
of the Holy Resurrection.[1] The domes were resplendent
with gold, and the buildings, from the natural formation of
the land, rose in tiers behind each other, intermingled with
cypresses and brighter trees in a manner which even now
makes the view of Constantinople from the sea one of the

*The princi-
pal build-
ings in the
city.*

[1] Constantine had been the founder of these churches. Probably at the time
when he named them he was still hesitating whether he should declare for Christianity or not, and hence he gave them names which would be suitable in either
event. The temple of Wisdom and the temple of Peace would have been reproductions of temples in Rome. At a later date popular belief assumed that these
churches were dedicated to saints. In the Middle Ages the official name of Hagia
Sophia was 'the Great Church of the Divine Wisdom of the Incarnate Word.'
These churches are perhaps the most striking illustrations of Constantine's vacilla-
tion, but they are not the only ones. His statue at Constantinople represented
him as Apollo, but the emblems of the Crucifixion served as rays. Under its
column, which still exists in Constantinople, and is known as the Burnt
Column, were buried the ancient palladium of the Elder Rome and a piece of
the true cross. Some of the coins of Constantine have on one side the monogram
of Christ, and on the other Apollo, with the inscription 'Sol invictus.' Hagia
Sophia was rebuilt by Justinian. The present Hagia Irene was probably built in
the ninth century. Both these churches remain. Hagia Anastasia, which might
have become the temple of the pagan feast of the resurrection of nature, no longer
exists.

most charming and impressive in the world.   Churches, columns, palaces, castles, towers, statues, and masses of houses, rose before the spectator in picturesque confusion. When the traveller landed the narrow streets and overhanging houses did not produce the same disagreeable effect upon him that they do upon the modern visitor to Constantinople, because he was unfamiliar with better streets, while the signs of abundant wealth, both public and private, filled him with amazement.   The whole Empire had been put under contribution for the adornment of the capital.   The temples and public buildings of Greece, of Asia Minor, and of the islands of the Archipelago, had been ransacked to embellish what its inhabitants spoke of as the Queen City, and even Egypt had contributed an obelisk and many other monuments.

The Great Church was at once the most prominent object in the city and the most interesting and characteristic.   Its noble dome still remains the wonder and the admiration of architects.   Its internal arrangements and its symmetrical proportions have never been excelled.   Not only was it the model for all subsequent Eastern church architecture and the noblest church then existing in the world, but it was the centre of the life of the capital.   The history of what passed within its walls and in its courts is the history of Constantinople from the time of its construction to that when it was stripped of its glory and became the chief temple of a rival creed.

Hagia Sophia.

The builders of the Great Church had plundered other famous edifices in order to decorate what was intended to outstrip the glory of Solomon's temple, and in order to complete what remained for nearly a thousand years the masterpiece of Christian architecture and the dominant model for all churches in Eastern Europe.   They had transported the eight large columns of green granite from the temple of Diana at Ephesus ; the eight porphyry columns, with beautiful white capitals and pedestals, had been brought from the Roman temple of the Sun of Aurelian ; the twenty-four columns of granite which support the galleries had come from Egypt.   The church was full of costly objects which had

been sent from every part of the Empire, while the Byzantine
architects had covered the ceiling with gold and mosaic
pictures which, even in their present form, mutilated in
accordance with the requirements of Moslem nakedness, give
an idea of the rich and magnificent effect which they must have
produced on the spectator six hundred years ago.   The altar
and the tabernacle were, even amid so much that was gorgeous, conspicuous by their splendour.   The octagonal tower
surmounting the tabernacle had over it a golden lily upon the
imperial orb and cross.   The screen secluding the Bema or
chancel contained twelve silver columns.   The patriarchal
throne and those of the seven priests were covered with the
same precious metal.   Within the vestries were an immense
number of chalices and vases and 42,000 robes embroidered
with pearls and precious stones.   Twenty-four Gospels,
written on parchment with all the skill of the East, were
preserved in massive gold cases.   The chandeliers were of
gold, and everything belonging to the interior of the church
was on a similar scale of magnificence.   Add to this that the
ceremonial had been arranged with a view to splendour, that
barbarous envoys had been so stricken by the magnificence
of this ceremonial and by the sense of awe and majesty which
it produced that they reported what they saw to be supernatural, and we may realise the effect which the service in
Hagia Sophia produced upon visitors from the West.[1]   The
walls of the building were veneered with beautiful slabs of
marble, arranged so as to produce a general effect of richness
and a harmony of tone, while the whole of the interior gave
an impression of unity and beauty such as even no Gothic
cathedral produces, and which makes a modern authority in

[1] See Stanley's *Eastern Church*, p. 299.   The author remarks that the Byzantine historian of the visit of the Russian envoys to S. Sophia gives the reply of
the guides, 'What ! do you not know that angels come down from heaven to
mingle in our services?' without any observation, and that the effect was a striking
one produced on a barbarous people by the union of religious awe and outward magnificence.   He observes also that a like confusion supports the supposed miracle
of the Holy Fire at Jerusalem.   As to the latter, whatever may have been its
origin, it is now purely and simply a fraud, and that the Greek Church should still
retain a service in which God is thanked for sending the fire is the worst piece of
evidence I know of against that Church.

architecture doubt whether any Christian church exists of
any age whose interior is even now so beautiful as this marvellous creation of Byzantine art.[1] Seen by Sir John Maun-
deville in 1322, and when it had been considerably injured, it
impressed him as 'the fairest and noblest church in the
world.'[2]

But while the Great Church of the Divine Wisdom was
the crown of so much that was beautiful and magnificent,
there were other buildings which claimed the attention of
travellers. It was surrounded with edifices which were characterised with Byzantine splendour. Near at hand to the Other
north-east was the imperial palace, a mass of buildings be- buildings.
tween St. Sophia and the Marmora, and occupying a site
which, from its choice by Constantine down to the present
day, has been renowned at once for wonderful beauty and for
the many and great events with which its history is crowded.
The Imperial Square—the ancient Forum, or Augusteon—
adjoined the Great Church and the palace, and was surrounded by a double colonnade. Opposite the church, and
upon a pedestal of bronze resting on seven arches, rose an
equestrian bronze statue of the Emperor Justinian, of colossal
size; his right hand extended threateningly to the East,
while in his left he held an orb as symbol of universal
dominion. Near at hand, to the south, was the imperial hip- The hippo-
podrome, the structural portion of which has almost entirely drome.
disappeared, but of which there are still sufficient remains to
enable us to see that it was nine hundred feet long and half
that width. Its rows of seats in white marble, and probably
after the beautiful model of those found in the theatre of
Bacchus at Athens, have long since disappeared. The
materials of which the portion set apart for the spectators
was formed have been taken away to be used in the construction of neighbouring mosques and buildings. In 1201,

---

[1] Fergusson's *History of Architecture*, vol. ii. p. 321. See also in the *Nineteenth Century* of December, 1884, an article by the same author on 'The Proposed New Cathedral for Liverpool,' in which he says (p. 911): 'S. Sophia . . .
which is the most beautifully proportioned interior of any church yet erected for
Christian purposes anywhere.'

[2] *Early Voyages in Palestine*, p. 130.

however, the hippodrome was probably but little changed
from what it had been for several centuries. Commenced by
Severus, successive emperors had added to it and adorned it.
There were then in it the famous bronze horses which now
adorn the church of St. Mark in Venice, an obelisk of
Egyptian syenite still standing in the centre, and which we
learn from an inscription upon the base had been set up again
by the Emperor Theodosius after it had lain a considerable
time on the ground. Near to this obelisk stood a pyramid,
which marked the goal of the chariot races. Probably on the
other side of the obelisk stood the famous column of the Three
Serpents,[1] a monument which had been an ancient relic when
it was brought to Constantinople. It dated back to the time
of the Persian invasion of Greece, and had served at Delphi
to support the golden tripod which the Greeks found in the
enemy's camp after the battle of Plataea, and which they had
dedicated to Apollo. Seen in position at Delphi by Hero-
dotus and Thucydides, it had been placed in the hippodrome
by Constantine, and was probably looked on by the Byzantine spectators with similar awe to that with which the Turks
have always regarded it—an awe which has probably been the
main cause of its preservation.

The
column of
Constan-
tine.

Near the hippodrome to the west was the noble column
of porphyry, which still stands as the Burnt Column, but which
in 1200 had been recently restored, according to the still
legible inscription, by the most pious Emperor, Manuel Comnenos. In other parts of the city were other columns, while
statues, some of which were of the best period of Greek art,
were probably more numerous than in any city now existing.
Beyond the hippodrome, the traveller would have met on
every hand solid constructions, which bore witness to the
wealth of the city. The north-eastern corner, now known as
Seraglio Point, was one mass of churches, baths, and palaces.
Behind it, and near the church of the Divine Wisdom, rose,
besides the buildings already mentioned, the great palace of

---

[1] The column still exists, but the heads have disappeared. Various untrustworthy reports are given as to their disappearance. One of them remained *in
situ* until 1621. A portion of one has recently been recovered, and is in the
Imperial Museum at Stamboul.

the Senate, and some of the most famous of what are now called Turkish baths. On the further slope, towards the Marmora, were the beautiful church built by Justinian, and called now Little Hagia Sophia, the palace of the Patriarch, called the Tricline, on account of the three flights of stairs by which it was approached, and other buildings. To the west of these buildings were the law courts, the palaces of the nobility, with other columns and statues. The remains of the baths and of some of these palaces still bear witness to the solidity of their construction, and the stateliness, and especially to what I may call the modernness, of their design.

The shore of the Golden Horn from Seraglio Point, throughout half its distance, was occupied by foreign and native merchants, whose vast stores were crowded with merchandise. The other half, up to the point where the wall turned southwards to form the landward defence of the city, was occupied by monasteries and by churches, which appear to have been enclosed by a wall, while the enclosure was known as the Petrion. The Petrion.

There was yet another species of wealth than those furnished by commerce and the other sources I have named, which cannot be passed over. Constantinople was conspicuous in the eyes of the Crusaders more for its treasure in relics than in works of art. The men of the West were too ignorant to understand the work of Phidias or of Lysippus. But they were connoisseurs in relics. During many years the churches of the West had been striving with each other to obtain possession of these Christian mementoes. When at rare intervals a traveller had returned from the East who had obtained possession of such an object, he was regarded as a benefactor of the Church. The relic was received by the community to which it was destined with solemn procession and religious services. In many instances the possession of a relic made the fortune of the church or monastery where it was contained. The search after relics became almost a craze, like that after new varieties of tulips or old china. Constantinople was the greatest storehouse—perhaps I may say manufactory—of such relics. Its population was the

Wealth in relics.

richest among Christian states, and its wealthy citizens were
proud of such possessions as evidences of their wealth, and
were glad to purchase the favour of the Church by bequeath-
ing them.   But Constantinople had never possessed so many
relics as at the time of the fourth crusade, and these stores of
wealth were always to be seen by those who wished.[1]   The
unceasing turmoil in which Asia Minor and Syria had been
kept by the Saracens and Turks had made the Christian
populations ready to transfer their wealth to the strongest
city in the world, but especially to take sacred relics out of
reach of the infidel.   In the East as in the West, the
churches, or the buildings adjoining them, were often used as
storehouses for the deposit of articles of value.   They were
strongly built and safer than ordinary houses from fire and
thieves.   The Church had from early times preserved these
deposits with extraordinary legislation, of which we have still
traces in our law of sacrilege, and it has been suggested that
the number of relics was exaggerated by Latin travellers who
visited Constantinople in consequence of the great store of
wealth which they saw in the churches.   But, however this
may be, it can hardly be doubted that not even in Rome
itself has there ever been amassed so great a number of
articles of veneration as existed in Constantinople at the opening of the thirteenth century.   The treasure of sacred relics in
the city was immense, says one writer.[2]   There were as many
relics in the city, says Villehardouin, as in all the rest of the
world put together.[3]   We may despise the veneration of
relics because we doubt the authenticity of the objects.   But
we are dealing with the Ages of Faith, and the Crusaders fully
believed both in their genuineness and usefulness.   'For my
part,' says La Brocquiere,[4] 'I believe that God has spared the
city more for the holy relics it contains than for anything else.'

---

[1] Ingulphus, *History of Croyland.*

[2] 'Lectiones S. Petri Insulensis,' *Exuviæ Sacræ*, vol. ii. p. 9.

[3] Villehardouin, p. 192. Many similar statements might be quoted, *e.g.*
Matthew Amalphitanus, *Exuviæ Sacræ*, 171 : 'Erat enim Constantinopolitana
civitas plurimorum sanctorum consecrata reliquiis et munita corporibus, quorum
præsidio primatum gloriæ meruit inter omnia regna.'—'Histoire de la saincte
larme,' *Exuviæ Sacræ*, vol. i. p. 189.

[4] Bohn's Translation, p. 341.

The city which guarded so much wealth and such valuable The city walls treasures was encircled with strong walls and towers, which gave it a strength such as no other city in the world possessed. On the side bordered by the Sea of Marmora and that by the Golden Horn, access to the walls could only be made by an enemy who had command of the sea. On the landward side there were two walls with strong towers at short intervals, and along more than three-fourths of the length a third wall and a ditch. These walls terminated at the Marmora end in a fortress, now occupied by the famous Seven Towers, and at the Golden Horn end by another near the imperial palace of Blachern. The walls were lofty, the inner one sixty feet high, and the ditch between them thirty-five feet broad and twenty-five feet deep. Even in their present condition they give a good idea of the resistance which could be offered by their defenders at a time when cannon were unknown, and constitute perhaps the most superb mass of ruins in Europe.

To enable the city to stand a siege there were underground Cisterns. and other cisterns for the storage of water which are still magnificent in their ruin, and one at least of which has not to this day been explored. Some of these were supplied through subterranean pipes which invaders were unable to discover. 'These cisterns,' says Manuel Chrysoleras with pardonable exaggeration, 'resemble lakes or even seas.' Those which were uncovered were surrounded with large trees.[1] At ordinary times the city was supplied by the ancient aqueducts which had been restored by the Emperors Valens and Justinian and the first of which still gives the main supply of water to Stamboul.

Most of the palaces and public buildings in Constantinople were of white stone, but everywhere then, as now, there was a general use of marble, such as might have been expected in the chief city situated on the Marmora.

There was, no doubt, another side to this picture. While Dwellings of the poorer class. the nobles and the merchant princes of the capital occupied marble palaces, the workmen and the poorer classes were

[1] Eleven large cisterns are enumerated by Constantius; the best known now is that called the Thousand and One Columns.

crowded into the narrowest streets, and were left, as a writer of the time of Manuel remarks, to stench and darkness.[1] The houses of an inferior class were built of wood, as indeed they have always been in the same city on account of the absence in the neighbourhood of Constantinople of any other cheap building material. Palaces crowded the hovels together as they did in all the cities of Western Europe for centuries after that with which I am concerned. It was indeed the very wealth of Constantinople, as compared with that of Paris or any Western city, which made the distinction between the luxury and poverty more visible than that with which Western writers were familiar. What they saw in the capital of the East, their descendants were destined to see in Venice, Marseilles, Paris, and London.

Constanti-
nople a
city of
pleasure

Life among the wealthier classes of Constantinople and its neighbourhood must have been on the whole very pleasant. There were villas on the neighbouring shores of the Bosphorus, on the Marmora towards San Stefano, and on the shore beyond Chalcedon, where one might escape from the great heat of summer and spend half the year in a country life, while the well-built palaces of the city were warm and comfortable in winter. The inhabitants appreciated these privileges and were proud of the Queen of Cities. The Byzantine noble when compelled to leave it longed to be back again. He loved the sacred city and the Marmora, where the zephyrs blew so softly, where the fountains were so pleasant, the baths so delicious, where the dolphins and other varieties of fish disported themselves on the surface of the waters, and where the nightingales and other singing birds made delightful music for those who flocked from all parts of the world to hear it.[2] Constantinople was a city of business, but it was likewise a city of pleasure. Everything that wealth could buy could be secured within its walls. As in our own days men who have acquired money in remote regions flock to Paris or London to take part in the luxurious life of these capitals, so the Cyprian, the islander, the trader from many a remote province or country, went to Constantinople as the place where

[1] Odon de Deuil.   [2] Nicetas, *Alexis Comnenos*, iii. 1.

he could make the best investment of his money in pleasure. But the inhabitant of what the Western writers then called Romania had a greater inducement to go to Constantinople than the inhabitant of Manchester or Marseilles to go to London and Paris. Property is in modern times as safe in these provincial cities as in the capitals of the countries in which they are situated, but property at Smyrna or elsewhere in Asia Minor was liable to attacks from the Turks ; property in Mitylene or others of the islands of the Ægean and along the seaboard of the Empire had to be continually protected from the pirates who were already infesting the neighbouring seas. No city was regarded as so secure as Constantinople, and amidst this security the wealthy man could find rarer silks, finer linen, and purer dyed purple, richer furs, dishes of greater delicacy, and wines of more rare and costly vintage than in the provinces. Precious stones and jewellery of every kind, including those ropes of pearls which are yet to be seen in daily wear at Damascus and other remote cities of Turkey, and to the display of which the inhabitants of Eastern Europe, like those of Asia, have always attached great importance, might be more safely worn, could be shown to more people, and would be more highly appreciated than in the provincial towns. The Crusaders regarded the luxurious dresses of the Byzantines as marks of effeminacy, just as a Turcoman horde clothed in sheepskin marching upon Paris would be sure to regard the luxury of the capital as a sign that the manliness had departed from the nation. The Byzantines looked on the rough and ill-dressed Crusaders as rude and uncouth barbarians, unskilled in science, ignorant of art and literature, and entire strangers to the luxuries of civilisation. The Crusaders are never weary of calling attention to the luxury and the wealth of the inhabitants of Constantinople, and Nicetas himself, the chief Byzantine historian of this period, tells several stories against his own countrymen of the fault found by the Crusaders with the effeminate character of this luxury. We may be sure, however, that the Byzantine point of view was far different. All the pleasures of nature and of art were his. The climate was safe from the great heat of Smyrna or the

cold of even a few miles further north on the Black, that is,
the rough, bleak Sea.   The Golden Horn, the Marmora, and
the Bosphorus were bright during six or seven months of the
year with gaily-decked and graceful caiques, probably not
much unlike their present representatives, except that they
were higher in the stem and stern, and thus more graceful in
form.   Carefully trained oarsmen from the Greek islands or
from the neighbouring shores were to be had at a cheap rate,
and each noble family had its own crews with gay distinctive
badges.   The ruins now existing in the neighbourhood of
Constantinople show how largely the nobles led a villa life on
the borders of the sea.   No city in the world is so largely
gifted by nature with the requirements for a happy life.   The
bright sky, the blue, tideless waters of the Marmora, the vine-
producing shores, the forests which even yet have not been so
far destroyed as to drive away the nightingale, the flights of
quail which pass the city twice every year and still fall
occasionally in the streets of Constantinople, the never-failing
supply of fish and other food, the presence of birds of beautiful
plumage and song, all contributed to the joyous life of this
city of pleasure.

Cere-
monials
carefully
studied.
Leaving out of consideration for the present the childish
and effeminate exhibitions of pomp which were direct imita-
tions of the barbaric magnificence of Eastern courts, we may
yet recognise that the pageants of the imperial court must
often have been extremely beautiful.   In Church and State
alike ceremonial had been carefully studied.   Let us suppose
that the Emperor, having passed out of the Golden Gate, which
was near the southern end of the wall running nearly north
and south, and forming the base of the triangle within which
Constantinople is enclosed, and having inspected his troops
along the range of this landward wall, finds himself at the
Golden Horn termination of the wall on the height above
what is now known as Eyoub—on the spot, that is, where
tradition asserted that Eyoub, the companion in arms of
Mahomet, was killed during the Arab siege of Constantinople
in 668.   The view before him is the finest to be had from
land of the city.   Cape behind cape and dome behind dome

arise in picturesque beauty until they terminate in what is now known as Seraglio Point.   Beneath him were the palace and towers, and beneath them again the prisons of the Blachern.   Above him float the imperial banners, with the crescent, the ancient emblem of Constantinople, on some, the imperial eagle or the white lion on others.   As he prepares to go down to the Golden Horn, the troops are drawn up to do him honour.   There are Dalmatians under their national flags, clothed in the brilliantly embroidered dress which even yet is the most picturesque in Europe, and armed with swords and lances.   There is a company of the Scholarii, or guards of the palace, composed of nobles, some of whom were clothed in rose-coloured tunics, and another of the body guard, chosen from the Scholarii on account of their stature and strength, and known as Candidati, from their light and beautifully embroidered garments, and yet another of the Macedonians of the great heteria, with swords, silver belts, gilded shields, and doubled-edged axes likewise gilded.   Near the Emperor is a company of his foreign guards, composed of Scythians,[1] Englishmen, and others of a kindred race, whose light hair and beards mark them as of Northern origin, and belonging to the famous Warings or Varangians.   They are armed with huge double battle-axes or bills, and, under their own acolyth, cluster about the Emperor, who puts more trust in their sturdy arms and northern fidelity than in either the noble Scholarii or the gaudy troops of Macedonians.

The oarsmen of the imperial trireme stand at the water's edge, bearing the imperial gonfalons emblazoned with gold, while the imperial standard, similarly embroidered, is carried before him.   The trireme bears, as its figure-head, the imperial eagle with outspread wings, of shape not unlike what has come down to us from imperial times in many of our own cathedrals.   The oarsmen in the imperial livery are well matched, and, as soon as the Emperor has taken his seat beneath the canopy, pull at once with a bold stroke out into

[1] The term Scythians is used very vaguely, but probably usually indicated the tribes, not Tartars, of Central Asia, who are now represented by the so-called Tekè Turcomans.

the midst of the Golden Horn, each man taking care not to lift his eyes to the imperial face.[1] The trireme is spread with rich carpets. The nobles are richly clad in silk. The attendant caiques are hardly less graceful or brilliantly ornamented than that of the Emperor. Their occupants vie with each other in the display of silks, richly embroidered in pearls and in jewelry. As they glide along the Golden Horn strains of music are heard, and the procession passes along, interrupted occasionally by the shouts of pleasure-seekers in other caiques, or of Venetian or Genoese passing across to Pera or Galata.

Learning not neglected. Nor amid such luxury was science, art, and literature forgotten. Constantinople had long been the asylum of scholars and of artists. From the time when Constantine had issued his edict for the transport to the city which he had chosen as the New Rome of the chief works of art which had embellished the cities of Greece and Asia Minor, columns, statues, and busts had continued to be sent to the capital, until travellers who visited the city in the twelfth or thirteenth centuries were amazed at the number of works of art which they saw around them. As the seat of the most important Patriarchate of the eastern division of the Empire, the great Christian writers flocked to the capital, and every monastery had its collection of manuscripts. At various times in the history of the New Rome the Hellenic spirit of philosophy seemed on the point of mastering that of Christianity ; and the treasures of ancient Greek literature, intelligible to the people in a language which had been comparatively but little changed, were reproduced and stored up, to become the seed for a new harvest of learning. If the sensual and sensuous pleasures which Constantinople offered in greater profusion than any other European city were not enough for the better minds of the time, they could find satisfaction in having access to more literature of a better quality than any other city could afford.

[1] The same custom has been handed down to modern times. Indeed, there can be little doubt that the famous procession of the Sultan to mosque by water is a pretty close reproduction of the imperial journey. The Sultan's caique for state ceremonies still has the Roman eagle with outstretched wings at its bow.

The subtle Greek intellect was too often inclined to waste its
strength on the useless distinctions of a hair-splitting philosophy or theology which has become to us intolerable and
almost incomprehensible; but even while accepting the waste
of intellectual strength and the valuelessness of the subjects
usually discussed, one is compelled to admit that the fact that
a considerable proportion of the population took an interest in
these subtleties implies an amount of education and of literary
development to which the men of the West were almost altogether strangers.   The interest, too, which the great mass of
the population took in the discussion of religious questions
shows an intelligence which, entertained by men possessed of
the acuteness of Greek thinkers, must in all likelihood have
led to a great religious movement for reform of doctrine that
would have amounted to an Eastern reformation, which would
probably have profoundly modified Western Christianity, had
circumstances allowed it to be developed.

In former times religious questions had occasioned infinite
discussion in Constantinople.   In the twelfth century the
popular interest in such discussions had altogether ceased.
The period in question had not, in the East at least, given rise
to any special religious or intellectual movement.   The disputes
which had raged in the early Church, and which had been
continued by the Blues and Greens, by many a heretical sect,
and by those who took part in the Iconoclast controversy, had
died out, and were represented either by what to most men
had already become incomprehensible articles of faith, or by
persecuted sects banished into the mountains of the peninsula
or the recesses of Asia Minor, where, like the Paulicians, they
were destined to linger on for centuries longer.   During the
eight long centuries between Constantine and the thirteenth
century there had been burning controversies, in which the
city had displayed an intellectual life and activity, a popular
interest in abstract questions as keen and as vivid as that
shown by the inhabitants of London during the time of Charles
the First, and not less eloquently than justly pointed to by
Milton as a proof of a quick and bold spirit among his
countrymen.   Religious belief was understood to have been

Absence of
interest in
intellectual
questions.

settled for all time. The centuries which were to bring inquiry and doubt had not yet dawned. The Church was part
of the established order of things. Religion was one of the
institutions over which the Emperor presided almost as absolutely as over law. No inquiry into the subject was necessary.
It had been decreed by the Emperor as had law, and had
even a higher, and if possible a more indisputable, authority
and sanction. As all that subjects had to do with laws was
to obey them, so also all that they had to do with religion
was to avail themselves of the advantages which it offered.
Baptism into the Church, which was the spouse of Christ, re-
generated the body ; the administration of the sacraments
kept it pure ; and no one doubted that when man's earthly
course was run, the purified body, having thus been made
capable of resurrection, would rise again. The plan of salvation was simple of apprehension, was universally accepted
was easy to follow. Religion thus sat very lightly upon the
inhabitants of the Empire, gave them no anxiety, and, I am
disposed to believe, did not very much influence their conduct.
There was no enthusiasm, there were no burning questions,
no zeal, and very little piety. If a comparison were to be
instituted between the religious condition of the Empire and
anything existing in modern times, I should again refer to
Russia. The way in which the Orthodox Church is accepted
by the great mass of the peasants, the wonderful manner in
which its practices are interwoven with the habits of the
people, and form part of the military, naval, and civil discipline of the Empire, are all reproductions of the condition of
things which the elder branch of the same Church had presented in the twelfth century in the New Rome, except that
the Slavonic spirit is, and ever has been, of a more serious
tone than that which has prevailed among those either of
Greek descent or who have come under the influence of Greek
literature. The Greek spirit of Arianism, which was defeated
at Nicæa, ultimately conquered throughout Eastern Christendom, and substituted the Hellenic for the Hebraic aspect of
Christianity.

The explanation of much of the difference in regard to

the position of religion in modern times and in the West, and that which existed in the twelfth century, is to be found in the results which arose from the facts, first, that the teaching of the Orthodox Church was unquestioned, and, second, that the Emperor was head alike of Church and State.   The first weakened the intellectual side of the Church; the second welded religious observances into the national life.   Nominally we have and have had in England the theory of a head of the State in things spiritual as well as in things temporal. Actually the sovereign has never been generally regarded as possessing such predominance as is accorded to the Czar or was accorded to the Emperors in Constantinople.   As I have already pointed out, the Emperor, when he ceased to be officially recognised as divine, had acquired a position over the Christian Church which gave him very nearly divine attributes.   If it be said that such a regard was incompatible with his being in theory an elected sovereign, I may point to the fact that the Pope's position certainly loses nothing by the fact that he too is elected.   The ruler of the East was Emperor and Pope in one.   That the head of the State was at once the head of the Church explains also what in the West would be regarded as the strange mixture of things temporal and spiritual in Constantinople.   The churches were the great treasure-houses and the great depositaries of merchandise. The markets were usually about their doors.   Hagia Sophia, in the capital, was not merely the greatest church in Christendom, but was the centre of the life of the city.   I do not forget how great a part our own parish churches and cathedrals played during the middle ages in the social and municipal life of the people.   But in the New Rome Hagia Sophia was at once the minster and the town hall—the patriarchal church and the chamber for the election of the Emperor, the meeting place for councils of the Church and for the inhabitants who wished to depose an unpopular Emperor.   Amid the marvels of its luxury, its spacious narthex and yet outer courts and outbuildings were applied to the purposes of commerce and the ordinary requirements of a great city.   The priests, who, it must be remembered, are always married, and the churches were both largely employed in the secular life of the city. Contracts were registered by the priests. The sanctions of the Church were employed to enforce fair dealing, and an amount of honesty was thus secured in trade which, for the period, was remarkable.

Monas-
eries. For those who sought a more severe religious practice the monasteries were open and existed in great numbers. In the capital the district of the Petrion contained several, while outside the walls and on the neighbouring hills were others, the ruins of which show that at one time the number of monks must have been very great. In the Eastern Church, however, monasticism has never assumed the strict and gloomy forms which the great Western orders of monks have given to it.

Wealth such as I have attempted to describe, luxuries which were almost unknown unless by name in Western Europe, a city which was the storehouse of art and of learning, all imply an amount of civilisation which, when compared with that which prevailed during the time of Richard the First and John in England, may justly be called high.

Sense of
security in
the capital. Nor must it be forgotten that that which constituted the most essential element in the civilisation of the capital and its neighbourhood was its security. We read in Benjamin of Tudela, and in other Western as well as in Greek writers, of the abundance of which he saw the signs as he passed through the Empire, of the confidence which, in spite of invasions on all the frontiers, the population had in the power of the government to protect it. At a time when feudalism had organised the great masses of the West into armed populations, and looked upon commerce and the exercise of handicraft with the contempt of ignorance, the inhabitants of the Empire were freely carrying on trade or tilling the ground. There were within the Empire no feudal towers, with serfs and retainers ready at any moment to engage in private warfare, but a country full of farms, prosperous and secure. The *pax Romana* had been well maintained within the Empire, and around the capital had hardly yet been disturbed. More fortunate than its elder rival, the New Rome had never seen a hostile army within its walls. The shores of the Marmora were dotted with the pleasant villas of merchants and nobles, for the roads were good, and the capital to the last provided security for life and property.

In the foregoing pages I have endeavoured to describe the wealth and luxury of the city as it existed in 1200. The Crusaders were amazed at the many forms in which this luxurious wealth was displayed. To the inhabitants of Constantinople this luxury was the outward form in which civilisation showed itself—was, in fact, the natural result and the proof of civilisation. To the Crusader it was no more the sign of civilisation than was the display of a somewhat similar luxury to the English soldiers who in our own days entered Pekin. The countrymen of Richard the Lion-hearted, the contemporaries of the barons who secured our great charter, no less than the countrymen of Philip of France and Frederic Barbarossa, marvelled at what they saw ; but they felt that all the luxury was associated with much that was mean, debasing, and effeminate. They saw wealth, and with it cowardice, luxurious habits of life, lying and treachery, the glorification of the few at the expense of the many, and the absence of public spirit, with its corresponding results in the administration of government.

Side by side with the gorgeous pageantry of the court there was an amount of effeminacy which rightly impressed the Crusaders with a low opinion of the state into which the Empire had fallen. Native writers, as well as travellers from Western Europe, abound with stories showing to what a degree this effeminacy had been developed. It seemed to the men of the West, who counted courage as the highest virtue, as the virtue which implied almost all others, that the manliness had gone out of the race in consequence of its wealth. At times, no doubt, they were led into the mistake of underestimating the valour of their enemies, and of supposing that because they were luxurious they were cowards ; as when the Germans, who, under Conrad, King of Swabia, with a more numerous force had attacked the Roman army in 1147, were defeated by the superior strategy of the enemy they had despised.

Effeminacy of the ruling classes.

The influ-
ence of
Asia upon
society in
the capital. What the Crusaders found fault with were the results of a long period of decadence in social manners and life, the history of which it is not difficult to trace. The success of the New Rome in Asia had been the principal cause of its weakness, and largely contributed to its downfall. So long as the country had been able to keep its democratic organisation of municipalities—so long, that is, as the Greek idea of local government had continued, so long the Empire had been in little danger. After its conquests had been extended far eastward, its wealth caused the Emperors to be independent of the European provinces, and enabled them gradually to deprive the provincial towns and cities of their independence. The nobles of Constantinople governed the provinces of Syria and Asia Minor as sovereigns in everything but their subjection to the Emperor. The government in the capital fell gradually into the hands of men who had been used to these Asiatic modes of rule. The traditions which the Greek race had preserved of independent municipal rule were forgotten. All government was centralised in the capital, until the people in the provinces began to forget that the interest of Constantinople was also theirs. There were, as we have seen, new influences at work, the tendency of which was to make the government Venetian in character, but of these the Crusaders knew nothing. Even in the capital itself the influences of Asia were altogether baneful. The rulers had but few occasions when it was necessary to consult the wishes of the citizens. Wealth poured into the imperial treasury in such abundance that an appeal to the popular will for new taxes was rarely necessary. The citizens lost their interest in politics worthy of the name, and confined themselves in taking part in the many dynastic changes with which the later history of the Empire abounds. Even from the foundation of the New Rome its imperial government had been possessed with the ideas of luxury which had already weakened the elder city on the banks of the Tiber. A new government had been imported into Byzantium, a government which was Cæsarian and absolute in character, and which had even in Italy absorbed much of the effeminacy,

extravagance, and luxury of the East. The position, however, of the city of Constantine rendered it more liable than
its predecessor had been to be affected by the influences averse
to progress which have usually surrounded Asiatic princes.
The gorgeousness of the Persian and Indian courts came to
be reproduced on the Bosphorus, just as they were in the
cities even of the Mahometan caliphates on the Tigris and
the Euphrates. And as the New Rome claimed something
like universal dominion, it seemed natural to her citizens that
her splendour should eclipse theirs. Her conquests enabled
her to succeed in doing so.

Without attempting to trace how this result was brought
about, and especially without attempting to trace the long
series of events by which the ideas of absolutism and
centralisation gradually undermined the systems of local
government which had been preserved in the villages and
towns, it is necessary, in order to understand the position of
the imperial government at the end of the twelfth century, to
see what were the results of the influence of Asia on the
social life of the New Rome.

The first and most noxious of these results was the bring- Position of
ing into Europe of the Asiatic conception of the position of woman.
woman. I have ventured to express my opinion already
that the fatal curse of Mahometanism is that the position it
assigns to woman renders progress beyond a certain point
impossible. Family life in the European sense cannot exist.
Woman holds, and has everywhere held, under Moslem rule
an inferior position, and the inevitable result ensues after a
few generations that the whole race has become less moral,
less manly, and less intelligent. An observer ready to
examine all systems of religion with academical impartiality
would find a difficulty in pointing out any doctrine or practice
taught or permitted by the religion of Islam which should
prevent its followers from growing in civilisation, except it
were in the position universally assigned in practice among
Mahometans to woman. To regard her as existing only for
the purposes of pleasure or of propagation, and as necessarily
degraded in thought, and therefore requiring to be watched

lest she should be unfaithful, is to degrade her, and implies keeping her in ignorance, and shutting her off from the education obtained by contact with the world. But to degrade generations of mothers means also to degrade the race itself.

The New Rome by her proximity to Asia had acquired far too much of this Asiatic conception of the position due to woman. During long centuries the notion of her degradation had been spreading downwards from the court and the capital, and this in spite of the position which Roman law had assigned her. Fortunately for the descendants of the inhabitants of the Lower Empire, they were saved by their religion from the lowest depth which the Asiatic creed had permitted or caused. Christianity had never permitted polygamy, and the spectacle of hundreds of women kept together in luxurious imprisonment in Constantinople was reserved for later times and Asiatic courts.

But allowing for the absence of polygamy, the estimate of woman in the capital was altogether Asiatic in character. Nicetas, who as a monk regarded woman from a monkish point of view, finds fault with the wife of Alexis the Third, and incidentally gives an indication of the position of woman a few years before the time of the Latin Conquest. He says that he does not complain of her insensate luxury nor of her prodigal extravagance, but of her immodesty (which he explains to mean that she was shameless enough to wish to take a part in the government); that she gave her orders without waiting to see whether they were in accord with the wishes of the Emperor ; that when the latter received foreign ambassadors her throne was as high as his, and she took her seat covered with diamonds and precious stones. The nearest relations of the Emperor would carry her litter on their shoulders as if they were her slaves. The real cause of complaint against her is that she did not live in retirement at the palace, but that she allowed herself to be seen in public places and on public occasions, sometimes even unaccompanied by her husband.

A life very like harem life had been introduced at court

and amongst the nobles.   Women were secluded and treated *Something like harem life.*
in much the same manner as women in Asia.   Above all,
one of the worst institutions of Asia, that of eunuchs, had been
introduced.   If there be an institution which more than all
others tends to degrade both man and woman, and to prevent
the progress of a race, it is the one in question.   The eunuch
not unusually rises to be the chief confidant, and sometimes
the chief adviser, of his master, and if he does not attain so
high a position is pretty certain to be a person of great consequence in the household.   He is the chief channel for
intrigue, the principal instrument of corruption.   A savage
usually in origin, he is elevated to a position which enables
him, if in the imperial court, to sway the fate of a state.   His
power and influence act on the community like leaven.   The
continual renewal of relays of these savage or barbarian
servants is the continual renewal in the body of a community
of the virus and corruption of savage or barbarian morality,
and each eunuch is a centre of malign influence.

At the opening of the thirteenth century eunuchs had
long been known in the imperial city.   Wherever they are
mentioned we see that their influence was very considerable.
In the attack upon Prosacus by Alexis the Third in 1199, the
generals of the army strongly advised that the city should
not be attacked.   This advice was, however, overruled by
that of the eunuchs.[1]   They rose to be ambassadors ;[2] they
were named senators ; and within five years of the Latin
Conquest one had been appointed prefect of Constantinople.
At the displays in the hippodrome they took part with the
nobles.   When Alexis heard the news of the departure of
the crusade for Constantinople, which was destined to destroy
the city, his preparations against attack were of the feeblest.
He had given himself over to luxury, and had left the government of the Empire in great part to his eunuchs.   ' These
creatures,' says Nicetas, 'who guard the mountains and the
forests for the Emperors' hunting with as great care as the
old pagans guarded the groves sacred to the gods, or with a
fidelity like that with which the destroying angel guards the

---

[1] Nicetas, *Alex*. Book III.   [2] Cinn. VII. ii. p. 296.

gates of Paradise, threatened to kill any who attempted to cut timber for the fleet.'[1] When this prince fled on the first victory of the expedition, it was a eunuch who assembled the troops, seized Euphrosyne, the Empress, and her friends, took the blind Isaac out of prison, placed him on the throne, and sent across to Galata to inform the enemy of what had been done for the father of the young Alexis who was with them.

The court was filled with eunuchs, comedians, clowns, musicians, and mistresses. Nicetas incidentally mentions that the mistresses sat at the imperial tables with the Empress.[2] The shortest road to success or to employment in the State was through the influence of these court favourites. In the Church alone were learning and character aids to

Subservience of the Church.

promotion, but even in the Church the influence of the court was so greatly superior to that of the Patriarch, that the prelate of holy life, respectable character and attainments, was too often postponed to the favourite of a court mistress, buffoon, or eunuch. Indeed, one of the worst results of the Asiatic influences which had overwhelmed the court was the subserviency into which, as an institution, the Church had fallen. The Bishops of the Elder Rome had succeeded in becoming lords of the West in all that related to things spiritual as completely, perhaps even more completely, than the Emperors had succeeded in retaining their power as lords in things temporal. In the New Rome the Emperors had been more powerful. From the moment when Constantine had declared Christianity to be the religion of the Empire he and his successors had never relaxed their hold over the rule of the Church. The Church had become much more than in the West the reflection of the State. But the abuses which had infected the one had stricken also the other. Just as the Emperor changed his ministers when he liked, so also he endeavoured to change the rulers of the Church. He never succeeded to the same extent, but the success to which he attained shows how subservient the Church had become. Nicetas mentions, for example, that Isaac Angelos in his short reign dismissed four Patriarchs in succession : the first under the pretext that he had allowed certain ladies to leave a monastery whom Andronicos had forced to become nuns ; the second, although named by him, because he was old and feeble ; the third, although the Emperor had named him, on pretence that the nomination had been revealed by the Virgin, he dismissed in order to place the favourite of the hour on the patriarchal throne. The latter, however, was violently opposed, and in his turn had to give way to a new favourite.[1]

The history of the twenty years preceding 1200 is full of illustrations of the effeminacy and corruption of the times. The boy-Emperor, Alexis Comnenos, passed his life, says Nicetas, at play and in hunting, while the courtiers who were about the Empress were decked out, curled, and scented like women. The treasury was robbed to support the debauchery of the palace. Andronicos Comnenos, his successor, although, as we have seen, an old man, devoted himself largely to the shows of the hippodrome and to horse-racing. His orgies in his country palace on the shores of the Marmora, where he was accompanied by a number of mistresses, and spent days in drunken debauchery, were alternated with journeys to the city, where his visits were more dreaded than his absence, because it had come to be remarked by experience that each visit was attended by some act of striking cruelty. A feminine love of display was the characteristic of his successor, Isaac Angelos. He appeared every day in new robes. His table was a daily show of wasteful profusion. There were, says Nicetas, 'forests of game, seas of fishes, rivers of wine, and mountains of bread.' He went every other day to the Eastern, or, as it is now called, the Turkish, bath, making use there of the most exquisite perfumes. He went about glorious as a peacock, was fond of songs, and his gates were ever open to actors, buffoons, and jugglers. Though the revenues of the Empire had been for many years constantly decreasing, the palace expenditure had not been diminished, and the Emperor was forced to fall back on the usual resources of Eastern despots in order to provide for it. The coinage was debased. Taxes were largely increased. Officers were

Effeminacy of the later Emperors.

---

[1] Nicetas, *Isaac*, Book II.

sent to administer the government or to dispense what ought
to have been justice without any means to pay their own
expenses. They went forth, says Nicetas, like the apostles,
'without scrip or purse,' the Emperor knowing they could not
afford to be honest, but that they would bring tribute to the
palace. Churches were robbed. The sacred vessels were
taken for the use of the palace. The rich ornaments and
precious stones let into the binding of the Gospels were de-
spoiled. Liturgies and crosses were stripped in order to
supply necklaces and bracelets. When the ostentatious Isaac
was replaced by Alexis the Third, it was found that the new
Emperor gave himself up to idleness, under the impression
that work was inconsistent with the dignity of an Emperor.

The organisation for administering the government
throughout the Empire, including that of the administration
of justice, borrowed from Old Rome, remained almost un-
altered as to form. The law was still almost as excellent as
ever, but its administration was too often corrupt. The
situation had become very much as if English law were to be
transferred to the people of an Asiatic state, and left to them
alone to develop. There would be subtleness and ability
enough to work out any number of legal problems, but it is,
to say the least, doubtful whether such securities as Habeas
Corpus and trial by jury, which are spontaneous growths
due to the determination of the race to secure individual
liberty, could continue without the ever jealous spirit of
Englishmen, continually on the watch to prevent violations of
the rights of which they are the safeguard. The race which
has created them may be trusted to guard them. It is
questionable whether another race would be either likely to
appreciate or to show the spirit necessary to preserve them.
So in the East, the administrative system of the Elder Rome
was being worked in the Empire under the New Rome by
rulers whose later history, at least, had been far different from
that of its creators. So long as there were a sufficient
number of men who had come under Latin influence, or who
retained the old Greek spirit, the system worked well. But
the Latin spirit had gone out of the ruling race, as the Greek

municipal spirit had also been to a great extent crushed out in the provinces. It looks at times as if nothing but the forms of the old organisation had remained. The courts of law were no longer unreservedly trusted. The administration of every department of the government, as well as that of the courts of justice, was at times tainted with corruption. The imperial family itself shared directly in the profits of this corruption. We have seen how one Emperor sent out his emissaries without scrip or purse to plunder his subjects, and how another Emperor is charged with taking a share in the profits, if he did not actually fit out six vessels to engage in piracy upon the ships of his own people. Prisoners were let out of jail to work, and no doubt on occasions to steal for the jailer. Judges purchased their offices, and as a consequence sold their judgments.

Alexis the Third, who came to the throne in 1195, published an edict to the effect that public offices would no longer be sold, but would be given free to the fittest men ; but his historian, while adding that such a reform would be one of the most praiseworthy that could be conceived, is careful to add that his good intentions were not seconded by those nearest to him. The ring of Byzantine nobles rendered him for the time as powerless as the ring of pashas would to-day render a reforming Sultan. Nicetas states that the men who formed this ring became immensely rich from the presents of those who wished to obtain any concessions from the government through their intervention. The highest offices both in the cities and in the provinces were publicly sold. Money-changers, ignorant men, and even Scythians, were allowed to buy the title of Cæsar. Creditors were paid by delegations—or, to employ the word too well known in Constantinople now, *havales*—upon the provinces.

The population which would tolerate such a government and such humiliation was as far from the manliness of the barons who, a few years later, were to figure at Runnymede as they were from the virtue of the Roman legions of the Republic during its best period, or from that of the Greek Republics. In truth, it was not only the spirit which would

resent a national injury which had disappeared from the
Byzantine nobles, but the virtues of self-respect, patriotism,
and courage. The ruling classes had lost all trace of either
Roman or Greek spirit. Cunning and intrigue had come to
be recognised as the highest statesmanship. Treaties had
been made with foreign states in order to put them off their
guard and make them more easy to be attacked. Diplomacy
meant dissimulation, and perfidy was substituted for courage.
Government existed as machinery for squeezing money out of
the provinces. The natural results ensued among the people.
The old ideal of Rome as existing for the good of the public
had disappeared. Reverence for law and equity as synonymous with justice had perished. The Greek ideal of compact
states seeking the benefit of the whole community had been
lost. Asiatic influences had filled the governing classes with
the same lying and vainglorious spirit which has ever been
the fault of all Eastern courts, and made the people regard
such classes as the public enemy.

Prevalence
of super-
stition.

With the effeminacy which may fairly be attributed to
Asiatic influences there existed an amount of superstition
which, with some hesitation, I should attribute in great part
to the same source. Talismans were almost universally used.
No important expedition of state was undertaken without reference to the astrologers. If their predictions turned out correct
they were held in honour ; if they failed recourse was had to
others, but the belief in the possibility of discerning future
events by reading the stars remained unshaken. Faith in
magic was yet strong ; the statues about the city were all
regarded as exercising an occult influence on persons or
events. The figure of Minerva, which appeared to be beckoning towards the West, was destroyed by the mob on the approach of the Crusaders under the belief that it had exercised
some kind of influence in bringing them to Constantinople.
The Empress Euphrosyne, the wife of Alexis the Third,
ordered the bronze statue of the boar struggling with the lion,
one of the most famous groups in the city, to be mutilated in
order to secure the success of her divinations. During the reign
of Manuel a statue on the Arch of Triumph in Constantinople,

representing a Roman, fell down just after the declaration of war against Hungary, while another near it, representing a Magyar, remained standing. Manuel was proof against the superstition of his people, and insisted upon reversing the position, believing, says Nicetas, that by so doing he could change the fate of the two nations. The same writer tells us that even Manuel never failed to consult the astrologers in all his enterprises. Madmen were held in honour, and believed to be divinely inspired. Every church had its relics, and the belief in their intercession, or in that of the saint to which they had belonged, was of the most implicit kind. Certain pictures wept. The famous representation of the Virgin in the chapel of Blachern was only one among hundreds of miracle-working pictures. Each person had his charm, his relic, or some particular object of worship in which he trusted. Isaac Angelos had special confidence in the intercession of the Virgin, and went into ecstasies when he saw her portrait. Superstition saturated the life of the period. Certain days were sure to bring good luck, others to cause disaster. The stars had their meaning, and governed or showed the lives of individuals or of states. Eclipses and exceptional darkness portended events which the astrologers pretended to read. Nicetas notes with amazement that the conquest of the city was not attended by any prodigy, and appears to think that the absence of such an event was an additional proof of the judgment of heaven against the capital.

In spite of the horrible punishment which had been decreed by successive Emperors against the practice of demonology and divination—which, it must be remembered, did not mean an attempt to defraud, but the actual consulting with devils—there were still recognised professors of the mystery. The Emperor Andronicos consulted one of them, who, says Nicetas, had been initiated in these detestable mysteries from his earliest youth, and who had been punished as a sorcerer in the time of Manuel. His act of divination appears to have been the childish one, which still lingers as an amusement among us, of whirling round an infusion in a basin, and observing what letters are made by the sediment. The historian, while expressing his horror of the practice, has no doubt of its efficacy. The demon gave an answer, and the answer was necessarily right.

Destruction of the peasantry.

The luxury of the court, the degeneracy and effeminacy of the ruling class, were nowhere so disastrous in their effects as on the means of defence. Indirectly the accumulation of wealth in the hands of the nobles and governing classes in Constantinople contributed greatly to the loss of Asia Minor. During the tenth and eleventh centuries the cultivation of that portion of the Empire had been in the hands of a Greek-speaking peasantry. The nobles during the century which preceded the incursions of the Seljukian Turks had rapidly accumulated land. Peasant owners had almost ceased to exist. The estates were cultivated by slaves, whom successful wars enabled the nobles to capture or their wealth to purchase. The peasants had been both able and willing to fight for their hearths and homes. Serfs or slaves had, however, no wish to risk their lives for their masters. The result was that, when the hour of trial came, the enemy had to be met with the regular forces of the Empire. The means of meeting him by a peasantry which would harass his every movement, which would be continually on the watch to resist every settlement of a Turk or Tartar in the country, which would be as persistently and tenaciously hostile as the Montenegrins have been during five centuries, did not exist. The inroads of a barbarian host had no terrors to men who had been reduced to serfdom or to abject poverty, who had nothing to lose, and whose soil was possessed by nobles who were hard taskmasters. So far, indeed, from the enemy being greatly feared by the peasants, there were, as we have seen, many examples of whole villages submitting themselves to the Turkish rulers, alien in race, religion, and language, in order to escape the oppression of their own countrymen.

Weakening of the navy ;

The corruption of the capital left the navy in a disastrous condition. The hardy sailors of the Marmora and of the islands of the Ægean supplied a body of men who were always ready to make admirable crews for the imperial fleets.

But the ruling classes had been so long accustomed to meet the enemy on land that the navy had come to be gradually neglected, and at the time of the Latin Conquest was so weak that it took no part in the defence of the city. The Power which possesses the Bosphorus and the Dardanelles ought always to be strong at sea if it possesses also the islands of the Archipelago. Nowhere in the world has there been, or is there, a nursery of seamen which produces more sailors. Their quality, from the days of the heroes of Salamis down to those of the exploits of Kanaris, has always been excellent. And yet, in spite of such a resource, the Empire had for a century and a half previous to 1200 hired most of its fleets from the Venetians, and done its naval fighting in large part by deputy.

The fiction of keeping up a fleet continued, indeed, until the attack upon the city, but it was improbable that the fleet of an Empire which had done its fighting by deputy could cope with that which had been employed to do the actual work. When the hour of danger came it was found that the admiral, Michael Struphnos, brother-in-law of the Emperor Alexis the Third, had sold the stores, and had appropriated to his own use the supplies that should have enabled the fleet to put to sea.

The effeminacy produced by Asiatic influences was conspicuously and lamentably shown also in connection with the army. During long centuries the New Rome had preserved the traditions and the discipline of Roman army organisation, and even in 1204 these had not been altogether lost. But the spirit which made the Greek phalanx and the Roman legion victorious had disappeared. The breaking up of the Roman system of administration in the army, and, indeed, in the government generally, dates from the time of the Basilian dynasty, and especially from the reign of Leo the Sixth. The period is one of great external success and military glory, but this very success and prosperity facilitated the destruction of the municipal spirit which gave life to the Empire. It is at this time that we find the degeneracy of the Empire really beginning. The Emperors had become so powerful, and had been so influenced by the success of their Asiatic conquests, that they commenced for the first time to rule as Asiatic despots. The Emperors had found it so convenient to hire mercenaries, and so inconvenient to force their own subjects to take the field, that they had come to do a large part of their fighting by means of foreign substitutes. The Immortals, or Ἀθάνατοι, remind us at once of their Asiatic origin. The Waring guard had held a deservedly honoured position during two centuries before the Latin attack on Constantinople. Italian and other mercenaries also hired their services to the Emperors. The Spanish Jew, Benjamin of Tudela, says : ' The Greeks hire soldiers of all nations whom they call barbarians. They have no martial spirit themselves, and, like women, are unfit for military enterprises.' The judgment is too severe, but, even with a large allowance for exaggeration, it shows what was the opinion of an independent observer from the West of the decay of martial spirit. When the later Emperors went themselves to war they encamped in palaces of canvas, which recall the appliances of a Darius or other Eastern monarchs.

Emperors alien in blood, commanding soldiers hired from foreign nations, became at times the slaves of their own mercenaries, and had to buy their allegiance by large donatives. The dynastic struggles of the quarter of a century preceding the Latin Conquest caused the foreign mercenaries to become yet more powerful and to be yet more petted than they had been before. When, in 1195, Alexis threw Isaac into prison and ascended the throne, he scattered money and honours among his supporters with a lavishness which not only made the public honours cheap, but which emptied the public treasury. But even this prodigality was not enough, and the Emperor had to distribute a part of the public domain among the troops in order to assure himself of their good-will.

As we approach 1200 we find the weakness of the Empire from effeminacy and luxury continually increasing. Even Manuel, in 1175, was suspected of having bought off the opposition of the Venetians. Nicetas notes with something like horror that the Emperor Alexis the Third wished to buy peace ; that instead of fighting Henry, the successor of Frederic Barbarossa, he endeavoured to dazzle his ambassadors by the splendours of the court and by robes which were one mass of pearls and precious stones ; that the ambassadors bluntly replied that neither they nor their countrymen valued such things, but regarded them rather as suited to women ; that the Emperor levied a duty called the German tax in order to buy off the enemy ; and that when the senate, the clergy, and the commons refused to help him, he robbed churches and tombs of their treasures in order to raise the amount necessary. In truth, the martial spirit had gone out of the race.

The period with which we are immediately concerned, namely, the latter portion of the twelfth century, was one of mental stagnation. Men were occupied with matters of such political and immediate interest that they had little time for literature or thought. The nation had to meet foreign enemies on every side, and the soldier rather than the man of letters was the man to be honoured. It was a transition period between the time when scholars had poured out their floods of learning in the development and the definition of Christian theology, and the period of the new movement which led to reformation in religion and to the revolution in politics. Men were resting on the labours of their predecessors, and during the twelfth century made few valuable contributions to human knowledge. There were indeed signs of a better time, but the dawn was hardly yet at hand. The appreciation of works of art was still high, and was probably growing in strength. Byzantine architecture was taking more and more the beautiful forms under which it was to become known to the world as Gothic. The internal decoration of churches, and probably also of private dwellings, had attained a high development. The mosaics and frescoes of the churches of Constantinople were already renowned in Italy, whither artists had gone, and had already prepared the way for the rapid progress in these forms of mural decoration which was made in the twelfth and thirteenth centuries. The Church was represented by a fairly educated and married priesthood, whose influence tended to the education of the whole people. The very frequent

Period is one of mental stagnation;

but also of considerable mental culture.

references to Homer, the constant classical allusions, the quotations from Scripture show not merely comparatively widespread reading on the part of the Greek writers of this period,
but imply a corresponding amount of knowledge on the part
of those whom they hoped to find as readers. But it was in
the great body of the people that the most hopeful signs were
to be found. The municipal spirit developed among the Greek
race had leavened the populations of Constantinople and the
chief cities under Byzantine rule. The government of the
municipalities had never been altogether surrendered by the
people. The education given by the widespread commercial
habits of the merchants was developing the intelligence of the
people, with the result that they were never so intolerant in
religious matters as the people of the West, and would never
have tolerated among them a feudal system.

Probable develop-ment of the Empire. Commerce, indeed, was the great glory of the Byzantine
Empire. Commerce, with all its advantages and all its draw-
backs, was the characteristic feature of New Rome. The
wealth, the luxury, the tolerance, the development of household and of ecclesiastical art were largely due to commerce.
The neglect of the public weal, the lessening of interest in the
management of public affairs, the abandonment of the wealthier
classes to effeminacy and idleness, and the low ideal which
was thus presented to the poorer classes, was largely due to the
enormous increase of wealthy families which commerce had
enriched. Had the external foes of the New Rome been
fewer or had she been able to overcome them, there is reason
to believe that Europe might have seen the development of a
state in which there would have been an amount of material
comfort associated with family life such as is hardly yet to be
found in any European country. Side by side with this there
would have been an intellectual activity which would have
enabled the Empire to preserve the foremost rank among
European nations. On the Bosphorus would have been the
capital of an Empire which for twelve centuries after Christ
had preserved an unbroken tradition of order, of good government, of knowledge of Greek literature, of commercial prosperity, of literary and artistic development. The imperial

city had bridged over the dark centuries of turmoil which intervened between the pagan civilisations and those of Christianity. While the nations of the West had been in course of formation, the Roman Empire had in the East been continuing its history in almost unbroken prosperity. We may probably gain the best idea of the forms into which that prosperity would have developed by recalling what her great rival subsequently became. Venice, I repeat, was in her later history the reproduction on the Adriatic of what her former patron had been on the Bosphorus. The rule of the New Rome was over a wider area and under more difficult conditions than that of Venice, but the resemblance is not the less remarkable.

The condition of things in Constantinople at the moment it was attacked by the army of the West presents many resemblances, but with some all-important differences, to that which exists in the same city at the present moment. Then, as now, the people were oppressed, and in the practice of the government seemed to exist mainly for the purpose of paying taxes. Corruption had honeycombed every department of the state. Offices were bought and sold. The influence of the eunuchs was greater than that of ministers of state. Public debts were paid by delegations upon the provinces—a mode which then, as now, allowed the local government to share the plunder of the people. Money collected for the state was seized by the palace and diverted from its legitimate purpose. Effeminacy had taken possession of the ruling classes, and had done much to demoralise them. It would be easy to multiply the resemblance between the Constantinople of the twelfth century and the same city under the rule of the Ottoman Turks. The danger would be to make the pictures too closely resemble each other. The essential differences between them were of a vital character. There existed a public spirit in the capital which jealously protected private interests, and which was singularly unlike the apathy towards private wrongs which now exists. The people of Constantinople never forgot that they were the ultimate source of authority, that they could make and unmake Emperors. They

Comparison between condition of Empire under Greeks and under Turks.

allowed the members of the royal family to fight out their
differences, to intrigue against each other, to pay for the
support of their followers within the city, though even here
they interfered upon occasion when a ruler became altogether
bad.   In political affairs there was a public opinion which was
in marked contrast to the absolute indifference of the Turkish
population of the city in our own time.   The frequent in-
surrections were at least a mark of public interest in politics.
But public spirit was especially strong where it has been
under Ottoman rule the most strikingly weak.   The populace
was disposed to take too little interest in political changes.
Touch, however, a private individual, and the corporation or
guild to which he belonged would at once claim redress.   The
plunder of private persons by arbitrary exactions was what
the population would never submit to.   It had the trading
instinct, the respect for property, the feeling of the necessity
for solidarity, which the great trading communities of Europe
have always possessed—the feeling which made the Venetians
and the Genoese regard the robbery of one of their merchants
as the business of state ; but to this in the minds of the
dweller in the New Rome was added a wider sentiment, since
he remembered with pride that he was a Roman citizen.
Nicetas records an incident, happening within the last two or
three years of the twelfth century, which shows how completely
the popular feeling was opposed to arbitrary dealing with
citizens.   There dwelt in the capital a banker named Kalomodios, who during long years and under difficult circumstances had acquired great riches, to which he greedily clung.
His reputation for wealth was widespread, and had exposed
him to the wiles of some of the nobles, who wished to share
it.   A number of these seized Kalomodios.   When the merchants heard of what had been done, they went in a body to
the Great Church, found the Patriarch, and threatened to
throw him out of the window if he did not take steps to release
the banker.   The Patriarch sympathised with the mob, promised to do his best, and succeeded in snatching this sheep
with the fleece of gold from the teeth of the wolves who
would have stripped him.   The voluminous annals of Con-

stantinople under the Empire are singularly free from attempts against the property of private individuals. So long as the merchant did not take part in conspiracy or revolution, his property within the city was safe. The explanation of the fact is to be found partly in the deep-seated respect for law—a respect which made even tyrants like Andronicos go through the form of a trial before he sent his victims to death or to blindness—partly in the remains of a healthy municipal spirit, which made the people act together against any unusual act of injustice to one of their number, but, above all, in the instinct developed by trade that the security of private property is the first necessity for commercial success. This latter is a feeling which the Turk never shares or has shared. He himself rarely engages in trade. In the capital a Turk is almost certain to be in the employ of the state, and he is almost as certain to regard traders as persons to be plundered. The Turkish attitude towards commerce has had much to do with the impoverishment of one of the most fruitful countries in Europe. In this respect the history of the city at its worst period before 1200 presents a favourable contrast to that which it has always presented under Turkish rule. To squeeze a wealthy rayah or a pasha has for centuries been the readiest resource of a Sultan or a favourite in pecuniary difficulties. The practice is not yet forgotten, although the publicity which is afforded by foreign journals, and especially the fact that as soon as a man begins to amass wealth he takes care to obtain the protection of a foreign Power in order to avoid such squeezing, has largely lessened the practice.

Nor does the fall of the Empire resemble that of the Ottoman Turks. The rule of the first fell after long centuries of struggles with external enemies, and after a long period of success which had helped to demoralise the conquerors. Its rule had been weakened by dynastic struggles, due in part to the fact that the people were progressive, and that a more modern form of government—that of oligarchy— was being evolved from the older one of an absolute sovereign with divine attributes. The Ottoman Empire has lost successively its possessions in South Russia, in Hungary, in

Roumania, Servia, Greece, Bulgaria, Asia Minor, and Africa in consequence of the incapacity of its rulers to govern, and, above all, of their powerlessness to absorb conquered races or acquire the habits of commerce, manufacture, or civilisation. One Empire fell, after an honourable existence of eleven centuries, the most civilised Power in Europe ; the other, inheriting such civilisation, has been powerful only to destroy, and will leave its territories far in the rear of the least progressive country in Europe and Constantinople the most backward of European capitals. So long as the armies of the present rulers were fed from the boundless supplies of men in Central Asia, so long as the harems were filled with European captives, and the supply of rulers kept up from Christian sources on the female side, so long was their military triumph secure, and their government at least better than organised brigandage. When these supplies were cut off and the Turkish race and religion were left to their own resources, decline immediately commenced, and is rapidly bringing the rule of the Ottoman Turk to its end.

Signs of better things.

The essential difference between the condition of the Empire even under the Comneni and that of the Turkish Empire is to be found in the results produced respectively by the religion of Christ and of Mahomet. The Christianity of the Empire would have provided a means of regeneration, or would not have prevented the natural spirit of the population from developing itself. The religion of the Ottoman Turks is a hindrance to advancement. I am fully alive to the low condition into which the Orthodox Church has now fallen, though it was by no means so low seven hundred years ago. But I repeat, that if that Church had fallen as low as that of Abyssinia, it would still, as a philosophical system accepted and entirely believed in by the people, be superior as a civilising force to Mahometanism, because at least it would not have been a hindrance to progress. As a fact, however, the Greek Church was still the preacher of morality, the torchbearer of civilisation, and the faithful guardian of the treasures of ancient Greece. The monks of Mount Athos were already multiplying the manuscripts which were to bring about a

revival of learning in the West. Amidst the general indifference to public morality, priests and monks could be found
whose lives and teaching were long protests against the
general corruption. The work of Nicetas Choniate—our
principal Greek authority on the history of the Latin Conquest
—is imbued with a religious spirit—religious in the sense that
he believed that God rules the world and will punish national
immorality, that morality implies progress and immorality
the reverse. He and others with him protested in the
strongest manner against the corruption in government, the
dissoluteness of the court, the absence of morality in statesmanship. In reading the history of his own times we are apt
sometimes to forget that these protests were written in the
thirteenth and not in the nineteenth century. The abuses in
the state and the cruelty of the Emperors were hateful to him.
But for the fact that we meet with passages showing that his
religion partook of the superstition of his age, we should
hardly remember that he was the contemporary of what he
records. The very discontent, amounting to querulousness,
which runs through the whole of his narrative, and which is
found in other contemporary, or nearly contemporary, writers,
is one of the most hopeful signs of his time. That he and so
many of his contemporaries were profoundly dissatisfied with
the condition of the Empire gives reasonable hope that, had
the Latin invasion turned out otherwise than it did, there
would have been a national movement towards reform or
revolution. This movement, as in Western Europe, would
probably have first been felt in religion, and the Eastern
Church might again have taken the lead in shaping the creed
of Western Europe. For, in spite of the subserviency into
which the Church had fallen, its nominal masters were obliged
to respect the opinion of its governing bodies. The disgust
felt by Nicetas over the frequent change of Patriarchs made
by Isaac Angelos, and the excuses which that Emperor had to
make use of in order to justify his action, show that the influence of the Church was still great. The lethargy was
already passing away ; discontent at the prevailing corruption
was widespread, both in Church and State. We, who have

seen an Italy resurgent and Greece and Bulgaria re-entered among civilised nations, may well refuse to believe that an intelligent people, who were at that time the first in civilisation, would not have shaken off their religious and political apathy, would not have recovered the strength which they had expended in resisting external attacks, and would not have had their reformation in religion and their democratic revolution in politics.

CHAPTER VIII.

THE PREPARATIONS FOR A CRUSADE.

THE fourth crusade began to be preached in 1197. The earlier successes of the third crusade, notwithstanding the quarrels of its leaders, had led the Christians of the West to believe that the progress of Mahometanism might yet be checked. In 1187 Saladin had captured Jerusalem. Guy of Lusignan had been taken prisoner. Many brave Templars and Hospitallers, with many a nameless soldier of the West, had suffered martyrdom rather than renounce the faith. The fall of Jerusalem had been the immediate cause of the third crusade. Our own Richard the Lion-hearted, whose sole claim to be remembered is his skill as a captain of Crusaders, Philip of France, one of the ablest of French kings, and Frederic Barbarossa, the Swabian Emperor of Western Rome, had, as we have seen, united to reconquer Christian territory in Syria. Acre had been besieged, and after a two years' resistance, which had cost the Crusaders 300,000 men, had surrendered to Richard and Philip. Saladin had been defeated at Ascalon. Other places had been captured. But the victories and the results of the expedition fell far short of what might reasonably have been hoped for from the preparations which had been made by the three great sovereigns of the West. Jaffa had been taken by storm, but had been recaptured, and its Christian garrison massacred. Frederic was drowned in 1190. The quarrel between Philip and Richard had been espoused by their followers. In 1192 the English king quitted Syria, was shipwrecked, imprisoned, and went through some, at least, of the adventures which have associated the name of that sovereign with poetry and romance.

Philip had returned home the same year. The victories which the Crusaders had gained would be altogether barren if help were not shortly sent to the Christians in Palestine. The supplementary expedition had been a failure. The Crusaders who had remained behind, aided by the Armenian, Greek, and Syrian Christians, were doing their best to hold the territory which had been conquered, but every year saw that territory decreasing. Every traveller returning from Syria brought a prayer for immediate help from the survivors of the third crusade. It was necessary to act at once if any portion even of the wreck of the kingdom of Jerusalem were to be saved. Innocent the Third and some, at least, of the statesmen of the West were fully alive to the progress which Islam had made since the departure of the Western kings.

In 1197, however, after five years of weary waiting, the time seemed opportune for striking a new blow for Christendom. Saladin, the great Sultan, had died in 1193, and his two sons were already quarrelling about the partition of his empire. The contending divisions of the Arab Moslems were at this moment each bidding for the support of the Christians of Syria. The other great race of Mahometans which had threatened Europe, the Seljukian Turks, had made a halt in their progress through Asia Minor. We have seen that their Empire was also divided against itself. Moreover, the great Asiatic horde which was shortly under Genghis Khan—perhaps the Prester John of the middle ages—to threaten the Empire which the Seljukians had carved out of the eastern dominions of the New Rome, was already approaching, and the Seljukians were compelled to turn their attention to the formidable enemy of their own race which was threatening their rear.

Other special circumstances which rendered the moment favourable for a new crusade, combined with the profound conviction of the statesmen of the West of the danger to Christendom from the progress of Islam, urged Western Europe to take part in the new enterprise.

The reigning Pope, Innocent the Third, was the great moving spirit of the fourth crusade. He came to the pontificate in 1198, when he was thirty-seven years old. Innocent Innocent the Third. was a man versed in the learning of his age, and of unceasing and untiring energy. His restless activity forced him to take interest in every question of the day. To be interested in a question meant for him to be actively engaged in its solution. There was not a country in Europe in whose affairs he did not take a prominent part. Quarrels between kings, between barons; disputes, as in the case of our own John, between kings and their subjects; differences between abbeys and monasteries in the most remote countries, were examined personally and decided upon finally by him. The decision once taken, he took care to have it obeyed. Nothing escaped his vigilance. No question was too large or too small to engage his attention. His vast correspondence is one of the marvels of the middle ages. His negotiations, not only with European sovereigns and their subjects, but with Leo the Great, King of Armenia, with the Bulgarians and with the Wallachs, were unceasing. His legates and cardinals were in every country, laying down the law of the sovereign Pontiff, scattering interdicts, issuing anathemas.[1] He, perhaps, more than any other Pope, secured that the occupant of the pontifical chair should be listened to throughout Europe as one speaking with authority, that the Pope should be an independent sovereign, that the Church should owe obedience to the Pope alone among earthly sovereigns, and that the ruler of Rome should own no superior but God. It is probably right to call the determination to carry out these designs ambition; but to understand the energy with which they were executed, one is forced to give Innocent credit for having believed that they were objects which it was desirable in the interests of mankind to attain. In his opinion he was called upon by divine right to govern Europe, to repress disorder, to put down civil war, to divert the fierce energy of Northern warriors away from anarchy into useful channels. The world was turned upside down. The Holy Roman Empire was divided against itself. What is now Germany was the scene of constant and bloody wars. Italy was

[1] *Hist. de Philippe Auguste II.*, by M. Capefigue.

divided. Everywhere there was anarchy and confusion. Our
fathers were right, no doubt, in opposing Innocent's designs
in England, in seeing principally in his policy towards King
John an attempt to advance the claims of the Papal See
against the rights of Englishmen. Matthew Paris says that
John knew the Pope as the most ambitious and proudest of
men, a man insatiable after money and capable of every
crime to obtain it,[1] but history does not bear out his judgment. Two schools of historians have discussed the character
of Innocent. He stands before one as a clever Italian, an
intriguing, ambitious priest, meddling in every business to
advance the interests of the Church ; and before the other
party—that, namely, which believes in the Roman Catholic
Church as the divine institution of the world—as the priest
full of supernatural energy, of ability, and of success, the
model Pontiff, the type pre-eminently of the Vicar of God.[2]
Judging the man by the circumstances of his time, and
putting aside his trivial weaknesses, one sees a clear-headed
statesman who knew his own purpose and was tenacious of
its realisation : one of the men who stamp their character
upon the world's history in unmistakable outlines. It is in
considering the amount of useful work done and the beneficial influence exerted by such Popes as Innocent, that we
who are outside the Church of Rome come to understand how
the belief in the inspired character of the Pope's official conduct has grown up. The character given of Innocent by a
contemporary is borne out by his conduct during the fourth
crusade—' a man of much discretion and kindliness, young
indeed in years (he was thirty-seven when made Pope), but
old in prudence, ripe in judgment, adorned by the uprightness
of his character, of a noble race and commanding presence, a
lover of what was right and good, a hater of iniquity and vice,

---

[1] *Eccles. Hist.* Book LXXVII.

[2] ' Cet homme dans la force de l'âge, qui devait, sous le nom d'Innocent III.,
lutter avec un invincible courage contre tous les adversaires de la justice et de
l'Eglise, et donner au monde peut-être le modèle le plus accompli d'un souverain
pontife, le type par excellence du vicaire de Dieu.'—Montalembert's *Hist. de
Sainte Elisabeth.*

so that he was called Innocent rather from his merit than from chance.'[1]

But for us the important point is that during the eighteen years of his reign the most absorbing thought of Innocent, the purpose to which he most constantly adhered, was the deliverance of the Holy Land.[2] His first act after he had ascended the pontifical throne was to announce to Monaco, the Patriarch of Jerusalem, his intention of proclaiming a crusade. Six months later he ordered the crusade to be preached, first in Italy and then throughout the rest of Europe. He sent letters to all princes, announcing to them his firm resolution to consecrate all his energy to this object. 'Who is there,' said he, 'who would wish to shrink from the danger of the Cross when he remembers Him who bound Himself to the Cross to deliver us from the enemy? Arise, therefore, ye faithful; arise, gird on the sword and the buckler. Arise, and hasten to the help of Jesus Christ. He Himself will lead your banner to victory.'[3] As an inducement to those who were ready to join in the holy war, he promised pardon for past sins. He placed the lands of the princes and the goods of the Crusaders under the protection of the Holy See during their absence; he declared that those who borrowed money for the expedition should be exempted from the payment of interest. Princes were invited to compel the Jews, who were the principal money-lenders, to remit the payment of interest to intending Crusaders. Rulers were urged to forbid the Jews to engage in any business in case of their refusal. Those who could not themselves take up the Cross were asked to provide substitutes, or at least to contribute to the expense. All who refused to give were warned that they incurred a grave responsibility. He ordered the clergy peremptorily to contribute a fixed portion of their revenue. He forbade the Venetians to furnish the Saracens with iron, ropes, wood, arms, galleys, ships, or any munitions of war whatever. Richard of England had made war on Philip of

The deliverance of the Holy Land was the great object of his life.

---

[1] Gunther, chap. vii.
[2] Hurter's *Hist. de Inno. III.* vol. i. p. 218, and elsewhere.
[3] Epist. i. 302.

France. Innocent sent a cardinal to France to conclude a
treaty for five years between the two sovereigns, and wrote
himself to his legate in France : ' If men perish, if the
churches are weakened, if the poor are oppressed, if the
French and the English incur danger on account of their
kings—all this is of less consequence than the loss of Palestine, than the extermination of the Christian name ; and yet
this is what will happen if these kings prevent their warriors
from going to reconquer what has been lost, from protecting
those who have been threatened.' If the treaty were not
accepted by the two kings, his firm resolution and that of
his cardinals was to place the kingdom of the offender under
an interdict, and to forbid, with the utmost rigour and severity,
without regard to privileges and indulgences, the celebration
of divine worship. Innocent pointed out that the time was
opportune. ' By the dissensions which divide the Saracens,
the Lord gives to Christian people the signal for the
crusade.' [1]

Innocent, in his determination to leave no stone unturned
for the accomplishment of his purpose, wrote also to Alexis,
the Emperor in the New Rome, asking for his aid. ' Who,'
he asked, ' can do more than you, seeing your nearness to the
field where the battle must be fought, your riches and your
power ? Will your Majesty put all other considerations on
one side, and come to the help of Jesus Christ and of the
country which He has won by His blood ? The Pagans will
flee before you, before your army, and you—you will share
with the others in the pontifical favours.' The assumption
of an authority was not likely to be welcome at Constantinople, but the letter shows at least how strong was the determination of the Pope to make the expedition a success.
Legates were sent to the New Rome to negotiate with the
Emperor and the Patriarch on the subject of the expedition
and of the union of the two churches. The letter and the
legates were treated with the utmost respect. The haughty
tone of the Pope's letter and the experience which the Greeks

---

[1] Hurter, *Inno. III.* p. 315. The same idea appears repeatedly in many of
the Epistles of Innocent.

had had of the last crusade were not likely, however, to produce a favourable reply. The Emperor Alexis, in his answer,
recalled that when Frederic, a few years earlier, had promised
upon oath to pass through the Empire peaceably, he had violated his promise. He had done great injury ; he had fought
Christians as well as Pagans, and yet, in spite of this, Alexis
claimed that the Greeks, out of veneration for the object of
the expedition, had furnished him with all that was necessary.
Notwithstanding this just cause of complaint, Alexis concluded this part of his letter by promising that if the Empire
were able to preserve its tranquillity, he would favour the
efforts which should be made for the delivery of the Holy
Sepulchre.

As to the old question of the union of the two churches,
the reply was that the best union would be brought about by
each giving up its own will and submitting to the divine will.
If the Pope wished to submit the doctrines in controversy to
the examination of a Council, the Orthodox Church would
take part in it. While admitting the zeal of the Pope for
the glory of God, Alexis could not conceal his astonishment
at hearing the Pope call the Roman Church the Universal
Church, and the common mother of all the churches. That
title belonged to the Church of Jerusalem. The old jealousy
between the two Romes was not to be overcome, and, as
usual, found vent in the religious questions which divided the
two churches. Little aid was to be hoped for Constantinople,
but only little had been expected.

Meanwhile in Western Europe the efforts of Innocent had
met with more success. In every church a box had been placed
to receive the gifts of those who had the holy cause at heart,
and a Mass was ordered to be said weekly for the givers.
Innocent again addressed himself to Philip of France. Christ
Himself, he repeated, had given the signal for the crusade.
Philip ought not only to permit his subjects to leave, but to
force them to quit their homes on so important a mission.
Innocent did all that he could in every European country, in
order that the effort about to be made might prove successful.

The preacher of the new crusade, the Peter the Hermit

who made known the Pope's wishes to the people of France
and of Flanders, was a priest named Fulk, of Neuilly. If we
can imagine a Wesley or a Whitefield with middle-age surroundings, we may obtain a glimpse of his character and of
the secret of his influence. If, as Gibbon alleges, he was
illiterate, his ignorance was not observed by his contemporaries. It is true that after his ordination he had been
reproached with ignorance ; but in consequence of this reproach, or of his desire for knowledge, he went to the
University of Paris, and returned to his parish to become
a distinguished preacher. He was full of zeal and enthusiasm. Like many of the great preachers of the churches,
he regarded his own time as especially given over to wickedness. Contemporaries of his, monks and priests, had persuaded themselves that the world was shortly to come to an
end, and that the mad confusion and anarchy of the time
was one of the signs of the end. Fulk found in this belief
the greater reason for putting right that which was wrong.
He denounced iniquity in high places with the utmost fearlessness. Clergy and prelates felt the bitterness of his speech.
In spite of ignominious treatment, threats, and imprisonment,
he warned nobles and kings alike that they were travelling
rapidly on the broad way to hell. He denounced the new
custom of lending money, which the Lombards had introduced into France, and spoke fiercely against avarice and
sensuality. No danger could terrify him, no threat make
him keep silence. His fervour made him popular with the
people. At times his audience became so excited that
men threw off their garments and offered their belts to the
preacher, publicly confessing their sins and asking for public
punishment. The people, rich and poor, came at last to hear
him gladly. His fame had already reached Rome. Here,
then, was the man whom Innocent had need of. His enthusiasm, his energy, his fearlessness, his apparent disinterestedness were to be made use of, as the Church of Rome has
so often utilised the undisciplined enthusiasm which other
churches have driven into opposition. The Pope commissioned him to preach the Cross in France, ' to use the gift of

eloquence which God had given him for the good of the Holy
Land.' Fulk executed his commission in Normandy, Flanders,
and Burgundy. His reputation as a preacher, a healer of
the sick, and a worker of miracles had preceded him, and
crowds everywhere went out to hear him and to be influenced
by his preaching. According to the popular belief, virtue
went out of him, and his clothes were sometimes torn to rags
from the struggles of the masses to touch them in order that
sickness might be healed. It is easy to say that Fulk lent
himself to the imposture, but it is more probable that he, like
other middle-age revivalists, believed himself to be a divine
instrument, and the marvels attributed to him to be proofs of
his mission. It must be said in favour of Fulk that he was
willing to turn the popular enthusiasm into a useful channel.
'My garments,' said he, when the crowd pressed upon him,
'are not blessed, and have no charm about them ; but look,
I am going to bless and give virtue to this man's cloak.' At
the same time, seizing upon one belonging to a bystander, he
made the sign of the Cross upon it, in token that the wearer
would join the crusade, and each one hastened to snatch a
portion as a relic. His influence was marvellous and at
times strangely exercised. If the crowd were too noisy, he
obtained silence by solemnly cursing the noisiest. Sometimes
he would lay about him lustily with his stick, while those who
were wounded would kiss their wounds or the blood as sanc-
tified by the man of God. Wherever he preached great
numbers took the Cross, or contributed to the expenses of
the crusade.

His greatest success was in the conversion of Theobald
of Champagne. This nobleman, a nephew of Richard of
England and of Philip of France, a young man of twenty-two,
was already renowned in arms and in song. Eighteen hundred knights did homage as his vassals. During the truce
between the Kings of England and France, he had called
together a brilliant assemblage to engage in or witness a
tournament. Fulk invited the knights to gain a more lasting
glory by joining in the crusade. Theobald, Count Louis
of Blois, and Simon de Montfort, father of our English hero

Theobald
of Cham-
pagne.

of the same name, with a host of others, accepted the
Cross.

Theobald, Earl of Champagne, was selected from his rank
and ability to be the leader of the expedition.   In his train
were Geoffrey of Villehardouin, with many others of high rank.
Under Theobald, the leaders were Baldwin of Flanders, whose
wife was the sister of Theobald, Baldwin's brother Henry,
Louis Earl of Blois, Simon de Montfort, and Count Hughes
de St. Paul.

It may be mentioned here that the intention of the Crusaders, and probably also of Innocent, was that Richard of
England should be the leader of the expedition.   His death,
however, in April 1199, put an end to this design.   In one
respect, however, his death contributed an element of success.
Many of the French barons had joined him against Philip
of France, and there can hardly be a doubt that but for
his untimely death he would have defeated Philip.   The
hostility between the two sovereigns had been bitter.   'The
devil is loose ; take care of yourself,' had been Philip's warning to John when Richard had been released.   The French
barons who had fought on the side of Richard were glad on
his death to escape the vengeance of Philip by joining the
crusade.   Among those who had been detached from the
side of Philip by Richard, and had joined the revolt of the
Bretons against him, was Theobald of Champagne himself,
the appointed leader of the crusade.   Baldwin of Flanders
had in like manner declared for Richard, and probably joined
the crusade the more readily on account of his death.

At the opening of the year 1200 a considerable number
of nobles and others had undertaken to join the crusade.
France and Flanders contributed the largest share, but Germany also furnished a considerable contingent.   During the
year many meetings or parliaments of the leaders of the
expedition had been held, but they had been adjourned
because the number of Crusaders was not judged to be
sufficiently large to justify the leaders in making arrangements
for the transport of the army beyond sea.   Towards the end
of the year, however, a parliament was held at Soissons, in

which it was agreed that the time had come when preliminary
arrangements might be undertaken for the chartering of
a fleet. The decision arrived at was that six messengers
should be sent to treat with Venice, with full powers to make
such agreements for the transport of the army as they deemed
necessary. Shortly after, the messengers set out on their
journey.

Venice was chosen as being the city which was likeliest
to furnish, if not the only city which could furnish, the large
fleet of transports and convoys necessary. But the choice
was in many respects an unfortunate one, and ultimately led
to the failure of the fourth crusade. We have seen that
Venice had occupied a neutral position between the East and
the West. On many occasions she had owned allegiance to
the New instead of the Old Rome, and although at the end
of the twelfth century she had her special reasons for hostility
towards her former protector, she was as little inclined as
ever to render obedience either to the Pope in spiritual things,
or to either of the rival claimants for the Empire in the West
in temporal things. The thunders of Innocent, which shook
every other Western state, fell harmlessly upon Venice. The
struggles between Guelfs and Ghibelins, whether in Germany or
Italy, aroused comparatively slight attention among her people.
Innocent early in 1201 had declared for Otho, a nephew of
Richard of England, the Guelphic claimant for the Empire of
the West, and had declared against Philip of Swabia, whom
he had threatened with the penalties of the Church. But
Venice cared little for such threats, and was ready to ally
herself with Philip. Her great interest was to have a monopoly of the carrying trade by sea, and in order to preserve
this she was ready with equal indifference to supply Crusaders
and Infidels with contraband of war, or to transport the one
or the other and their property whither they would.

Venice was now in the first springtime of her splendour.
The islands, which had themselves been constructed on the
marshes, were already covered with stately buildings. The
city had increased in wealth as Constantinople had declined.
The monopoly over the seas once possessed by Constantinople

Choice of
Venice as
port of
departure.

had long since been shared by the Republic, which recognised in the annual ceremony of the Bucentaur that her wealth was derived from commerce. She had been, as we have seen, specially favoured in the New Rome. The tone of her civilisation was that of Constantinople rather than that of any Western city. Her wealth, her distinction as a city whose civilisation was more advanced than that of any Western rival, were derived from her intercourse with the New Rome. The very aspect of her streets were a reproduction of what had been seen on the Golden Horn. Her famous church, dedicated to St. Mark, was but a reproduction on a smaller scale of the still more famous church of the Divine Wisdom of the Incarnate Word which existed in Constantinople.

The Crusaders of this and of former expeditions were profoundly impressed with the prosperity and magnificence of Venice. The New Rome was still the royal or imperial city ; but both cities evidently opened to the Crusaders new worlds of wealth, luxury, and civilisation. They marvelled much, says Robert de Clari, at the great riches they found in Venice,[1] and numbers of contemporary writers bear testimony to the astonishment which her civilisation excited.

Hostility of Venice towards Constantinople. Of late years the Venetians had had difficulties with the New Rome. We have seen that these difficulties arose, in great measure, from the fact that the influence of Venice in Constantinople was no longer sufficient to exclude that of the other Italian republics. Isaac Angelos had, in 1187, and again in 1189, as we have also seen, concluded a new alliance, assuring to Venice her old privileges, together with the payment of a considerable indemnity. The consideration for the valuable concessions offered by the Emperor was that the Venetians should place their fleet at the disposition of the Empire, even in the case of a war against the Emperor in the West. This treaty was confirmed in 1199 by Alexis the Third. In the spring of 1200 a quarrel took place at Constantinople between the Venetians and their great rivals the Pisans. The Venetians complained that their treaties had been violated ; that the subsidies

---

[1] Rob. de Clari, c. x.

promised by the Emperor had not been paid ; above all, that the Pisans had been favoured at their expense.[1] The Doge, during the summer of the same year, sent an embassy to Alexis to demand the payment of arrears and the renewal of commercial privileges. Another embassy was sent six months later, and, indeed, the whole year was occupied with negotiations, which served only to show that it was improbable that the Republic should regain her supreme influence on the Bosphorus. But the hostility to Constantinople reached its height when the Venetians learned that Alexis had, in May 1201, received an embassy from Genoa, and was negotiating with Ottobono della Croce, its leader, for the concession of privileges for trade in Romania which Venice had hitherto regarded as exclusively her own. From this time the Doge appears to have determined to avenge the wrongs of his state on the ruler who had ventured to favour his rivals.

The Doge of Venice at this time was the famous Henry Dandolo. He was already a very old man,[2] but full of energy, greedy of glory, exasperated against the Empire, and devoted to the interests of the Republic. He was able to command with equal success an army or a fleet. Though he was nearly, if not quite, blind, he devoted an amount of attention and ability to the cares of government which places him in the first rank of Venetian administrators. The New Rome was the special object of his hatred. The general belief after his death was that his eyes had been put out by order of the Emperor Alexis during his visit in 1172 or 1173 to Constantinople.[3] What is certain is that he bore against the Empire an inextinguishable hatred, which made him willing to embrace any project directed against its capital city. He possessed the entire confidence of his fellow-citizens. His influence in

Dandolo.

---

[1] Nicetas, 712.

[2] Du Cange makes Dandolo ninety-two in 1200 ; but neither Villehardouin nor Andrea Dandolo use terms which would imply so great an age.

[3] Daru, *Hist. of Venice*, i. 201. Authorities are divided as to whether he was blind or only of weak sight. ' Visu debilis et visu aliqualiter obtenebratus,' says Dandolo. Sanutus, Villehardouin, and Gunther say that he was altogether blind. The *Chron. of Novgorod* says that he was blinded with a burning glass by Manuel.

Venice was so great that when he subsequently embarked with the Crusaders his son was appointed Regent during the absence of his father.

Messengers arrive in Venice.

The six messengers chosen by the Crusaders at Soissons arrived at Venice in February 1201. Four days after their arrival they were introduced to the Council and the Doge, in a palace which was *bien riche et beau.* ' Sire,' said their spokesman, ' we are come to thee on behalf of the noble barons of France, who have taken the sign of the Cross to avenge the shame of Jesus Christ, and to reconquer Jerusalem if God wills it. And because they know that no men can help them so well as you and your men, they pray that for God's sake you will have pity on the Land of Outremer, and on the shame of Jesus Christ, and that you will labour that they may have ships of war and transports.'

The Council took a week to consider what should be their reply. At the end of that time, the delegates of the Crusaders were informed that the Venetians were willing to provide ships to carry 4,500 horses, 9,000 esquires, 4,500 knights, and 20,000 infantry, together with provisions for nine months, in consideration of a payment of four marks per horse and two per man. The total sum therefore to be paid, reckoning the Venetian mark at a little over two pounds sterling, was about 180,000*l.*[1] This contract was to hold good for a year.

Contract for transport accepted.

Besides this the Venetians promised to add for the love of God fifty armed galleys, in consideration that half of the money captured should belong to them. The terms were accepted by the delegates, were again submitted by Dandolo to the Council, and were approved. A solemn service was held in St. Mark's, and much enthusiasm displayed at the conclusion of what each believed a good bargain. Villehardouin, whose narrative of the crusade has long been the chief authority on the subject, was himself the spokesman of the delegates, and thanked the Venetians, on behalf of his brethren, that they had taken pity on Jerusalem, which was in slavery to the Turks, and that they were ready to aid in

---

[1] M. de Wailly estimates the mark at fifty-two francs. So also does Sismondi. See also Heid.

avenging the shame of Jesus Christ.   The contract was signed early in April 1201, was referred to the barons, and was ratified at Corbie in the middle of May.

It had been decided from the first that the expedition should be directed towards Egypt as the best base of operations against the Mahometans in the Holy Land, though the plans and contract signed by the Venetians and the delegates contained the statement simply that the destination should be 'for the deliverance of the Holy Land.'   The decision taken in the Council was kept secret from the army, to whom it was simply announced that the Crusaders would go beyond the sea.[1]   Charts of the route were prepared and sealed, and it was agreed that the Crusaders should be in Venice by St. John's Day, 1202.   *Destination, Egypt.*

The Doge and his Council on the one side and the delegates on the other swore solemnly to observe the terms of the arrangements entered into.   The contract was then sent to the Pope, who approved it conditionally.

Innocent could not see without distrust the contract made with those who had shown their readiness to serve either Christians or Moslems, provided they paid.   He would have preferred that the Pisans or the Genoese had been selected, and it was only on finding that no such arrangement could be made that he consented to accept the Venetians.[2]   The conditions upon which he insisted showed the distrust which he entertained.   He stipulated that there should be no attack made against a Christian state, and that a legate should accompany the army and watch over the expedition, in order to see that this article was complied with.[3]   *Innocent accepts the arrangement conditionally.*

The leaders of the crusade had decided, as we have seen, that their operations should be directed against Egypt. Many considerations induced them to arrive at this conclusion.   The passage through Romania had been found during previous crusades to be long and costly.   Even when the Dardanelles had been passed, there remained the terrible   *Reasons for choosing Egypt.*

[1] Villehardouin, c. iv.   [2] *Inno.* Epist. ix.
[3] 'Conventiones illas ita duceret confirmandas ut videlicet ipsi Christianos non laederent, apostolicæ sedis legati consilio accedente.'—*Gesta Inno.* No. 84.

march through Asia Minor, where the Turks hindered the
progress of the Christians at every step, and where fever had
rapidly thinned their ranks.   The terrible experience of the
last crusade had been that the great German army, after
winning every battle it had fought, had, by the time it reached
the Holy Land, melted away.   The leaders wished to avoid
this long and fatal route, and desired to be landed at some
place where they could strike at the enemy before the army
had been weakened by repeated contests, and wearied and
demoralised by long marches through an unhealthy country.
No place offered so many advantages from this point of view
as Egypt.   A short sail over a pleasant sea and the Crusaders could be landed fresh and vigorous and prepared for
battle.   The cost of transporting an army to Alexandria
would be far less than that of taking it to any other part of
paynimrie.

The sea was the safest and most easily guarded road to
keep open between the invading army and Europe.   Alexandria was a base of operations which might be kept with
surety against the enemy, while its port would always be open
to supplies of men and means of warfare from the West.   A
footing once obtained, Egypt could better support the army
of Christendom than any other country.   Its perennial
wealth had been the mainstay of the Arabs in their marvellous conquests over Syria and Northern Africa.   Moreover,
while the renown of Egypt was spread throughout Islam and
Christendom alike, the enemy could be more advantageously
fought in the densely-populated delta than in the wide and
thinly-peopled regions of Syria.   Probably too it was known
in Europe that the Egyptian Arabs had lost their early
vigour, that the climate had told upon them, and that they
were already becoming an unwarlike race.   The occasion,
however, in 1201 was peculiarly favourable for an attack on
that country.   Saladin had conquered it, had abolished the
Egyptian Caliphate in 1171, and had done all that he could
to exhaust its resources.   On his death, in 1193, his two sons
had quarrelled about the division of his Empire.   The one ruling
in Egypt asked the aid of the Christians in Syria against

his brother. The civil war which followed had still further weakened Egypt. But an exceptional and remarkable circumstance rendered an attack upon Egypt still more opportune. During five successive years the Nile had ceased to fertilise the country.[1] The result of this unprecedented calamity had been famine and distress. The population had been largely reduced. The wealth and strength of the country had been greatly diminished. To these considerations have to be added the fact that if Egypt were once in the hands of a crusading army, it could be held against all invaders, and its wealth turned against Islam. Every Mahometan country would feel the loss of Egypt. A wedge would have been driven into the long stretch of Moslem territory between the Atlantic and India. Islam would have been cut in two and its wealth used to reconquer and hold Syria.

The desirability of striking at Islam through Egypt, the very centre and fulcrum of Moslem power, had been recognised from the time of Godfrey by a succession of warriors and statesmen. Innocent the Third was especially impressed with the necessity of making the attack through Egypt. He called particular attention to the exceptional opportunity which the time presented from the accidental or, as he believed it, the providential impoverishment of the richest country in Islam, from the failure of the Nile to overflow, and from the division of its rulers. Even without these accidental advantages no other spot offered so many advantages for the attack. No other country, if conquered, would be so great a loss to Islam. These considerations, in fact, seem to have been so generally recognised that it is doubtful whether any other plan was seriously considered. It was to Babylon, as the Crusaders generally called Egypt, that the expedition was to go, because. says Villehardouin, 'one could

---

[1] 'Quod utique si fecissent' (*i.e.* take Alexandria), 'sperabile satis erat tam ipsam magnificam civitatem quam et maximam ipsius totius Egypti partem, facile compendio, in eorum potestatem posse transferri, eo quod totus fere populus terrae vel consumptus fame perierat, vel squalebat penuria, propter sterilitatem eiusdem videlicet terrae, cui Nilus frugiferas aquas, quibus eam rigare solet, annis, ut aiunt, jam quinque subtraxerat.'—Gunther, *Exuviæ Sacræ*, vol. i. p. 71.

more easily destroy the Turks there than in any other
country.'[1]

The choice having been made, it will become necessary to
ask why the original plan was abandoned How did it happen
that an expedition prepared with great care, and proposing
under such favourable circumstances to strike at the heart
of Moslem power, turned away from its object and attacked
the capital of Eastern Christendom ? The question is one
which was asked by all Europe at the time and has never
been altogether satisfactorily answered, although in our own
time the laborious industry of German and French scholars
has succeeded in bringing to light a mass of evidence hitherto
unknown bearing on the question. The conclusion to which
this evidence appears to me to point will, I hope, become
clear in subsequent pages.

The agreement between the delegates of the Crusaders and
the Venetians was ratified, as we have seen, in May 1201.[2]
The crusading army was to arrive in Venice not later than
the 24th of June, 1202. In the interval between these dates
many events happened. Theobald, Earl of Champagne, the
young noble who had taken the Cross on the preaching of
Fulk, who had probably been induced to do so partly in
order to escape the vengeance of Philip of France, who had
been elected leader of the expedition, and in whom all had
confidence, died in May 1201. His loss was the more serious
that his great wealth was no longer available for the purposes
of the crusade. A payment in advance which had been
promised to Venice could not be met. The leaders were
divided as to the course to be adopted for the conduct of the
expedition. None among them possessed either position or
ability sufficient to indicate him as the leader. After considerable delay the leadership was offered to the Duke of
Burgundy, and on his refusal to Count Theobald of Bar, who
also refused. Then a parliament of the Crusaders met at

Death of
Theobald.

---

[1] Villehardouin, sec. 30.

[2] In the same month Innocent had invited the dignitaries of the Venetian
Church to contribute towards the crusade from the church revenues. See
Archives de l'Orient Latin, i. p. 383.

Soissons, and Villehardouin proposed Boniface, Marquis of
Montferrat.   The proposal was finally though reluctantly
accepted.   From the first it was evident that Boniface had not
the confidence of the Crusaders, and his election was the first
severe blow given to the success of the expedition.   Fulk
himself affixed the Cross to the shoulders of Boniface in the
church of Our Lady at Soissons, and, as the great preacher
died in May 1202, he disappears from this history.[1]   The
appointment of Boniface was in August 1201.   Two months
later he was at the court of Philip of Swabia,[2] on the invitation of that sovereign.   What was the object of his visit may
never be accurately known.   But subsequent events raise the
presumption that Philip either had the design of an attack
upon Constantinople before this visit, or formed such a design
at, and in consequence of, his interview with Boniface.   Philip,
the head of the house of the Waiblings, or, as the name was
now beginning to be spelt in Italy, Ghibelins, had married
the daughter of Isaac Angelos, the Emperor of the New Rome,
who was at this moment a prisoner in Constantinople deprived
of his eyesight, though allowed to go about the city of which
he had once been the ruler.[3]   The son of Isaac and heir to
the throne—whom we may conveniently call after the fashion
of the time young Alexis, to distinguish him from the reigning
usurper Alexis in Constantinople—had made his escape[4] from
the capital.   He left the imperial city in the spring of 1201, arrived
in Sicily and sent messengers to Germany announcing his safe
arrival.   Allowing three months for the news to reach Philip,
there was ample time for the messengers of Philip to reach
the Marquis of Montferrat, and for the latter to have been at
the Swabian court in October.   Boniface remained with
Philip until January or February 1202, and then left with an
embassy for Rome, sent thither in order to induce Innocent the
Third to take up the cause of young Alexis.[5]   In the spring of

Appoint-
ment of
Boniface,
Marquis of
Montferrat,
as leader.

His visit to
Philip.

[1] Villehardouin, c. ix.   [2] Gesta Inno. III. c. 84.   [3] Nicetas, p. 712.
[4] One author states that the wife of the Emperor Alexis pitied the young
man, and gave him notice that her husband determined to kill him.   Anon.
Caietanus, Ex. Sac. 152.
[5] Gesta Inno. III.

the year the latter received letters of recommendation to the Crusaders from Philip.[1] It therefore appears clear that, from the beginning of 1202, the leader of the expedition had become aware of the facts connected with the claims of Alexis. Subsequent evidence indicates that even at this time he had promised Philip to aid him.

At the time appointed—namely, the 24th of June, most of the leaders of the expedition had arrived, according to the arrangement, in Venice. Baldwin of Flanders, Hugo Count of St. Paul, Geoffrey of Villehardouin, perhaps Boniface, and many also from Germany were present, while the Abbot Martin and others from that country were on their way thither.[2]

---

[1] Nicetas says (p. 715) ' from Philip and the Pope,' but the latter is doubtful ; from Πάπα Ρώμης τῆς πφεσβυτέρας καὶ τοῦ ρηγὸς 'Αλλαμανίας Φιλίππου.

[2] M. Jules Tessier contends that the Crusaders could never agree upon the destination of the expedition. He admits that the most intelligent of its leaders proposed to attack Egypt, but he insists that the majority of the army were in favour of going to Syria. In support of this contention he (1) calls attention to the fact that the charter-party made with the Venetians makes no mention of either Syria or Egypt ; (2) he quotes Villehardouin (par. 49) and claims that the 'grant peril' of which the Flemings stood in fear was of going to Egypt, and (3) he quotes the reply given to the speech of the Abbot of Citeaux (Villehardouin, par. 96), 'In Syria you can do nothing.' The first of these arguments is inapplicable if the contention is well founded, that it was intended to conceal the destination of the expedition. Later on I give a different interpretation to the 'grant peril' phrase, while the argument founded on the reply to the Abbot appears to me to fall when connected with the surrounding circumstances. Gunther's statement that the resolution to attack Egypt was adopted unanimously (' Hii quidem omnes uno consensu in hoc convenerant, ut petentes Alexandriam ') is probably too sweeping. See La Diversion sur Zara et Constantinople, par Jules Tessier. (Paris, 1884.)

CHAPTER IX.

ARRIVAL IN VENICE.

MANY of the pilgrims had only left home between Easter and Whitsuntide, 1202. The ordinary road taken was over the Mont Cenis and through Lombardy to Venice.

Meantime a fleet had left Flanders for the Mediterranean with a great number of Crusaders. The leaders of this detachment had sworn to Baldwin that they would join the division coming from Venice at the first convenient place after hearing of its whereabouts. Baldwin and the other leaders of the crusade who had already arrived at Venice soon learned with dismay that many pilgrims had gone by other routes to other ports, and that thus it would be impossible to provide the number for whose passage the delegates had undertaken to pay the Venetians. Those present were unable to raise the amount agreed upon. They did their best by sending messengers here and there to persuade the pilgrims to come to Venice, and to point out to them that Venice was the only port from which they could start with a fair prospect of success. Villehardouin was himself sent on such an expedition, and succeeded in persuading Count Louis with a great number of knights and men-at-arms to come to Venice from Padua, where they had been encountered. Others were also brought in to Venice; but a considerable number had already left by other routes before they could be overtaken. Never, says Villehardouin, has a finer army collected than that which was at length gathered at St. Nicolo di Lido, the island where the Crusaders were lodged by the Venetians. No man had seen a finer fleet than the Venetians had prepared. The only fault to be found with it was that it could take an army three

Non-arrival of a considerable number of the Crusaders in Venice.

times as large as that which had assembled.   The Venetians
had kept their part of the bargain.   'What a misfortune,'
exclaims the Marshal, 'that so large a portion of the Crusaders
had sought other ports !   Had they come to Venice the Turks
would have been put down ; Christendom would have been
exalted.'

Crusaders
unable to
pay.

The Venetians, having done their part, now asked for
payment of the passage money according to the terms of the
contract.   This, however, could not be raised.   Many pilgrims
had come without money ; others were already sick of the
enterprise, and, according to Villehardouin, hoped that the
money would not be found.   Baldwin of Flanders, Earl Louis,
and the Marquis and the Earl of St. Paul did their utmost by
borrowing to raise the amount promised.   But when all was
done, when many a beautiful vessel of silver and of gold had
been taken to the Doge's palace, when two collections had
been made, 34,000 marks out of the 85,000 stipulated for were
still wanting.

So far we are on safe ground.   All contemporary accounts
agree that the contract with the Venetians was broken ; that
a large amount was wanting to complete the sum agreed upon
to be paid as freight ; and that, even after every effort had been
made to raise this sum, about 35,000 marks still remained
due.   From this time forward we are upon doubtful ground.

Official and
non-official
versions of
the cru-
sade.

The authorities upon whom we have to rely differ widely.
The account given by Geoffroi de Villehardouin, Marshal of
Champagne, may be taken as the type of what has been aptly
called the official versions of the expedition, and of these it
ranks undoubtedly the first.   Besides these versions, the
labours of a number of historians, from Du Cange in the
seventeenth century down to Count Riant, who has ransacked,
and is ransacking, the libraries of Europe in search of evidence
relating to the fourth crusade, have brought a large amount
of evidence to light which may be conveniently classed as
that of the unofficial versions.   The official version of what
passed in Venice is that which has been generally received by
modern historians until our own time.   Villehardouin states
in few words that the Doge, when it had become clear that

the Crusaders could not pay the stipulated sum, proposed that they should agree to assist the Venetians in recapturing Zara, in Dalmatia, from the King of Hungary ; that the Crusaders were divided as to whether this proposition should be accepted ; that those who were tired of the enterprise opposed, but that the majority accepted it.

So far the official account given by Villehardouin and followed by others. The diversion of the enterprise was due solely, according to these writers, to the simple fact that the Crusaders could not pay 34,000 marks. Villehardouin, whose history of the crusade is much longer than that of any other contemporary writer, skips over in a few short paragraphs the events which happened between the arrival in June and the alliance to attack Zara. The transaction was, according to him, the simplest possible. The Venetians had completed their part of the contract ; the Crusaders were unable to pay their fare ; the Doge made a proposal which was accepted. At this point it becomes necessary to examine such other testimony as exists, in order to learn whether the diversion was due to the simple cause which is assigned for it by the great apologist for the crusade. The intention was, as we have seen, to go to Alexandria. 'But this praiseworthy design,' says Gunther, 'was hindered by the fraud and malice of the Venetians.' ' The Crusaders were received treacherously,' says Rostangus, 'by those to whom they had come, who would not allow them for a long time to pass beyond sea. They refused to carry them beyond sea or to allow them to leave St. Nicolo di Lido unless they paid the uttermost farthing.' The leaders and the Crusaders generally appear, as we have seen, to have done their best to pay. But the number for which the city had furnished transport was largely in excess of that which had been brought together by the end of June. Out of 4,000 knights and their attendants, only 1,000 had assembled. Of the 100,000 foot soldiers provided for, there were not more than 50,000 or 60,000 on the Lido. The Crusaders argued that those who had come and were ready to pay ought not to be forced to pay for those who had not come. The Venetians claimed their pound of flesh. Resistance

was useless ; the Crusaders were prisoners. The Doge, according to Robert de Člari,[1] told the Crusaders plainly, ' If
you do not pay, understand well that you will not move from
this island, nor will you find anyone who will furnish you
meat and drink.' It was upon this threat that the leaders had
borrowed what they could to pay their jailers. It was after a
second collection for payment, in July 1202, that there was
still about one third of the freight, or, according to Robert de
Clari, 36,000 marks, unpaid. Shortly afterwards the Crusaders
were persuaded to accept a compromise, which on the whole
could not be considered as unfair. Dandolo was understood
to have proposed that out of the share of the first spoil which
fell to the Crusaders in fighting the common enemy—that is,
the Moslems—the sum due to the Venetians should be deducted. This proposition was gladly accepted.

Proposal made to the Crusaders. Subsequently this promise was changed into a proposal
for an attack upon Zara. This city lies on the opposite coast
of the Adriatic to Venice, was the capital of Dalmatia, and
belonged to the King of Hungary, who had himself sent aid
to the Crusaders. It had been rising in importance for many
years. The Venetians alleged that its inhabitants had often
of late made piratical attacks upon their ships. Possibly the
charge was true, but the real reason of the hostility felt towards
it was a jealousy of its commercial prosperity. The non-
official versions represent the Zara expedition as forced on
the Crusaders. The official versions represent the Crusaders
as gladly consenting to pay the Venetians out of the spoils
taken at Zara falling to their share. The story of Villehardouin is not at variance generally with those of other
contemporary writers. Its chief fault is a suppression of disagreeable facts. His object in writing the story of the crusade
was to show that the expedition had not been so complete a
failure as a crusade as the world had taken it to be. We

[1] *La Prise de Constantinople*, by Robert de Clary, or Clari, is by far the most
valuable contemporary account which modern research has brought to light on the
Latin Conquest. The MS. was printed in 1868 by Count Riant, but only for
private circulation. It was not really published until 1873, when Charles Hopf
brought out his *Chroniques Greco-Romanes*. Robert de Clari was present at the
conquest of Constantinople.

must look to others for the unpleasant facts. The author of the 'Devastatio'[1] states that the troubles of the Crusaders began even before their arrival in Venice. The Lombards charged them heavy prices for victuals. When they reached the city they were cast out of the houses and compelled to go to Lido. The Crusaders were there treated in every respect as captives. Provisions were sold to them at famine prices. A sistarius of corn cost 50 soldi.

The Venetian rulers gave orders that no one should ferry any of the foreigners out of the island. The want of provisions and the sense of their helplessness created a panic among them. Those who could escaped. Some went home ; some hastened to other ports in the hopes of finding ships for Egypt or Syria. The summer heats caused a terrible mortality among the crowded host, so that, according to the same author, the living could scarcely be found to bury the dead. According to Robert de Clari, the Doge himself came to recognise that the Venetian policy of pushing the Crusaders in their distress too far was mischievous. 'Sirs,' said he, addressing his council, 'if we let these men go home we shall be looked on as rogues and tricksters. Let us propose to them that, if they will pay us the 36,000 marks out of their share of the first conquest they make, we will transport them beyond sea.' There was no proposal here to take Zara or to attack Constantinople. The *Outre-mer* to which they were to be transported was understood to be the land of the infidel. The conquests they were to make were to be the lawful spoils of a crusading war. There was nothing whatever in the suggestion to make it unacceptable to the Crusaders who gave heed to their vow. Hence, when the Doge, having obtained the consent of the Venetian council, submitted the proposal to them, they accepted it gladly. A way had been found out of their difficulty. They were to leave the fever grounds of the Lido, were to go over the sea to fight the infidel and to fulfil their vow. On the announcement of the proposal their

---

[1] *Devastatio Constantinopolitana.* This is another MS. brought to light by recent research, though its existence has been long known. See *Chroniques Greco-Romanes*, par Charles Hopf.

camp was illuminated and there were other manifestations of joy.[1]

It is difficult to determine precisely when this proposition was made. Probably it was in the last week of July 1202. The 24th of June was the latest time appointed for the arrival of the pilgrims. The second attempt to collect the balance due had been made probably in the middle of July. Shortly afterwards came this proposal, which was joyfully accepted. Villehardouin speaks only of one proposal, namely, that to help the Venetians to capture Zara. If his account is to be reconciled with that of the non-official writers, the explanation is that the attack upon the Christian city was at the time carefully concealed from the mass of the Crusaders, a policy which was continually pursued throughout the expedition. Robert de Clari, as we have seen, represents the proposal quite otherwise, and the fact that it was joyfully welcomed shows that the Crusaders were told nothing of an attack upon a Christian city as part of it. Another writer [2] states that the Venetians kept the Crusaders prisoners for three months, and would not allow them to return home, and when after that time their substance was nearly consumed, then they were compelled to go to Zara. We learn from a German writer [3] that after much complaint, both on the side of the Venetians and on that of the Crusaders, it was at length agreed that the Venetians should go with the pilgrims, and that whatever was gained should be equally divided, but that from the part going to the pilgrims the balance due for freight should be deducted for the Venetians.

We may rest assured that the pilgrims did not accept joyfully the promise to go to Zara, because, as we shall see, the crusading spirit was far too strong in the army for them yet to tolerate the idea of an attack upon a Christian city.

The conclusion at which I arrive after a comparison of the authorities is either that there were two distinct proposals, one made in July for the payment out of the proceeds of lawful spoil, and a subsequent one made some weeks later for payment out of the spoil to be taken at Zara ; or that, if the

---

[1] Robert de Clari.   [2] Anon. Suessionensis.   [3] Anon. Halberstadt.

proposal to attack Zara were made in July, it was made only
to the leaders, and was carefully concealed at first from the
mass of the Crusaders. Robert de Clari's account points to
the existence of two proposals. After speaking of the illumi-
nations on the Lido when the Doge's first proposal was made
and accepted, he states that the Doge afterwards went to the
camp and declared that the winter was lost, and that it was
too late to go to *Outre-mer*. Then the secret was let out.
'Let us do the next best thing. There is a city near here
called Zara, which has often defied us, and which we are
going to punish if we can. If you will listen to me we will
pass the winter there until Easter, and then we will go to
Outre-mer at Lady Day. Zara is full of provisions and
riches.' Then this author adds : 'The barons and leaders of
the Crusaders assented to the Doge's proposal. But this
proposal was not known to all the army.'[1] Robert probably
believed that there were two proposals, and that even the last
was kept secret from the host.

The account of Robert is borne out by the evidence to
which I have already called attention. Assuming that the
portion of the proposal made during the last week of July,
referring to an attack on Zara, was kept secret, as to which
there can be little doubt if it be admitted that Zara was
mentioned in July, the next month was spent in negotiations.
There was a party opposed to its acceptance as soon as the
attack was mentioned. Here again we are on solid ground.
Villehardouin tells us that discord sprang up as soon as the
Venetians refused to carry them beyond sea until they paid.
He says that those who declared they wanted to leave Venice
to go to other ports did so because in reality they desired
that the army should break up, and therefore struggled
against the acceptance of the proposition. The unofficial
writers tell us why they did so. 'In truth,' says Gunther,
'the proposal to attack Zara seemed to our princes cruel and
iniquitous, both because the city was Christian and because
it belonged to the King of Hungary, who, having himself
taken the Cross, had placed himself and his, as the custom

Opposition to the proposal to attack Zara.

[1] Robert de Clari, c. xiii.

is, under the protection of the Pope.   While the Venetians
were constantly urging us to accept the proposal, and we on
the other hand were earnestly refusing, much time was lost.'
Why was time lost?   The same writer answers, ' Because our
men thought it altogether detestable and a thing forbidden
to Christian men that soldiers of the Cross of Christ should
march to pillage Christian men with slaughter and rapine
and fire, such as usually happen when a city is attacked,[1] and
therefore refused their consent.'

There was no idea of abandoning the crusade.   The
expedition to Zara was probably, though by no means certainly, regarded even by the leaders who were in the secret
merely as a means of payment, in order that when it had been
captured the Crusaders might go about their proper business.
The third great mistake of the campaign had, however, been
made ; the second being the failure to bring sufficient men to
comply with the terms of the charter-party entered into with
the Venetians.   The third blunder was the more serious.
The leaders of the first great crusade had declared under
the walls of ancient Nicæa that it was no part of their
business to fight Christian princes, that their work was to
fight the infidel, and they had readily given that city into
the hands of Alexis.   The enthusiasts of the fourth crusade, who had left their homes in order to fight against
Christ's enemies, had no heart for the new undertaking, and
though they did not know all the adventures it would lead
them into, we can see from Villehardouin himself that they
would have preferred to return home rather than violate
their vow.

On the 22nd of July [2] Cardinal Peter Capuano, the Pope's
legate, arrived in Venice from Rome.   Bishop Conrad, and
probably others, required that the propositions of Dandolo
should be referred to him.   He at first protested against the
proposal,[3] because, as Gunther says, he thought the attack upon
Zara ' a lesser evil than the abandonment of the crusade, the
vow of the Cross unfulfilled, and the return home with ignominy

[1] Gunther, c. vi.   [2] *Devastatio.*
[3] *Gesta Inn.* i. c. 86.

and sin.'¹ Cardinal Peter sent away all the sick, the useless hangers-on, and the women.²

The dissatisfaction among the Crusaders was at that time daily increasing. Some were for abandoning the expedition altogether. Many poor men who had brought but little with them and had nothing left for the journey quitted the army and went home. 'Certain powerful and rich men, not influenced by poverty,' says Gunther, ' so much as frightened by the horror of committing such a crime (as attacking a Christian city belonging to a crusading king), hesitated, and much against their will turned back.' Some of these went to Rome in order that they might be absolved from their vow or have its execution postponed. Others wished to leave Venice in order that they might embark for Alexandria or Syria from other ports.

Cardinal Peter's protest was followed by an earnest request that the expedition should be sent off as early as possible to Alexandria. His mission as legate was to accompany the army, to urge it to leave for Alexandria, to prevent it from going to Zara, to settle the differences between the Crusaders and Venetians, and generally to represent Innocent the Third. The Venetians, however, received him coldly. The Doge and the council told him that if he wished to accompany the Crusaders in order to preach to them he could do so : if he wished to go as envoy of the Pope he had better stay behind.³

News of what had been done in Venice reached the pilgrims who had not yet arrived in that city, and created consternation among them. Many of the German pilgrims in particular declared the expedition against Zara iniquitous and went home, and all further supply of Crusaders was thus cut off.⁴

Meantime the leader of the expedition, the Marquis Boniface of Montferrat, who had left Venice during July, returned to the city. Probably the treaty with the Venetians was concluded in the middle of August. The Cardinal again protested, and, having committed the German pilgrims to the

---

¹ Gunther, vi.   ² *Devastatio.*
³ *Ep.* VII. 203 ; *Gesta*, 85.   ⁴ Gunther.

care of Bishop Conrad and the Abbot Martin, the latter of
whom had avoided Venice when he learned the proposal of
the Doge, left for Rome.   The Cardinal, however, seems to
The Cardi-
nal yields. have vacillated.   He protested but yielded.   When he found
that the Venetians would not give way unless the Crusaders
would go to Zara, he seems, according to Gunther, to have
considered it more venial and less inexpedient to accept the
Zara proposal than to allow the expedition to be abandoned.[1]

He, therefore, insisted on the promise that the Venetians
would not only transport the army to Alexandria after the
Zara expedition but would themselves join in the crusade.
The author of the Halberstadt MS. confirms the version of
the Cardinal's conduct.   The Cardinal, in reply to Bishop
Conrad, declared that the Pope would rather the terms of the
Venetians were accepted than the expedition should be abandoned.   He advised Conrad to bear with the insolence of the
Venetians, and appointed him, together with four Cistercian
abbots, to go with the army to represent the Pope.   In the
same way Abbot Martin was advised by the Cardinal to remain with the army.   Gunther says that when the Abbot saw
that the expedition would necessitate the shedding of Christian
blood he was at a loss what to do.   He begged the Cardinal
to absolve him from his vow and to allow him to retire to the
quiet of his cloister.   The Cardinal, however, flatly refused,
and ordered him in the Pope's name to take charge of the
German pilgrims.   He was further enjoined by the Cardinal
to go with the army wherever it went, and to use his influence
with that of the other religious leaders to prevent all attacks
upon Christians and their territory.

The Vene-
tians join
the
crusade. On Sunday, the 25th of August, there was an imposing
ceremony in Saint Mark's, the object of which was probably
partly to delude the pilgrims into the belief in the good faith
of Dandolo and the Venetians, and partly to give a pretence
to them to join the expedition.   At the Mass, which was of
unusual solemnity, Henry Dandolo ascended the pulpit and
addressed the Venetians :—' You are allied with the bravest
men on earth.   I am old, and weak, and infirm ; as you see,

[1] Gunther.

I have need of rest ; still, I know of no one more capable of
taking command of your undertaking than I. If you wish
that I should take the Cross and that my son should remain
here to replace me, I will go with you and the pilgrims for
life or death.' The assembly cried, ' Come with us, for God's
sake.' Many in the congregation, both Venetians and pilgrims, shed tears as the old man was led to the altar, and a
cross, made especially large so that it might be seen by all,
was affixed to his breast. Dandolo from this time became, Henry
Dandolo.
perhaps, the most conspicuous actor in the fourth crusade.
His personal influence was immense. We have already seen
that his hatred of the New Rome was intense, that he had to
revenge private injuries as well as the wrongs of Venice.
From the moment when he took the Cross he towers above
all the leaders in the great host which his fleet was shortly to
transport to the Bosphorus. The venerable figure of the old
man at the altar pledging himself to go with the Crusaders
and to share their fortunes imposed on many. Others, however, reflected that he had not entertained the idea of going
with the army until the proposal to attack Zara had been
accepted, and such distrusted his new-born enthusiasm for
Christianity. A brave man—' de bien grand cœur,' says Villehardouin—but one also who knew the interests of Venice and
cared for nothing else ; a statesman of the Italian type before
Mazzini and Cavour had taught or shown a more excellent
model. Capable of venturing upon bold and dangerous enterprises, he had all the ability necessary to carry them through.
Self-reliant to the last day of his long life, he was yet able to
avoid arousing the easily-awakened jealousy of the Venetian
oligarchs. He was virtually dictator of Venice, and possessed
the entire confidence of the Republic through his successful
management of its affairs. He intrigued, kept his plans secret
from his countrymen, deceived the Crusaders, and yet always
succeeded in his designs. Lying and intrigue were indeed
held to be fair by the rules of that Italian statesmanship
which Machiavel reduced to a science. The best Italian
statesman was the one who could best succeed in the purpose
he had taken in hand. That faith should be broken, that

craftiness should be continually necessary, were merely the incidents necessary to success. In Venetian politics, right or wrong had no meaning, except in the sense that everything which advanced Venetian interests was right, everything which made against them was wrong. Dandolo never appears to have felt himself under any obligation to tell the truth, or to respect either his oath as a Crusader or his pledged word to the pilgrims. Provided the Republic could be benefited, all means were lawful. If a man ' de bien grand cœur,' yet also a statesman without conscience and an unscrupulous man.

The arrangements having been definitely made in conformity with which the Crusaders and the Venetians were to attack Zara, the preparations for sailing were rapidly pushed forward. For the moment discontent appears to have been hushed. The Crusaders even, who had objected to making war upon a Christian city, were delighted at any change which would get them out of the steaming and fever swamps of the Lido.

CHAPTER X.

DEPARTURE TO, CONQUEST OF, AND STAY IN ZARA.

THE expedition against Zara left Venice in two divisions, one which started on the 1st and the other on the 8th of October. The whole fleet consisted of four hundred and eighty sail. The departure of the second and great division, containing the army of Crusaders, was one of the most picturesque sights which even Venice can ever have seen. The Republic of the lagoons has always cherished a love of artistic display, and nowhere can any spectacle be set amid surroundings which more completely enhance its beauty than amid the waters where the Queen of the Adriatic rises from the sea. The time had not yet come when her rulers thought it necessary to check lavish display of colour and undue extravagance. The dwellings and storehouses of her people were already palaces. Her citizens had already grouped themselves into guilds, each with its own characteristic dress, so that brilliancy of colour was already a striking feature of a Venetian crowd. The silks and velvets of the East were set off with precious stones and jewelry, while over all the southern sun shed a light which, reflected from the waters, did not make their gorgeousness seem out of place. Robert de Clari describes with evident enjoyment the scene as Dandolo and the Crusaders left. Each of the nobles had a ship for himself and his esquires, while attending it was the sailing barge for the horses. Each ship was girt around by the bucklers of the knights, and looked as if it had a belt of steel. The Doge had fifty galleys, which had been fitted out at his own cost or at that of the city. The one in which Dandolo voyaged was vermilion coloured, like that of an emperor. Four trumpeters with trumpets of silver attended him from his vermilion tent to his galley, and with the bearers of cymbals contributed to the popular demonstration on the departure of the expedition. The priests and monks were stationed in the castles at the cross-trees of the vessels, and solemnly chanted the *Veni, Creator Spiritus.* So beautiful a sight as this departure, says Robert, had never surely been seen. A hundred trumpets with many other instruments of music gave the signal for sailing. When the vessels were in the open sea and had spread their sails, when the rich banners and gonfalons of so many earls and nobles were unfurled by the wind, while as far as the eye could reach the Adriatic was covered with ships, the beauty of the spectacle was at its greatest. It was remarked, and truly, says Robert, that never were there so many such beautiful ships assembled together.[1] Even here, however, he is careful to point out a jarring note. Very many, both great and small, deplored the sin which was being committed and the great joy which prevailed.[2] They crossed the sea, says another writer, with great speed but with sad hearts.[3]

Arrival at Zara.

On the 20th of October Dandolo made a triumphal entry into Trieste. Both divisions united a few days afterwards at Pola. The united fleet arrived off Zara on November 11. On the same day the harbour was captured and the army landed. The city was the wealthiest on the eastern shores of the Adriatic, and the metropolis of Dalmatia and Croatia. It is situated on a peninsula, and was well fortified. It had formerly owned allegiance to Venice, but had shaken off her rule, and was now under the protection of the King of Hungary. On the 12th a deputation proposed to surrender everything to Dandolo if the lives of the citizens were spared. While the proposal was being considered some of the Crusaders, at the head of whom was Simon de Montfort, told some of the deputation that they had only to fear the Venetians.

---

[1] Rhamnusius estimated the fleet to consist of 480 vessels, composed of 50 galleys, 240 transports for troops, 70 for provisions, and 120 huissiers for the horses. Nicetas says 240, composed of 110 huissiers, 60 galleys, and 70 transports for provisions. I suspect the larger estimate is obtained on the fair supposition that there must have been an equal number of transports for the troops.

[2] Robert de Clari, ch. xiii.   [3] Gunther, i.

'I am not here,' said he, ' to do harm to Christians. I wish you no ill, and, on the contrary, would rather protect you against those who would hurt you.'[1] The well-meant interference proved mischievous. The deputation returned to the city. The negotiations were interrupted, and the terms on which the people of Zara had proposed to surrender were withdrawn. The Venetians proposed to attack the city, and lest the Crusaders should make further delays in what Gunther calls this hateful and detestable business, the Venetians commenced the siege at once. The people of Zara, in anticipation, probably, of this attack, had obtained letters from the Pope, excommunicating any who should do them damage. These they sent to the Doge and the leaders of the army. The Doge declared his intention to disregard the threat, and most of the barons expressed their determination to follow his example. The discontent and indignation of the better part of the Crusaders found at length a mouthpiece. A council was held. The Abbot of Vaux, a Cistercian monk, could no longer control his indignation. In the council held in Dandolo's tent he suddenly rose, and in a bold, clear voice said, ' I forbid you in the name of the Pope to attack this city. It is a city of Christian men, and you are Crusaders. You have another destination.' The Venetians would have murdered him if he had not been protected by Simon de Montfort and by other nobles. Dandolo was greatly annoyed. He charged the Crusaders with having prevented him from taking possession of the city, and claimed the fulfilment of their promise to aid him in conquering it. The majority of them thought themselves bound to help Dandolo, and promised to do so. Simon de Montfort, however, and many other pilgrims declared that they would not act against the apostolic command, and that they had no intention of being excommunicated. Notwithstanding these protests, the letters of the Pope, and the threats of the Pope's representatives, the city was attacked.

It was captured in five days, namely, on the 24th of November, 1202. The pilgrims and the Venetians entered into it, and

Capture of Zara.

[1] Petri, *Val. Cern. Hist. Albig.*, c. 19.

Zara was mercilessly plundered. Its churches were pillaged and many houses destroyed. The inhabitants were barbarously treated. Some were beheaded, others were banished, while a great number fled to the mountains to save their lives. Dandolo was not content with punishing the citizens of Zara. His intention was to bring it again under the rule of the Republic, and for this purpose considerable time was necessary. Hence, shortly after the conquest, he proposed that the army should winter in Zara. 'The winter,' said he to the leaders, 'is coming on. We cannot budge from here until Easter, because we shall not be able to find provisions in any other place. The city is rich and well supplied with everything. Let us divide it.'[1] The proposition was accepted ; the spoil was shared, and the Venetians and Crusaders took up their quarters for the winter in different portions of the city, the Venetians near the harbour, the Crusaders inland.

Dissatisfaction of the Crusaders.

Meantime the dissatisfaction between the Venetians and the leaders on the one side and the great body of Crusaders on the other was daily increasing. The latter had persuaded themselves that when Zara was taken they would at once be permitted to go on their pilgrimage. They had violated their vow, and had fallen under the sentence of excommunication. The religious portion of the army in particular was greatly embittered against Dandolo and their own leaders. Within three days of the capture of the city the Venetians and the Crusaders were fighting against each other in a quarrel which lasted several hours,[2] and in which a hundred persons were killed and many were wounded. There was not a street where the fight was not going on. As fast as the leaders stopped the fighting in one quarter their attention was called for in another. Everywhere the Venetians had the worst of it. All the authority of the leaders of both sides was required to put an end to this quarrel. What was its immediate cause it is perhaps impossible to learn. The author of the 'Devastatio' says that the barons kept the spoil to themselves, and did not share it with the poor men of the army. The explanation is

[1] Villehardouin, ch. xviii.
[2] A day and a night, says Robert de Clari.

possible, and is in accordance with the policy which was followed throughout the expedition until its end. The leaders were in league with the Venetians, while the mass of the Crusaders, who had set their minds on pilgrimage, saw only that they were being made use of to benefit the Venetians and their own leaders. What is certain is that the army was already considerably demoralised, and that some at least of the leaders joined with a large body of the pilgrims in distrusting the Venetians. The quarrel increased the bitterness of feeling between the opposing sections. A large number of the Crusaders were anxious to leave for Egypt or Syria ; a large number, Villehardouin says, were tired of the expedition and wished to return home.

During the weeks which followed there was great and continual dissatisfaction between the Venetians and the Crusaders. Possibly there is truth in the statement of Villehardouin that many wished the army to break up and were anxious to return home. They had not come out to fight either the King of Hungary or the Emperor of Romania, as it began to be whispered they were to be called upon to do. They had no desire to give their services to the traders of Venice. The great French chronicler wishes to leave the impression that the disaffection was merely wanton and without just cause. The narrative, however, of every independent contemporary, and especially of the 'poor knight,' Robert de Clari, shows that abundant cause existed. The expedition had already fallen under the expressed censure of the Church. Each man knew without such official censure that in taking part against a Christian city he had violated his oath, and had been untrue to the pledges he had given and the convictions which had led him to join the enterprise. The treatment the Crusaders had received on the Lido, their loss of the autumn, their journey across the Adriatic, 'with great speed but with sad hearts,' in the interests of Venice, had been borne in the hopes that on the capture of Zara a way might be found for a speedy departure *outre-mer*. But the pilgrims now saw that their allies cared nothing for the object of the pilgrimage, and were mainly bent on recovering

territory and destroying a rival, while they believed that their
own leaders were bent upon amassing the largest possible
amount of spoil from a Christian people.   They themselves
were suffering much from cold and hunger,[1] and would
have been content so to suffer if it were in the execution of
of their vow.   Now, however, both their spiritual and their
temporal interests were being sacrificed.   Those who thought
most of the first found themselves under the ban of excommunication, and those who might have been disposed to disregard spiritual censure found that they were being used to
benefit the Venetians while others obtained the spoil.   Hence
there were daily desertions.   The strictest orders were given
that none should leave the camp.   These orders, however,
were insufficient to check the evil.   A thousand went without
leave.   The clamour for permission to go away was so great
that the leaders judged it well to give permission to another
thousand.   Many merchant ships went away filled with
soldiers.   One had five hundred on board, who were all
drowned.   Another detachment tried to return home through
'Slavonia'—that is, through Dalmatia and Styria—but after
being badly assailed by the peasants had to return to the
army.

It should be noted also that this anxiety to leave the
army was mainly caused by the desire of the deserters to be
about the business for which they had left home.   The object
of most of those who left the camp was to get to Syria or
Egypt.

[1] *Devastatio.*

CHAPTER XI.

THE PLOT.

PART I.

THUS the winter of 1202-3 passed slowly away, in discontent among the Crusaders, in smouldering suspicion against their chiefs, and in animosity towards the Venetians. Suspicion was in the air—suspicion by the Crusaders that they were to be made the tools of Venice in the future as they had already been in the immediate past—a new suspicion also that Philip of Swabia, King of the Romans, was about to unite with Dandolo against the Pope of Rome, that their own leader, Boniface, had already betrayed them, sold them as an army to assist his kinsman Philip in fighting against the head of the Church. The proof of treachery was not complete, but sufficient was known to justify the suspicion and to account for the uneasiness. The soldiers who had been carried away from their native countries on a wave of religious enthusiasm, who had come out to fight for God and His cause, had already violated their oaths, and felt themselves powerless to get out of the trap into which they had been led.

Leaving the Crusaders at Zara, I propose now to narrate the facts which justified the suspicion of the army, and to attempt to point out what was the plot against the object which the Crusaders had in hand.

Before doing so it is necessary to call attention to the reasons which are assigned by contemporary writers for the two circumstances which marked the diversion of the fourth crusade from its intended purpose. The two circumstances were, first, the attack upon Zara, and, second, the expedition to Constantinople.

These circumstances are described, as we have already seen, by two sets of contemporary historians, who may be classified roughly as official and non-official writers. In the first class I have already stated that the graphic and singularly interesting account written, dictated, or revised by Villehardouin takes the highest rank. The writer describes what he saw or heard. All the official accounts are open to the objection that they are the work of men who were either themselves leaders or were under the influence either of the leaders of the expedition or of Philip of Swabia. They are all pleas of men writing for the defence. Their testimony is therefore not impartial, and may fairly be examined with suspicion. When they wrote, the crusade from which Europe had hoped so much had failed miserably in its object, had begun by destroying a Christian city, and had ended by destroying a Christian instead of a Moslem state. The Pope had indignantly condemned the conduct of the Crusaders, and in doing so had probably expressed the opinion of the conscience of Western Europe. The writers in question had to explain the change of a crusade into a buccaneering expedition as best they could.

The reason they assign for the diversion of the crusade to Zara is, as we have seen, that many of the Crusaders having taken ship elsewhere or having refused to leave home, the number of those who reached Venice was far below that which the delegates had contracted for ; that the Venetians insisted upon their bargain, until at length they made a fair proposal by means of which the Crusaders would be able to pay the 34,000 marks which were still due to the Republic under the contract for transport. These writers add that those who opposed this proposal did so because they wished to break up the enterprise. The chief of them, Villehardouin, begins his excuses for the failure of the expedition with the departure of the Flemish fleet already mentioned. He tells us that this fleet was a very fine one, was very well provided, and contained a great number of well-armed men. Baldwin of Flanders, however, did not go with it, but went overland to Venice. The command of the fleet was given to Jan de

Neele and two others.[1] The pilgrims had great confidence in
the fleet, because, says Villehardouin, the greatest number of
their sergeants-at-arms were on board. Jan de Neele and
the other officers in command had promised Baldwin that
after they had passed the Straits of Gibraltar they would join
the army which had collected at Venice in whatever place they
learned it had gone to. Villehardouin says that they had broken
their word to their lord ' because they were afraid of the great
peril in which those at Venice were engaged.' The meaning
of the phrase is doubtful. It probably signifies that those in
the fleet deserted the enterprise in order to avoid the peril to
which those in Venice seem to have exposed themselves.[2] If
the writer meant the peril or danger of being delayed in
Venice, then a comparison of the dates at which the troubles
in Venice began with that of the arrival of this fleet at
Marseilles will show that no such fear could have influenced
the fleet. The messengers announcing the arrival of the
fleet in Marseilles reached Venice probably in January 1203.
They declared that the fleet proposed to winter at Marseilles
and asked for orders. Baldwin, after consultation with the
Doge, sent word to them to leave at the end of March and to
proceed to Methroni, at the south-east of the Peloponnesus, to
meet the Venetian fleet. 'Alas!' says Villehardouin, 'they
acted so ill that they did not keep their word, but went away
to Syria, where they knew that they could do no good.'[3] The
truth probably is that they had heard how the Crusaders had
been tricked and turned away from their purpose, and therefore decided that they at least would go forward to fight the
Moslem. If they were not strong enough to make an
attempt on Egypt, they could at least give aid to the
Christians who were in Syria. If Villehardouin's suggestion
means that the Flemish fleet could have been of use to the
army for the purposes of the Crusade, it is dishonest. The
bargain for the attack on Zara was concluded before the
fleet reached Marseilles. The capture of Zara had been

[1] Villehardouin, x.
[2] This is the meaning which Du Cange gives. See *Observations on Villehardouin*.   [3] Villehardouin, c. xxi.

made in November.   The contract to attack Constantinople was made at latest before the fleet reached the Adriatic. The fact is that Villehardouin seizes upon the very slightest shadow of evidence to afford proof of the necessity of abandoning the expedition to Egypt.

The story of Villehardouin and his school, which attributes the diversion of the crusade to the want of men and to the pressure of the Venetians, is in the main true, but it is not the whole truth.   We have to turn to the non-official historians of the expedition in order to supplement and check the narrative of the official writers.   The former are less open to suspicion than the latter.   They had fewer motives for misrepresentation.   But even they were disposed to make the best of a bad business.   They had no sympathy either with the Zarans or the Venetians.   At the same time they were themselves Crusaders or derived their information from Crusaders, and were desirous of showing that the crusade had done something useful, if it were only the punishment of a nation which had refused to recognise the supremacy of the Pope.   One advantage, however, they undoubtedly possess over the official writers.   They do not consider themselves bound to conceal the conduct of Venice.   The explanation they give of the diversion of the enterprise is that it was due solely to the conduct of the Republic.   Enough might have been gathered from a careful search of the authorities known to exist even in the time of Gibbon to raise a strong presumption against the good faith of Dandolo, Boniface, and Philip of Swabia.   But it has been reserved to our own time to complete the evidence against them ; to prove almost already to demonstration that the expedition was diverted from its purpose through the cupidity and treason of Venice, and that from this cause the army was converted into a band of robbers, who were to commit the great crime of the middle ages by the destruction of the citadel against which the hitherto irresistible wave of Moslem invasion had beaten and had been broken.

Bearing in mind the difference in weight to be attached to the two classes of witnesses, it becomes necessary to put together their evidence.

The messengers of the Crusaders arrived in Venice in the middle of February 1201.[1] Their treaty with the Venetians for the transport of an army to Egypt was made in the middle of March.[2] News of the signature of this treaty reached Malek-Adel, the Sultan of Egypt, very shortly afterwards, and filled him with alarm. The weakened condition of his country, due to natural causes and to the divisions in his own family, made it of the utmost importance that the crusading army should be diverted from Egypt. An army very much inferior to the great hosts of the last expedition would inevitably conquer Egypt. Accordingly, Malek-Adel set to work not only to repair his defences but to buy over the Venetians. In the autumn of the same year two envoys were sent from Venice to this Sultan, possibly at his request, were received by him with great distinction and occupied themselves at once with framing terms of peace, which later on took the form of a commercial treaty.

Negotiations between Venice and Egypt.

Meantime the Crusaders had been collecting. According to their contract with Venice, they were to be in that city and the transports were to be ready by St. John's Day, the 24th of June, 1202. On the 13th of May, 1202, the envoys of Venice had concluded their treaty with Malek-Adel. This treaty assured to the Venetians, in addition to many other privileges, a district or quarter in Alexandria, and to the pilgrims who visited the Holy Sepulchre under Venetian protection safety for their lives and goods. The Sultan sent an emir, named Sead Eddin, to Venice to secure its confirmation. His mission was successful, and the treaty was secretly ratified in July 1202.[3] The signature of this treaty gives the explanation of the diversion of the fourth crusade from Egypt and of its subsequent failure. Venice was henceforward playing a double game. She had signed her agreement of March 1201 with the Crusaders, in accordance with

Treaty with Malek-Adel.

---

[1] 'La première semaine de caresme.'—Villehardouin.

[2] Villehardouin, c. vi.

[3] Carl Hopf. See the very able examination of the date assigned by Carl Hopf in *Innocent III., Philippe de Souabe, et Boniface,* par le Comte Riant, p. 124. Extracted from the *Revue des Questions Historiques.*

which she was to transport the army of the West to Egypt.
She now signs a secret treaty with the enemy who was to be
attacked.   The successes which Pisa and Genoa had obtained
over her in Constantinople were to be compensated by her
successes over them in Egypt.   The price of her triumph
was the betrayal of Christendom.   It was impossible to keep
faith both with the Crusaders and with the Arabs.   The
signature of the treaty with the Sultan of Egypt meant that
faith was to be broken with the followers of the Cross, and
·was therefore the immediate cause of the diversion of the
enterprise from Egypt.   The Crusaders at the time and for
years afterwards suspected treachery, and some of the contemporary writers did not hesitate to accuse Venice of
betraying the expedition.   But there is no evidence to prove
that even any of the leaders had any certain knowledge that
a treaty had been signed, by which the services of the Venetians in carrying the army to Egypt had become impossible.
The presence of Sead Eddin in Venice, in July 1202, possibly
gave rise to doubts as to the good faith of the Republic,
though the presence of an envoy from the Sultan may have
been concealed or may have been disregarded amid the
multitude of visitors to the great centre of Eastern trade in
Western Europe.   If such doubts arose, the conduct of the
Venetians to the Crusaders while at Lido increased them,
while the attack upon Zara brought conviction into the
minds of a large body of the army that they were not being
fairly dealt with by the Venetians.   It is probable that the
belief that Venice was not acting fairly was one of the causes
of the ill-feeling which showed itself in the riot between the
Venetians and the Crusaders within a week after the occupation of the city.   But the secret of the treaty was well kept.
The interest of Dandolo was, on the one hand, not to allow
its provisions to transpire, and, on the other, to take advantage of every circumstance in order to divert the attention of
the Crusaders from Egypt.   Henceforward, and without any
explanation being suggested, we find that the Crusaders
speak rather of going to Syria than to Egypt.   The arrival
of a smaller number of Crusaders in Venice than had been

contracted for gave a plausible excuse to Dandolo, first, to delay the departure of the expedition, then to divert it towards Zara, and afterwards to keep it there during the winter. We have seen that he entirely succeeded. From the ratification of the treaty with the Sultan of Egypt, in July 1202, the intention was to divert the expedition from its intended attack upon Egypt, the weakest and at the same time the most important point under Moslem sway.

The evidence in support of an understanding between Venice and the Sultan, by which Venice was to prevent an attack upon Egypt, is already weighty, and will probably be conclusive when a more careful examination has been made of the Venetian archives. Charles Hopf, the greatest of German authorities on all that relates to the history of the East during the middle ages, and who had amassed large stores of materials for his historical works, appears to have had a copy of this treaty in his possession.[1]

The treaty is mentioned by one of the earliest historians of the crusade. Arnold of Ibelino, the probable author of the 'Continuation of the History of William of Tyre,'[2] gives an account which is full of detail and which there is no reason to regard as seriously inaccurate. He says that when the Sultan of Babylon, as the ruler of Egypt was then generally called, from the fortified town on the Nile which he usually occupied, heard that a great fleet had been chartered by the Christians to proceed to Egypt, he sent for the cadis and priests to take council with him how he should save his country from the Christians who were coming. He made various proposals for the defence of the country. Then he sent messengers to Venice with rich presents to the Doge and the inhabitants. The messengers were charged to ask for the friendship of the Venetians, and to promise that if the Christians were diverted

[1] He has given an analysis of it in vol. lxxxv. of the *Encyclopédie d'Ersch et Gruber* (Leipzig, 1867), p. 188. Unfortunately on his death his collection was either dispersed or at any rate has not been made available to historical students. See a very valuable examination of the whole subject in the appendix to Comte Riant's *Innocent III., Philippe de Souabe, et Boniface*, Paris, 1875.

[2] Known as *L'Estoire de Eracles Empereur*, pp. 250-252. *Rec. des Croisades*, vol. ii.

from their plan of an attack upon Egypt the Venetians should receive great treasures and large privileges in the port of Alexandria. The messengers went to Venice, and, as we have seen, succeeded.[1]

The explanation, therefore, of the diversion of the crusading army from Egypt is to be found first and mainly in the treason of Venice. In order to obtain advantages of trade over her Italian rivals she had accepted a treaty which made it impossible for her to conduct the army of the Cross to Egypt. The Crusaders grumbled, suspected treachery, and did all they could to fulfil their vows, but all in vain. Venice had a fixed and definite purpose. Circumstances enabled her to force the Crusaders to go to Zara, and the winter once lost it became easier to divert the expedition from its original purpose than it had been a year previously. We shall now have to examine how it came about that

[1] One MS. of Ernoul or Arnold says, 'et lor manda que se il povent tant faire que il n'alassent mie en la terre d'Egypte il lor donroit granz tresorz et granz franchises on port d'Alissandre.' Another, 'En nulle maniere qu'il destornassent les Chrestiens qu'il n'alassent.' All the MSS. quoted in the *Recueil* agree generally on these points. Two MSS. given by Buchon in *Le Livre de la Conqueste* (Paris, 1845) give additional details, though one is probably only a variation of the above. One of them says ' La nouvelle de ceste emprinse, dit-il, s'espandi moult loins. Quant li soudan d'Egypte, qui avoit esté frére Salehadin et qui avoit son neveu de Damas déshireté entendi ces choses, il s'en ala en Egypte et fist moult bien garnir les forteresses ; puis envoia en Venisse et manda aux Venissiens que, se il povoient tant faire que il destournassent les crestiens d'aler en Egypte, il leur donroit dou sien largement ; et grans franchises averoient en ses pors. Avec ce leur envoia biaux dons ' (MS. Supp. 34, quoted in Buchon). The other says ' Or vous dirai du soudan de Babilone, qui freres avoit esté Salehadin qui le tére d'Egypte avoit saisie après sen neveu quant il fut mors et qui sen autre neveu avoit desherité de la tere de Damas et de la tere de Jherusalem qu'il fist. Quant il oï dire que li Crestien avoient levé estoire pour venir en le tere de Egypte, il fit mettre boines garnisons en le tere de Damas et de Jherusalem pour son neveu que il avoit desherité. Et a dont s'en ala li soudans de Babilone en Egypte, pour prendre conseil coment il porroit mix le tere garnir encontre les Crestiens vaillans qui venoient en se tere. . . . Puis fist appareillier messages ; et si lor carqua grant avoir, et si les envoia en Venisse. Et si manda au duc de Venise et as Venisiens salut et amistié—et si lor envoia moult grans presens. Et si lor manda que—s'il pooient tant faire as Franchois que il n'alaissent mie en le tere de' Egypte, que il lor donroit grant avoir, et si lor donroit grant franquise el port d'Alixandre. Li message alerent en Venise et si fisent moult bien che qu'il quisent as Venissiens—et puis si s'en repairicrent arrière en Egypte.'—MS. No. 7488⁵ (quoted also from Buchon).

Dandolo was enabled again to prevent the Crusaders leaving for Egypt, and in so doing to carry out at once his part of the treaty with Egypt and to revenge his own wrongs and those of Venice against Constantinople.

PART II.

It now becomes necessary to examine one of the most interesting intrigues that have ever influenced the course of European history. During the winter at Zara the discontent of the Crusaders increased daily. The pilgrims saw their chance of being landed in Syria or Egypt rapidly diminishing. Apart even from the suspicion of Venetian treachery, they remembered that their contract with the Republic was only for a year, and expired in June. They had already seen that the Venetians adhered to the strict letter of their agreement in regard to payment. They would be equally exacting in regard to time. The expenses of the expedition had moreover exhausted the provisions and money they had brought with them. Even the money which the barons had been able to borrow was nearly spent. It was already difficult to obtain provisions.[1] If a further demand should be made for extra payment after June the army would be unable to meet it. Villehardouin insists that many attempts were made in presence of these difficulties to break up the expedition. Many of the Crusaders wished to return home; many more wished to leave for Syria in order to accomplish the vow which they believed would be impossible of execution if they remained with the Venetians. But while Dandolo was well content that the attack upon Egypt had been temporarily avoided, he had his own reasons for preventing the break-up of the army. So far he had been successful. But his own work was only half done. The expedition had been diverted from Egypt. Venice had gained time. Still, if the Venetians kept their part of the bargain, it was quite possible that the army should be landed in Egypt, and should be able to fight its way to sustenance

Expedition only temporarily diverted.

[1] Robert de Clari, xvi.

and victory. If the army broke up, the Crusaders might re-
unite, and, with the aid of the Genoese and Pisans, the great
rivals of the Venetians, still attack Egypt. Such a result
would be the humiliation of Venice and the discomfiture of
Dandolo. The great Doge had long since provided against
any such mishap. There is reason to believe that even before
the expedition left Venice he had determined to make use of
the crusading host against Constantinople. A conspiracy had
already been formed between Dandolo, Boniface, the commander-in-chief, and Philip of Swabia, which was to result in
the greatest blow yet given to Christendom.

Events in
Constanti-
nople.

In order to understand how this conspiracy had been
formed, we must recall briefly what had been passing in the
imperial city. The reigning Emperor was Alexis the Third.
He had deposed his brother Isaac in 1195, and after putting
out his eyes had imprisoned him in the dungeons of the
Diplokionion, or in the tower of Anema. Isaac's son, Alexis,
was allowed his liberty. At a time when Alexis the Third
had apparently determined to kill young Alexis, his nephew
and the lawful heir to the throne, the wife of the usurper
warned Isaac of the contemplated crime. Isaac, according to
the same authority, counselled his son to leave the city at
once, and to escape to his sister, the wife of Philip of Swabia.
Young Alexis, either disguised as a common sailor or hidden
in a box carefully disguised,[1] fled from Constantinople in a
Pisan ship, and escaped the diligent search which was made
for him by the imperial police. This was in the spring
of 1201. Contemporary Western writers, who have been
followed in this respect by all historians until the present
day, speak of young Alexis as the son of Isaac by Margaret, daughter of Bela of Hungary, his second wife.
This marriage took place in 1185. Alexis, therefore, in
1200, could not be older than fourteen or fifteen.[2] He

[1] *Chron. Novgorod*, p. 93: 'Conductus est in navem ibique dolio tribus fundis instructo reconditus.' The story of Nicetas is different.

[2] Two facts are opposed to the accepted statement that Margaret was the mother of Alexis : (1) that the reigning Emperor wrote to Innocent the Third that the youth was not *porphyrogenetos* ; and (2) that, according to Nicetas (p. 481), Mar-garet was only ten years old in 1185 ; 'τὸν μείρακα ἤδη ἀμείβων,' *Geo. Acrop.* p. 6.

had sent messengers to his sister (or more probably his half-sister), the wife of Philip, imploring the help of her husband. He made his way, according to Villehardouin, to Ancona,[1] in Italy. His movements, however, after leaving Constantinople, are doubtful. The balance of the evidence of contemporary writers seems to show that he went direct to Philip of Swabia,[2] after calling at Sicily, and possibly taking Ancona on the way. According to one writer, he was in July at Warzburg, where Philip held his court.[3] Apparently he continued with Philip until the end of the year, where, as I have already mentioned, he would have seen Boniface. In the summer of 1202 he was in Hungary,[4] probably on his way to the Pope with a request for aid. In August, or the beginning of September, he was at Verona.[5]

In order to understand why he had returned to Italy, we must trace the events which had happened in the interval between his flight from Constantinople and his arrival in Hungary. Young Alexis had appealed, as we have seen, to his sister and her husband Philip. The Swabian king wished for many reasons to help him. Philip, who claimed to be King of the Romans, was the head of the party opposed to the Pope. On the death of the Emperor Henry the Sixth, the Pope and other princes had refused to recognise his infant son Frederic as his successor. Philip, brother of Henry, on failing to have his nephew recognised, had succeeded in having himself elected Emperor by one party, while Otho of Brunswick had been selected by the Guelfs. The Pope opposed the pretensions of Philip, and had carried his opposition to such an extent that in March 1201 Philip had been excommunicated. The result to the pretender had been very serious. His subjects were absolved from their obedience. Many nobles and ecclesiastical princes had withdrawn from or were wavering in their allegiance. Others, like the Bishop of Halberstadt,

Philip of Swabia.

---

[1] Villehardouin, xv. c. 70.

[2] Gunther, viii. ; *Chronique de Morée*, p. 10, and *Chronaca di Morea*, p. 416 ; *Chroniques Greco-Romanes* of Charles Hopf. ; Rigord, p. 55 ; *Chronista Novgorodensis*, 93 ; *Chron. Gr.-Rom.* of Hopf ; and others.

[3] Böhmer, *Register Imperii*, p. 12.   [4] *Continuatio*, 28.

[5] Villehardouin, xv. c. 70.

had joined the crusade in order to avoid the necessity of choosing between their temporal and their spiritual lord.

Philip was a delicate, fragile looking man of the blond German type, whose appearance suggested weakness. The physical weakness at least was more apparent than real. He could hold his own in the manly pursuits of his time. He had been brought up by his father for the Church, and had been carefully trained in the monastery of Adelsburg, founded by a vassal of the House of Hohenstaufen. His education or natural temper made him a narrow churchman, a man ready for intrigue and for persistent petty opposition—a man, too, full of ambition. His great chance of recovering influence was to show that notwithstanding the Pope he could hold his own. If in so doing he could thwart the great object of the Pontiff's life, not only would he have succeeded in triumphing over his rival, but he might expect that those who had deserted him would return to their allegiance.

His ambi-
tion.
The arrival of messengers from Alexis corresponding with the collection of the crusading army appears at a very early period to have suggested the idea to Philip that the crusade might be made use of, under the pretext at least of assisting his brother-in-law. Philip had, however, selfish reasons which disposed him to help young Alexis. He seems to have persuaded himself that he had a right to the imperial throne of the East through his wife, and one of his dreams was that it might be possible to unite the two empires of the New and the Elder Rome in his own person. Thus the indignation which he had a right to feel at the deposition and imprisonment of his wife's father urged him to a course which coincided with that which his own ambition would dictate. Add to this that the disastrous result of the last crusade had been most keenly felt in Germany, and that any movement against the Empire in the East was sure to be popular with his own subjects, and we see that the motives which urged Philip to assist young Alexis were exceedingly strong. If he could help him by turning the crusade into a weapon against the reigning Emperor in Constantinople, he would at the same time succeed in recovering the allegiance of those of his own subjects whom

the Pope's excommunication had caused to waver. He could let the Pope see that he was more powerful than his rival, and even Innocent might think it well to side with the stronger claimant. His own power would be enormously increased. He might be not only the triumphant leader of the Ghibelin party, but lord of the East and of the West.

Impelled by such motives, the appointment of Boniface, Marquis of Montferrat, to the command of the crusading army on the death, in May 1201, of Theobald of Champagne, supplied the instrument he required. If Boniface could be induced to act with him, a successful attack might be made on Constantinople, and his plans appeared assured of success. Boniface, as Robert de Clari is careful to point out, was a relative of Philip. His father was William of Montferrat, who had played an important part on the Ghibelin side. This William had married Sophia, daughter of Frederic Barbarossa, and sister or half-sister of Philip.[1] In the contest for the imperial throne, which had commenced on the death of Henry the Sixth in 1197 between Philip and Otho of Brunswick, Innocent himself had sent Boniface with the Archbishop of Mayence to try to arrange their differences. The mission had, however, failed. Not only was Boniface acquainted with the affairs of Philip, but he had occasion to be well versed in what was passing at Constantinople. The family of Montferrat was well acquainted with the East. Six of its members had contracted marriages with the imperial family. William, the father of Boniface, had four sons, each of whom connected his name with the history of the crusades, and three of them very closely with that of Constantinople. These sons were William, surnamed Longsword, Conrad, Reynier, and Boniface.

Boniface, Marquis of Montferrat, and the connection of his family with the East.

The eldest was for a time the hope of the Crusaders. The family was related to those of the Roman Emperor in the West, the King of France, and other powerful princes. He married in 1175 the daughter of Baldwin the Fourth, the King of Jerusalem, and received in dowry the earldoms of Jaffa and Ascalon, but died two months afterwards.

---

[1] See genealogical table of the family of Montferrat, *Du Cange*, 309, Paris ed.

The second son, who became Marquis of Montferrat on the death of William, was that Conrad whom we have seen in Constantinople, aiding the Emperor to resist the attack upon the city by Branas. We have seen also that after his marriage with Theodora, sister of Isaac, he refused to follow the Emperor to Adrianople, was dissatisfied with his honours, and went to Palestine in 1187, where he played a most important part during the next four years, and especially distinguished himself in the siege of Tyre. After marrying Isabella, to the disgust of the Archbishop of Canterbury and other churchmen, and after having quarrelled with Richard, and having been named King of Jerusalem, he was killed by one of the assassins in 1192. Robert de Clari alleges that Isaac behaved treacherously to Conrad even when he had organised an army of Latins to oppose Branas ; that when the marquis went out of the city to meet the rebel the Emperor shut the gate upon him instead of following with his own troops. Nicetas distinctly contradicts this statement, and states that the Emperor himself commanded the right wing and Manuel Camyzes the left wing. It is not improbable that the story of Clari is one which only passed into circulation about the time of the capture of Constantinople, when the family and partisans of Montferrat found it convenient to find grievances against that of Isaac.

Reynier, the third son of William of Montferrat, younger brother of Conrad and elder brother of Boniface, had married Maria, daughter of the Emperor Manuel. He was at the time a beardless boy, and she a woman remarkably robust, and thirty years of age.[1] The Western writers declare that he received as dowry the kingdom of Salonica, though no Greek writer mentions a fact so important. He died without children after the murder of Conrad, and his only surviving brother was Boniface.[2]

Thus the leader of the expedition, if we are to judge by

[1] Nicetas, 222.

[2] A charter of 1204 states that Boniface sold to the Venetians his rights to the fiefs given by Manuel to his *father*, probably a mistake for his brother (*Tafel et Thomas*, i. 513).

narratives which were written by men whose object was in most cases to find an excuse for the conduct of Boniface, had family grievances which made him hostile to Constantinople. He considered himself *de jure* King of Salonica as inheritor of the dowry of Reynier. He had also, if Clari is to be believed, to revenge the attempt upon the life of his other brother Conrad. Philip and he had therefore each his own reason for wishing to attack the Emperor Alexis. It is by no means improbable that they had discussed and decided upon a plan of attacking the Empire during the time that Theobald of Champagne was still alive.[1] The election of Boniface had taken place in June 1201. In August he took the Cross and was solemnly invested with the title of Captain of the Christian Army. Shortly afterwards, as we have already seen, he left Burgundy for the court of Philip of Swabia, which was then at Hagenau, where he arrived at the end of the year, and where he probably found young Alexis. It is in the highest degree probable that he had taken this long journey on the invitation of Philip, and it is equally probable that the object of Philip was to urge him to make use of the crusade to restore the Emperor Isaac, or to place his son Alexis on the throne. It is, however, impossible to do more than surmise what passed during the weeks which Boniface spent at the court of Philip. The 'Gesta' of Innocent the Third state that a treaty was concluded between them by which the crusading army was bound to place young Alexis on the throne at Constantinople.[2] The existence of such a treaty is not improbable, but as no mention is made of it by other contemporary writers, such an agreement either never existed or was kept secret, or, what is more probable, was merely an understanding which it was unnecessary and undesirable either to disclose or to reduce to definite form in writing. While there is nothing in the subsequent story of the crusade to indicate

[1] See on this point the examination by Count Riant in *Inno. III. Phil. et Boniface*, pp. 36, 37. This author believes Boniface to have been the secret agent of Philip, even before he was appointed to the command of the crusading army. See, however, the arguments on the other side in M. Jules Tessier's *Diversion sur Zara et Constantinople*; Paris, 1884.

[2] *Gesta Inno. III.* No. 83.

that Philip and Boniface had not a complete understanding,
there is a large amount of evidence to suggest that they had.
It is especially noteworthy that several contemporary writers
speak of Philip having assumed the direction of the expedition from the time he was visited by Boniface.

Young
Alexis visits
Rome.

The struggle between the Pope and Philip in regard to the
use to be made of the fourth crusade began with the opening
of the year 1202. Well knowing that the object dearest to
the heart of Innocent after the success of the expedition was
the union of the Eastern and Western Churches, Philip sent
Alexis to Rome [1] to ask for aid, and to put this union now,
as always in these and all subsequent negotiations, in the front
as the chief advantage to be gained in return for such aid.

In January or February 1202, Boniface himself left the
court of Philip with an embassy for Rome. His mission
from the King of the Romans was twofold, to urge the Pope
to assist Alexis and to present the protest of the German
nobles against the Pontiff's support of Otho. By putting in
the front the promise of young Alexis to aid in bringing
about the union of the churches, the Pope might be induced
to support him. If he did so he could hardly continue to
support Otho, since Philip's influence with the army would
then be too powerful to be disregarded. If the Pope refused,
it remained to be seen what could be done through Boniface
with the Venetians and the Crusaders.

Boniface
visits
Rome.

Boniface reached Rome early in March 1202.[2] Alexis
had already been received in solemn audience by the Pope,
the cardinals, and the Roman nobility. He had asked for
justice against his uncle. He urged that the whole city
desired that he should become Emperor, and he insisted much
upon his power to bring about a union of the two churches.
The Pope seems to have hesitated as to the answer which he
should give. The offer was tempting, and especially perhaps
because Alexis insisted that he had a large party devoted to
his interests in the New Rome which would be ready to rise
on his approach.[3] The Pope concluded by distinctly refusing

---

[1] *Chron. di Morea.*   [2] March 11, Winkleman, p. 256.
          [3] *Chron. Novgorod.*

to promise any aid to Alexis. On the arrival of Boniface the proposals were again submitted, but with a like result. Shortly afterwards the latter left Rome in deep disappointment, having altogether failed in the accomplishment of his and Philip's designs.

From the moment of the failure in Rome, Boniface turned his attention to the execution of his designs by means of the army under his command. After a short visit made by himself and Alexis to Boniface's domains at Montferrat, we find the Pretender at Verona, the city which commands the Brenner pass, by which the German pilgrims came, as well as the road through Lombardy along which the Crusaders coming from France must needs travel.

On August 15, 1202, Boniface arrived in Venice. He found the army, as we have already seen, on the Lido in a state of the greatest distress. Forbidden to leave the island, plague-stricken, in need of provisions, wishing to be about their sacred business, they regarded the Venetians as the cause of all their ills. But they could hardly look upon Boniface with great affection or confidence. He had been chosen only after the command had been refused by several others. He had seen less of the army than Baldwin of Flanders and others who had done their best to lessen the troubles of the Crusaders, and who had at least shared them. *He goes to Venice.*

Early in September an embassy arrived in Venice from Alexis in Verona. A meeting took place between the messengers of Alexis and the leaders of the army. The proposals of Alexis were submitted. A reply was given that a message should be sent to Philip with Alexis, who had sent word that he was going to his uncle. The message to Philip was in these words: 'If Philip will aid us to recover the land *d'outre-mer* we will help Alexis to recover his own land.'[1] *Proposals from Alexis.*

It is clear that the mass of the Crusaders knew little or nothing of this embassy or of this message. Probably Dandolo on the part of the Venetians, Boniface the commander-in-chief, and three or four of the leaders, including Villehardouin himself, were alone in the secret. It did not suit the

---

[1] Villehardouin, sec. 72.

conspirators yet to reveal their project, and we shall see that when it was made known to the army it was made to appear that the proposal to go to Constantinople was a quite recent suggestion, due to the necessities in which the Crusaders found themselves after wintering at Zara, instead of part of a well-planned conspiracy.

Still no definite agreement with the Crusaders and with Venice was yet arrived at. The project of Alexis had been favourably received; had been accepted in principle by the leaders. Almost immediately afterwards, and probably in September, Boniface again left the army, and remained absent until after the conquest of Zara. During a part at least of this time he was at Rome, where also was Cardinal Peter Capuano. Thus, while the crusading army was leaving Venice, its two chiefs, one in temporal and the other in spiritual things, were absent.

Boniface appears to have won over the Cardinal entirely to his views. In spite of the way in which Peter Capuano had been treated by the Venetians, he appears on this visit to Innocent to have made light of the expedition to Zara; to have spoken of it as a merely temporary incident, the punishment of a half heretical people by the occupation of their city, and as a punishment which would not entail the shedding of Christian blood. What is perhaps more remarkable is that in this visit to the Pope the Cardinal rather than Boniface seems to have been the chief advocate in favour of the proposal to help Alexis.[1] It is easy to see what would be the arguments used. The Crusaders were short of money: had spent what they had, had been unable to borrow more, and had been compelled to agree to the Zara arrangement in order to get rid of their obligations to the Venetians. Boniface would be careful to point out that the arrangement with Venice expired in June, and to urge that an expedition to Constantinople, with the object merely of restoring young Alexis, would be the only means of supplying money for the expedition; the only means of buying over the aid of the Venetians, without whom it could never reach either Egypt or

---

[1] Inno. III. *Epist.* viii.

Syria, and in short the only means of preventing the crusade from absolute failure.

Innocent remained firm ; refused to give any approval to the Zaran expedition ; disavowed the legate's approbation, and sent to the army an injunction to restrain them from accomplishing their unrighteous purpose. In reference, however, to the project for giving aid to young Alexis, the arguments of Cardinal Peter and of Boniface made more impression. The Pope indeed formally refused to sanction the proposal. He did more. Knowing that the Cardinal agreed with Boniface, he forbade him to return to the army. But, notwithstanding this attitude of opposition, he appears to have thought it desirable at this time to keep the question in suspense. An embassy had been sent to Venice by the Emperor Alexis the Third to endeavour to bring about an alliance with the Republic. It was, however, too late, and was treated with ignominy. From Venice it appears to have gone to Rome. The Emperor seems from the first to have suspected the designs of Philip, of Boniface, and of Dandolo, and his embassy was the bearer of a golden bull asking for the aid of the Pope against these designs. Innocent regarded the opportunity as favourable to his own plans. The great inducement which the young Alexis had offered to obtain the Pontiff's support was the union of the churches, an object only less dear to Innocent than the success of the crusade. While promising aid to Alexis, the reigning Emperor, he did so conditionally upon this union being brought about. At the same time he sent word to the army distinctly forbidding the Crusaders to attack Romania.

The messengers sent to Philip by the Crusaders in Venice during September, to submit the proposition for assisting Alexis, arrived in Germany in October. Probably about the same time Philip would hear of the failure of the negotiations at Rome. This ill news would, however, be more than counterbalanced by the tidings of the great obstacle put in the way of the crusade by Venice. If the Republic could thus divert the expedition from its object, there was every reason to hope that with Dandolo's help he would be able to turn its energy

and refuses.

Embassy reaches Philip.

to the accomplishment of his purpose. Henceforward Philip acted more boldly, and was recognised by all as taking the leading part in the direction of the crusade. He negotiated the agreement that was to be made for aiding young Alexis. He acted at once as his guardian and guarantor. He sealed on his own behalf the treaty when concluded. In November the messengers of the Crusaders left Philip, accompanied by German plenipotentiaries. They arrived at Venice in the middle of December, and on the 1st of January, 1203, made their appearance at Zara, whither they had followed the army.

Alexis left the court of Philip probably at the same time as the messengers for Zara, but appears to have diverged in order to visit his uncle Emeric, king of Hungary.

Boniface reaches Zara.

In the middle of December Boniface had arrived at Zara. If the account of Robert de Clari is to be trusted, something like a comedy was arranged between him and Dandolo. The latter saw that the pilgrims were uneasy. The leaders were aware that they had not provisions enough for an expedition to Egypt or to Syria, and they had given out that even if they had they could do nothing when they reached either of these two countries. Dandolo therefore said to them : ' Sirs, in Greece [1] there is a bountiful supply of all things. If we can find a reasonable occasion to go there and to take provisions and other things, then we can easily manage to go *outre-mer*.' Then uprose Boniface, Marquis of Montferrat, and explained that at Christmas time he had been in Germany at the court of Philip, where he had seen young Alexis, whose father had been treacherously driven from his throne. ' Whoever,' said Boniface, ' has this young man can go into the land of Constantinople and take provisions and what is needed.' [2] Hence, according to Robert, the messengers were sent to Alexis in order that by inducing him to come the Crusaders might have *boine acoison, rasnauvle ocaision*, to go to Constantinople.

On New Year's Day, 1203, the messengers returned from Philip, accompanied by those whom that king had sent.

---

[1] Greece and Romania are used as synonymous terms by many of the Western writers.

[2] Robert de Clari, xvii.

Henceforward it was impossible to keep the object of their mission secret.

The organisation of the Crusaders for the purpose of taking a decision was not unlike that which prevailed throughout most European states.[1] Substitute the leaders and the great barons for the king, the lesser barons of the army and the knights for the lords, and the whole army for the commons, and the parallel will be complete. The leaders took the initiative. Then the parliament of lesser barons and knights had the proposition submitted to them, and lastly the commons of the army had to give their approval. The leaders had been consulted at Venice, and had accepted in principle the proposal to aid Alexis in return for his subsequently assisting the army. At Zara the proposition in a definite shape had to be submitted to the parliament of lesser barons and knights.

The day after the arrival of the two embassies from Germany, namely, on the 2nd of January, this parliament was held, to consider the proposals of Philip. The leaders of the expedition and their great barons—French, Flemish, German, and Lombard—were present. There were also as of right the bishops and abbots who were with the army. It is probable, too, that Dandolo and his council also attended, since they, too, had taken the Cross. The five bishops were, with one exception, likely to be favourable to the plans of Philip. Of the four Cistercian abbots, two were partisans of the King of the Romans, and two believed that it was shameful to divert the crusade from its lawful object ; one of the latter, the Abbot of Vaux and Cernay, as we have seen, had had the courage, at the risk of his life, to read the letters announcing excommunication against those who had taken part in the capture of Zara. The French barons were divided. The most important, Baldwin of Flanders, Louis of Blois, and Hugues of St. Paul, were under the influence of Philip. The barons of Lombardy, as might be expected, were under the same influence through Boniface. The leader of those

Proposals are submitted to parliament of barons.

[1] *Eclaircissements à Villehardouin*, p. 463, par M. de Wailly. This writer suggests that the form was specially copied from that of Venice.

who were in favour of loyally carrying out the expedition as
Innocent intended was Simon de Montfort, who appears to
have exercised a considerable influence, but who was intem-
perate and rash. The German barons were divided. Those
who had taken the side of Otho in his dispute with Philip
were probably among the pilgrims who had gone to the Holy
Land by other routes. Those who had left Germany for the
purpose of avoiding the excommunication which the Pope
had pronounced against Philip, and had left, in most instances,
against his wish, were unwilling to excite his anger by opposition to his designs. Those who were not under his suzerainty,
like the great barons of Belgium and of Franche Comté,
were more independent. The Venetians, under Dandolo, no
doubt went into the parliament to accept a foregone conclusion. The expedition to Romania would require an extension
of time for the employment of the fleet chartered from Venice,
and would therefore greatly enrich the Republic. Dandolo
knew that its great advantage would lie in its enabling him
to keep his promise towards the Sultan of Egypt, since, if
the Crusaders ever fought against the infidel, it would be in
Syria and not in Egypt. All the Venetians hoped that the
Republic would thus be enabled to punish Constantinople, and
at least to obtain better concessions from the Empire than
any other Italian state ; while, finally, the desire of Dandolo
to be revenged upon the Empire would be gratified.

Definite
proposals
are sub-
mitted.

The place of meeting was a palace occupied by Dandolo.
The messengers were introduced, and explained that they
had come from Philip. Villehardouin professes to give the
words of their message : ' My lords, says the King, I shall
send you my wife's brother. I put him in the hand of God
and in yours. Since you are fighting for God, for right, and
for justice, you ought, if you can, to restore to their inheritance those who have been wrongfully dispossessed. If you
are willing, he, Alexis, will make with you the best agreement that anybody ever made, and will give you the most
powerful aid for conquering the Holy Land. In the first
place, if God allows you to restore him, he will place the
whole of Romania under obedience to Rome. Moreover, he

knows that you have exhausted your substance and are poor. He will give you, therefore, two hundred thousand silver marks and provisions to all in the army, small and great. He will personally go with you into the land of Babylon, or, if you prefer it, will send there ten thousand men at his expense, and will keep them there for a year ; and for the rest of his life he will maintain, at his own expense, five hundred knights in the Holy Land as a guard. My lords, we have full powers to conclude an agreement on these terms, provided you are also willing. And remember that so good an arrangement was never offered, and he who refuses it will show that he has no wish for conquest.' These are the terms of the proposal as given by Villehardouin. There were other conditions which regarded the Venetians, and which may on that account have been omitted by the marshal. The advances made to the Republic were to be repaid. The contract for the freight of the Venetian transports was to be renewed for another year on its expiration in June, and the Republic was to receive one hundred thousand marks.[1]

The messengers had brought with them letters from Philip, ordering the Germans under his rule, under strict injunctions,[2] to support the proposal for the restoration of Alexis. He promised the French and Flemings that if Alexis should come to his own, he would always keep open a road through Romania safe and free.[3]

The meeting was adjourned until the next day. When it took place the division of opinion amongst the barons became at once evident. The Abbot of Vaux, who represented the

---

[1] *Ernoul, Chron.*, Halberstadt. Robert de Clari and others mention the ships and victuals for another year.

[2] ' Theothonicis autem, pro eo quod sui juris esse videbantur, hanc rem securiosius et imperiosius injungebat ; marchionem, cognatum suum, ejus, quæ inter eos erat, commonebat propinquitatis ; Flandrenses atque Francigenas et Venetos, et aliarum regionum homines, omni precum molimine sedulus exorabat, certissime promittens, si ille, auxilio ipsorum, sedem suam reciperet, peregrinis omnibus, tam per Theothoniam quam per totam Græciam, tutam ac liberam in perpetuum patere viam. Accedebat etiam ad hoc quod idem juvenis certissime pollicebatur, si viribus eorum restitutus foret, eis in commune argenti trecenta marcarum millia se daturum.'—Gunther, c. viii. *Exuviæ Sacræ.*

[3] Gunther, p. 77, *ib.*

party which Villehardouin insists was desirous of breaking up the army, declared that he and his friends would not agree to the proposal, though even this writer tells us that they gave as their reason that they had not left théir homes for such work as that proposed, and that they wished to go to Syria. Those, says Gunther, who were anxious for the success of the Cross earnestly dissuaded the rest from accepting the proposals of Philip. They urged that the restoration could not be effected without bloodshed. The plan, says this writer, seemed foolish and dishonest ; foolish, because a few foreigners were not likely to take a city so well fortified and so populous, and where there was sure to be much slaughter ; dishonest, because they were departing from the holy purpose to which they had pledged themselves. I give the answer of the Venetian party in Villehardouin's own word's : ' Beaux seigneurs, you can do nothing in Syria, and you can see *that* by those who have left us and gone to other ports. Remember that it is either by the land of Babylon or by Greece that the Holy Land will be recovered if it ever be recovered. And if we refuse this proposal we shall be disgraced for ever.' Feeling ran high. As I have already said, the Cistercians or White Friars were themselves divided. The Abbot of Loos and others spoke in favour of accepting the agreement in order to keep the army together, and as a means by which the expedition might best succeed in obtaining its object.

Proposals are accepted.

The Abbot of Vaux replied that all this was wrong. Whether they succeeded or not, they were at least bound to do what was right. Boniface, Baldwin of Flanders, and others, declared that they would be ashamed to reject the offer. Their influence overwhelmed all opposition, and the result was that the agreement was accepted upon the conditions already mentioned.[1]

The two leaders mentioned, together with the Earl of St. Paul, swore to observe the treaty, and did their best to induce the French barons to do the same. Only eight, however, consented to sign. Among the whole of the leaders only the seals of sixteen could be obtained.[2]

[1] Villehardouin, ch. xix. and xx.
[2] *Ib.* 99.

Upon the signature of this agreement the messengers from Philip left Zara. They were accompanied on their journey homewards by two Crusaders, who were to bring young Alexis to the camp. Part of the arrangement was that the Pretender should join the crusading army within a fortnight after Easter, that is, not later than the 20th of April.

The news of this arrangement could not be altogether concealed from the Crusaders, and increased the dissatisfaction already felt. Only the barons, however, had any definite knowledge of the agreement. The project, which had been approved in principle at Venice by the leaders, had now been advanced a great step further by its acceptance in the parliament of the barons and knights. It had not, however, been submitted or even published to the army, whose approval was nevertheless necessary. Such particulars as had leaked out increased the number of deserters and raised a bitter opposition. Many of the people, says the author of the 'Devastatio,' assembled and conspired together and swore they would not go into Romania.[1] The most notable opponent was again Simon de Montfort. He and his followers determined to refuse to follow Boniface, and when, a little later, the expedition left Zara, they went to Hungary, where they were well received by the King.[2]

Meantime the leaders of the crusade had become anxious to make their peace with Innocent. They had allowed themselves to be persuaded by the Venetians into an attack upon a Christian army. They had violated their oaths, and had incurred the terrible penalties of excommunication. The strong party in the army which had protested against the attack upon Zara would naturally represent the facts in their own light to the Pope, while the King of Hungary would claim restitution of his territory, compensation for the injury done to him, and the punishment of the offenders. Accordingly, during the last days of December, the leaders of the expedition sent Nivelon, Bishop of Soissons, and John de Noyon to Rome to represent their case to the Holy See, and to ask for absolution. They were authorised to speak on

Attitude of Innocent the Third.

[1] *Devast.*, p. 88. [2] Gunther, p. 13.

behalf of the Crusaders only—not on behalf of the Venetians. They were accompanied by the German abbot Martin, whose object was to obtain the Pope's permission to return home.

Innocent had been put on his guard, and could not be unprepared for the tidings which they were charged to convey to him. He knew enough of what had gone on at Venice to suspect Dandolo. The propositions which had been submitted to him in November by Boniface had warned him that the leader of the army would be ready to play into the hands of the Venetians, in return for their support of Philip's designs in favour of young Alexis. It is probable that the proposals for a truce among the Western princes made by Innocent at this time were due to his desire to place difficulties in the way of the execution of these designs. If Otho could gain time by means of such a truce, he could form a league which might be sufficiently strong to occupy all the energy of Philip. Accordingly, when Bishop Nivelon and John de Noyon arrived in Rome, in the early part of February, the Pope was ready to hear their news. Before their arrival he had sent to Peter Capuano, who was in the neighbourhood of Zara, a solemn bull of excommunication against the Venetians, together with a letter which he was directed to forward to the army. 'Satan,' said he, 'has pushed you to flesh your swords upon a Christian people. You have offered to the devil the first-fruits of your pilgrimage. You have not directed your expedition against Jerusalem or against Egypt. Loyalty to the Cross you bear, respect for the King of Hungary and his brother, and to the authority of the apostolic see which gave you on this subject precise orders, ought to have prevented you from doing such wickedness. We exhort you to put a stop to the destruction, and to restore all the plunder to the envoys of the King of Hungary. Unless this be done you will be liable to the excommunication which you have incurred, and you will be deprived of all the benefits of the crusade which have been promised you.' The letter further required that the Crusaders should give written declarations under seal that they would not again attack Christian nations. The pardon granted to them was to be conditional on such declarations being made and observed. In particular they were to pledge themselves not to attack Greece, either under pretext that they would thus be able to bring about the union of the churches or to punish the crimes committed by Alexis the Third.

When the messengers arrived from the army, they did their best to excuse the conduct of the Crusaders, but they spoke to a man who was their superior in intelligence, and who probably was to a considerable extent behind the scenes. One of the knights who accompanied Nivelon and John de Noyon refused to explain the matter as the majority wished ; in doing which, says Villehardouin, he perjured himself. The others excused themselves to the Pope by saying that the Crusaders had done the best they could under the circumstances. They laid all the blame on those who had not come to Venice, and had thus placed the army at the mercy of the Republic. They declared that to help the Venetians against Zara was the only way of keeping the army together, and that in so doing they believed they had been acting in conformity with the Pope's wish.[1] Innocent expressed to the deputies his deep grief at the conduct of the Crusaders. *Report made to Innocent.*

Probably there were many interviews and much long and anxious consideration on the part of the Pope during the days which followed their arrival. They had left Zara, as we have seen, before the signature of the agreement for the restoration of Alexis (January 2), but they were probably aware that such a convention was contemplated. The conditional form of the absolution shows that the Pope had either heard from some other source of this pact, or believed it to be probable. After some time, he addressed to the barons a second letter. This was especially intended to influence the great body of the army. The Pope attempted indirectly to appeal to the rank and file against the leaders. The soldiers were not to be led away by any excuses. Innocent knew that they were not in the secret of the leaders. They at least had little to gain by the execution of Philip's projects, and cared nothing *He appeals to the army.*

---

[1] *Epist.* vi. 100 : ' Reminiscens de consilio vestro multa dissimulanda fore loco et tempore si Veneti ad dissolutionem stolii aspirarent.'

for political intrigues.   Hence, the Pope's policy of making
the absolution conditional upon their not again attacking a
Christian country was likely to have, as we shall see that it
had, a considerable measure of success.   Pardon was to be
granted provided they did not attack the Greeks.   The Pope,
addressing the leaders, did not offer them the usual saluta-
tions.   He was perforce compelled to grant them absolution if
the expedition to which he had attached so much importance,
and from which he hoped so much, were to have any chance
of success.   But even in doing so, he did not spare his reproaches.   He admitted the excuse of necessity which the
deputies had pleaded.   But reparation was necessary, and
this could only be made by restoring the whole of the booty.
He declared that the absolution given by the bishops was not
valid.   Cardinal Peter was instructed to receive their oaths to
be obedient henceforward to the Pope's orders, and Innocent
again declared that it was only on such an oath being sworn
and kept that the excommunication could be raised.   Those
who had offended must show their intention not again to invade a Christian country unless they were resisted, and must
ask pardon from the King of Hungary for the wrong they had
done him.

The sole concession which the Pope would grant was that
in case of need the army might take provisions from the
territory of the Greek Emperor.   Alexis was, however, to be
requested to give permission.[1]

At the end of March, Nivelon, Bishop of Soissons, left
Rome, the bearer of this conditional absolution.

[1] 'Nullus itaque vestrum sibi temere blandiatur, quod terram Græcorum occu-
pare sibi liceat vel prædari, tanquam minus sit apostolicæ sedi subjecta, et
quod . . . imperator Constantinopolitanus, deposito fratre suo, et etiam ex-
cæcato, imperium usurpavit. Sane, quantumcunque in hoc vel aliis idem imperator
et homines ejus jurisdictioni commissi, delinquant, non est tamen vestrum de
ipsorum judicare delictis, nec ad hoc crucis signaculum assumpsistis, ut hanc
vindicaretis injuriam, sed opprobrium potius crucifixi cujus vos obsequio spe-
cialiter deputastis. Monemus igitur nobilitatem vestram . . . quatenus nec
decipiatis vos ipsos, nec ab aliis decipi permittatis, ut, sub specie pietatis agatis
illa, quod absit ! quæ redundent in vestrarum perniciem animarum. . . . In
Terræ Sanctæ transeatis subsidium, et crucis injuriam vindicetis, accepturi de
hostium spoliis quæ vos, si moram feceretis in partibus Romaniæ, oporteret for-
sitan a fratribus extorquere.'— *Epist.* vi. 101.

Meantime Boniface and the leaders became anxious to explain to the Pope why they had concealed from the army his bull condemning their conduct. The messengers who had gone to Rome to ask for absolution would soon return, and would no doubt be aware of what the Pope had written. It would no longer be possible to conceal from the army the decision of the Pope, nor from the Pope the fact that his former letter had not been published. The barons had argued, no doubt, that to have published it would have greatly strengthened the malcontents ; that with daily desertions, with a desire openly expressed by many to break up the expedition, with the bitter feelings existing between the pilgrims and the Venetians, a statement of the Pope's solemn and formal condemnation would have put an end to the expedition. In the communication which Boniface and the other leaders sent to Rome they urged, by way of excuse, that everything had been done with the object of still carrying out the lawful designs of a crusade, and they protested that it was their intention to be obedient in the future to the pontifical orders.

When this communication reached Rome, the Pope knew the particulars of the plan to divert the crusade into an expedition against the New Rome. He knew that young Alexis had been sent for, and that his bull of excommunication had been intercepted. Instead of the deeds under seal he had asked for, he received but vague promises. For the moment he was bewildered.[1]

Both he and his Council saw the danger in which the crusade was placed of failing altogether.[2]

The hesitation of Innocent was, however, of short duration. He declared that the Crusaders had no right to interfere in the internal affairs of Constantinople.[3] He warned

Innocent's decision.

[1] ' Cœpit vehementissime dubitare quid in tanto negotio esset agendum.'— *Gesta Inno.* 93.

[2] ' Dominus papa cum omni clero suo, nunciisque nostris, aliisque quamplurimis, vehementer expavit, metuens ne maligni hostis invidia, hac occasione, vel totius nostri exercitus machinaretur interitum, vel saltem crucis negotium impediret.'— Gunther, viii.

[3] ' Vos nullam in Græcos jurisdictionem habentes.'— *Epist.* viii.

them once more against being induced to attack Romania on the pretence of necessity.[1] The messengers from the army were sent back with letters from Innocent, in which the Crusaders were ordered to swear to be obedient, and were again warned that, if they refused, the absolution granted to them for their attack upon Zara was *de facto* null. A special clause in the oath to be taken contained a pledge that those who took it would not attack Greece. Cardinal Peter Capuano was deprived of his post as papal representative with the expedition. The letters of the Pope to the army were given into the charge of John Faicete and John de Friaise. Among them was one ordering that the bull which had formally excommunicated the Venetians should at once be published. John Faicete persuaded some of the leaders to send their written promises under oath to Rome. The influence of Boniface appears, however, to have been sufficient to prevent these promises from being generally made. A few were forwarded in an incomplete form during April.

Innocent was yet sanguine that the crusade would soon leave for Egypt. Though he had abundant evidence which showed him that influences were at work to prevent the crusade accomplishing its legitimate object, he did not know how strong these influences were. Though he had a profound distrust of Venice, and would not grant the Venetians his absolution, he could hardly have believed that she had become a traitor to Christendom. He had seen an army collected together with the utmost care, its plan of action carefully considered, submitted to himself, and adopted ; and he knew of no reason why this plan should be abandoned. We have now to see the last step which had to be taken in order to divert the expedition from its purpose.

[1] ‘ Cessantibus potius occasionibus frivolis et necessitatibus simulatis.’ *Epist.* vi.

CHAPTER XII.

IN the beginning of April 1203 the bearers of the Pope's message arrived at Zara. That message consisted of two parts : first, a confirmation of the absolution which had been granted by the bishop ; and, second, the formal order that the Crusaders were not to attack the Greeks except in case they refused to sell them provisions.[1]

The first part of the message was communicated to the army. There is no evidence to show that the second was, and there is much to suggest that it was not. It had been arranged that Alexis should join the army on the 20th of April. He might arrive at any day, and it would then be no longer possible to conceal from the great host the secret arrangement which had been concluded in January. His arrival would, therefore, be extremely inopportune. The disaffection in the army was great. The example of Simon de Montfort and others, whose departure I have already mentioned, had been largely followed by many who were unwilling to violate their oaths. The Pope's order not to attack Greece, if, as I have suggested, it were kept secret, might become known. The ill-feeling between the army and the Venetians, which had shown itself by the rioting immediately after the capture, still existed. All were weary of inaction, and wished to be

---

[1] 'Quod si forsan ea vobis contingeret denegari . . . possitis et vos cum timore Domini sub satisfaciendi proposito, ad necessitatem tantum, ea sine personarum accipere læsione' (*Epist.* vi. 102). ' Permittebat etiam eis ut, de maritimis locis Romaniæ, quam alluit id mare, cibos inemptos, id est, absque pretio, moderate tollerent, qui eis ad annum et dimidium possent sufficere ' (Gunther, No. 8). 'Ne autem victualia vobis desint, charissimo in Christo filio nostro, Imperatori Constantinopolitano scribimus, ut . . . victualia vobis faciat exhiberi ' (*Epist.* vi. 102).

on their way to fight the common enemy. If Alexis should arrive the army would then learn that the leaders proposed to divert the enterprise from its lawful purpose. Accordingly, every effort was made to send the Crusaders a stage further before his arrival. On the 7th of April the army left the city of Zara, and prepared to embark. The Venetians destroyed its walls, towers, and palaces, and razed the city to the ground.[1]

Zara destroyed.

The army and its convoy set sail from Zara for Corfu on the 20th of April. Dandolo and Boniface had arranged to remain behind to await the arrival of Alexis. Two galleys were left for their use. The Pretender arrived on the 25th of April, five days after the date which had been appointed. Without loss of time the two leaders and their charge embarked to follow the expedition. On their way they called at Durazzo, where a demonstration was made in favour of young Alexis. The inhabitants surrendered the city and swore fealty to him. On May 4 they arrived at Corfu. They found the army already encamped before the town. Every opportunity was taken to impress the Crusaders with the importance of having with them the 'lawful heir,' as Boniface called Alexis. Every possible honour and mark of respect was shown to him. His tent was pitched in the midst of the army, near to that of Boniface, who assumed from this time forward the part of his protector and guardian.

Army leaves for Corfu.

The arrival of Alexis rendered all further attempts at concealment useless, because it was now necessary formally to submit the change of plan to the approval of the host. It was clear to every man that the leaders intended that the expedition to Egypt should be postponed till the young man now among them was placed upon the throne of the New Rome. The pretence was still kept up that after this was accomplished the army would go upon its appointed mission. The great mass even of those who approved, and even perhaps some of the leaders themselves, believed that such a course was possible. What was certain was that they must go first to Constantinople. The barons and Dandolo assembled, and

Anon. Halberstadt p. 14.   Exuviæ I. *Devastatio*, p. 88.

before them Alexis solemnly ratified the convention of Zara. He promised them 200,000 marks. He would pay the cost of the navy for a year, would himself accompany them on their pilgrimage as far as he could, would maintain during his life an army of 10,000 men in the Holy Land, and would provision the army of pilgrims for a year.[1]

The convention had, however, now to be submitted to the army, which had hitherto been kept as far as possible in the dark. When this was done the dissatisfaction among a large portion immediately broke out. There were many men, no doubt, in so large a host who were willing to go in search of adventure or of plunder, and who cared little whether this were to be found in Syria or in the rich capital of the world. The majority of the Crusaders had, however, left their homes in no such spirit, and were righteously indignant when they found they had been duped by their leaders and the Venetians. They had been duped in many ways. They had taken up the Cross at the call of Innocent. The Pope, as they knew, believed the moment opportune for striking at Islam, and had thrown all his exceptional energy into the fulfilment of this the great design of his life. Innocent's influence had been cast against Philip of Swabia, and in favour of Otho. Yet from the moment of the election of Boniface they suspected that they had been duped into opposing the Pontiff's great design, and into supporting Philip's cause in Western Europe against the Pope. They recalled that immediately after his appointment Boniface had visited his relation Philip, an excommunicated prince, the avowed enemy of Innocent, and had remained with him for many weeks. In the army were many partisans of Otho, the rival of Philip, and they could not but see that in the subsequent conduct of Boniface he was doing that which would be looked on favourably by Philip as well as severely condemned by the Pope. Others had been wiser than they. Many Crusaders, as we have seen, had taken ship at Marseilles rather than trust themselves to the Venetians and to Boniface. Some of their German fellow-pilgrims had refused to leave home, or had returned, because

The convention submitted to the army,

---

[1] Robert de Clari, xxxii.

they foresaw that antagonism between Philip and the Pope was certain from the moment that Alexis was in Lombardy and Boniface in command. They recalled the treatment of the army while on the Lido, by which they were duped into consenting to fight for Venice ; the constant and ever-increasing rumour of an expedition into Romania, which was to be for the profit of the leaders and of Philip ; the destruction of Zara ; the fight between the Venetians and the Crusaders after the city was captured ; the Pope's censures, which could not be altogether unknown ; his absolution, strictly conditional upon their not repeating the offence ; the opposition of Simon de Montfort and so many of the army, who were determined to find their way to the Holy Land by other routes, because they were convinced that Boniface and Dandolo had no intention of carrying out the great plan which Innocent had approved. All their recollections showed them how completely they had been deceived, increased the discontent, and caused it now to culminate when all disguise was abandoned, and it became known to everybody that a convention had been entered into, by which, in spite of the Pope's express command, their destination had been changed from Egypt or Syria to Constantinople.

and arouses great opposition. In the short time which passed between the arrival of Alexis with Boniface and Dandolo in Corfu and the agreement subsequently arrived at, probably many meetings and much discussion took place. The Doge insisted much upon the necessity of obtaining the help which Alexis had promised, and pointed out that they had now a lawful excuse, a ' *raisnauvle acoison*,' to go to Constantinople, because they had the rightful heir. The leaders of the opposition, however, took the view they had adopted from the beginning. ' Bah ! ' said they, ' what have we to do in Constantinople ? We have to make our pilgrimage, and purpose to go to Babylon or Alexandria. Our transports are only chartered for a year, and half of that is already past.' [1] Their duty was clear ; they had not left home for plunder but for pilgrimage, and upon pilgrimage they would go. The same author gives the

[1] Robert de Clari, § xxxiii.

reply of the party of Philip : 'What shall we do in Babylon or in Alexandria, when we have no provisions or means of getting them ? Surely it is better to take the *raisnauvle acoison* to obtain meat and means for our journey than to go there and die of hunger.' The bishops were asked whether it would be a sin to go to Constantinople, and, as they were on the side of the Marquis, replied that it would not, because as they had the lawful heir they could help him to conquer his own and to be avenged of his enemies.[1] Nothing was said at Corfu of the union of the Churches. This pretext had only been put forward so long as it was hoped that the Pope might be won over.

The malcontents, however, united together, and decided to leave the army and join Count Gautier de Brienne, who then held Brindisi. Villehardouin mentions by name twelve great chiefs who joined the popular party, and he asserts that there were many others who had secretly agreed to join them, and that they had with them more than half the army.[2] The malcontents had formed a parliament of their own, had separated from their brethren, and occupied a valley at some distance from the rest of the army. Their cry was '*Ire Accaron*,'[3] a cry which probably indicates that the leaders of the dissentients recognised that with their diminished numbers it might be safer to go to Syria than to Egypt.

The danger was great. There was every appearance that the expedition would be broken up. The Marquis of Montferrat and the barons who were in his counsels were greatly troubled. 'If,' said the Marquis, 'these men leave us, after those who have already gone on many occasions, our army will be ruined and we can conquer nothing. Let us go to them, and fall at their feet, and beg their favour ; that, for God's sake, they will have pity on us, and will not dishonour themselves, and that they will not prevent us from delivering the Land of *Outre-mer*.'[4]

[1] Robert de Clari, xxxiii. and xxxix.

[2] Villehardouin, xxiv.

[3] 'Inter nos fuit magna dissensio et ingens tumultus : omnes enim clamabant Ire Accaron.'—*Epist. H. S. Pauli*, Tafel and Thomas, i. 304.

[4] Villehardouin.

The leaders acted on the advice of the Marquis. They went in a body to the valley in which the parliament of the malcontents was held, taking with them young Alexis and the bishops and abbots. When they arrived, the opposition barons were on horseback, but, on seeing the leader of the expedition and the bishops approach unattended, dismounted and went to meet them. The barons fell at their feet, wept copiously, and declared they would not rise from their knees until the others promised that they would not leave the army.

A com-
promise
is effected. Then, according to the melodramatic description of the Marshal of Champagne, there was a wonderful scene. Dandolo and Boniface and all with them wept. If Villehardouin is to be credited, there was never a greater flood of tears ; those from Dandolo and the leaders being mostly of the crocodile sort. The opposition leaders were filled with pity, and wept sorely when they saw their lords, their relations, and their friends fallen at their feet. They withdrew, conferred together, and after some time returned with a proposal for a compromise. They would consent to remain with the army until Michaelmas Day, provided that the leaders would solemnly swear on relics that after that day they would provide them with a fleet, in good faith, at a fortnight's notice, with which they might go to Syria.

This proposal was accepted. The leaders swore to observe the conditions. Apparently, immediately afterwards the convention of Zara was adopted by the whole of the army. The authors of the ' Continuation of William of Tyre ' allege that, in addition to the terms accepted by Alexis at Corfu, there were secret conditions by which Boniface of Montferrat and Baldwin of Flanders were each to receive 100,000 marks, and others of the chief barons smaller sums.[1] In other words, they were bribed to divert the crusade to the support of the cause of Alexis. Henceforward, some of the chief opponents became the firm supporters of Alexis.[2] The

---

[1] Ernoul, p. 361. This statement is confirmed by the fact that in the charter by which in 1204 Boniface ceded the island of Crete to the Venetians he includes the sum of 100,000 marks formerly promised to him by Alexis.

[2] Villehardouin, 284.

pilgrim host had now been changed from a crusading army into a filibustering expedition, and its history in the future is that of their adventures in sacking the noblest and richest city of the middle ages.

As soon as the convention of Zara was ratified, the leaders lost no time in hurrying on the preparations for embarkation. The quicker the evil deed could be done the better.

CHAPTER XIII.

FROM CORFU TO CONSTANTINOPLE.

THE expedition left Corfu on the 23rd of May, Whitsun eve. Villehardouin is again in raptures at the beauty of the spectacle presented by the fleet. It looked, says he, like one which could conquer the world. The sails of the vessels dotted the ocean from the shore to the verge of the horizon, so that the hearts of men rejoiced within them. All went well as far as Negroponte and Andros, at which latter island the leaders with young Alexis landed and received the submission of the inhabitants. The Marquis of Montferrat everywhere presented young Alexis to the population, and did his best to make the journey an imperial progress. On arrival at the Dardanelles the leaders and those vessels which had arrived with them waited a week until the galleys and the transports came up. They occupied the time in plundering the neighbouring country and gathering in the harvest, their own stores having run short. Then they sailed again, and on the 23rd of June anchored off the abbey of San Stefano, about twelve miles to the south-west of Constantinople and on the Marmora. The domes and churches, the walls and towers of New Rome were at length in sight. The view from San Stefano is not the most picturesque which can be obtained of the imperial city, but even in these days it is sufficiently imposing. The Crusaders were amazed at the sight before them. They could not have imagined, says Villehardouin, that there could have been in the world a city so rich as that which the high walls and higher towers now before them girt entirely round. No one would have believed that there could have been so many rich palaces and lofty churches if he had not seen it with his own eyes. Nor would

Expedition arrives before Constantinople.

he have credited that the city which was the sovereign among cities could have been so long or so broad. 'Be sure there was not a man who did not tremble, because never was so great an enterprise undertaken by so small a number of men.'

The Doge and the leaders landed and held a parliament in the church of San Stefano. Dandolo advised that before any attack was made the fleet should sail some ten miles away to the Princes' Islands, and that a stock of provisions should be gathered from the neighbouring coast. The advice was accepted and the leaders embarked once more. In the morning, however, there was a southerly wind which made a journey to the islands dangerous, but which took them pleasantly right under the walls of Constantinople into the Bosphorus. The walls are built at the water's edge, and were crowded with spectators as the fleet passed. The ships anchored off Chalcedon, probably in front of the present English cemetery.[1] The army disembarked, and formed an encampment upon the Asiatic shore, the city of Constantinople being in full view and only a mile distant. The harvest in the neighbouring country had been gathered in, and was at once seized by the Crusaders 'comme gens qui en avaient grand besoin.' The leaders took possession of a splendid palace belonging to the Emperor. On the third day the fleet went a mile further up the Bosphorus to Scutari and there anchored.

The Crusaders waited nine days in order to take in provisions and make their arrangements for an attack. During this time a skirmish took place on the Asiatic shore with a small body of imperial troops, who were completely routed, and the Crusaders obtained a considerable quantity of booty.

Meantime the Emperor was filled with alarm at the arrival of the Venetian fleet and the great Frank army. On the tenth day after their arrival he sent a messenger named

---

[1] This is usually spoken of as being at Scutari. It is, in fact, in a village between Scutari and Kadikeui, called Hyder Pasha, the latter being the name of a village, and not, as the Judicial Committee of the Privy Council stated recently, the name of a 'respectable Turkish gentleman.'

Embassy
from Em-
peror.
Nicholas Roux, a native of Lombardy, across the Bosphorus with letters of credence to the leaders. The barons met in council. The messenger announced that he had been sent by the Emperor to learn why they had come into his territory. 'You are Christians and he is a Christian. He knows well that you are on your way to deliver the Holy Land. If you are poor and needy he will willingly give you provisions and what he has, but on condition that you leave his territory. He has no wish to do you any harm, though he can do it.' The statement implies that he had no knowledge of their intention. It may fairly be presumed that such knowledge as he had was of a very vague character. He certainly had officially no knowledge. It is possible, and indeed probable, that spies or others had hastened on to Constantinople as soon as the destination of the army had been made known at Corfu. It is unlikely that more than a suspicion of what was going on can have been communicated to him at any period before the arrival of the army in that island.

Answer of
the
Crusaders.
Canon de Bethune replied to the imperial messenger on behalf of the Crusaders. He denied that they had come into the land of Alexis, because the occupant of the throne was not the rightful Emperor. The land belonged to his nephew, who was with them, the son of Isaac. The message he was to take back to his master was, that if Alexis would surrender his crown and Empire to his nephew, they, the Crusaders, would ask young Alexis to pardon him and to give him enough to live upon luxuriously. If the messenger did not return with an answer accepting these conditions, he had better not dare to return at all. The leaders seem to have been under the impression that there existed within the city a strong party in favour of Alexis. No doubt Philip, and possibly young Alexis himself, had done their best to persuade them that such was the case. The barons de-termined to give this party the opportunity to declare itself. The nephew of the Emperor should be shown to the people of Constantinople.

Accordingly they manned and armed all their galleys. Dandolo and the Marquis of Montferrat and young Alexis went on board one of them, and a crowd of barons and knights into the others. The walls of Constantinople then, as now, came down to the water's edge through two-thirds of their extent. The tideless waters of the Marmora and the Golden Horn are deep enough within ten feet of the walls to float larger vessels than the great galleys of the Venetians. The procession crossed the Bosphorus. The walls were crowded with spectators. The boats went quite near and then stopped. 'Here,' proclaimed some one on board the galley containing Alexis, 'here is your rightful lord. We have not come to do you any harm. We will protect you if you do what you ought. He whom you obey rules you wrongfully against God and law. You know how disloyally he behaved to his lord and his brother, how he put out his eyes and usurped his Empire. Here is the real heir. If you do not acknowledge him we will do the worst we can against you.'

The proclamation was received with laughter. The only answer given, and that in derision, was, 'We know nothing about him. Who is he?'[1]

The Crusaders returned to Scutari. Next day a parlia- ment was held to consider what steps should be taken for attacking the city. It was agreed that the army should be divided into seven parts. Baldwin of Flanders was appointed to lead the van, because of the great number of archers and crossbowmen who were under his command. The Marquis of Montferrat was to bring up the rear with the Lombards, Tuscans, Germans, and men from the country between Mont Cenis and Lyons.

The business in hand was felt to be a serious one. There was apparently no longer any disaffection. The consciences of all had been quieted or their scruples overcome by the prospect of rich booty. All that remained was to fulfil their part of the contract and to receive their reward. But many a stout heart quailed at the prospect of the difficult undertaking before them. No Spaniards under a Cortez or a Pizarro ever had an apparently more hopeless task, and, to

[1] Robert de Clari, xi.

the credit of the filibustering host, it must be added that none
ever succeeded more completely in the work of destruction
before them. The bishops and clergy in the army exhorted
the soldiers to confess and make their wills. Solemn religious
services placed the army under the protection of the saints.
Then the embarkation commenced. The knights with their
chargers went once more on board the huissiers or transports,
which were so constructed that either large ports or a portion
of the bulwarks opened readily, and could allow the knights
to ride across the gangways while mounted. The rank and
file, on board the larger ships, followed. The galleys were
manned, the fighting men clothed in battle array, and the
vessels themselves made ready for action. Alexis was
attended by numerous troops, and was treated with every
mark of respect. The next morning at daylight, everyone
being in his place, the trumpets sounded ; the signal for
starting was given, and the expedition set out on the last
stage of its journey to the imperial city. The knights had
their helmets laced, their armour on, while their horses were
arrayed in battle gear. Each galley took in tow one of the
The army huissiers with knights on board. The crossbowmen and
crosses the
Bosphorusy archers went first to keep clear the coast for landing.[1] No
other order of precedence was observed. The vessel which
could get over first did so. The distance from Scutari is
under a mile, and was soon covered. The knights, though in
armour, leaped overboard while the water was still up to their
waists, and, lance in hand, made for the shore. They probably landed near the modern Tophana, or between it and
the mouth of the Golden Horn. Some of the troops of the
Emperor saw the fleet approach, but they turned and fled
from the bowmen before the cavalry was landed. The dis-
embarkation was allowed to go on without interruption.

The entrance to the Golden Horn, the harbour of Constantinople, was guarded by a chain thrown across from the
city to Galata. On the Galata side, the end of this chain
was protected by a tower spoken of by the Western writers

[1] Robert de Clari, xli.

as the tower or castle of Galata.[1] The slope of the hill
behind it was the Jewry of Constantinople. Near it also
were probably Genoese and other Italian quarters, the whole
forming already a wealthy suburb. The Crusaders encamped
in the Jewish quarter, and prepared for an attack. It was
necessary for the protection of the expedition that the ships
should be brought within the harbour, and the Venetians
urged that an attempt should be made next day to capture
the tower within which the Galata end of the chain was fas-
tened.[2] The council of war agreed to this proposal, and
determined that such an attempt should be made immediately.
Fortune favoured them, and gave them their first success on
the following day. In early morning the ordinary guard of
the tower, assisted by a detachment which had crossed the
harbour, instead of remaining on the defensive, made a foolish
attack upon the invading army. The Greeks were far less
numerous than the enemy, and were completely overpowered
by the Crusaders. Many were killed ; others were driven
into the water and drowned. The remainder fled, and endeavoured to regain the protection of the castle which they
ought not to have left. The enemy, however, pressed them
so hard that they were unable to close the gates. A severe
struggle took place, and the superior weight of the knights
triumphed. The castle was captured. While this attack on
the watch tower had been going on by land, the Venetian
ships were doing their best to break the chain which was
stretched across from Galata to the city. The capture of the
tower gave the army command over this chain. It was at
once broken or loosened. The fleet entered swiftly into the
Golden Horn, attacked the imperial galleys, captured some
and sank the others.[3] The surprise was complete ; the victory,
both by land and sea, brilliant and unexpected. It is hardly
too much to say that it was the beginning of the end, because
the weakest portion of the walls were those facing the Golden

and takes possession of Galata.

The fleet is surprised.

[1] This must not be confounded with the present Galata tower, which is at the
apex and highest point of the triangle formed by the walls of Galata, and was
not built until two centuries later.
[2] Robert de Clari, xlii.   [3] Nicetas, p. 719.

Horn and within the harbour. The Greeks scarcely realised at the time how great was their loss, but the elation among the Venetians and the Crusaders showed the importance they attached to the event.[1] Readers will remember that in 1453 the defence of the harbour was so strong, by means of the chain and the fortifications, that Mahomet, in despair of breaking through, had to obtain possession of the harbour by transporting his boats over the neck of land between the modern Tophana and the valley now known as Cassim Pacha. Galata was then, however, a walled city, and the Turkish ships were probably much smaller than those of Venice.

Venetians and Crusaders were rightly of opinion that the advantage they had gained should be immediately followed up by a general attack. No attempt at negotiations appears to have been made. A bold, sudden attempt was to be made before the Emperor should have time to organise a defence Four days only were spent in Galata, and these were occupied in transporting their stores, in preparing for battle, and in determining upon the plan of attack. The Venetians were naturally in favour of making the principal assault by sea.

Arrangements for an attack by land and water. Their proposal was to take their ships close up to the wall on the north side of the city, and throw out ladders from the ships to the walls—a feat quite capable of execution, as subsequent events showed. The Crusaders as naturally preferred fighting on land. The difficulty was overcome by the arrangement that the Venetians should attack by sea, while the army endeavoured to effect an entrance through the landward walls. The army passed round the head of the Golden Horn, crossing by a stone bridge which the Greeks had destroyed, but which the Crusaders were able, by working day and night, to repair in time for the attack. On the fifth day after the capture of the port, the army took up its position opposite the palace of Blachern, which was at the north-west corner of the walls, facing on one side towards the Horn, on another landwards.[2] This was the one position where fleet and army could bring their forces to act simultaneously on contiguous portions of the defences. The palace occupied the corner,

had many outworks, and, though it had no fosse, it was
strongly fortified. The position taken up by the army was
at Gyrolemna. No camping-ground could have given the
Crusaders a better idea of the wealth and strength of the
capital. The hill behind them enabled them to have, perhaps,
the most picturesque view of the beautiful city they were
about to attack. Point beyond point stretched out, under the
July sun, into the blue waters of the Golden Horn. In the
immediate foreground were the new walls which Manuel had
built to fortify Blachern.[1] Behind these walls rose the superb
palace of the Emperors, which had now, rather than the palace
of Bucoleon, or, as the Crusaders called it the Lion's Mouth,
on the side of the Marmora, become their favourite dwelling-
place. Churches, the great law courts, columns, and towers
rose one behind the other in infinite confusion, until, on the
last hill, was the church of the Divine Peace, adjoining that
which was at once the richest and most beautiful building of
all, the great temple dedicated to the Divine Wisdom of the
Incarnate Word. The strength of the city might be judged
from its landward walls, which were immediately before them.
The wide moat, except on the immediate descent to the
Golden Horn, was well filled with water, though this had to
be kept up by a long series of dams, while a wall immediately
behind it could only be assailed from the bed or the waters
of the moat itself. When these obstacles were passed, there
remained a second and a third wall, each higher than the
former. The short distance between the towers with which
each of these walls are studded enabled the occupants to have
an enemy well within range even of the simple machines with
which, in that age, stones could be hurled upon an invader.
All that the best mechanical science of the most civilised
nation in Europe could do towards making the triple walls
strong had been done Nor were these fortifications untried.
Again and again in the history of the city they had proved
stronger than the power of any invader. Not to speak of
less important sieges, it may possibly have been known to
some of those who now sat down before these walls that the

[1] Nicetas, p. 311.

great horde of Arab invaders which had been checked in its
hitherto irresistible progress had been encamped on almost
precisely the same spot which Boniface and Baldwin now
occupied.   The site is among the most interesting in the
world.   Occupied, within a half-century, by two invading
hosts of Arabs which had spent their strength before the
virgin city, and which had been as completely defeated by
the Romans as were the Moors who had crossed the Pyrenees
by Charles Martel, it was destined to be the place from which
the city was to be destroyed by Western Europeans.   Two
centuries and a half later it was to witness a greater triumph
over the city—a victory which was to inflict upon the Balkan
peninsula four centuries and a half of barbarism.   The army
of Mahomet, the second of the Ottoman house, was encamped
on the same corner, and effected its entrance at a point very
little outside the grounds which were enclosed within the
palace walls of the Blachern.   On a portion of this historical
site the mosque of Job, or Eyoub, now marks the supposed
burying-place of the great leader of the chief Arab attempt
upon the city.   The mosque is regarded with more sanctity
than any other now in the city.   No unbeliever is allowed to
enter it.   Within it is kept the sacred banner of the prophet,
and no Sultan is considered invested until he has been girt
with the sword of Osman, which is treasured within its sacred
walls.

As soon as the crusading army had taken up its position
at Gyrolemna, the Greeks within the city sought to harass
them.   Their efforts, however, were feeble.   Several sorties
were made under the command of Theodore Lascaris, son-in-
law of the Emperor.[1]   The Crusaders enclosed their camp with
palisades until their preparations were completed.   In the
meantime the Venetians had drawn up their fleet in such a
manner as best to co-operate with the army.

On the 17th of July everything was prepared for an assault.
Three out of the seven divisions guarded the camp under the

---

[1] The sorties were made most commonly from a gate above the palace of
Blachern, probably therefore from the very same gate which in 1453 was the first
to fall into the hands of the Ottoman Turks.

leadership of Boniface, while the remaining four made the attack under the orders of Baldwin. The outside wall, an outwork of the imperial palace, near if not actually on the sea, was defended partly by Pisan auxiliaries,[1] but mainly by the Waring guard, *les Anglois et les Danois*, as the Western historians call them. This was the position first attacked by the army. Two scaling ladders, or probably wide platforms, were thrown against the wall. The assault was '*fort et bon et dur*,' and by sheer force fifteen of the boldest among the Flemings managed to win a position on the wall. There they fought shoulder to shoulder with their swords against men of their own race armed with Danish bills. The struggle on the wall was fierce. The Warings steadily recovered ground, drove their daring assailants back, and captured two of them. The Crusaders were not able again to gain even a temporary foothold on the walls. The first attack had failed on the landward side.

The first attack is made,

On the seaward side the Venetians were more successful. The brave Dandolo, old and blind, the gonfalon of St. Mark flying proudly over his head, directed the attack from his own galley. No precaution that long experience could suggest was neglected by him. The ships had been carefully cased and covered with raw hides so as to resist the famous Greek fire. Scaling ladders, or rather bridges, had been provided in great numbers, which could reach from the ships' cross-trees to the walls. These were formed of the ships' yards, with sails and skins, so completely protecting the fighters that it was almost impossible for arrows to reach them. They were so wide that three knights could advance abreast.[2]

The fleet was drawn up in line three crossbow shots long opposite the walls. The order was given to advance as near the shore as they could get. This was done under a tremendous discharge of stones from mangonels placed on the towers. In spite of this opposition the ships pushed boldly ashore. Their stems were moored to the land, and anchors were thrown out from their sterns. Each huissier had a

---

[1] Nicetas mentions the Pisans and the Warings. Villehardouin speaks only of the latter.   [2] Robert de Clari, xli.–iii.

mangonel. The stones thrown in immense quantities by the Romans were returned by the Venetians, and the return shots were better aimed. The Venetians succeeded during the attack in destroying the outer wall of the palace with a battering-ram.[1] The bolts came in abundance from the crossbows. The scaling-ladders thrown out from the ships' tops were so close to the walls that the contending soldiers fought together with lance and sword. A fierce hand-to-hand fight went on for some hours without interruption. The galleys had at first not ventured to run their bows on to the land, but had remained astern of the transports. Dandolo determined that everything should be dared. He commanded his own crew to put him on shore on the narrow strip of land a few feet broad, between the walls and the water, and threatened his followers with death when they hesitated to obey. The old man and those with him leaped on shore. When the men in the other galleys saw the gonfalon of St. Mark carried on shore over the head of their fearless leader, they rushed to defend him. The enthusiasm spread throughout the fleet. Numbers of men from the transports and the barges leaped into their boats or into the water and landed. The order was given that a general attack of all the Venetians should be concentrated upon a short distance of the walls. A battering ram was brought to bear against one of the towers. Those who worked it were defended by a crowd of crossbowmen. While this thundered at the walls below, hundreds of men were fighting from the scaling-ladders, and trying to win or to hold a position on the walls. Presently the gonfalon of St. Mark was seen flying from one of the towers. For awhile the defenders were panic-stricken and fled. Immediate advantage was taken of this success. Twenty-five towers were captured by the Venetians before the Greeks could rally. The invaders pushed beyond the walls, but a new detachment of the imperial troops, consisting of Warings and Pisans,[2] came up and drove them back to the towers, but from the latter even the Warings were not able to dislodge them. In order to render their hold on the fortifications less liable to

---

[1] Nicetas, p. 721.   [2] Nicetas, p. 720.

attack, or perhaps, as Villehardouin asserts, in order to cover their retreat, the Venetians set fire to the neighbouring buildings. The fire spread rapidly, and burnt a large mass of buildings.

While this fighting about the seaward towers was going on, a sortie of the imperial troops took place from the gate of St. Romanos, at a considerable distance from the camp. The Crusaders immediately abandoned their attack, and drew themselves up behind their palisades. Villehardouin alleges that against their six battalions the imperial troops were forty, and an even greater discrepancy is represented by Robert de Clari.[1] The former adds, however, that they could only be attacked in front. The tidings of this incident were at once conveyed to Dandolo, who immediately withdrew his forces from the towers and hastened with as many men as he could muster to help the Crusaders. The Emperor brought his troops opposite to the pilgrims. Neither side dared to begin the attack. After considerable marching and countermarching the imperial troops commenced to retire. The Crusaders rode slowly after them, but no fighting took place.[2] This movement was watched by the ladies of the palace, who crowded the windows and walls.

The results of the general attack had on the whole been in favour of the defenders. The army of the Crusaders had been beaten back. The Venetians had indeed obtained possession of twenty-five towers, but they had not been able to hold them. The great loss to the citizens was occasioned by the fire lighted by their enemies.

and fails.

---

[1] Ch. xliii.

[2] The account of this sortie given by Robert de Clari represents it as occupying a considerable time and engaging much more attention than the reader of Villehardouin would suppose.

CHAPTER XIV.

FLIGHT OF THE EMPEROR ALEXIS AND RESTORATION OF ISAAC.—
REVOLUTION IN THE CITY.

THE most useful ally of the invaders was the spirit of indifference and discontent which reigned within the city.
While this spirit paralysed the efforts of the defenders, there
was probably also a small but active, although secret, party
in favour of Isaac and of young Alexis. The latter had
made many promises to his friends within the city, and had
urged them to assist him.[1]

Feeling within Constantinople. The dissatisfaction with the ruling Emperor was great,
and was doubtless increased by this party. The enemy
without had not asked for possession of the city. There
was nothing said even about an occupation. All that was
demanded was that a young prince, who undoubtedly had
claims to the throne if his father were dead, should replace
Alexis the Third. There was indeed a payment to be made,
though it is doubtful whether the terms of the convention
with Alexis were at this time known within the city, and
even if they were the payment might perhaps be avoided,
or at least levied on the provinces. At any rate, it was
better to come to an arrangement with the enemy when his
demands were so reasonable than to fight.[2] Moreover, there
was now a distinct threat that if an arrangement were not

---

[1] Gunther, xiii.: 'Cives itaque magnificæ urbis, territi fuga regis sui, quem
etiam plerique nec prius propter scelera perpetrata satis dilexerant, simulque per
nuntios a juniori Alexio promissis ac precibus frequentibus attentati, nostris quo-
que, contra spem suam, comminantibus excidium urbis, nisi illum legitimum here-
dem regni in regem susciperent, patentibus portis, illum cum toto exercitu infra
mœnia pacifice admiserunt.'

[2] Nicetas says (p. 721) that the object of the assault was, ὡς ἢ τῶν κατὰ
σκοπὸν ἐπιτευξόμενοι ἢ τούτων διαπεσόντες ἐς συμβάσεις βλέψοντες· ἀμφότερα γὰρ
ἡ φήμη διπταμένη λαμπρῶς ἐκώτιλλεν.

made the city would be destroyed.[1]   Accordingly there was considerable murmuring within the city.   The many dynastic troubles within the experience of the inhabitants made them think lightly of a change of rulers.   Alexis the Third had done nothing to make himself respected.   He was now informed that if he did not deliver his subjects from the enemy, they would declare for the younger Alexis, and would make him Emperor.[2]

In spite, however, of these threats, I am disposed to think from the narrative of Nicetas, who knew better what went on within the city than any of the Western chroniclers, that the great mass of the inhabitants of Constantinople were indifferent rather than hostile to the Emperor.   The majority of the inhabitants had long lost all interest in dynastic changes.   The experience of the last generation had accustomed them to see one sovereign deposed and another placed on the throne, until they had come to look on depositions or attempts to obtain the throne as matters with which they had little concern.   Apathy in regard to political changes very closely resembled that which exists now in Constantinople.   I have been present in the city during the deposition of two Sultans.   The most striking characteristic in the circumstances attending these depositions was the utter indifference of the great body of the native, and especially of the Moslem, population to the change which was being made.   There was a small but active party which took action, but beyond this there was comparatively very little excitement ; no resistance, no rioting, no expression of dissatisfaction.   When newspaper correspondents and foreigners generally were aware that a revolution was in preparation, it is impossible to believe that thousands of Turks and rayahs were in ignorance of the fact.   The general feeling among the Sultan's subjects was one of indifference.   If the conspirators failed it would go hardly with them.   If they succeeded it would go hardly with the Sultan.   *That* business only regarded the parties concerned.   Beyond a vague belief that any change could hardly be followed by a worse

[1] Gunther, xiii.   [2] Ròbert de Clari, ch. l.

condition of things than had existed, there was no public sentiment on the matter.   In 1203 the frequent dynastic troubles
and the influences of Asia had brought the people to the
same indifference to any mere change of government.   The
inhabitants in the besieged city knew that a few years before
Isaac Angelos, who was still in prison, though his eyes had
been put out, had been deposed by the present ruler, Alexis,
just as the Turks of to-day know that a deposed Sultan is
imprisoned somewhere on the Bosphorus, but in neither case
did they regard the matter as of any consequence.   The
besieged in 1203 knew that the son of Isaac, the young
Alexis, had persuaded the Venetians and a body of Latins,
through the influence of his sister's husband Philip, to assist
him to regain possession of the Empire, and that he and his
friends were now outside the city walls.   The Latins did not
wish to capture the city.   Even if they did, stronger armies
than this had tried to do so and had failed.   If the invader
won there would be a new Emperor—that was all.   Indeed,
why should the citizens care ?   They had no love for the
reigning sovereign nor he for them.   When he heard that
young Alexis was coming with a band of Venetian pirates,[1]
he made no preparations for resistance.   He was a mere idle
lover of luxury, an Eastern Charles the Second, who thought
only of the ills of to-day ; an essentially weak man, too sentimental to be a successful ruler.   He shrank from inflicting
the cruelty of ordinary punishments, and still more from that
which was necessary to make him a strong despot.   Though
he had not hesitated to depose his brother, he was either
conscience stricken or pretended to be so, and continually upbraided himself.   The eunuchs, says Nicetas, who
guarded the royal forests with as much care as the Destroying
Angel guarded Paradise, threatened to kill anyone who ventured to cut timber for the construction of vessels.   The
Emperor's brother-in-law had sold all the navy stores.   Those
who thus robbed the public seemed rather thereby to gain in
the estimation of their sovereign.   The Emperor appeared
more amused than frightened with the preparations of which

---

[1] Nicetas calls them πειρατικοί, p. 715.

he heard, and it was only after he learned of the proclamation of his nephew which had been made at Corfu—and this
he could only have learned a few days before the arrival of
the expedition in the Bosphorus—that he concerned himself
with the means of defence. But even then the voluptuary
and the drunkard could not set himself with sufficient energy
to meet the danger. When the expedition had arrived and
the Crusaders were encamped opposite the imperial palace,
he wished to withdraw from the city. His relatives, however, and the ring which always surrounds an Eastern despot
urged him to resist on their account. It was they who forced
him to make a show of defence. The bravest among them
was the Emperor's son-in-law, Theodore Lascaris. When, as
we have seen, the seaward towers around Blachern were
taken, and a part of the city set on fire, his subjects openly
reproached him with cowardice, and it was then, probably,
that the threats of which Robert de Clari speaks were
uttered. Perhaps it was under the influence of these threats
that he had been induced to lead his army outside the walls
on the occasion mentioned. Lascaris begged hard to be
allowed to attack the Crusaders.[1] The Emperor, however,
was either afraid or possibly believed that as the city never
had been captured it never could be.[2]

The retreat, according to Nicetas, encouraged the Latins.
It strengthened the party of Isaac within the city. Even indifferent men argued that if there were no arrangement there
should at least be fighting, and if an army more numerous
than the invaders had yet been forbidden to attack, it was
time to change their sovereign. The cowardly voluptuary
had, however, no intention of making resistance. The same
night he fled ignominiously from the city. He told Irene,
his daughter, and several other women of his intention; took
ten thousand pieces of gold, a number of precious stones and
imperial ornaments,[3] and embarked, deserting his wife and
children, his throne and people.

The Em-
peror
leaves the
city.

---

[1] Nicetas, p. 722.
[2] Nicetas charges the Emperor with cowardice, and is probably right; but he
is so continually unfair, not only to Alexis but to all the Comneni, that his
account has to be received with caution.   [3] Nicetas, p. 723.

The flight of Alexis filled the city with alarm. Constantine, the minister of finance, however, assembled the troops

and declared for Isaac. The blind old Emperor was led, or rather carried, out of prison, placed upon the throne, and once more treated as the Emperor of Rome. As soon as he understood the situation he sent the news of his release to his son, to the leaders of the Venetians, and to the Crusaders. His great anxiety was to hear once more his son's voice.

The Venetians and Crusaders could scarcely believe the tidings of the flight of the Emperor and the restoration of Isaac, and suspected treachery. Boniface of Montferrat called a council. The news had been brought during the night, and the leaders immediately armed themselves, as Villehardouin says, 'parcequ'els ne croyent pas beaucoup les Grecs.' Boniface and the Venetians had apparently never contemplated that such a step as a restoration of Isaac would have been taken. In the negotiations directly with Philip, in the pact of Zara, in the proceedings at Corfu, no writer gives the slightest indication that a thought had ever been given to the possibility of the restoration of the old Emperor. If the design of Philip and of Boniface had not been to join the imperial dominions of the East and West, as I venture to think that it was, the Swabian king at least intended to keep his hold over Constantinople through the young Alexis. The desertion of the Emperor Alexis was a gain to the party of Philip, but the resurrection of Isaac from the tombs of the Blachern was a severe blow. This party had posed before their deluded followers as the asserters of right. They had dwelt on the justice of punishing a usurper who had deposed and blinded the anointed of God. They had pointed to young Alexis as the exile deprived of his rights and fleeing for his life ; the bishops had expressly authorised the siege on the ground that the Crusaders might punish a wrong and defend the right. Boniface and Dandolo had urged the importance of having with them ' the rightful heir.' The very existence of Isaac seems to have been ignored. Perhaps even there were doubts whether he still lived. If he did he was blind, and by a well-recognised practice could not be

Emperor. The sentiment of chivalry to help the weak against the strong, the oppressed against the oppressor, had been roused, but always in favour of Alexis and not of his father. In a night all this was changed. The oppressor had fled. The Crusaders learned that one who had been oppressed far more than the youth among them had been brought out from his dungeon, and was now occupying the throne of which he had been wrongfully deprived. The first order was to arm, the first thought probably to snatch the prize out of the hands of Isaac. Reflections, however, soon convinced the party of Philip that this could not be done at once. For the moment they would have to acquiesce in the settlement which had been arrived at. The simple-minded Crusaders would be unable to find fault with the citizens for placing the father of Alexis on the throne, of which he undoubtedly was, according to Western notions, the rightful occupant. The only pretext for remaining in Constantinople would henceforward be that they wished to be paid according to their bargain. Isaac had sent word, says Villehardouin, that he was willing to ratify the promises that had been made by his son.

Boniface was probably unwilling to allow Alexis to escape from his influence, but replied that the heir to the throne would not be permitted to enter the city until these promises had been formally confirmed by the father. Accordingly, Villehardouin himself and Matthew of Montmorency, chosen to represent the Crusaders, with two Venetians, were sent to convey a reply to this effect to Isaac. At the gate of the city the messengers dismounted, and passed through a lane guarded on each side by Warings, *les Anglois et les Danois*, with their axes, to the palace of Blachern. When they entered they saw before them Isaac and his wife, the sister of the King of Hungary. The messengers, after being received with every honour, told the Emperor that they wished to speak to him in private on behalf of his son and the leaders of the army. Accordingly, the Emperor, his wife, the chancellor, and the interpreter, with the four messengers, passed into a private room. It had previously been arranged that Villehardouin should speak on behalf of the messengers, and

Deputation from expedition enters the city.

he gives us the substance of what he said. He called attention to the service which the army and the Crusaders had
rendered to his son, and to the fact that they had kept their
part of the bargain. As to his son, he would not be allowed
to enter the city until he had given security for the execution
of the obligations he had undertaken. Young Alexis now
asked through them that Isaac should confirm the contract
which the youth had made, both as to substance and manner
of execution. 'What is the contract?' said the Emperor. 'I
will tell you,' said Villehardouin. 'First and foremost, there is
the promise to put the Empire of Romania under obedience
to the Pope; afterwards to give 200,000 silver marks to the
army, and provisions for a year to small and great; to transport 10,000 infantry and cavalry in the proportion that we
shall designate in his vessels, and at his expense, into Egypt,
and to keep them there for a year; and to maintain in the
Holy Land, and at his expense, during his life, 500 knights to
protect it. This is the contract which your son has made.

Contract of
Alexis con-
firmed by
Isaac. He has confirmed it on oath by charters with pendent seals,
and by the guarantee of King Philip of Germany, your son-
in-law; we now ask you to confirm it.' 'Of a surety,' replied
the Emperor, 'the convention is very hard, and I don't see
how it can be carried out, but still, you have done so much for
him and me, that if one gave you the whole of the Empire
you would have deserved it.' The result of the interview was
that the father confirmed his son's agreement by oath, and by
letters patent with the gold seal or imperial bull. The
messengers returned to the camp bearing the precious document. Probably the same day young Alexis was conducted
by the chief barons into the presence of his father. The
Greeks received him and his friends with great feasting and
rejoicing, and with every mark of respect.

The revolution had been accomplished rapidly. Alexis the
Third had fled on the night of the 18th of July. Next day
Isaac had been placed on the throne, and had again been
allowed to see his son. During the next ten or eleven days
there appear to have been many negotiations between the
Emperor and his son on the one side and the leaders of the

expedition on the other. The great result which Boniface obtained was that Alexis should be associated with his father as Emperor, and as a joint occupant [1] of the throne. Apparently, before this decision was accepted by Isaac, and probably as a condition precedent, it was arranged that the Crusaders and Venetians should retire across the Golden Horn.

On the 1st of August, 1203, young Alexis was crowned Emperor together with his father Isaac in the Great Church with the usual pomp. He at once set about the payment of the 200,000 marks promised to the Venetians and Crusaders. Enough was received to enable each Crusader to pay back the price that had been paid for his passage at Venice.[2] The treasury, however, was empty. The drain upon the resources of the population in order to pay the foreign army was naturally unpopular. The young Emperor was not secure of his throne. He accordingly proposed to the barons a new arrangement. The agreement between the Venetians and the army was to terminate at Michaelmas. The new Emperor declared with simple truth that he could not pay within so short a term ; that he would lose his throne if the Crusaders left him, and would be killed by his own subjects ; and that the Greeks hated him on account of his friends the Crusaders. If they would stay till the following Easter he would bear their expenses up to that time, and would pay the Venetians their freight for the fleet for a year. If these terms were accepted, his revenues after harvest would have come in from the provinces, he would be able to pay what he had promised, to preserve his throne, and to go with them, or at least to send an army.

It is found impossible to pay the expedition within time stipulated.

Then the old trouble once more broke out. The party of the Marquis recognised, says Villehardouin, that the Emperor's statement was true, and that his proposal was the most advantageous one possible under the circumstances. On the other hand, the bargain at Corfu had been that after Michaelmas those who had come out for Holy War, and had no wish to join in an expedition against a Christian city, should be free to go, and should have a fleet provided for

Differences in the army.

<hr />

[1] Villehardouin, § 193.   [2] *Ibid.*

their transport to Syria. The compromise had been confirmed by the most solemn oaths. This party now claimed
its fulfilment. 'Baillez-nous les vaisseaux, ainsi que vous
nous l'avez juré ; car nous voulons aller en Syrie.' Dandolo
and Boniface readily accepted the imperial proposal. The
first, because of the treaty with Malek Adel, not to introduce
the Crusaders to Egypt, for though Syria was spoken of it
was by no means clear that the original plan would not be
adhered to ; the second, with the object of serving Philip and
himself. They could now use stronger arguments than at
Corfu. They had begun the business and must finish it. It
was dangerous to go down to Syria or to Egypt in winter.
They could do nothing at that season even if they were there.
The cause of the Lord would be lost. 'Wait till March, and
we can then leave the Emperor in a good position. We can
then go with plenty of money and of provisions.' Again and
again Villehardouin insists that the aim of the malcontents
was to break up the army. 'They cared,' says he, 'neither
for better nor for worse, provided that the army should be
divided.'

Once more it is worth recalling that his object is to
explain why the army of Crusaders did not accomplish its
object. The Venetians accepted the proposal, and bound
themselves to hold the fleet in readiness for a year from

Postpone-
ment de-
cided on.

Michaelmas. The opposition, feeble now in comparison with
what it had been at Corfu, found itself in far too small a
minority to prolong its resistance, and thus the proposal of
Alexis was accepted by the Crusaders also.

Position of
Alexis.

In truth, the position of the young Emperor was exceedingly critical. He had gone himself to Galata to make his
proposal, and although he probably wished that it should not
be published, it is pretty certain that its tenour would be
known within the city. If he indeed stated that his subjects
hated him on account of his having been brought there by
the Crusaders, and would kill him if he were left without
their help, he probably told the truth. Nicetas says that the
new Emperor had changed the ancient faith, and had re-
nounced the ancient rites of the Romans to follow the new

laws of the Pope. The Crusaders had probably been cajoled into the belief that to bring the Greeks into subjection to Rome would be a success which would ensure for them the Pope's absolution. The hint of such an intention had become known, and was of itself sufficient to arouse the hostility of every member of a Church as jealous of foreign interference as that of Rome. But the great cause of hatred towards Alexis was, no doubt, because he was associated with the enemy. So long as the question had been merely one of a change of ruler, public opinion had hardly existed. There is no reason to suppose that the citizens had known of the agreement which had been made by Alexis. Now, however, that he was on the throne, and had made unheard of demands for money, with which to pay his supporters, now that the process of robbing the churches and extorting large sums from the wealthy citizens had commenced, and now that one of the conditions which this youth had accepted was that he was to place the Church of the New under that of the Elder Rome, popular sentiment was altogether against him. If the invaders were to be bought off at once, it would have to be with money raised in the city itself. If the payment could be postponed, a large portion might be raised in the provinces.

It is possible also that Boniface saw that he had blundered in consenting to allow Alexis to enter the city. The latter was a weak youth, who, so long as he had been with the Crusaders, had been under the influence of his guardian. Now that he had become Emperor, Mourtsouphlos and a few others, who took the lead among the citizens, became his advisers. From them he soon learned how difficult was the execution of the contract which he had signed. It became important to Boniface to place the young Emperor again under his own guardianship and influence. After all Isaac was weak, blind, and old. He could not last long. He might probably easily be deposed. Provided that young Alexis would do what was wanted, the designs of Boniface and of Philip might yet not miscarry. With the object, partly of recovering his lost influence and partly of preventing his falling

Boniface and Alexis leave for Adrian-ople.

under that of the popular leaders within the city, Boniface and a portion of the army agreed to go with Alexis to Adrianople, in order to pursue the late Emperor, Alexis the Third, who had fled to that city, and to help also young Alexis to reduce his subjects to submission. Boniface probably recalled the influence which he had obtained at Corfu and in the islands of the Ægean, while accompanying Alexis as guardian. It might be hoped that again he would have the youth entirely in his power, and that thus the design of Philip to obtain either direct sovereignty over the Empire, immediately or at some later period, could be carried into effect. Accordingly, the proposition to accompany Alexis was accepted, by the advice, says Villehardouin, of the Greeks and the French. Baldwin of Flanders remained behind in command of the remainder of the army.

A second fire in Constantinople.

During the absence of Alexis a second fire, more destructive than the first, broke out within the city. The fire deserves to take rank among the great historical conflagrations of the world. Even Constantinople, which has always been particularly liable to great fires, never saw its like. In the value of the wealth consumed, in the influence of the fire in striking terror into the population and exasperating them against the invaders, and in thus influencing the fate of the Empire, few similar disasters can compare with it in interest. The circumstances attending it are also remarkable, as throwing light on the relations existing during the joint reign of Isaac and Alexis the Fourth between the citizens and foreign invaders. Shortly after the arrival of the Crusaders, the mob attacked the wealthy Pisan quarter within Constantinople and on the shores of the Horn. It was not surprising that they should have done so. Nicetas says that the untaught masses did not distinguish between friend and foe. They knew that the invaders were all Latins—that is, members of the Western Church, that the fleet which was in the harbour was from Venice ; and it was natural that a mob should not make the distinction between the inhabitants of one or another Italian city. Many houses belonging to the Pisans were destroyed. The wealthier portion of the population did what they could to assist the Pisans to save their property, and to explain to the mob that though Italians they were not allies of the Venetians. On the other hand, it is, to say the least, highly probable that a considerable number of the Pisans had fraternised with the Venetians, and had thus awakened the hostility of the Constantinopolitans. Greek and Frank writers agree in saying that Crusaders and Venetians went over in considerable numbers from Galata [1] to see the rich palaces, the richer churches, and the other marvels of the imperial city. The Italians and Burgundians in the army spoke the same language as the Pisans, and it is probable that even the Frenchmen did not find much difficulty in making themselves understood by them. This alone would tend to make them sympathise with the Italians, and when it is remembered that they were all of the Church of the Elder Rome, and that the people among whom they were living had long been jealous of their commerce, it is easy to see that there were many common sentiments and interests which worked towards bringing the Latin inhabitants and the invaders together. Nicetas tells us expressly that the Pisans and Venetians were reconciled, and adds that the reconciliation was the work of Isaac.[2] The consequences of the attack made upon the Pisan quarter were twofold : first, this understanding with the Crusaders was improved ; and, second, many of the Pisans were so alarmed that they fled across the Golden Horn to Galata, and took up their residence with their fellow-countrymen and co-religionists. Meantime, whilst constant and daily visits were paid by the foreigners to the Great Church and the marvels at the east end of the city, the old Emperor was receiving daily visits from the Italian and crusading chiefs at the Blachern palace in the west. They were received, to the disgust of the Romans, says Nicetas, as saviours of the Empire and as benefactors. The Emperor melted down the statues and even the sacred vessels of the churches, in order to supply their insatiable greed.

---

[1] Pera and Galata are always confused by the Western writers, or rather the present distinction did not exist. All was Pera *across* the Horn. The immediate slope was Galata. [2] Nicetas, p. 731.

For a few days the growing hostility between the citizens and the invaders was restrained.   But on the 19th of August an incident occurred which gave the spark necessary to cause an explosion.   Some of the Flemish soldiers, accompanied by Venetians and Pisans, crossed the harbour in order to pillage the Saracens.   Under the system of capitulations, which has always prevailed in Constantinople, these Arab and other Moslem traders were allowed to have their own quarters and their own mosque even within the city.   This building stood near the Pisan quarter, on the northern slope, and between the church of the Divine Peace [1] and the sea.   Probably the Crusaders regarded the existence of such a building as a cause of offence, just as a London mob in the seventeenth century so regarded the existence of a Roman Catholic chapel in their midst.   We may fairly conjecture also that the Pisans regarded it as a special object of detestation, because it had been built in the neighbourhood of their khans for the use of rival traders as well as miscreants.   The Flemings and Crusaders looked upon the wealth of the Moslems as their lawful prey.   The Saracens were found in their mosque and were surprised. The Christian mob rushed in upon them, and at once, at the point of their swords, made them give up all the property that could be found.   Their Roman neighbours came, however, to their assistance.   A disgraceful riot took place, in the course of which the robbers set fire to the city in several places.   The fire commenced near the mosque, and was carried by a strong north wind [2] across the peninsula to the Marmora.   Then the wind changed, and a new district was devastated.   The fire lasted two days and nights. [3]   A large

Attack upon a Saracen mosque.

[1] Nicetas, p. 733.   [2] Nicetas, p. 733.

[3] So says Villehardouin. Others say eight days, and the continuator of William of Tyre nine days. All accounts agree that the fire was of a terrible character. Nicetas implies that it occurred before the departure of Alexis with Boniface. This may be so, but he is always so violent against the Emperor that it is impossible to trust his statement. For example, in this place he affirms that while Isaac was greatly troubled at this sad accident, Alexis, ὁ τῆς πατρίδος δαλός, who had a face like that of the greatest incendiary, the Destroying Angel himself, would have liked to see the whole of the city reduced to ashes (p. 734). The statement of Villehardouin that the fire was during the absence of Alexis is

portion of the richest and most thickly populated quarters of the city was entirely destroyed. A wide belt across the peninsula from the harbour to the Marmora was left a heap of ruins. The width of the fire was at one time, according to Villehardouin, half a league. The inhabitants of this burnt strip lost everything they had. The houses, says Nicetas, were enriched with many precious ornaments, and were full of various kinds of valuable property. No one, says the Marshal, can estimate the amount of the wealth which was destroyed, while many men and women perished in the flames.[1] The barons and leaders regretted the fire, 'furent bien tristes et eurent grand pitie,'[2] when they saw these beautiful churches and splendid palaces being consumed and the great commercial streets burning, but they could do nothing.

The natural result of the fire was to intensify the ill-feeling which existed between the Latins and the citizens. The brutal soldiery of the West had caused the fire, and had been brought into the city by Italian colonists. It was not surprising that the citizens no longer cared to protect any Italians within their walls. None of the Latins, says Villehardouin, dared remain any longer in the city. They escaped with their families and such property as they could save from the fire, and, crossing the harbour, took up their abode with the Crusaders. Fifteen thousand thus fled.

On the 11th of November the Emperor Alexis returned to Constantinople, and was welcomed by the Crusaders, and, according to Villehardouin, by his own subjects. The old friendly relations between the young Emperor and the host which had accompanied him from Corfu continued for a time. Alexis, however, soon lost the respect of both his own subjects and the pilgrims. He had come into his Empire. His one idea was to enjoy it. But the condition of the city made this impossible within its walls, and for enjoyment he had to return to his old comrades. He passed days and nights in

Return of Alexis from Adrianople.

confirmed by the *Chronique de Munic* (Tafel and Thomas). See also Eracles, *Recueil,* p. 270.
[1] Villehardouin, § 204. [2] *Ibid.* § 203.

drinking bouts with the invaders and at play. He was 'hail-fellow, well met' with all. He allowed those who were at the gaming table with him to take off his imperial diadem, and to replace it by one of their own woollen caps. He soon became despised, says Nicetas, by every honest man, both among the Romans and among the Crusaders.

Condition of Isaac.

Meantime his wretched father was filled with jealousy at the honours accorded to his son. Isaac appears to have been almost entirely ignored by the Western host—partly, no doubt, because of his feeble condition, and partly because Boniface and Dandolo found a readier instrument in Alexis. He complained that he was not treated with sufficient respect, that his son was intriguing against him. Probably his long imprisonment, his sufferings as a common prisoner, and the loss of his eyesight combined to make him ill-tempered, and had injured his health. He became more than ever the victim of superstitious fears. The monks by whom he was surrounded promised that he would become the lord of a great empire, that he would recover his eyesight, that he would be cured of gout or rheumatism, to which he was a martyr, and Isaac was weak enough to believe them.[1] The astrologers persuaded him to transport into the Great Palace from the hippodrome a statue of the Calydonian boar, under the belief that by so doing his enemies would be destroyed, as the enemies whom the original boar was sent to attack had been rent in pieces.

Confusion in the city.

Since the fire the condition of the city had been one of confusion. The Romans hated Crusaders and Venetians as the cause of all their ills, especially of the heavy taxation and of the two fires. A trivial incident, mentioned by Nicetas, shows how great was the irritation. The mob broke up one of the finest statues in the city, a representation of Minerva in bronze, which stood in the great square of Constantine. The statue faced to the West, and in the imagination of the people appeared to be beckoning the natives of the West towards New Rome.

The Crusaders were still encamped in Galata, and after

[1] Nicetas, p. 737.

the flight of the foreign residents do not appear to have
entered the city. They were becoming impatient to be paid.
Alexis let them have what he could. But the money only
came in driblets,—' pauvre petits payements,' as Villehardouin
calls them. Alexis was doing his best to satisfy his former
friends. Their protection had become as dangerous as their
enmity, and Alexis would probably now have been glad to
get rid of them. The two Emperors endeavoured again to
levy a tax upon the city, but the people rose against it. They
therefore did their best to raise the sum necessary from the
wealthy class of the population, and by melting down the gold
and silver vessels, chandeliers, and other valuable metallic
furniture of the churches. Meantime the Crusaders were
helping themselves. They were naturally, says Nicetas, the
enemies of every kind of beauty. They went about in bands,
and plundered the beautiful villas of the wealthy nobles and
the rich churches which were on the neighbouring shores of
the Marmora. It pleased them even to burn and destroy
many of the villas. The inhabitants resisted, and sent to
the city for soldiers to defend their homes. No help
was, however, there to be obtained. The monk-ridden and
imbecile old Emperor was powerless. The worthless and in-
experienced youth was unable or unwilling to assist them.
Reproaches were addressed almost daily by the Crusaders to
the Emperors, but without effect, except to bring in new
' pauvre petits payements.'[1] Indeed, during November and

[1] Villehardouin, xlv. Villehardouin says Alexis commenced to pay immediately
after the coronation (1st August, 1203). The payments to the army enabled those
who had not paid to repay what had been paid for them at Venice (xl.).

Robert de Clari states that 100,000 marks were paid, of which half went to
the Venetians, together with 34,000, balance of unpaid freight, while the rest—*i.e.*
16,000 marks—repaid the Crusaders who had advanced money to the Venetians
for their poorer brethren's passage.

Gunther declares that half of the promised sum was ordered to be paid :
' Dimidiam promissæ pecuniæ partem principibus nostris benevole ac liberaliter
numerari jussit ' (xiii.).

Nicetas says that, in conference between Dandolo and Mourtzouphlos in St.
Cosma, the Doge demanded immediate payment of fifty centenaria of gold, or
about 120,000 marks (p. 751).

One-fourth, therefore, of the promised sum of 400,000 marks agreed to a
Zara appears to have been paid almost immediately after the coronation, 1st August.

December 1203 and January 1204 the confusion within the
city and the anxiety without were of a kind which we, who
have seen Paris besieged, may fairly realise. The rule of the
city was rapidly slipping out of the feeble hands of Isaac and
those of his son. The imperial orders were disobeyed. The
demoralisation of the populace, caused by taxation, by the
interruption of commerce, though the city was not yet besieged,
and by the fires, had ruined half the traders, and increased
daily. The foreign residents had left. The ordinary business
of life was at a standstill. The troops were divided in their
allegiance ; the Warings remaining faithful to the Emperors,
the Greek troops being some on the side of those who were
clamouring for the deposition of Isaac and Alexis, some
probably willing to recall Alexis the Third, and some few
willing to remain faithful to the reigning sovereigns.

Dissension
and anxiety
in the
army.

Across the Golden Horn the condition of the invaders
was one of extreme anxiety. The opposition wanted to be
gone about their lawful business. Their provisions were
running short, and had to be replenished by raids upon the
surrounding country. Dissension and dissatisfaction were
increasing daily. Alexis had declared that it was impossible
for him to execute his promises, and the Crusaders knew that
what he said was true. The citizens dared, says Gunther, to
forbid the Emperor to take from his own property and give it
to foreigners. The Crusaders, on the other hand, he declares,
were loth to attack the city because they had no hope of
success. They were in such danger that they were not safe
around the city, nor could they leave without great risk.
Hence it came to pass, says this writer, that ' our men determined to besiege the city from which they could not flee.'[1]
Another author describes the situation of the army in equally
striking terms. The Franks were between the hammer and
the anvil.[2]

The invaders, however, had the great advantage over the

Then came in the 'pauvre petits payements' during September, October, and
December. Probably in all there was little if anything short of 200,000 paid by
the end of the year.

[1] Gunther, x.-xv.
[2] Rostan gnus of Clugny, p. 133, *Exuviæ Sac.*

citizens that they had two leaders who knew precisely what they wanted, and who intended to make every sacrifice in order to succeed. Though the chiefs and the soldiery might be restive, there was yet a military and a feudal discipline. There never appears to have been a murmur of discontent among the Venetians. Gunther again and again insists on the determination of the Venetians, 'who drove us earnestly this way, partly because of the promised reward, and partly from their desire to obtain the dominion of the sea.' The expedition, which, he adds, had been undertaken to please King Philip, was now solely directed by Boniface and Dandolo. The brave old leader, whose tenacity of purpose it is impossible not to admire, ruled the host by his nod, and, in spite of want of provisions, of secret disaffection among the troops, and of open opposition, was neither to be frightened nor wearied out of the accomplishment of his purpose. Boniface had blundered, had lost his hold over Alexis, and seems, since his return in the beginning of November from Adrianople, to have been gradually losing ground. Still he, too, had his object, for which he was prepared to make every sacrifice, and so long as Dandolo was willing to hold out he, too, would defy disaffection and opposition.

Ostensibly, all that Boniface wanted was to be paid. In reality, nothing was further from his desire. No other grievance remained.[1] No other pretence is alleged by any writer. The great chance of making payment impossible was to insist upon its being made at once. The Emperors were doing their utmost, and Isaac had scandalised the Greeks by selling church ornaments to raise money.[2] The revolution within the city might result in the substitution of a strong man in lieu of the two feeble occupants of the throne. In such case, not merely would the great conspiracy of Philip and Boniface fail, but payment itself might be altogether lost, or terms might be offered to the Crusaders which the malcontents would have sufficient influence with the army to cause to be

Doubtful whether payment was desired.

---

[1] This reason is assigned in Villehardouin, Gunther, the *Halberstadt Chron.*, and Rostangnus.

[2] Nicetas and *Chron. Novgorod.*

accepted. Whether payment were made or the latter alter-
native adopted, the invaders would have no pretence to
remain longer before the city. There were, therefore, many
reasons, some of which weighed with the army, while others
had especial influence with Boniface, in favour of demanding
immediate payment and of precipitating a struggle.

A struggle
is precipi-
tated. The barons, therefore, held a parliament, at which Dandolo
was present, and determined to send a deputation to the
Emperor, in order to bid him pay or to publicly insult him by
defying him to battle. The Venetians and the barons each
chose three of their number for this bold mission. Among the
latter was Villehardouin himself. The six rode round the harbour to the palace of Blachern girded with their swords. The
Marshal points out that they adventured much and went in
great peril on this enterprise. They descended at the palace
gate, and were admitted into the imperial chamber. The
Emperors, seated on their respective thrones, side by side, together with the Empress, Isaac's wife, and a large assembly of
nobles, received them. The messengers reminded the Emperors
of their oaths. ' We come,' said Conon de Bethune, addressing
apparently only Alexis, 'to summon you in the presence of
your barons to fulfil the agreement made between you and
us. If you fulfil it, well ; if not, take note that the barons
will recognise you neither as lord nor as friend, but they will
consider themselves free to take that which belongs to them
in any way in which they can get it. They give you notice
that they will do you no harm till they have defied you.
They will not betray you ; it is not the custom in their country
so to do. You have heard what we have said, and you will
take counsel upon the matter as you like.'

The noise which this public challenge made in the city
was great, as no doubt Boniface and Dandolo intended that
it should be. The messengers returned to the camp, thinking themselves fortunate, as Villehardouin admits, that they
had escaped with their lives. It is hardly necessary for
him to add, that the Greeks took this defiance as a great
insult, and remarked that no one had hitherto dared to
challenge the Emperor of Constantinople in his own palace.

There was now open hostility between the inhabitants and the invaders, and each side prepared to oppose the other. The Greeks made a night attempt to burn the Venetian fleet. They prepared seventeen boats, set fire to the wood and various combustibles with which they had been loaded, and at midnight on New Year's Day, when a strong southerly wind was blowing, turned them adrift. The attempt, however failed. A few persons were injured, and a Pisan merchantman was burnt with her cargo ; but the Venetians with their boat-hooks managed to push the burning ships away from them to the mouth of the harbour, where the strong current which is always running soon carried them out of the way of doing harm. A week after the Greeks made a sortie with their cavalry, but were repulsed.

Open hostilities commence.

Within the city the confusion increased daily. The people were convinced that they had nothing to hope from either Emperor. They had at length awakened to a sense of danger. The question was no longer one of a mere change of rulers, but one of fulfilling a contract to which they were no party, of paying a band of robbers who were without the walls for a service which their young Emperor had requested, but which they had not desired, and for which they certainly had no reason to be grateful. What they wanted was a ruler who would not allow them to be plundered. They saw an enemy which had already done them grievous wrong, and were burning to be delivered from him. The policy of Alexis seemed to the citizens to be to sacrifice everything in order to keep on good terms with their enemies. Even the Crusaders admitted that he was doing what he could for them. He was divided between loyalty to his own subjects and fear of displeasing Philip of Swabia and his late companions.[1]

Revolution in the city.

[1] Gunther (xv.) says : ' Videres eum graviter anxiari, quasi medium inter suorum nequitiam et amorem nostrorum, et gratiam Philippi regis, quem si nostros vel falleret vel læderet, graviter metuebat offendere. Cum ergo ad tantum facinus non facile posset impelli Murciflo ille, cujus superius fecimus mentionem, cujus consilio pater ejus cæcatus, et ipse in carcerem retrusus fuerat, eum propria manu suffocavit, dicens : " Minus esse malum, si solus ipse presenti vitæ foret exemptus, quam si totius Greciæ opes ad ignotos quosdam homines ejus stultitia transferrentur " (ch. xiii.).

The leaders of the citizens had asked the Emperors to take the offensive, to attack the Crusaders, and make an end of the matter, but these Emperors were either unwilling or afraid to do so. The attempt on the ships was apparently the result of a popular impulse. The same popular sentiment urged the party to get rid of their imbecile rulers. The impulse seems to have been general, for amidst the popular movement no attempt appears to have been made to suppress the rising which took place against the government. During some time the people were undecided as to the course they ought to adopt. Meetings were held in the Great Church, and each day saw the confusion increase. As day by day passed, however, one man was steadily coming to the front. A certain Alexis Ducas, a member of the imperial family, and nicknamed Mourtzouphlos, on account of his meeting eyebrows, headed the discontented party, and became the leader of the revolution.   He had for a long time been known as the bitterest opponent of the Latins.[1]

On the 25th of January, 1204, an extraordinary meeting of the inhabitants was held in Hagia Sophia. The senators were there, and the members of the college of pontiffs and other high dignitaries of the Church. The senate was a survival of the early days of the New Rome, and had long since ceased to exercise any real authority.   In the midst of the anarchy which now prevailed public opinion turned for support to its mere semblance of power, and senators and pontiffs were forced by the threats of the multitude to deliberate on the election of a new Emperor. They wished to temporise, but the multitude protested that they could not and would not live under the actual government.   The names of the members of the reigning family and of other nobles were gone through, and apparently submitted to the public assembly of the citizens.   The meeting, however, could not agree upon a choice.   Those who were selected refused to act. Some of the magistrates present were themselves asked to become Emperor. A second and a third day were spent in these meetings. Finally the choice fell upon a young man named

[1] Villehardouin, p. 221.

Nicolas Kanabos, who was, however, chosen against his will. Alexis and Isaac knew what was going on, but were powerless. Isaac was ill. Alexis, alarmed for himself, seeing that whoever the next Emperor might be the citizens were at least determined that he should no longer reign, feeling that power was rapidly slipping away from him, and that but for the presence of his foreign guards his own life would be in immediate danger, took what under the circumstances was perhaps a natural act, but what was nevertheless justly regarded by the citizens as an act of treason. He sent to the Marquis of Montferrat, and invited him to fill the palace of Blachern with Frenchmen and Italians, in order to defend his life and maintain him on the throne. This treason to the city cost him both his throne and his life.

On hearing of what Alexis had done, Mourtzouphlos decided that the time had come for him to act. The minister of finance was in his favour, but the imperial guard of the Warings, who knew that their duty was to defend the Emperor, constituted a serious obstacle to any attack on the occupant of the throne. It is probable that, as foreign mercenaries, they were by no means favourably regarded by the people. The very fidelity for which, as we have seen, they were so justly esteemed by the imperial family, even in the time of Anna, made their opposition on the present occasion the more probable. The object of Mourtzouphlos was now to secure the person of Alexis, either by inducing him to leave the palace or by withdrawing the Warings themselves. The latter course was found to be the easier. The Warings were therefore deceived, and led to believe that in leaving the palace they were to fight for Alexis. The guards being thus withdrawn, Mourtzouphlos undertook to secure Alexis. As *Protovestiarios*, he had the right of entrance to the palace. This he made use of, entered, and, according to the narrative of Nicetas, told the young Emperor that there was a mob coming to the palace and ready to tear him in pieces on account of his proposal to introduce the Crusaders into the city. Alexis fell into the trap. His only thought was to save himself, and instead of remaining in his palace and

Alexis is deposed and a new Emperor proclaimed.

awaiting the return of the Warings, he wrapped himself up so as not to be recognised, and followed Mourtzouphlos out of the palace walls. When he reached the tent of the leader he was immediately put in irons and sent to prison. Mourtzouphlos seized the imperial insignia, assumed the vermilion [1] buskins, and was saluted as Emperor.

Kanabos was abandoned, and the elect of the citizens was crowned with the usual formalities in Hagia Sophia. Isaac, already very weak, died on hearing the news of his son's arrest. Alexis did not survive him beyond a few days. He was imprisoned, and on the 1st of February he also died. Whether his death was a natural one, as his successor affirmed, or whether, as Nicetas and Villehardouin declare, he was strangled, it is impossible and immaterial to say.

The new Emperor, Mourtzouphlos, had an impossible task to perform, but he set himself to work in a vigorous manner to organise the defence. The treasury was empty. Everything was in confusion. The army was disorganised. Such navy as had existed had already been destroyed. A large portion of the city was in ruins from the fires. He at once ordered a heavy contribution from the wealthy classes, and insisted upon the money being paid. He immediately set energetically to work to improve the defences. Men worked day and night in heightening the walls on the harbour side, and in fortifying the gates on the landward side. The Emperor encouraged citizens and soldiers by his presence, now at the works, now in leading the attacks that he organised upon the foraging parties of the enemy. His conduct confirmed him in the confidence of the people. He was hampered, however, by the old aristocratic spirit of the wealthy nobles. To them he was objectionable because in such a time he refused to recognise their privileges. He insisted on their help, and subjected them together with the rest of the inhabitants to the severity of discipline of a city in a state of

---

[1] Vermilion and not purple was the imperial colour in the New Rome. The Œcumenical Patriarch still signs with vermilion ink, maintaining in this as in several other matters the traditions of the Empire. The Western writers generally speak of vermilion, though sometimes also of scarlet, tents, &c., as if no distinction were made between the two colours.

siege. They feared his voice, says Nicetas, like death. His energy seems to have entirely won the confidence of the imperial guard. They probably resented his conduct in withdrawing them from the palace while he obtained possession of Alexis ; but when they subsequently learned that the Emperor had proposed to bring in the enemy, they consented to join Mourtzouphlos.[1] There were doubtless men among them who had left England rather than endure Norman tyranny, and such men had now no wish to treat Normans and Frenchmen as friends. Had the Gambetta of this revolution been able to have delayed the attack upon the city, it is possible, and even probable, that he would have saved it. The writers on the side of the Crusaders and Venetians speak of the new Emperor in a manner which shows that they believed they had now a much more formidable opponent to deal with. His great object was to save time. The enemy also saw, however, that in their interest no time should be given him.

The deposition of Isaac and Alexis gave Boniface and Dandolo the excuse they wanted. So long as the 'right heir' and his father were reigning within the city, the only pretext which the leaders could put forward for remaining before it was the merely mercenary one that they were waiting to be paid. Now, however, that they were deposed, that Isaac was dead, and Alexis, their late guest, a prisoner, and now murdered, as they believed, the leaders could again pose as the defenders of the right, as the avengers of the injured. 'Never,' says Villehardouin, 'was so horrible a treason committed by any persons as the deposition and imprisonment of young Alexis.' All agreed, he adds, that the murderer had no right to reign, and that all who had consented to the deposition were accomplices in the murder. The clergy once more used their influence at the bidding of Boniface, and preached to the Crusaders that war in such a case was lawful and right ; and added that if they intended to conquer the

Effect of revolution upon invaders.

---

[1] The author of the *Chronicle of Novgorod* charges Alexis, when the Greeks sent their fire-ships against the Venetians, with having given notice to the Franks beforehand. *Ch. Nov.* p. 96.

land and place it in obedience to the Pope, they would have
the Pontiff's indulgence.   Crusaders and Venetians alike
appear to have been content with this assurance.   We shall
see presently that, while some were appealed to on the ground
that it was their duty to punish murderers, a more substantial
inducement was held out to all by the prospect of a rich
harvest of plunder.

The city was divided.   To understand its division it must
be remembered that the citizens knew little or nothing of the
plans of the enemy.   Boniface appears, on the death of young
Alexis, to have been regarded in the city as a candidate for
the imperial throne which his ward had lost.   The death of
the latter would probably increase the resentment of his
friends ; and the nobles, who formed the bulk of his party in
the city, never worked heartily for Mourtzouphlos.   This was,
no doubt, the party which, as we shall see later, hailed Boniface
as king.   Mourtzouphlos had had as yet insufficient time to
organise his forces, but meantime was acting bravely, was
superintending and pushing on the repairs, and was harassing
the enemy.   The Crusaders and Venetians, on their side, were
equally active.   During the days which followed the accession
of the new Emperor, and before the death of Alexis, an incident
occurred which is worthy of note.[1]

Fighting was going on daily.   The neighbouring country
was scoured in order to lay in a stock of provisions preparatory
to the attack and the siege.   One of these raids was made
during the end of January as far as Philies,[2] near the Black
Sea entrance of the Bosphorus, where Henry, the brother of
Baldwin, Earl of Flanders, led an expedition and captured
great quantities of cattle and provisions.   Mourtzouphlos,
hearing of their departure, endeavoured to surprise them.   A
sharp skirmish took place, in which he was defeated
and narrowly escaped being taken prisoner.   The imperial

[1] Gunther says that Mourtzouphlos did his utmost to conceal the death of
Alexis, and sent messengers continually, in the name of the young Emperor, asking
the leaders of the army to enter the city, but that Dandolo persuaded them not
to go.

[2] Possibly Kilios.

gonfalon [1] was captured, and a banner which represented the Virgin, by which the Greeks set great store.[2]

Profiting by the occasion presented by this defeat, Boniface appears to have entered into negotiations with the Emperor in order to save the life of Alexis.[3] All hope of carrying out the design of Philip of Swabia was not lost so long as the life of Alexis was safe. The message may even have been given in the form in which the Russian monk reports it : 'Give us Alexis, and we will depart and allow you to remain Emperor. We have been forced to come here through necessity.' The answer was that the application was too late. Alexis was dead.[4] It is impossible to tell what was the full signification of this message, but, read in the light of the surrounding circumstances, it appears to me to point to a distinct divergence between the Crusaders and the Venetians. Boniface and Dandolo found themselves forced to work together, but each distrusted the other and was jealous of him. At this moment the great object of the first was to save the life of his pupil ; that of the second was to make an arrangement with Mourtzouphlos impossible. A mission had arrived from the Holy Land, with which was Abbot Martin, urging the Crusaders to lose no time in going to the aid of those who were fighting the Saracens. The old spirit of dissatisfaction was once more showing itself. Possibly already some news of the intention of the Pope, as shown by a letter ordering them to leave for the business of the crusade, had reached them.[5]

The design of placing Alexis on the throne was at an end with the death of the young man, and even if Boniface had knowledge of the arrangement made between the Venetians

(Margin note: Negotiations between Mourtzouphlos and Boniface.)

---

[1] Codinus says that the Emperors had twelve ensigns which were used in public ceremonials, one or two only of which were employed when the Emperor took the field. The emblem of the city has always been the crescent, probably derived from the horns of a bull (βοῦς), which was the symbol of the Turanian race, as that of the lion was of the Arian. Each regiment had its own flag or βάνδον, whence we still speak of a band of soldiers.

[2] Villehardouin, 227-8, and Nicetas, p. 751.

[3] *Chron. Novg.* 95 ; *Chron. Grec.-Rom.*, Hopf.

[4] '*Iste obiit* ; *venite et videte*,' *ib.* 95. See also Epist. Baldwin, *Cron. Altinat.* p. 192.   [5] Inn. III. *Epist.* vi. January 23.

and the Sultan of Egypt, he had no interest in prolonging the stay before Constantinople. The failure of the object of the expedition had added largely to the number of the malcontents, and it may well be that Boniface felt inclined to give way to them. If this were so we can well understand the jealousy which undoubtedly soon displayed itself towards Dandolo. But the latter was now master of the situation. The Crusaders were almost as much at the mercy of the Venetians as when they were on the Lido. Provisions were short. January and February are in Constantinople cold and stormy months. The Venetians could urge the necessity of waiting for fine weather before they embarked. Their money was spent. They were to some extent as one writer says, ' between the hammer and the anvil,' and were compelled to follow as Dandolo led. The next negotiation was therefore one in which there is no evidence that Boniface took any part, just as in the one already mentioned there is nothing to show that Dandolo had any share. Each leader was playing for his own hand. The common bond of union had not yet been found.

Attempt to capture the Emperor.

A meeting took place between the Emperor Mourtzouphlos and Dandolo in order professedly to discuss conditions of peace. The meeting was held at the monastery of St. Cosma, which was about half a mile without the walls of Blachern.[1] The Doge asked for immediate payment of fifty centenaria of gold,[2] and imposed other conditions which were exceedingly hard, among which probably was obedience to the Romish Church. Dandolo must have known that his conditions were certain to be refused. While the two leaders were together, a detachment of the Crusaders' cavalry made a descent from an adjoining hill with the object of capturing the Emperor, and would have succeeded if he had not fled. Some of his body guard were indeed captured.[3]

[1] The monastery of St. Cosma is repeatedly mentioned by the Byzantine writers. Du Cange, *Cos. Christ.* p. 127, discusses with his usual deluge of learning where it was situated, and arrives at the conclusion I have adopted. The position agrees with that given by Nicetas, who says that Dandolo crossed in a galley, while the Emperor rode thither.

[2] Nicetas, p. 751.

[3] Nicetas (p. 752) is the authority for this statement. It is not improbable,

No further attempt at negotiation appears to have been made either by the Venetians or the Crusaders. Boniface had failed, and had probably no wish to come to an arrangement when he learned that Alexis was really dead. He could no longer carry out the design of Philip to unite the two Empires. Two courses were open to him : to go with the Crusaders to Egypt or to Palestine, or to throw in his lot with Dandolo. His oath, the wishes of the better portion of his troops, the command of the Pope, the call from the messengers who had come from the Holy Land, urged him in one direction. But to leave Constantinople was to admit himself beaten, and to be submitted to the reproaches of the Crusaders for the failure of the expedition up to the present. The chances of success against the infidels were now far less than they had been. Even supposing that Boniface knew nothing of the treaty between Venice and the Sultan of Egypt, the difficulties before a crusading host were largely increased. The expedition organised with so much care by Innocent had been divided, and all who had taken part in it had up to the present time been unfortunate. The messengers with whom Abbot Martin had arrived told how the Flanders fleet, which had wintered in Marseilles, and which had more Crusaders on board than those who were before Constantinople, had failed in Syria. Great numbers had been stricken down with country fever and had died. The rest had returned home. They related also how those who had gone to Prince Bohemund in Antioch, who was fighting for the Armenians against the Turks, had been slaughtered or captured to a man.

The Venetians, moreover, were not yet paid, and would never consent to transport the army. It would be necessary, if Boniface wished to lead his army against the infidels, either to pay the Venetians or to fight them. To do the one was impossible. To do the other was inexpedient. If the Crusaders defeated Dandolo, his army would be at the mercy of the Greeks. If Dandolo should succeed, he was equally ruined. The Crusaders at least were between the hammer and the anvil.

and indeed is likely enough, if Gunther's story is true that the Emperor had tried to decoy the leaders into the city.

Advantages of acting with Dandolo.

The second course, on the other hand, to throw in his lot with Dandolo, offered innumerable advantages. The richest city in the world was before them. Its inhabitants were divided. Its defences had already been proved to be vulnerable. Its soldiers had shown themselves less valiant than his own host. The Crusaders and Venetians alike would fight heartily in order to have the looting of such undreamt-of wealth as they had already seen. The disaffected in the army, who were uninfluenced by the bait of plunder, could be brought over under the plea that the dearest object of Innocent, after the defeat of the miscreants, was the union of the two Churches, and that in attacking the Greeks they were punishing them generally for their schism, and specially for their share in the deposition of their lawful ruler. The temptation of plunder, added to the excuse that they were in the path of duty and of obedience, would overcome the most scrupulous. And then, the greatest inducement of all to Boniface presented itself. If the city were captured a new Emperor would have to be chosen. Who so certain of success as he? He was the chosen leader of the crusading army. Baldwin of Flanders and the other princes of the army had never pretended to dispute his supremacy. He had hitherto carried everything before him. The malcontents at Venice, at Zara, at Corfu, and before the city had been powerless. He had but to triumph once more, and he would be Emperor of the New Rome. He had done his best, as even Philip must admit, for young Alexis. The Swabian king could not blame him if, after all his loyal efforts, he should now fight for himself. The prospect was too dazzling to admit of indecision. He threw in his lot heartily with Dandolo and declared for the siege.

An attack is decided on.

In conformity with the practice followed throughout the expedition it became necessary to assemble a parliament to decide on the next step. This met probably in the early days of March. We have no information as to what went on in reference to the proposal to attack the city. What is certain is that the parliament agreed to it. We know also that the meeting was long and stormy. 'On y parla assez, en avant et en arrière,' says the Marshal. The result arrived at confirms the natural presumption that there were two, and probably even three, parties. The interest of the Crusaders was opposed to that of the Venetians. But the Crusaders were still, as they had always been, divided. The malcontents who had been opposed to the expedition to Constantinople distrusted and were disgusted with Boniface, and, though they were not able to have their own way, were sufficiently powerful at least to thwart his plans. It was decided that if the city were taken six Venetians and six Crusaders should be elected to form a committee to choose an Emperor.[1] A proviso was, however, added that all the twelve delegates should solemnly swear on holy relics that they would elect the candidate whom they believed to be the best in the interest of the world. The other provisions show that the parties were pretty equally balanced. It was agreed that if a Frank [2] should be elected Emperor the Patriarch should be chosen by the Venetians, and *vice versâ*. The Emperor was to receive one-fourth of all that should be captured within the city and throughout the Empire, together with the two imperial palaces of Blachern and the Lion's Mouth. The remaining three-fourths were to be divided equally between the Venetians and the Crusaders. The gold and silver, the cloth, the silk, and all the rest of the booty captured were to be abandoned to the host, and to be collected together for the sake of a fair division. When this should have been accomplished a new committee of twenty-four, chosen by the Venetians and the Crusaders, was to be named to divide the Empire into fiefs, and to define the feudal service which the holders should render to the new Emperor. It was further resolved that no one should lay hands on priest or monk nor plunder the churches or monasteries. The division of the spoils of the Empire, including the carving out of the fiefs, was to be finished within a year, and therefore to be completed before the end of March 1205. After the capture of

Decision as to division of spoil if city were captured.

---

[1] Robert de Clari says twenty were chosen, ten from each (clxviii.).

[2] The term 'Franchois' is used by all the contemporary writers to designate Frenchmen, Flemings, Germans, and Burgundians. The term 'Frank,' which is still used in the Balkan peninsula, in much the same sense, is therefore a convenient one.

the city all were to be free to leave it who wished to do so up to that date. After it, however, all who remained were to be bound to accept the suzerainty of the Emperor.[1]

The bear's skin having thus been divided, it only remained to capture the bear.

The Crusaders and Venetians had been pressing on their works for the attack upon the city with all their might. Rewards were offered to those whose scaling ladders and covered gangways, to be thrown out from the ships' cross-trees to the walls, were first ready. The machines were prepared for hurling stones. Battering-rams, balistæ, mangonels, and all the engines known to the military science of the time for attacking a walled city were got ready. There was no longer any question of leaving for the Holy Land. The lust of gain had fallen upon the whole of the army, and while they were making preparations for the attack they were already planning out the best course for a division of the spoil.

---

[1] The agreement is given in Tafel and Thomas, pp. 444 and 452; Villehardouin, pp. 234-5; Rhamnusius, iii. ; Innocent, *Gesta*, p. 90.

CHAPTER XV.

THE ASSAULT, CAPTURE, AND PLUNDER OF THE CITY.

THE preparations which the leaders had been pushing on
during several weeks were completed by the 8th of April, and
that day was chosen for an assault upon the city. A noteworthy change of plan had been made from that which had
been acted upon nine months before. Instead of attacking
simultaneously a portion of the harbour walls and a portion
of the landward walls, Venetians and Crusaders alike directed
their efforts against the defences on the side of the harbour.
The horses were embarked once more in the huissiers. The
line of battle was drawn up ; the huissiers and galleys in
front, the transports a little behind, and alternating between
the huissiers and the galleys. The whole length of the line
of battle was upwards of half a league,[1] and stretched
from the Blachern to beyond the Petrion.[2] The Emperor's
vermilion tent had been pitched on the hill just beyond the
district of the Petrion, where he could see the ships when
they came immediately under the walls. Before him was the

Prepara-
tions for the
attack.

---

[1] Robert de Clari says it was a league long (lxx.)—a statement which cannot
be true.

[2] The Petrion, which is repeatedly mentioned by contemporary writers, was
a district built on the slope of a hill running parallel to the Golden Horn for
about one-third of the length of the harbour walls eastwards from Blachern. It
had apparently been a neglected spot during the early centuries of the history of
Constantinople, but had lately come to be the residence of numerous hermits, and
the site of several monasteries and convents. A great part is now occupied by
the Jewish colony of Balata.—Du Cange, Cons. Ch. Dr. Mordtmann, of Constantinople, has carefully examined the question, and has published the result of
his inquiry in Constantinople. Nicetas says that the ships reached from Blachern
to the monastery of Everyetis. This monastery was near, and below the present
mosque of Sultan Selim.

district which had been devastated by the fire. On the morning
of the 9th the ships, drawn up in the order I have described,
passed over from the north to the south side of the harbour.
The Crusaders landed in many places, and attacked from a
narrow strip of the land between the walls and the water.
Then the assault began in terrible earnest along the whole
line. Amid the din of the imperial trumpets and drums the
attackers endeavoured to undermine the walls, while others
kept up a continual rain of arrows, bolts, and stones. The
ships had been covered with planks and skins so as to defend
them from the stones and from the famous Greek fire, and,
thus protected, pushed boldly up to the walls. The transports
soon advanced to the front, and were able to get so near the
walls that the attacking parties on the gangways or platforms,
flung out once more from the ships' tops, were able to cross
lances with the defenders of the walls and towers.[1] The
attack took place at upwards of a hundred points until noon,
or, according to Nicetas, until evening. Both parties fought
well. The invaders were repulsed. Those who had landed
were driven back, and amid the shower of stones were unable
to remain on shore. The invaders lost more than the defenders. The heightening of the walls had made their
capture more difficult than at the previous attack. Before
night a portion of the vessels had retired out of range of the
mangonels, while another portion remained at anchor and
continued to keep up a continual fire against those on the
walls. The first day's attack had failed.

The leaders of both Crusaders and Venetians withdrew
their forces to the Galata side. The assault had failed, and it
became necessary at once to determine upon their next step.
The same evening a parliament was hastily called together.
Once more, in the presence of defeat, the old differences
showed themselves. Some advised that the next attack
should be made on the walls on the Marmora side, which
were not so strong as those facing the Golden Horn. The

---

[1] The author of the *Devastatio* and Robert de Clari speak enthusiastically of
the ingenuity of the Venetians, as shown in the construction of these platforms or
scalas, and of the other machinery for attack.

Venetians, however, immediately took an exception, which everyone who knew Constantinople would at once recognise as unanswerable. On that side the current is always much too strong to allow vessels to be anchored with any amount of steadiness, or even safety. Villehardouin's irritation at the suggestion shows how bitter the opposition still continued. There were some present, he says, who would have been very well content that the current or a wind—no matter what —should have dispersed the vessels, provided that they themselves could have left the country and have gone on their way.

It was at length decided that the two following days, the 10th and 11th, should be devoted to repairing their damages, and that a second assault should be delivered on the 12th. *A second assault decided upon.* The previous day was a Sunday, and Boniface and Dandolo made use of it to appease the discontent in the rank and file of the army. Once more, as at Corfu and before the first attack upon the city, the bishops and abbots were set to work to preach against the Greeks. They urged that the war was just, because Mourtzouphlos was a traitor and a murderer, a man more uisloyal than Judas ; that the Greeks had been disobedient to Rome, and had perversely been guilty of schism in refusing to recognise the supremacy of the Pope, and that Innocent himself desired the union of the two Churches. They saw in the defeat the vengeance of God on account of the sins of the Crusaders. The loose women were ordered out of the camp, and for better security were shipped and sent far away. Confession and communion were enjoined, and, in short, all that the clergy could do was done to prove that the cause was just, to quiet the discontented, and to occupy them until the attack next day.[1]

The warriors had in the meantime been industriously repairing their ships and their machines of war. A slight, but not unimportant, change of tactics had been suggested by the assault on the 9th. Each transport had been assigned to a separate tower. The number of men who could fight from the gangways or platforms thrown out from the tops had

[1] Robert de Clari, lxxii.

been found insufficient to hold their own against the defenders. The modified plan was, therefore, to lash together, opposite each tower to be attacked, two ships containing gangways to be thrown out from their tops, and thus concentrate a greater force against each tower. Probably also the line of attack was considerably shorter than at the first assault.

The second assault.

On Monday morning, the 12th, the assault was renewed. The tent of the Emperor had been pitched near the monastery of Pantepoptis,[1] one of many which were in the district of the Petrion, extending along the Golden Horn from the palace of Blachern, about one-fourth of its length. From this position he could see all the movements of the fleet. The walls were covered with men who were ready again to fight under the eye of their Emperor. The assault commenced at dawn, and continued with the utmost fierceness. Every available Crusader and Venetian took part in it. Each little group of ships had its own special portion of the walls with its towers to attack. The besiegers during the first portion of the day made little progress, but a strong north wind sprang up, which enabled the vessels to get nearer the land than they had previously been. Two of the transports, the 'Pilgrim' and the 'Parvis,' lashed together, succeeded in throwing one of their gangways across to a tower in the Petrion, and opposite the position occupied by the Emperor.[2] A Venetian, and a French knight, André d'Urboise, immediately rushed across and obtained a foothold. They were at once followed by others, who fought so well that the defenders of the tower were either killed or fled. The example gave new courage to the invaders. The knights who were in the huissiers, as soon as they saw what had been done, leaped on shore, placed their ladders against the wall, and shortly captured four towers. Those on board the fleet concentrated

---

[1] The remarkable church of this monastery still exists as a mosque, and is known as 'Eski imaret Mahallasse.' It still bears witness to its having been arranged for both monks and nuns. It is on the Fourth Hill, just above the Phanar.

[2] Nicetas, p. 753.

their efforts on the gates, broke in three of them, entered the city, while others landed their horses from the huissiers. As soon as a company of knights was formed, they entered the city through one of these gates, and charged for the Emperor's camp. Mourtzouphlos had drawn up his troops before his tents, but they were unused to contend with men in heavy armour, and after a fairly obstinate resistance the imperial troops fled. The Emperor, says Nicetas, who is certainly not inclined to unduly praise the Emperor, who had deprived him of his post of *Grand Logothete*, did his best to rally his troops, but all in vain, and he had to retreat towards the palace of the Lion's Mouth. The number of the wounded and dead was 'sans fin et sans mesure.' An indiscriminate slaughter commenced. The invaders spared neither age nor sex. In order to render themselves safe they set fire to the *The third fire.* city lying to the east of them, and burnt everything between the monastery of Everyetis and the quarter known as Droungarios.[1] So extensive was the fire, which burned all night and until the next evening, that, according to the Marshal, more houses were destroyed than there were in the three largest cities of France. The tents of the Emperor and the imperial palace of Blachern were pillaged, the conquerors making their head-quarters on the same site at Pantepoptis. It was evening, and already late, when the Crusaders had entered the city, and it was impossible for them to continue their work of destruction through the night. They therefore encamped near the walls and towers which they had captured. Baldwin of Flanders spent the night in the vermilion tent of the Emperor, his brother Henry in front of the palace of Blachern, Boniface, the Marquis of Montferrat, on the other side of the imperial tents in the heart of the city.

The city was already taken. The inhabitants were at *The city captured.* length awakened out of the dream of security into which seventeen unsuccessful attempts to capture the New Rome had lulled them. Every charm, pagan and Christian, had been without avail. The easy sloth into which the possession

---

[1] It was the quarter about the gate in the harbour walls, now known as Zindan Capou, near the dried fruit market.

of innumerable relics, and the consciousness of being under the protection of an army of saints and martyrs, had plunged a large part of the inhabitants, had been rudely dispelled. The Panhagia of the Blachern, with its relic of the Virgin's robe, the host of heads, arms, bodies, and vestments of saints and of portions of the holy Cross, had been of no more use than the palladium which lay buried then, as now, under the great column which Constantine had built. The rough energy of the Westerns had disregarded the talismans of the Greek Church as completely as those of paganism. In vain had the believers in these charms destroyed during the siege the statues which were believed to be of ill omen or unlucky. The invaders had a superstition as deep as their own, but with the difference that they could not believe that a people in schism could have the protection of the hierarchy of heaven, or be regarded as the rightful possessors of so many relics. During the night following its capture the Golden Gate, which was at the Marmora side of the landward walls, had been opened, and already an affrighted crowd was pressing forward to make its escape from the captured city. Others were doing their best to bury their treasures. The Emperor himself, either seized with panic or finding that all was lost—as, indeed, everything was lost so soon as the army had succeeded in obtaining a foothold within the walls—fled from the city. He, too, escaped by the Golden Gate, taking with him Euphrosyne, the widow of Alexis. The brave Theodore Lascaris determined, however, to make one more attempt. His appeal to the people was useless. Those who were not panic-stricken appear to have been indifferent. Some, at least, were apparently still dreaming of a mere change of rulers, like those of which the majority of them had seen several. Theodore turned his attention to the Waring guard, but before any attempt at reorganisation could be made the enemy was in sight, and Theodore himself had to fly. The Crusaders had expected, according to the Marshal, another day's fighting, and knew nothing of the flight of Mourtzouphlos. To their surprise, they encountered no resistance. The day was occupied in taking possession of

Flight of the Emperor.

their conquest. The Byzantine troops, including also the Warings, laid down their arms on receiving assurances of personal safety. The Italians who had been expelled took advantage of the entry of their friends, and appear to have retaliated upon the population for their expulsion. Two thousand of the inhabitants, says Gunther,[1] were killed, and mostly by these returned Italians. As the victorious Crusaders passed through the streets, women, old men, and children, who had been unable to flee, met them, and, placing one finger over another so as to make the sign of the Cross, hailed the Marquis of Montferrat as King,[2] while a hastily gathered procession, with the Cross and the sacred emblems of Christ, greeted him in triumph. The people had known him as the guardian of Alexis. Besides those who yet believed that all the change which would be made would be that of the sovereign, there were some among the number who had been the partisans of young Alexis, and who believed that they were therefore entitled to share in the favour, or at least in the clemency, of Boniface. It was, therefore, natural that he should be hailed as king.

Montferrat hailed as King

The Marquis had led his division along the shore of the Horn round to the palace of Bucoleon. The occupants surrendered it. The ladies of the court, including one who had been the sister of the King of France and another the sister of the King of Hungary, had fled to the fortress of this palace on the capture of the city. While Boniface took possession of the Bucoleon, Henry, brother of Baldwin, occupied the Blachern.

Then began the plunder of the city. The imperial treasury and the arsenal were placed under guard ; but with these exceptions the right to plunder was given indiscriminately to the troops and sailors. Never in Europe was a work of pillage more systematically and shamelessly carried out. Never by the army of a Christian state was there a more barbarous sack of a city than that perpetrated by these soldiers of Christ, sworn to chastity, pledged before God not to shed Christian blood, and bearing upon them the emblem

Plunder of the city.

[1] Ch. xviii.   [2] Gunther, xviii.

of the Prince of Peace. Reciting the crimes committed by the Crusaders, Nicetas says with indignation:[1] 'You have taken up the Cross, and have sworn on it and on the holy Gospels to us that you would pass over the territory of Christians without shedding blood and without turning to the right hand or to the left. You told us that you had taken up arms against the Saracens only, and that you would steep them in their blood alone. You promised to keep yourselves chaste while you bore the Cross, as became soldiers enrolled under the banner of Christ. Instead of defending His tomb, you have outraged the faithful who are members of Him. You have used Christians worse than the Arabs used the Latins, for they at least respected women.' An immense mass of treasure was found in each of the imperial palaces and in those of the nobles. Each baron took possession of the castle or palace which was allotted to him, and put a guard upon the treasure which he found there. 'Never since the world was created,' says the Marshal, 'was there so much booty gained in one city. Each man took the house which pleased him, and there were enough for all. Those who were poor found themselves suddenly rich. There was captured an immense supply of gold and silver, of plate and of precious stones, of satins and of silk, of furs, and of every kind of wealth ever found upon earth.'

The sack of the richest city in Christendom, which had been the bribe offered to the Crusaders to violate their oaths, was made in the spirit of men who, having once broken through the trammels of their vows, are reckless to what lengths they go. Their abstinence and their chastity once abandoned, they plunged at once into orgies of every kind.

The Greek eye-witness gives the complement of the picture of Villehardouin. The lust of the army spared neither maiden nor the virgin dedicated to God. Violence and debauchery were everywhere present; cries and lamentations and the groans of the victims were heard throughout the city; for everywhere pillage was unrestrained and lust unbridled. The city was in wild confusion. Nobles, old men, women,

[1] Nicetas, p. 759.

and children ran to and fro trying to save their wealth, their honour, and their lives. Knights, foot soldiers, and Venetian sailors jostled each other in a mad scramble for plunder. Threats of ill-treatment, promises of safety if wealth were disgorged, mingled with the cries of many sufferers. These pious brigands, as Gunther aptly calls them, acted as if they had received a licence to commit every crime. Sword in hand, houses and churches were pillaged. Every insult was offered to the religion of the conquered citizens. Churches and monasteries were the richest storehouses, and were therefore the first buildings to be rifled. Monks and priests were selected for insult. The priests' robes were placed by the Crusaders on their horses. The icons were ruthlessly torn down from the screens or were broken. The sacred buildings were ransacked for relics or their beautiful caskets. The chalices were stripped of their precious stones and converted into drinking cups. The sacred plate was heaped with ordinary plunder. The altar cloths and the screens of cloth of gold, richly embroidered and bejewelled, were torn down, and either divided among the troops or destroyed for the sake of the gold and silver which were woven into them. The altars of Hagia Sophia, which had been the admiration of all men, were broken for the sake of the material of which they were made. Horses and mules were taken into the church in order to carry off the loads of sacred vessels and the gold and silver plates of the throne, the pulpits, and the doors, and the beautiful ornaments of the church. The soldiers made the chief church of Christendom the scene of their profanity. A prostitute was seated in the patriarchal chair, who danced and sang a ribald song for the amusement of the soldiers. Nicetas, in speaking of the desecration of the Great Church, writes with the utmost indignation of the barbarians who were incapable of appreciating and therefore respecting its beauty. To him it was an 'earthly heaven, a throne of Divine magnificence, an image of the firmament created by the Almighty.'

The plunder of the same church in 1453 by Mahomet the Second compares favourably with that made by the Crusaders of 1204.

The sack of the city went on during the three days after the capture.[1] An order was issued, probably on the third day, by the leaders of the army for the protection of women. Three bishops had pronounced excommunication against all who should pillage church or convent.[2] It was many days, however, before the army could be reduced to its ordinary condition of discipline. A proclamation was made throughout the army that all the booty should be collected, in order to be divided fairly among the captors. Three churches were selected as depôts, and trusty guards of Crusaders and Venetians were stationed to watch what was thus brought in. Much, however, was kept back and much stolen. Stern measures had to be resorted to before order was restored. Many Crusaders were hanged. The Count of St. Paul hung one of his own knights with his shield round his neck because he had not given up the booty he had captured. A contemporary writer, the continuator of the history of William of Tyre, forcibly contrasts the conduct of the Crusaders before and after the capture. When the Latins would take Constantinople they held the shield of God before them. It was only when they had entered that they threw it away, and covered themselves with the shield of the devil.[3]

The experiences of Nicetas.

I have already mentioned that the Italians resident in Constantinople who had returned to the city with their countrymen were conspicuous in their hostility to the Greeks. Amid this resentment there were examples, however, that

---

[1] 'Tres dies gladiis sævibant.'—Clari, lxxx.

[2] 'Sed cæca cupiditas, quæ facile persuadet, ita manus eorum victrices victas tenuit, ut non solum ecclesias violarent, immo etiam vascula, in quibus sanctorum reliquiæ quiescebant, impudenter effrangerent, aurum inde et argentum et gemmas turpiter evellentes ; ipsas vero reliquias pro nihilo reputabant. Quo audito, seniores exercitus doluerunt valde, timentes ne talis victoria eis in exitium verteretur ; habito igitur consilio, legatus, qui vicem apostolici gerebat, cum archiepiscopis et episcopis, sub districti anathematis interminatione precepit, ne quis sibi retineret reliquias, sed omnes in manu bonæ memoriæ Guarneri, tunc Trecensis episcopi, libere resignarent. Inter quas inventum est caput gloriosi martyris, nudum quidem, nisi quod circulus argenteus ipsi capiti circumductus erat, et supra, in modum crucis extensus, totum comprehendebat, in quo erat scriptum antiquis literis græcis, quæ adhuc ibi apparent : ΑΓΙΟΣ ΜΑΜΑΣ, quod interpretatur Sanctus Mamas.' Can. Lingonensis, *Exuviæ Sac.* i. 29.

[3] *L'Estoire de Eracles*, p. 275, *Recueil.*

former friendships were not forgotten. The escape of Nicetas himself is an illustration in point. He had held the position of *Grand Logothete*,[1] but he had been deposed by Mourtzouphlos. When the Latins entered the city he had retired to a small house near Hagia Sophia, which was so situated as to be likely to escape observation. His large house, and probably his official residence, which he is careful to tell us was adorned with an abundant store of ornaments, had been burnt down in the second fire. Many of his friends found refuge with him, apparently regarding his dwelling as specially adapted for concealment. Nothing, however, could escape the observation of the horde which was now ransacking every corner. When the Italians had been banished from the city Nicetas had sheltered a Venetian merchant with his wife and family. This man now clothed himself like a soldier, and, pretending that he was one of the invaders, prevented his countrymen or any other Latins from entering the house. For some time he was successful, but at length a crowd, principally of French soldiers, pushed past and flocked within. From that time protection became impossible. The Venetian advised Nicetas to leave, in order to prevent himself from being imprisoned and to save the honour of his daughters. Nicetas and his friends accepted the advice. Having clothed themselves in skins or the poorest garments, they were conducted through the city by their faithful friend as if they were his prisoners. The girls and young ladies of the party were placed in their midst, their faces having been intentionally smeared in order to give them the appearance of being of the poorest class. As they reached the Golden Gate the daughter of a magistrate who was one of the party was suddenly seized and carried off by a Crusader. Her father, who was weak and old, and wearied with the long walk, fell, and was unable to do anything but cry for assistance. Nicetas followed and called the attention of certain soldiers who were passing, and after a long and piteous appeal, after reminding them of the proclamation which had been made against the

---

[1] This office still exists. The principal duty of the person who holds it is to recite the Creed in great religious services when the Patriarch officiates.

violation of women, he ultimately succeeded in saving the maiden. The entreaties would have been in vain if the leader of the party had not at length threatened to hang the offender. A few minutes later the fugitives had passed out of the city, and fell on their knees to thank God for His protection in having permitted them to escape with their lives. Then they set out on their weary way to Silivria. The road was covered with fellow-sufferers. Before them was the Patriarch himself, 'without bag or money or stick or shoes, with but one coat,' says Nicetas, 'like a true apostle, or rather like a true follower of Jesus Christ, in that he was seated on an ass, with the difference that instead of entering the New Sion in triumph he was leaving it.'

Division of the spoil.

A large part of the booty had been collected in the three churches designated for that purpose. The Marshal himself tells us that much was stolen which never came into the general mass. The stores which had been collected were, however, divided in accordance with the compact which had been made before the capture. The Venetians and the Crusaders each took half. Out of the moiety belonging to the army there was paid the fifty thousand silver marks due to the Venetians. Two foot sergeants received as much as one horse sergeant, and two of the latter sergeants received as much as a knight. Exclusive of what was stolen and of what was paid to the Venetians, there were distributed among the army 400,000 marks, or 800,000*l.*, and 10,000 suits of armour.[1]

The total amount distributed among the Crusaders and Venetians shows that the wealth of Constantinople had not been exaggerated. 800,000*l.* was given to the Crusaders, a like sum to the Venetians, with the 100,000*l.* due to them. These sums had been collected in hard cash from a city where the inhabitants were hostile, and where they had in their wells and cisterns an easy means of hiding their treasures of gold, silver, and precious stones—a means traditionally well known in the East—and in a city half of which had been recently

[1] Du Cange's version says *chevaucheures*, or beasts of burden. I adopt that of M. Wailly.

burnt in three great fires. As we have seen, abundance of booty was taken possession of by the troops which never went into the general mass. Sismondi[1] estimates that the wealth in specie and movable property before the capture was not less than twenty-four million pounds sterling.

The distribution was made during the latter end of April. Many works of art in bronze were sent to the melting-pot to be coined. Many statues were broken up in order to obtain the metals with which they were adorned. The conquerors knew nothing and cared nothing for the art which had added value to the metal. The weight of the bronze was to them the only question of interest. The works of art which they destroyed were sacrificed not to any sentiment like that of the Moslem against images which they believed to be idols or talismans. No such excuse can be made for the Christians of the West. Their motive for destroying so much that was valuable was neither fanaticism nor religion. It was the simple greed for gain. No sentiment restrained their cupidity. The great statue of the Virgin which ornamented the Taurus was sent as unhesitatingly to the furnace as the figure of Hercules. No object was sufficiently sacred, none sufficiently beautiful, to be worth saving if it could be converted into cash. Amidst so much that was destroyed it is impossible that there were not a considerable number of works of art of the best periods. The one list which has been left us by the Greek *Logothete* professes to give account of only the larger statues which were sent to the melting-pot. But it is worth while to note what were these principal objects so destroyed.

Destruction of works of art.

Before doing so, however, let me again point out that Constantinople had long been the great storehouse of works of art and of Christian relics, the latter of which were usually encased with all the skill that wealth could buy or art furnish. It had the great advantage over the Elder Rome that it had never been plundered by hordes of barbarians. Its streets and public places had been adorned for centuries with statues in bronze or marble. In reading the works of the historians of the Lower Empire the reader cannot fail to be

[1] II. p. 405.

struck alike with the abundance of works of art and with the appreciation in which they were held by the writers. First among the buildings as among the works of art, in the esti-

Plunder of Hagia Sophia and other buildings and works of art.

mation of every citizen, was Hagia Sophia. It was emphatically the Great Church. Tried by any test, it is one of the most beautiful of human creations. Nothing in Western Europe even now gives a spectator, who is able with an educated eye to restore it to something like its former condition, so deep an impression of unity, harmony, richness, and beauty in decoration as does the interior of the masterpiece of Justinian. All that wealth could supply and art produce had been lavished upon its interior — at that time, and for long afterwards, the only portion of a church which the Christian architect thought deserving of study. ' Internally, at least,' says a great authority on architecture, ' the verdict seems inevitable that Santa Sophia is the most perfect and most beautiful church which has yet been erected by any Christian people. When its furniture was complete the verdict would have been still more strongly in its favour.' [1] We have seen that to Nicetas, who knew and loved it in its best days, it was a model of celestial beauty, a glimpse of heaven itself. To the more sober English observer, ' its mosaic of marble slabs of various patterns and beautiful colours ; the domes, roofs, and curved surfaces, with gold-grounded mosaic relieved by figures or architectural devices ' are 'wonderfully grand and pleasing.' [2] All that St. Mark's is to Venice, Hagia Sophia was to Constantinople. But St. Mark's, though enriched with some of the spoils of its great original, is, as to its interior at least, a feeble copy. Hagia Sophia justified its founder in declaring, ' I have surpassed thee, O Solomon,' and during seven centuries after Justinian his successors had each

[1] Fergusson's *Hist. of Arch.*, vol. ii. p. 321. I may add that at Mount Athos, where Byzantine architecture fled after the fall of the capital, and where it became crystallised, I have seen how completely the remark is borne out that the furniture must have greatly improved the appearance of a Byzantine church. In the churches of some of the monasteries—that, for example, at Vatopedi—a visitor may see what Byzantine architecture was at its best, and may reconstruct the decoration of such beautiful churches as the Karkrie jamisi at Constantinople.

[2] *Ibid.*

attempted to add to its wealth and its decoration. Yet this, incomparably the most beautiful church in Christendom, at the opening of the thirteenth century was stripped and plundered of every ornament which could be carried away. It appeared to the indignant Greeks that the very stones would be torn from the walls by these intruders, to whom nothing was sacred.[1]

Around the Great Church were other objects which could be readily converted into bronze, and the destruction of which was irreparable. The immense hippodrome was crowded with statues. Egypt had furnished an obelisk for the centre. Delphi had given its commemoratory bronze of the victory of Platæa. Later works of Pagan sculptors were there in abundance, while Christian artists had continued the traditions of their ancestors in a style by no means so debased as Western writers have, until recently, believed it to be. The cultured inhabitants of Constantinople appreciated these works of art, and took care of them. In giving a list of the more important of the objects which went to the melting pot, Nicetas again and again urges that these works were destroyed by barbarians who were ignorant of their value. Incapable of appreciating either their historical interest or the value with which the labour of the artist had endowed them, the Crusaders knew only the value of the metals of which they were composed.[2]

The Emperors had been buried within the precincts of the church of the Holy Apostles, the site of which was afterwards chosen by Mahomet the Second for the erection of the mosque now called by his name. Their tombs, beginning with that of Justinian, were ransacked in the search for treasure. It was not until the palaces of the nobles, the churches, and the tombs had been plundered that the pious brigands turned

[1] A most interesting account of the plunder of Hagia Sophia is given in the *Chronicle of Novgorod*. See *Chroniques Greco-Romanes*, par Charles Hopf. The author evidently knew the church well. Another interesting account is given in *Peregrinus*, by Antony, Bishop of Novgorod ; *Exuv. Sac.*, ii. p. 218.

[2] The bronze, or 'Corinthian copper,' was formed of copper, gold, and silver. The stand of the tripod of Platæa still remains in the hippodrome, and was probably spared on account of the inferior quality of its metal.

their attention to the statues. A colossal figure of Juno,
which had been brought from Samos, and which stood in the
forum of Constantine, was sent to the melting pot. We may
judge of its size from the fact that four oxen were required to
transport its head to the palace. The statue of Paris presenting to Venus the apple of discord followed. The Anemo-
dulion, or Servant of the Winds, was a lofty obelisk, whose
sides were covered with bas-reliefs of great beauty, representing
scenes of rural life, and allegories depicting the seasons, while
the obelisk was surmounted by a female figure which turned
with the wind, and so gave to the whole its name. The bas-
reliefs were stripped off and sent to the palace to be melted.
A beautiful equestrian statue of great size, representing
either Bellerophon and Pegasus or, as the populace believed,
Joshua on horseback, commanding the sun to stand still, was
likewise sent to the furnace. The horse appeared to be
neighing at the sound of the trumpet, while every muscle was
strained with the ardour of battle. The colossal Hercules of
Lysippus, which, having adorned Tarentum, had thence been
transported to the Elder and subsequently to the hippodrome
of the New Rome, met with a like fate. The artist had expressed in a manner which won the admiration of beholders
the deep wrath of the hero at the unworthy tasks set before
him. He was represented as seated, but without quiver or
bow or club. His lion's skin was thrown loosely about his
shoulders, his right foot and right hand stretched out to the
utmost, while he rested his head on his left hand with his
elbow on his bent knee. The whole figure was full of dignity ;
the chest deep, the shoulders broad, the hair curly, the arms
and limbs full of muscle.

The figure of an ass and its driver, which Augustus had
had cast in bronze to commemorate the news brought to him
of the victory of Actium, met with the same fate.

For the sake of melting them down into money the barbarians seized also the ancient statue of the wolf suckling
Romulus and Remus ; the statues of a sphinx, a hippopotamus,
a crocodile, an elephant, and others, which had represented
a triumph over Egypt ; the monster of Scylla and others ;

most of which were probably executed before the time of Christ.

To the same period belonged the eagle struggling with a serpent, which was ascribed to Apollonius Tyanensis. Nicetas describes with glowing admiration the statue of Helen. ' What shall I say of Helen, of elegant stature, with snowy arms and beautiful form ? Why could she not soften the barbarians ? —she who formerly had led all spectators captive ; a statue clothed in a robe which graced rather than concealed her charms, her brow clear, her hair flowing gently to the wind, her graceful lips slightly opened as if about to speak, arched eyebrows ; a figure full of harmony, elegance, and beauty ; the joy of beholders, a pleasure to the eyes, such as makes it impossible to give an adequate description for posterity.' This statue was destroyed by men who knew nothing of its original. There must be added to these the graceful figure of a woman who held in her right hand the figure of an armed man on horseback. Then near the eastern goals, known as the ' reds,' stood the statues of the winners in the chariot races. They stood erect in their bronze chariots, as the originals also had been seen when they gained their victories, as if they were still directing their steeds to the goals. A figure of the Nile bull in deadly conflict with a crocodile stood near. These and other statues were hastily sent to the furnace to be converted into money. We may judge of the value and artistic merit of the bronze statues which were destroyed by the specimens which remain. The four horses which the Emperor Theodosius had brought from Chios and placed in the hippodrome escaped by some lucky chance the general plunder, and were taken to Venice, where they still adorn the front of St. Mark's.

I have already alluded to the wealth of Constantinople in relics. As the city had become the storehouse of works of art, so also from the same causes it had drawn to it nearly all the relics of the Eastern world. There was even an additional reason why the relics should have flowed in greater number to the capital than did works of art, because faithful

Hunt after relics.

Christians felt bound to prevent them falling into the hands of the Moslem miscreant. This was a species of wealth which the Crusaders could much more readily appreciate than that which consisted merely in marble or bronze, to which the genius of the sculptor had added value. Even among the more conscientious of the soldiers it seems to have been held that the surest way to compensate for the breach of their vow was to steal a relic for the use of the church in the neighbourhood from which they had come. I have already said that the relics were usually encased either in coverings of silver or gold, to which the best art of the time had added value, and the caskets were often set with precious stones. The coverings would, of course, be preferred by us to the contents, but that is because we do not believe in the genuineness of the relics. To understand the feelings of the Crusaders we must remember that doubt as to their genuineness scarce entered their minds. Out of the great number of documents which have been collected together by the zeal of a recent writer, and which give minute accounts of the reception of these relics in the West, there are very few that speak of the value of the covering, and, even when they do so speak, it is only incidentally. The fragment of the true cross or the arm of the true saint was the gem ; the silver or gold covering was only the suitable casket to contain it.

The pillage of the relics of Constantinople lasted for forty years. More than half of the total amount of objects carried off were, however, taken away between the years 1204 and 1208. During the few days which followed the capture of the city the bishops and priests who were with the Crusaders were active in laying hands on this species of sacred spoil ; and the statement of a contemporary writer is not improbable, that the priests of the Orthodox Church preferred to surrender such spoil to those of their own cloth rather than to the rough soldier or the rougher Venetian sailor. On the other hand, the highest priestly dignitaries in the army—men, even, who refused to take of the earthly spoil—were eager to obtain possession of this sacred booty, and unscrupulous as to the means by which they obtained it. The holy cross was carefully divided by the bishops for distribution among the barons. Gunther gives us a specimen of the means to which Abbot Martin, who had had the German Crusaders placed under his charge, had recourse. The abbot had learned that many relics had been hidden by the Greeks in a particular church. This building was attacked in the general pillage. He, as a priest, searched carefully for the relics, while the soldiers were looking for more commonplace booty. The abbot found an old priest, with the long hair and beard common then, as now, to Orthodox ecclesiastics, and roughly addressed him, ' Show me your relics, or you are a dead man.' The old priest, seeing that he was addressed by one of his own profession, and frightened probably by the threat, thought, says Gunther, that it was better to give up the relics to him than to the profane and blood-stained hands of the soldiers. He opened an iron safe, and the abbot, in his delight at the sight, buried his hands in the precious store. He and his chaplain filled their surplices, and ran with all haste to the harbour to conceal their prize. That they were successful in keeping it during the stormy days which followed could only be attributed to the virtue of the relics themselves.

The way in which Dalmatius de Sergy obtained the head of St. Clement is an illustration of the Crusader's belief that the acquisition of a relic and its transport to the West would be allowed as a compensation for the fulfilment of the Crusader's vow. That knight was grievously afflicted that he could not go to the Holy Land, and earnestly prayed God to show him how he could execute some other task equivalent to that which he had sworn but failed to accomplish. His first thought was to take relics to his own country. He consulted the two cardinals who were then in Constantinople, who approved his idea, but charged him not to buy these relics, because their purchase and sale were forbidden. He accordingly determined to steal them, if such a word may be applied to an act which was clearly regarded as praiseworthy. The knight, in order to discover something of especial value, remained in Constantinople until Palm Sunday in the following year. A French priest pointed out to him a church, in which the head of St. Clement was preserved.[1] He went there in the company of a Cistercian monk, and asked to see the relics. While one kept the persons in charge speaking with him, the other stole a portion of the relic. On leaving, the knight was disgusted to find that the whole head had not been taken, and, on the pretext that he had left his gauntlet behind, a companion regained admittance to the church, while the knight again kept the monk in charge in conversation at the door. Dalmatius went to the chest behind the altar where the relic had been kept, stole the remainder, went out, mounted his horse and rode away. The head was placed with pious joy in the chapel of his house. He returned disguised some days after to the church in order, as he pretended, to do reverence to the relic, in order really to ascertain that he had taken the right head, for there had been two in the chest. He was informed that the head of St. Clement had been stolen. Then, being satisfied as to its authenticity, he took a vow that he would give the relic to the church of Cluny in case he should arrive safely. He embarked. The devil from jealousy sent a hurricane, but the tears and prayers before the relic defeated him, and he arrived safely home. The monks of Cluny received the precious treasure with every demonstration of reverent joy, and in the fullest confidence that they had secured the perpetual intercession of St. Clement on behalf of themselves and those who did honour to his head.[2] The relics most sought after were those which related to the events mentioned in the New Testament, especially to the infancy, life, and passion of Christ, and to the saints popular in the West. But the mass possessed by the imperial city ranged from the stone on which Jacob had slept, and from the rod which Moses had changed into a serpent, down to that of the latest opponents of heresy in Constantinople. Those connected with the life of Christ and His

---

[1] The church was popularly Rose, from the name, still common among the Greeks, of the former owner of the land, Τριακοντάφυλλον. The Turks preserve the name, and call the mosque occupying the same site Guljami. It was dedicated to St. Theodosia.

[2] I have taken this account from Hurter, whose authority is Dalmatius de Sergy himself. *Bibl. Cluniac.*

Mother existed in great number, and comprised objects supposed to be connected with almost every event of His life. There was the cross on which the Saviour had been crucified, the great drops of blood which He had shed in Gethsemane, one of His first teeth, and some of the hair of His childhood. The devout had venerated the purple robe, and could reverence also a portion of the bread which He had blessed at the Last Supper. But besides these there was hardly a disciple a saint, or a martyr of whom some relic did not 'exist. The greater portion of these objects formed part of the plunder of the city which was collected during the first few days after its capture, and which was officially divided amongst the invaders. Three-eighths were allotted to the clergy and monks who accompanied the Crusaders ; the remainder were bought or otherwise acquired subsequently, mostly by private persons. The officially certified relics first mentioned seemed to have come chiefly from the imperial palaces of Bucoleon and Blachern. Many of those which were collected after the scramble of the first few days were certified with imperial golden bulls. When they reached their destination they were received with great honour and ceremony. Princes attended and took part in the solemn procession which met them on their way to the church, where with solemn rites they were to be deposited. A sermon often followed, relating to the events with which the relic was supposed to be connected. In many instances an annual festival was appointed to celebrate the arrival of the relic, and occasionally the gift was made conditional upon the establishment of such annual festival in its honour. Lessons from the Old or New Testament appropriate to the saint, a relic of whom had been received, were selected for public reading on such festivals. Special services were framed to commemorate the event. Hymns were composed in honour of the relic.[1] In the case of the monastery of Selincourt, where a sacred tear of Christ had been carried,

[1] Count Riant has found eighty-five of such feasts of the relics of 1204, seventy-four of which commemorate the reception of the relic. Several of the hymns are curious ; a favourable specimen is that ' In festo susceptionis Sanctæ Coronæ,' p. 47, vol. ii. *Exuviæ Sacræ.*

the name was changed through the reception of this relic to that of the monastery of the Sacred Tear. A few of the more important objects of the same kind may be mentioned in order to show both the quantity which were received in the West and the honour with which they were regarded. The Venetians are accused by the author of the 'Continuation of William of Tyre'[1] of having taken an undue share of the spoil and of having concealed it in their ships. Many of the beautiful objects which had adorned the church of the Divine Wisdom went to decorate St. Mark's. The high altar of that church, with its columns of marble and its bronze gates, was one of the most valuable acquisitions. The Venetian church obtained also many pieces of sculpture, pictures, gold and silver vessels, and a mass of church furniture. The Venetians obtained the famous picture of the Virgin which was painted by St. Luke under the direct inspiration of the Holy Ghost.[2] In 1205 there were received at Soissons from its bishop, Nivelon, who was at Constantinople, the head of St. Stephen, the finger which St. Thomas thrust into the side of Christ, the crown of the head of St. Mark, a thorn from the crown worn by Christ, a large portion of the sleeveless shirt of the Virgin Mary, a portion of the garment with which the Lord girt himself at the Last Supper, the girdle of the Virgin and the arm of John the Baptist ; and a few months after the arrival of these a further consignment containing the head of St. John the Baptist, the head of St. Thomas, two great crosses made out of the true cross of our Lord, the head of St. James, with two other crosses made out of the true cross, the head of St. Thaddeus, and three other relics of lesser importance which are specified, together with a large number of others which are not specially mentioned, but which were distributed among the parish churches and convents mostly in the diocese of Soissons.[3] An anonymous account, probably

[1] 'Cel qui plus enblerent ce furent li Venecien qui l'emporterent par nuit à Cornes.'—*L'Estoire de Eracles : Recueil*, p. 275.

[2] Innocent III. apparently did not believe in the genuineness of this relic. Opinionem illam, tanquam superstitiosam, minime approbamus.'—*Ep.* ix.

[3] Anonymi Suessionensis, *Ex. Sc.* i. 8.

written about 1208, by a clerk of Halberstadt, tells another story of the bringing of certain relics from Constantinople. The whole of the population, laymen and clergy, and an immense number of people even from adjacent dioceses, came together on the occasion of the reception of these relics, which were borne by Conrad the bishop, who had himself come from Constantinople. Such a concourse, says the chronicler, was never seen before, and the rejoicing at the reception of the relics was such as might have been expected, seeing that they were destined to bring peace and safety to the country. If any relics could do this, surely those brought home by Conrad ought to have sufficed, since among them was some of the blood of Jesus from the true cross, from the sepulchre, from the crown of thorns, from His agony and bloody sweat, from His purple robe, from the sponge and reed, and from seven other sources ; the head of James the brother of Christ, and thirty other relics which are specially mentioned, besides many others, says the narrative, of martyrs, confessors, and virgins, which it would take long to name. By the side of such relics the further gifts of silk cloths in imperial purple woven with gold, and of a dress set with gold and silver and precious stones, seemed probably poor and almost unworthy of notice.[1] Amiens was fortunate to obtain possession of the head of St. John the Baptist, which was sent by Peter the Walloon.[2] Sens was even more successful, and received the crown of thorns worn by the Lord. Gunther tells us how the Abbot Martin, of Pairis in Alsace, transported many relics from Constantinople into that country, the principal one being a large portion of the true cross. Other relics which went to the glorification of this diocese were a trace of the blood of Christ, a further portion of the wood of the true cross, an arm of St. James, and fifty others which are enumerated.[3] The body of St. Andrew was taken to Amalfi.[4] The sacred tear already mentioned was taken to Selincourt, and the abbot was warned of the approach of the person bringing it by the

---

[1] Anon. Halberstadensis, *Ex. Sac.* 10.

[2] Richard of Gerberon, *Ex. Sac.* 35.

[3] Guntherus Parisiensis, *Ex. Sac.* i. 123.   [4] *Ibid.* 165.

ringing of the bells, a fact which could only be attributed to miraculous agency.[1]

It would be tedious and unprofitable to attempt to give a list of other relics which were taken from Constantinople. Some of these found their way to our own country. Two documents apparently derived from the same source are inserted in the chronicles of Rauel or Rudolph of Coggleshall and Roger of Wendower which have special interest for Englishmen. They give an account of a relic surreptitiously taken away from Constantinople, and are in fact the confessions of the author of the theft. The relic was a small cross cut from the wood of the true cross, and the writer had seen it in the hands of Baldwin of Flanders. The writer having stolen it, took it to Norfolk, and subsequently gave it to Bromholm. The gift made what had hitherto been the 'poor little house' of Bromholm a richly-endowed house, and enabled the monks to put up new and handsome buildings.[2]

The Crusaders were not indifferent to the value of the coverings of these relics, and while they looked after objects of veneration, kept a keen eye also on the reliquaries—the gold and silver ornaments of the church, church furniture, golden embroidery, silk cloths, and the beautiful bindings set with precious stones of the gospels and liturgies. The treasury of St. Mark's at Venice was filled, in 1205, with costly reliquaries received from Constantinople.[3] It is hardly possible to believe that the cunning workmen and traders of Constantinople did not palm off upon the Crusaders a good many relics which they knew to be fictitious. The objects could be manufactured so cheaply, and the critical spirit of

---

[1] Count Riant has collected 145 documents relating to relics sent to the West. See *Exuviæ Sacræ*.

[2] The story is told most fully by Roger of Wendower, and is illustrative of many similar stories. There appears to have been a practice in England like that which still prevails on the peninsula of Mount Athos. Pilgrims went from monastery to monastery to do reverence to the relics, and in each case they were expected to pay for the privilege of so doing. Such pilgrimages were, as they are still in the East, one of the chief sources of revenue for the monkish houses. *Radulphus*, ed. J. Stephenson, London, 1875, copied in *Ex. Sac.* ii. 284, where also see Roger of Wendower.

[3] *Ex. Sac.* xliii.

the Crusader was so slightly developed, that it would be beyond the power of human nature to let such a chance of profit escape.

In the years which followed the conquest Latin priests were sent to Constantinople from France, Flanders, and Italy, to take charge of the churches in the city. These priests appear to have been great hunters after relics. Thus it came to pass that there was scarcely an important church or monastery in most Western countries which did not possess some share of the spoil which came from Constantinople.

For some years the demand for relics seemed to be insatiable, and caused fresh supplies to be forthcoming to an almost unlimited extent. The new relics equally with the old were certified in due form to be what they professed to be. Documents duly attested and full of detailed evidence, sometimes doubtless manufactured for the occasion, easily satisfied those to whom it was of importance to possess certified relics. The 'poor little house of Bromholm,' which had been enabled from its possession of a cross made out of the sacred wood to become large and powerful, became the envy of many other poor little houses, and throughout the West the demand for relics which might bring profit to their possessors continued to increase. At length the church deemed it necessary to put a stop to the supply, and especially to that of the apocryphal and legendary acts which testified to their authenticity, and in 1215 the fourth Lateran Council judged it necessary to make a decree enjoining the bishops to take means to prevent pilgrims from being deceived.[1]

It is easy to ridicule the respect and veneration paid to the sacred tears, the numerous small crosses made from the holy wood, the heads, arms, and old garments of saints and martyrs. It is more difficult to understand how the men of the thirteenth century could have regarded these objects as genuine. It seems reasonable to suppose that many persons must have suspected their genuineness. The relics existed in such numbers, there were so many professing to be originals

Absence of sceptical spirit.

---

[1] ' Praelati non permittant illos qui eorum ecclesias causa venerationis accedunt vanis figmentis aut falsis decipi documentis.'—*Decr.* LXII.

of the same object, the wood of the true cross was so abundant, and the legends relating to the preservation of such
relics as, for example, the tear of Christ, were so extraordinary,
that it is almost incomprehensible that men's suspicions were
not generally aroused.   It must be remembered, however,
that we are dealing with the ages of faith, and that relics in
the East were not regarded with the same superstitious veneration as they were at the end of the twelfth century, and
subsequently by the masses in the West.   Neither earnestness
in religion nor belief in its superstitions were, or are, so intense in the Eastern as in the Western Churches.   In the East
I doubt whether relics have ever been regarded with the same
veneration as they were in the West.   The Eastern spirit was
less gross or more spiritual than that of the West.   The
tendency to drive a harmless and natural habit into a fetish
worship was much more common among the earnest men of
the West than among the more easy-going Christians of the
East.

Probably the Greek could never hate idol-worship with the
same amount of hatred as the Jew or the Western Christian,
and mainly for the reason that he never realised how completely some races can fall into it.   To St. Paul idol worship
was devil worship.   To our fathers, when they had once
come to see that the articles were spurious, relic worship was
idolatry.   But the Greeks both of the time of St. Paul and
their representatives of the middle ages regarded the creations of Greek art and the relics of the saints rather as
symbols than as objects of reverence, and, speaking generally,
were never in danger of converting the worship or respect
due to the person or thing symbolised into fetish worship.
Just as the men of the West had transferred much of their
ancient heathenism into the ceremonies and practices of the
mediæval church, so the Greeks had allowed their Christianity
to become saturated with the ideas of old Greek religion.
While there were probably gross and material views taken of
the Olympic gods and of the other deities recognised by the
ancient Greeks, it is doubtful whether there existed among
them, to any considerable extent, statue, picture, or relic wor-

ship in the modern sense of the term. Asiatics might vene-
rate a stone which had fallen from Jupiter, but such worship
was alien to the Greek spirit. But, even while remembering
these facts, anyone who is acquainted with the contemporary
writings of the twelfth and thirteenth centuries is forced to
recognise that even in the East in religious matters the spirit
of inquiry can scarcely be said to have existed. For many
years afterwards scepticism was unknown even in historical
or geographical matters. The wonderful stories told by our
early geographers are often scarcely more childish than those
related by our early historians. When a man of genius and
learning, like Milton, writing a century after the Reformation,
and contemplating even a reform of Reformation itself, could
yet accept the fables concerning English history which he has
transmitted to us, we may well cease to wonder at the spirit
of credulity possessed by rough Crusaders three centuries before the Reformation. The time came when an Erasmus,
enumerating the fragments of the true cross which he knew
to exist, could fairly and properly turn relic veneration into
ridicule, but at the opening of the thirteenth century we are
far from such a period.

CHAPTER XVI.

THE ELECTION OF A LATIN EMPEROR.

The candi-dates. NOW that the city was captured, the great question was the election of a new Emperor. The three chiefs of the expedition, the three most prominent men, and therefore the candidates whose names rose first to each man's mind, were Boniface, Marquis of Montferrat ; Baldwin, Earl of Flanders and of Hainault ; and Dandolo. There were others who hoped to be appointed, or at least to become candidates, but none of them ever had the least chance of success.[1] The great Doge would not allow himself to be put forward as a candidate. Whatever his own wishes may have been, it was in the highest degree improbable that even his great influence with the Republic could have persuaded it to allow any of its citizens to occupy so exalted a position as that of Emperor. Venice was fully alive to her own interest. To break the power of Constantinople, to weaken its influence over the territories adjacent to those of the Republic, to take away its trade, to obtain a considerable portion of its territory — all these were advantages. But it was not to the interest of the Republic to allow one of its citizens to occupy a throne which might render him or his successor a dangerous rival. Venice was already in difficulties with the Elder Rome, and had no wish to alienate Philip and everyone else who claimed or hoped to be the ruler of the New Rome. Moreover, it was not probable that Dandolo would have stood a good chance of being elected. A large portion of the Venetians themselves would have opposed his election, while the Crusaders would probably have for the

[1] Clari, p. 73.

moment put aside their jealousies in order to join in opposing
him. Public feeling against the Venetians was strong, and
the disaffection towards them was ready at any moment to
break out.

While, however, Dandolo did not propose to become a
candidate himself, his influence over the election was of the
utmost importance. He, indeed, was master of the situation.
It had been agreed that the Emperor should be elected by six
representatives chosen by the Venetians and six chosen by
the Crusaders. Dandolo had great and probably absolute
influence over the Venetians, and the fact that he had not put
himself forward as a candidate probably gave him considerable
authority with the rest. There were reasons why he should
have used his influence in favour of Boniface of Montferrat.
Dandolo and Boniface had been triumphant in their efforts to
divert the crusading army from its object : the first in order
to carry out the treaty with Malek Adel, the second in order
to accomplish the designs of Philip of Swabia and his own.
Their common intrigues at Venice and at Zara, their common
struggles with the Crusaders, who wished to be about their
lawful business while at Corfu and before Constantinople, and
their final success in spite of so much opposition, formed a
bond of union between them. Boniface was far more closely
allied with Dandolo than was Baldwin. Whether the assertion of a Venetian writer be true or not, that Boniface had
married a daughter of Dandolo [1]—and I see no reason to
doubt it – it is at least certain that the relations between them
had been of the most intimate kind. Since the capture of
the city the breach between the Crusaders and the Venetians
appeared to be continually widening. There was great dissatisfaction about the division of the spoil. The Crusaders
charged the Venetians with having conveyed plunder by night
to their ships instead of having given it up for distribution.[2]
Such a charge was more likely to be made by the Flemish

*The influ-
ence of
Dandolo.*

*Claims of
Boniface.*

---

[1] The younger Sanudo makes this assertion : 'Vite de' duchi di Venez.,'
Muratori, xxii. Du Cange, in his genealogy of the kings of Thessalonica,
mentions Constance de Suene as his first wife.

[2] See *L'Estoire de Eracles*, 275.

and French Crusaders than by the Lombards. The sympathy therefore of the Venetians was more likely to be with Boniface than with his rival. To these considerations others must be added. Boniface, with a noble figure and imposing presence which had caused him to be known as ' The Giant,' and with his great experience of war, was the popular type of an Emperor. Above all, he had been the recognised and official leader of the expedition. He had been solemnly appointed by the Crusaders, had shared his fortune with them, had led them to conquest and to plunder. His supreme authority had never been questioned. Moreover, he had been recognised by the inhabitants of the city as their ruler. The party of young Alexis would be on his side, and his marriage with Margaret or, as she now called herself, Maria, the widow of the Emperor Isaac, would increase his followers within the city. Not to appoint him was to condemn him. He was the one whose name would naturally first rise to each man's lips. To appoint another over his head was to declare that he no longer possessed the confidence of the host, but that he had been tried and had been found wanting.

Reasons against his election.

There were thus many reasons which indicated Boniface as the one likely to be elected Emperor, and some of them, as we have seen, were of a kind specially to recommend his appointment to Dandolo. There were others, however, which induced the great Doge to look unfavourably upon his appointment, and which made it necessary for him to act energetically if he wished to prevent it. The power such a position would give Boniface was too dangerous for the interests of Venice. His territory was too near Venice, and his relations with Philip were too intimate to allow the Republic to see him with equanimity the lord of the dominions to the west, east, and south of their possessions. Moreover, the Marquis was well known to have intrigued with the Genoese, the great rivals of the Venetians, in everything that regarded the trade of the Republic in the East; and although the interests of Boniface and the Venetians were for the moment united, he and their rivals might become the most formidable enemies they had ever faced were he Emperor of the East. If Boniface had been the husband of Dandolo's daughter, he was so no longer. His marriage with Margaret had taken place either during the days immediately after the capture of the city or, if not before the election, it was well known to the army that Boniface was engaged to the mother of young Alexis.[1] Not the least of the inducements to such a marriage was that his election would satisfy the Constantinopolitans. The eagerness and the confidence with which he had advanced his claims; the fact that the Greeks already recognised him as their master; that, as we have seen, they had already hailed him as Emperor; that they would probably have regarded his appointment much as our fathers looked upon the coming to the throne of the first Henry; and that they might possibly have become reconciled to his rule as that of one closely connected with the imperial family; the fact that his marriage would make him the guardian of the younger children of Isaac—all these circumstances showed that Boniface intended to lose no chance, that he had much to recommend him, and made it necessary for Dandolo to act with vigour if he did not wish him to be elected.

The election, on the other hand, of Baldwin, Earl of Flanders, offered many advantages to the Republic, and commended itself for many reasons to the Crusaders. His dominions were too far removed from those of Venice to make him a formidable opponent. He was only thirty-two years of age, and had had much less experience in war than Boniface. He was an amiable man, but wanting in the energy which characterised his rival. While, therefore, his personal charms and his nobility of blood, his cousinship to the King of France, and his descent from Charlemagne recommended him to the host, his want of the ability and energy of Boniface commended him to the Venetians. He appears to have been popular with the army generally, though it was among the Flemings and the French that, as might have been expected, his strongest supporters were found. As

Advantages to Venice of electing Baldwin.

---

[1] Villehardouin places the marriage about the time of the coronation, on the 16th. Count Riant thinks it took place earlier. Villehardouin's words are: 'Dedenz le terme del coronement.'

France had taken, as she continued to take, the leading part
in the Crusades, it was natural that the French should desire
one whose influence would commend itself to the French
people, rather than an Italian whose influence would only be
among a section of a people which had not played a prominent
part in these attempts to resist the Moslem.   There was yet
another consideration in favour of the election of Baldwin
rather than Boniface.   The Marquis from the first had played
the principal part in the intrigues for the diversion of the
enterprise from its lawful purpose.   Baldwin had indeed
acquiesced in what Boniface and Dandolo had arranged, but
the less active opposition of the Count of Flanders was likely
to make his election much more agreeable to the Pope than
that of the leader who had been the conspicuous opponent
of the orders emanating from Rome.   His election would
gratify that portion of the army which had been opposed to
the expedition to Constantinople, while even among those
who had willingly followed the lead of Boniface there would
be a considerable number ready to abandon him in order, now
that the plunder had been procured, to obtain the absolution
of the Pope.   There are reasons also for supposing that, after
young Alexis had been restored, Baldwin had placed himself
at the head of the party which urged that the Crusaders
should leave for the Holy Land, and, if this were so, not only
must he have had the support of those who had wished to
make their pilgrimage, but of all those who now desired to be
reconciled with the Church.[1]

Nomination of twelve electors.   A fortnight was spent before the Venetians and the
Crusaders could agree upon the choice of the electors.   Feeling
ran high.   No declaration appears during that time to have
been made by Dandolo as to whether he would consent to be
named or not.   It appears to have been understood that the
contest would be between Boniface and Baldwin.   As the
Venetians were to elect the same number of representatives
as the Crusaders, as Boniface evidently distrusted Dandolo,

---

[1] The official excuse put forward by Baldwin makes no mention of Boniface,
and is addressed to the rival of Philip, *Ottoni Dei gratia Romanorum regi et
semper augusto.*   Ernouil, I. vi. c. 19.

as the followers of Baldwin were sure to succeed in carrying a certain number of representatives out of the six to be chosen by the host, it had become evident to Boniface that his election was by no means safe. Accordingly, during the fortnight before the electors were chosen, negotiations went on with the object of securing something to Boniface in case he should fail in being elected. A compromise was at length made. To the original conditions for the election of an Emperor an additional article was added, to the effect that the one of the two candidates who was not elected should receive the Peloponnesus [1] and the provinces in Asia Minor still belonging to the Empire. The latter part of the concession was in reality very slight, because, as events showed, the Greeks were still sufficiently strong to hold their own against the Crusaders in those places in Asia Minor where the continually advancing tide of Turkish conquest had not already overwhelmed them. Even when this arrangement had been made Dandolo appears to have anticipated opposition on the part of Boniface in case the election should go against him. Guards were placed over the Bucoleon, and everything arranged so that the city should be given over to the Emperor named by the electors.[2]

At length each party had chosen its electors. The Venetians named six nobles ; the Crusaders chose six ecclesiastics.[3] The electors named by the Venetians were Vitale Dandolo, chief of the marines with the fleet, Querini, Contarini, Navagiero, Pantaleon Barbo and John Basegio, or, according to some writers, Michielo. Those named by the Crusaders were the Bishops of Halberstadt, Soissons, and Treves, the Papal Legate and titular Bishop of Bethlehem, the Archbishop-Elect of Acre, and Abbot Peter of Lucedio.

On the 9th of May the electors met. The place of meeting was the beautiful church of Our Lady the Illuminator, which was situated within the walls of Bucoleon.[4]

Meeting of electors to choose Emperor.

---

[1] Others say Crete.   [2] Rob. de Clari, p. 71.

[3] Rob. de Clari says each party chose ten.   Most authorities give six.

[4] τοῦ φάρου. Nicetas states that the meeting-place was the Church of the Twelve Apostles.

The twelve electors attended a solemn Mass, invoked the assistance of the Holy Spirit, and then swore upon the famous relics for which the church was renowned that they would choose him whom they believed in good faith to be the man they were most in need of, and who according to their conscience would make the best Emperor.

The palace of Bucoleon was filled with spectators. Venetians, Crusaders, and citizens were anxious to hear the verdict. The electors, says the Marshal, were placed in the rich chapel. The doors were locked from the outside, so that no one might communicate with them. The barons and the knights remained near at hand to learn what the decision should be.

We know the result of their deliberation. The indications of what went on are scanty. Hurter says that 'some were of opinion that as there was only one Pope so there should be but one Emperor, and that as Philip had been the cause of the expedition, so also he had through his wife Irene, the only daughter of Isaac, hereditary right to the throne.[1] If such a suggestion were raised, it was probably not at but before the meeting of the electors in the church of the Panhagia.

Dandolo declares for Baldwin. Venetian authors assert that the Bishops of Soissons and Troyes declared for Dandolo, and that at first the Venetian delegates were ready to vote for him. Justiniani affirms that when this proposition was made it was opposed by Pantaleon Barbo the Venetian delegate, who by his character, position, and influence with the Republic, had the greatest authority among them. A long discourse is given, which professes to be that delivered by Barbo, setting out the reasons why it would be dangerous to Venice that one of her citizens should be Emperor, and insisting that Dandolo himself would feel bound to refuse such an offer. The author of the 'Chronique de Romanie,' writing about a century later, says that the deliberations of the twelve electors were very long and very stormy. He adds that the Doge of Venice was proposed, and that on hearing the news he went to the church where the

---

[1] Hurter, *History Innocent II.*, 239. It is probable enough that such a suggestion was made by Boniface, or on his behalf, but Hurter gives no authority, nor can I find any to support it.

electors were sitting, knocked at the door, and addressed them. The author professes to give the substance of Dandolo's speech. He thanked them for the intended honour, declared that personally he was unworthy of it, asked them to withdraw his nomination, and prayed his friends to give their votes for Baldwin, whom the whole army judged to be worthy of the Empire.[1] The author of the ' Chronique ' is by no means a trustworthy guide as to details, but there can be little doubt that he represents fairly the substance of what was done. I am disposed to think that a declaration of the kind was made by Dandolo, but that it was made before the actual meeting in the palace chapel. Villehardouin represents the meeting as one held with closed doors, and leaves the impression that the electors were watched as carefully as the jury in the trial of the Seven Bishops. It is, however, clear that Dandolo's influence was thrown in favour of Baldwin.

The deliberations were long, and lasted far into the night, and this fact suggests that the electors had not met merely to register a foregone conclusion. Three out of the twelve are said by a contemporary writer to have been in favour of Boniface. We may fairly conjecture that after they found a decided majority against him they would endeavour to carry a resolution in favour of the election of Philip, as Hurter asserts they did. Such a course would have doubtless been the most agreeable to Boniface once his own chances were lost ; and such a course would have much to recommend it to the electors. *Philip probably proposed.*

The name of the Emperor of Rome had not yet lost its power. If the whole of Christendom could by one stroke be placed again under the rule of a Cæsar in things temporal as it was about to be in things spiritual, then indeed a great work would have been accomplished. The whole of the contemporary Western writers without exception advance as justification for the conquest of the New Rome the justice of punishing it for its schism, and the necessity of bringing about the union of Christendom under the rule of the Bishop of the *Reasons for such proposal.*

[1] *Chronique de Romanie*, from Buchon's *Collection de chroniques.* Paris, 1875.

Elder Rome. Hardly any other excuse is mentioned. No other in the eyes of the West was necessary. The Church of Christ ought to be in one fold and under one shepherd. It is difficult for us who live under a condition of things so greatly altered to conceive the overwhelming importance which the men of the thirteenth century attached to this visible union of Christendom ; and while we may admit that the Western writers were driven to find or to invent excuses for the destruction of Constantinople, it is impossible not to see that the union of the churches really possessed for them an importance which we can hardly comprehend. ' God delivered the city into the hands of the Latins,' says one Western writer,[1] ' because the Greeks had asserted that the Holy Ghost proceeded from the Father only, and celebrated the Mass with leavened bread.' ' By the wickedness of its long schism this city had provoked the Divine wrath.'[2] ' As the Crusaders knew that it was rebellious and odious to the Roman Church, they did not think that the forcing upon it another ruler would be displeasing either to the Pope or to God.'[3] Similar expressions occur in the contemporary accounts with great frequency and evident belief in their force.

This overwhelming sentiment in favour of the absolute and indispensable union of the Churches (a union, moreover, which the Crusaders knew would be the only fact which would tend to justify them to Innocent), applied also, though not to the same degree, to the union of Europe under one temporal head. It must be remembered also that the modern conception of a distinction between Church and State, between things temporal and things spiritual, hardly existed at the opening of the thirteenth century. The imperial power in the West was to a certain extent in commission; but the power of Cæsar had by no means passed away, and the electors in the chapel of Bucoleon, bound by their oaths to select the best man in the interests of Christendom, may well have seriously discussed the proposal to name Philip. The last crusade had been largely hindered

[1] Petrus Calo, writing about 1310 to the Roman Church.
[2] *Lectiones Bortens. : Exuviæ Sac.* ii.
[3] Gunther, xi.

because of the hostility which had been shown by the people under the rule of Constantinople. Were Philip Emperor, then not only could his troops pass in safety through Romania, but a large force could be selected from the Greeks themselves who would join the Crusaders. If any other were elected, then the old hostility would be shown, and though for a time Baldwin, or whoever else might be selected, would be friendly to the soldiers of the West who were fighting the battles of Christendom, yet every year would tend to make the interest of the Eastern Cæsar opposed to that of his Western rival. The remedy was to name Philip.

The reply of course was that Philip was King of Swabia, and, though he claimed to be Emperor, was opposed by Otho and disclaimed by the Pope. Still it may well be that Philip, as Hurter states, was proposed, that he was supported by the partisans of Boniface, and that the Venetians themselves may have hesitated over the rejection of such a proposal.

When after the long deliberations it became clear that Baldwin was the candidate of the majority, some further time was probably lost in determining that he should be the candidate named by all. It was evident that, in presence of the divisions among the Crusaders, it was in the common interest that the candidate selected should have as far as possible unanimous support. A resolution, therefore, by which he should be selected by all commended itself to all, and at length was carried.

At midnight the deliberations were at an end. The doors of the chapel were opened. The great crowd which had filled the palace-yard pressed near in order to see if they could obtain any indication from the faces of the electors of what their decision was.[1] The Doge, barons, Crusaders, Venetians, and citizens crowded round the electors to hear the new Emperor named. Nevelon, Bishop of Soissons, had been chosen by his colleagues to act as spokesman. 'Signors,' said he, 'thanks be to God we are all agreed upon our choice; ye have all sworn that you would accept him whom we should elect to be

Delibera-tions ended.

---

[1] Villehardouin, 260.

Emperor, and that you would support him against all opponents. This hour of the night which saw the birth of God sees also the birth of a new Empire.[1] We proclaim as Emperor Earl Baldwin of Flanders and Hainault.' The announcement was greeted with a loud cry of delight by the assembled crowd. Baldwin was raised upon a shield, according to the ancient custom, and carried from the palace into the Great Church. Boniface took part in this impromptu performance, and publicly showed his successful rival every mark of honour. The Emperor was placed on the golden throne set apart for the Emperors. The barons pressed forward to kiss his hand, and Baldwin was solemnly invested with the scarlet buskins.

Coronation of Baldwin.

Sunday, the 16th of May, that is, a week after the election, was fixed for the coronation, the preparations for which were made on a scale which astonished the Crusaders. As the Greek Patriarch had been deposed, the ceremony was performed by the Legate. Baldwin, seated on a buckler, was first raised on the shoulders of the chiefs ; then, descending, he was conducted solemnly to Hagia Sophia. He was escorted and followed by the barons and other officers of the army. Boniface bore in the procession the robe of cloth of gold with which he was to be invested. The Count of St. Paul followed with the imperial sword. At the church, or Great Minster, as the Western writers often called it, a solemn Mass was celebrated. The rite was a mixture of that of the Orthodox and Latin Churches. After the Trisagion had been intoned, the Legate, acting for the Patriarch, placed the imperial crown on the head of Baldwin, pronouncing at the same time the word ἄξιos—'he is worthy'—which was taken up and repeated by the other bishops and by the people. After the new Emperor had communicated, and had received all the imperial insignia, he headed a procession, escorted, right and left, by the Waring guard, armed as usual

---

[1] Du Cange *(Observations on Villehardouin)* discusses the meaning of the phrase 'in the hour in which God was born,' and concludes that this shows that the proclamation was made at midnight, which is the time when, according to common belief, Christ was born ; *dum silentium tenerent omnia.*

with their double-edged bills. The streets and houses through which the procession passed were decorated with the rich carpets which had escaped the three fires and the general plunder. Baldwin was thus conducted into the neighbouring palace of Bucoleon, and a Frank Emperor was seated, for the first time, on the throne of Constantine.

CHAPTER XVII.

CONCLUSION.

How the news was received by Innocent. IT remains to be told how the tidings of the conquest of Constantinople and the overthrow of the Eastern Empire was received by Innocent. The deviation at Zara and again at Corfu for the imperial city had been in direct opposition to the Pope's instructions. His absolution for the crime at Zara had been conditional upon no further attack being made upon the territory of any Christian nation. If the condition were not observed the absolution became *ipso facto* null. The Crusaders had been anxious that their first offence should be absolved by Innocent, but the leaders, doubtless, did their best to keep him in ignorance of the object of the expedition until it had been accomplished. The absolution had been conveyed to Corfu by Nivelon de Quierzy towards the end of April. The means of conveyance, however, were then so slow that the Pope only learned of what passed when it was too late to interfere with success. On the 20th of June, Innocent wrote to Boniface under the impression that the expedition, which had left nearly a month before, was still on that island.[1] Nearly two months later he appears to have been in doubt whether the fleet had really left for Constantinople.[2] It was not apparently until January 1204 that Innocent learned what was the destination of the crusade, although at that time the city had been captured and young Alexis restored.[3]

[1] *Inno. III. Epist.*, vi. 102.

[2] *Inno. III.*, vii. 130. ' Exercitus crucesignatorum in Græciam dicitur divertisse.'

[3] VI. 209. Within the recollection of men still living it was not unusual for ships to have to wait two months before being able to pass through the Dardanelles.

By the end of that month he had received the letters written at the end of August by the young Emperor and the barons, informing him of the first capture of the city on the 17th of July, and the coronation of the ward of Boniface on the 1st of August.

Innocent was indignant at the conduct of the Crusaders. He declared that to their first transgressions before Zara they had now added a second.[1] He reminded them that as they had deviated from their purpose they were still under the sentence pronounced upon them for the destruction of Zara. He informed them that that sentence could only be removed by the union of the two Churches becoming effectual and by the immediate departure of the Crusaders for the Holy Land.[2] The Venetians, being still under an unconditional excommunication, were not even addressed by the Pontiff.

When the city had been again captured, and when, in accordance with the agreement between the captors, the spoils of the New Rome had been divided, and a Crusading Emperor placed on the throne, the conquerors deemed it necessary to obtain the approval of Innocent. They rightly judged that the one extenuating circumstance would be in his eyes, as it, indeed, was in their own, the union of the Churches. Accordingly, almost immediately after his coronation, Baldwin addressed a letter to the Pope, giving the Crusaders' official version of what had taken place. With this letter Baldwin sent many presents, consisting of relics, of a golden cross, of chalices, of priestly garments in silk and velvet, all set with pearls and precious stones. The ship which conveyed the messenger in charge of the letter and the presents was captured off the Morea by a Genoese vessel, and the presents fell into the hands of the great rivals of Venice, who for a time seemed to have disregarded the fact that they were intended for the Pontiff. It was not until the Pope had protested energetically against the robbery and had

---

[1] *Ep. Inno.*, vi. 230; vi. 222.

[2] 'Nisi forsan ad extenuandam culpam et pœnam . . . quod de Græcorum inchoastis ecclesia, studueritis consummare. Ad recuperationem igitur Terræ Sanctæ totis viribus insistatis.'—*Inn. Ep.* vi. 230.

threatened an interdict that the *podesta* of Genoa consented
to restore them. The letter, which was intended not merely
for the Pope but for the Emperor in the West and its princes
and prelates generally, arrived in safety. It treated the capture of the city and the establishment of the Empire as
accomplished facts, and spoke of the future rather than of
the past. Innocent, the Emperor, princes, and prelates were
asked 'to stir up among the inhabitants of the West, of all
ranks and both sexes, the desire to come and share in the
immense mass of eternal and temporal treasures. Riches
and honours awaited all. The clergy should come in crowds
with the consent of their superiors, not to fight, but to organise
amid peace and plenty, for the good of the Church.' Baldwin
suggested that Innocent would be consulting his own glory,
and that of the Catholic Church, if he were to call a council
at Constantinople, and were himself to attend it, in order
that the New might be again united to the Elder Rome. He
reminded the Pope that, as he had already invited the Greek
Church while in schism to take part in a council, he might
now with greater effect preside over such an assembly. The
day of salvation had arrived—the day which old men and
Christians ought to celebrate ; the day destined to see peace
and union re-established. Other Popes for various reasons
had visited New Rome, why not he ? Baldwin declared that
the bishops, the abbots, and even the lower clergy had conducted themselves so honourably, so prudently, and so bravely
that it was only right that they should receive their reward
at the hands of the Lord. As for himself, who had been
judged worthy to be elected Emperor, he recommended the
Doge of Venice and his allies, the Venetians, to the Apostolic
benevolence. Baldwin intimated that before embarking for
the Holy Land he proposed to consolidate his dominion in
the new Empire and to introduce there the Latin rite.[1]

Innocent was placed in a situation of some difficulty. The
failure of the crusade caused him deep grief. The deviation
of the expedition was in flagrant violation of his orders. But
the city was captured. The great rival Church had been for-

[1] *Inno. Ep.*, viii. 147 ; vii. 153. Gesta, c. 95.

cibly brought into union or subjection. A Catholic instead of an Orthodox Emperor was seated upon the throne of the East. The schism, the obstinacy, the indifference of the Greeks had been punished. He had seen what so many of his predecessors had desired to see. Against the disobedience of the Crusaders were to be set off the advantages which might result from their conquest. The expedition had been crowned with success, and that success had so completely changed the situation that for a time Innocent was bewildered. His reply to the letter of Baldwin was at first in vague or general terms. He 'rejoiced at the success of Baldwin's arms.' He would take the Empire of Baldwin under the protection of St. Peter, and he ordered all the Crusaders to help Baldwin by their counsels and their deeds. He promised that he would do his best to furnish the clergy who were asked for. He urged upon Baldwin that the only way to make sure of his dominion was to make the subjection of the Greek Church to the Holy See complete. On the principle of rendering unto Cæsar that which is Cæsar's and unto God that which is His, he urged the new Emperor to be careful to preserve all Church property. The union of the Churches was evidently the one compensating fact which weighed against the disobedience of the Crusaders. Addressing the bishops and clergy in the expedition, he urged them to do their utmost to make the union complete. If they did this, there would soon be but one fold under one shepherd.

In the many letters in which Innocent speaks of the conquest, he leaves the impression that he is overwhelmed by the circumstances which had happened ; that, so far as the Crusaders are concerned, they have been guilty of sin, but that their acts and his own desires, in his opinion, have been overruled by a Divine interference, and that it is now his duty to make the best of a situation which has been created by a higher Power than his own. Above all, the conquest appeared to have brought about the union of the two Churches—a union which had now been accomplished by forcibly bringing the Eastern into subjection to the ruler of the West. But even this union had been the result of a violation of every right principle to the last. While, however, making every allowance for the fact that Innocent could hardly help feeling himself slighted by the intentional disregard of his injunctions and of his rights, the whole tone of his correspondence shows that he was filled with righteous indignation at the iniquities perpetrated by the Christian host which had destroyed the capital of Christendom. After many consultations with the eminent men by whom he had surrounded himself, Innocent wrote a letter on the conquest of the city which will ever remain as a monument of just scorn and the lofty statesmanship of the greatest man of his time.

His reproaches against the expedition.
'Since, in your obedience to the Crucified One, you took upon yourselves the vow to deliver the Holy Land from the power of the Pagans, and since you were forbidden, under pain of excommunication, to attack any Christian land or to do damage to it, unless its inhabitants opposed your passage or refused you what was necessary (and in such case you were to undertake nothing against the will of the Legate), and since you had neither right nor pretence of right over Greece, you have slighted your vow; you have not drawn your sword against Saracens, but against Christians; you have not conquered Jerusalem, but Constantinople; you have preferred earthly to heavenly riches. But that which weighs more heavily upon you than all this is that you have spared nothing that is sacred, neither age nor sex; you have given yourselves up to prostitution, to adultery, and to debauchery in face of all the world. You have glutted your guilty passions not only on married women or widows, but upon women and virgins dedicated to the Saviour; you have not been content with the imperial treasures and the goods of rich and poor, but you have seized even the wealth of the Church and what belongs to it; you have pillaged the silver tables of the altars; you have broken into the sacristies, stolen the crosses, the images, the relics, in such a fashion that the Greek Church, although borne down by persecution, refuses obedience to the Apostolical See, because it sees in the Latins only treason and the works of darkness, and loathes them like dogs.'

As the conquest was already accomplished, Innocent declared that the Crusaders might keep the land conquered by the judgment of God ; but its people must be governed with justice, must be maintained in peace and made to conform to religion. The property of the Church must be restored ; restitution and repentance must be shown for what was past, and the vow which the Crusaders had taken must yet be fulfilled.

I have insisted that the great object of Innocent's pontificate was to strike a blow at Mahometanism. He hoped against hope that by the conquest of Constantinople the cause of the Crusades might be advanced. Hence, in claiming from the Crusaders, after the conquest of the city, that they should fulfil their vow, he pointed out that 'the conquest of Greece would facilitate the conquest of the Holy Land,' and he reminded them that they themselves had made use of the argument that the shortest way to Palestine was through Constantinople rather than through Alexandria. Again and again he returns to the same idea, and, beyond the union of the Churches, the great practical benefit which Innocent sought to derive from what he elsewhere describes as 'an act of justice where wicked men have been made use of by God to punish other wicked men,' is that by means of Greece a heavier blow might yet be struck against the Mahometans. Baldwin had summoned the two Legates from Palestine. Innocent could not approve of their conduct in obeying the summons. ' If you have left in order to obtain aid for the Holy Land, we approve of what you have done ; if you have done so to assist in organising the Church of Greece, you have acted too hastily. We authorise you to remain at Constantinople on condition that you do not lose sight of Jerusalem, to which you were sent.' As the Venetians had been the instruments of diverting the expedition to Constantinople, Innocent's opposition to them was greater than it was to the Crusaders. By the former his wishes had been disregarded to the last. In accordance with the agreement for the division of the spoil, the Venetians named one of their own countrymen, Thomas Morosini, as patriarch. The arrangements for his appointment, and for naming Latin priests to the churches

Especially against the Venetians.

in Constantinople, had been made, not only without consulting Innocent, but in a way which Dandolo knew would be in defiance of what the Pope regarded as his rights. Innocent rejected Morosini, and declared his election by the Venetian canons of Hagia Sophia null and void, on the ground that laymen had no right to appoint an ecclesiastic to so high an office, and that the canons had not themselves been regularly appointed. The objection was not to the person, for Innocent at once named Morosini to the patriarchal see. Innocent declared that they had added to their offence the pillage of the temples and the iniquitous diversion of the ecclesiastical possessions. He continued even to refuse the request made by the Venetians to appoint the archbishop they had named to Zara. 'It is you,' he wrote, ' who have led the army of the Lord into a wicked path. Instead of fighting the Saracens, you have made war on Christians. You have despised the Legate, treated the excommunication with contempt, broken the vow of the Cross, sacked the treasures and the Church possessions at Constantinople. You have done your best to appropriate and make hereditary among you the Lord's Church by means of lawless treaties. Tell me yourselves how you can make up for the harm you have done to the Holy Land, since you have turned to your profit an army of Christians, so great, so noble, and so numerous, which had been brought together with so much pain and expense, and with which not only Jerusalem, but even a part of Babylon might have been conquered. For if it succeeded in taking possession of Constantinople and Greece, *a fortiori* it could have snatched Alexandria and the Holy Land from the pagans. . . . . Not only earthly might, but the will of heaven, would have placed the two cities in your power. . . . . Christianity was scandalised by your conduct towards Zara, and we cannot scandalise the whole Church by giving the pallium to the archbishop without having received satisfaction from you.' [1] As late as 1213 he reproached them with the crime of Zara.

Innocent refused the request made to him to exclude Dan-

[1] *Ep. Inno.*, ix. 139.

dolo, on account of his great age, from the performance of the vow to make the crusade. When he learned that Cardinal Peter had actually arrived in Constantinople to aid in the reorganisation of the Orthodox Church, he reproached him bitterly for his continual misconduct. He had removed the excommunication for the sack of Zara ; he had allowed the first siege of Constantinople ; he had absolved the Crusaders from their vow. Innocent formally charged him with having known, and even having formed, the plot in 1202 for the restoration of young Alexis.[1] 'When the Crusaders, after having consecrated themselves to the Saviour, have abandoned their route, drawn away by earthly attractions, were you free to change so holy and so solemn a vow, and to permit them to take another destination ? Think on it yourself. Disappointment, shame, and anxiety weaken us when we ask whether the Greek Church can enter into union with the Apostolic See when that Church has seen only the works of darkness among the Latins.' Innocent had heard that after a year the pilgrims in Constantinople were to be at liberty to return home. 'The Saracens,' he declares, 'who trembled after the fall of Constantinople, will they not throw themselves on you, like wolves on an abandoned flock, when they learn that the Crusaders will return during the year to their homes ? And we, how can we ask the people of the West to come to the aid of Palestine, even to the help of Constantinople, if they reproach us who are guiltless for what you have done, because the Crusaders have abandoned their vows, and have returned to their homes, loaded with the booty of an Empire which they cannot even defend. . . . . We do not wish to blame you further for the absolution which you have granted to the Venetians ; that will be the subject of a special letter. But we order you to return without delay to the Holy Land.' Boniface, who had been the leader of the expedition and its evil spirit, was in like manner not spared by Innocent. He was mean enough to endeavour to throw all the blame of the deviation of the expedition on Cardinal Peter, and a long letter endeavouring to justify himself in this manner was

---

[1] *Inno. Ep.* viii. 133.

carried to Rome by a special messenger.[1] His arguments
and excuses were answered by Innocent, who holds him responsible as the leader of the expedition for the horrors of
the plunder of Constantinople, and refuses to absolve him
from his vow to make the pilgrimage to the Holy Land.

In truth, the designs of Innocent had completely failed.
His long and careful preparations had been defeated by
Philip, Boniface, and Dandolo. All the efforts he had made
to strike a deadly blow at Islam had come to nought. The
preparations made at so much cost had resulted in an attack
upon Christians, and not upon Moslems. Constantinople
had been captured instead of Jerusalem. The opportunity,
so favourable from many causes, had been lost, and no other
presenting equal advantages was ever to occur again. The
internal quarrel between the Saracen leaders, and the weakening of Egypt by the non-rising of the Nile during a succession
of years, were accidental circumstances which were never repeated. The supreme moment for striking a blow at the
Saracens at a time when it could have been struck with effect
had passed. Innocent's energy was too great to allow him to
sit idle under the failure, but all his efforts were unable to
create an expedition equal in strength to that of 1202.
Innocent had been humiliated by Philip, and in order to
accomplish the design of his life was compelled to accept his
humiliation, and, by declaring for Philip, to acknowledge that
he had been defeated. On the other hand, the Duke of
Swabia had failed in the principal object of his intrigues, and
had only succeeded in defeating the plans of the Pontiff. But
though his design of becoming Emperor of East and West
had failed, he never ceased until his assassination in 1208
by Otho of Wittelsbach to intrigue against Baldwin and his
successor on the throne. He claimed the booty collected in
Constantinople as belonging to him, and took possession of a
considerable portion which had been taken into Germany.
When the short reign of Baldwin was terminated in 1205 by
his capture before Adrianople by an army of Bulgarians,
Wallachians, and Comans, and his subsequent death or

[1] *Inno. Ep.* viii. 133.

murder, Philip still hoped that he might be named to the imperial throne. When Henry, the brother of Baldwin, was named as his successor, Philip treated him as a usurper, continually spoke of his own rights through his wife, and appears to the last to have hoped that all Europe might again be brought under his rule, as the Cæsar universally recognised.

The great consolation of Innocent was that the union of the two Churches had been effected ; but, as we have seen, he doubted whether even this could be brought about effectually since the conduct of the Latins had outraged the members of the Orthodox Church. Subsequent events showed that he was entirely right. The Latin conquest of Constantinople caused so deep a hatred to the Church of the West that there was never a chance again of a union between the two being accomplished. Upwards of two centuries later futile attempts were made at Ferrara and Florence to bring about such a union in presence of the ever-constant danger of the Maho-metan progress, but the events of 1203–4 made the endeavour a ridiculous failure. Nor was the anticipation of the diffi-culties of union in the mind of Innocent without justification for other branches of the Orthodox Church. Russia was the great convert of the Greek Church. Innocent sent a mission to that country to invite its archbishops and bishops to sub-mit themselves to Rome, in order that their Church might not be left out of his fold, and called attention to the fact that the Greek Church, from which they had hitherto derived their aid, had now become united under him. The mission obtained no satisfactory result. The Russian remained loyal to the Orthodox Church. Its aversion to that of the Elder Rome appears even to have been increased by this mission, and in a short time it placed itself under allegiance to the Patriarch of Nicæa, who soon took the position which had been occupied by the Patriarch of Constantinople.

It is beyond my purpose to give an account of the rule of the Latin Emperors of Constantinople. The events which followed the capture of the city in rapid succession proved that the Crusaders had undertaken a task far beyond their

Conquest destroyed all chance of union of Churches.

Powerless-ness of Franks to govern Romania.

powers, even if they had been united. But dissatisfaction at once began to show itself, and the struggles among the captors themselves greatly weakened their power. Boniface and his friends seem to have believed themselves outwitted by Dandolo and the partisans of Baldwin. Within a few days of the coronation of the new Emperor a tumult was raised between the rival factions.[1]

Quarrel between Baldwin and Boniface.

The leaders themselves were soon at variance. In accordance with the arrangement by which the candidate who should not be elected Emperor should have the Morea and the Roman territory in Asia Minor, Boniface became entitled to these possessions. I have already stated that the latter, at least, was a concession of territory which it was beyond his power to conquer. He therefore made application to exchange it for the principality or kingdom of Salonica. His hereditary claim to this part of the Empire as the heir of

---

[1] *Chron. of Romania*, edition Buchon, p. 73. The Greek in which this is written is one of the most curious specimens existing of the mediæval form of that language. The Marquis of Montferrat becomes ὁ μαρκέζης τοῦ Μονφέρα ; he becomes king or Ῥήγας τῆς Σαλονίκης πόλης. The French are Φραντζέζοι. Baldwin is Μπαλδουβίνος, just as in modern Greek the sound of *b* is always represented by Μπ. The language of Nicetas contains many words of Western origin. I had prepared a long note on the subject of the Greek language of the twelfth century, but Professor Freeman's paper on ' Some points in the Later History of the Greek Language' in the *Journal of Hellenic Studies* of Oct., 1882, says all, and more, than I could say on the subject, and says it much better. I am inclined, however, to doubt whether his assertion (p. 390) that Anna and Nicetas ' are always using words which could never have been the first words that came into their heads ' is true. To this day islanders in the Archipelago, Greeks around Trebizond and other places in Asia Minor, have preserved in their dialects great numbers of words which even those well acquainted with modern Greek do not recognise, although they are words which will be found in Liddell and Scott. Many also of the words used in modern Greek, though not usually found in a classical dictionary, are old, and had already come into general use in the time of Nicetas. Thus, he writes κρασίον for wine, φεγγάριον for moon, νέρον for water.

The pages of Nicetas show that the Latin Court of the early Emperors had left a great number of words in the language, and that Nicetas and his readers were quite familiar with the sight of Romance words in a Greek form. Some of these are very curious. Thus, φρέριος for brother, *frère*, used of the brethren or friars of Jerusalem ; τάβλιον for table, καβαλλάριος for cavalier, δοὺξ and δούκας for duke, μαρκέσιος for marquis, σκουτάριον, σκάλα, σέκρετον, σάγιττα, ῥὴξ for *rex* (the king in a pack of cards is still in modern Greek called ῥήγας), πόρτα, κουστωδία, κόμης, ἰνδικτιών, δομέστικος, βούλλα for *bulla*, βίγλα for *vigilia* (which shows that in the twelfth century at least β was sounded as it is now, *v*).

Reynier, to whom Manuel Comnenos was alleged to have given certain rights, and the restoration of which inheritance had been promised to him at Corfu by his ward, and the fact that it adjoined the territory of the King of Hungary, to whose sister he was now married, were put forward as reasons in favour of such an exchange. Boniface had a sufficient party to enable him to make his claim in the form of a demand. The new arrangement was a violation of the agreement which had been come to, but Baldwin did not feel strong enough to refuse it. Mourtzouphlos and Alexis were at large. The country might yet offer opposition to the new rule, and a division between the Crusaders themselves might supply the opportunity which each of these ex-Emperors needed in order to regain Constantinople. The question was much discussed, spoken of, says the Marshal, in many ways, but at length Baldwin gave an evasive answer, which Boniface construed into a consent to the exchange. Then Boniface did homage. The difficulty, however, was not as yet at an end. Baldwin, leaving Constantinople in charge of Dandolo, marched against Mourtzouphlos and Alexis. Boniface was to have accompanied him, Baldwin apparently not having confidence in his fealty. After leaving Adrianople the Emperor arrived at Mosynopolis,[1] where he determined to await the coming of his powerful subject. On his arrival the latter begged Baldwin to allow him to leave at once for Salonica, in order to take possession of his signiory, and requested the Emperor not to ruin him by going there himself. Baldwin, however, refused. A defiance followed. Boniface declared that if the Emperor went into his country when he, Boniface, was quite able to conquer it for himself, it could not be for his benefit. 'If you go, understand clearly that I shall not go with you, and that I shall separate myself from you.'[2] The Emperor replied that even on such terms he would go

---

[1] Mosynopolis is, I believe, the present Mastanly, a village to the north of the Rhodope, distant about two days' journey, as Villehardouin describes it, from Adrianople, and to the west of that city. Du Cange (*Observations on Villehardouin*, p. 158), says it was formerly Maximianopolis, and places it at the mouth of the Maritza or Hebrus.

[2] Villehardouin, 277.

to Salonica. The breach was a serious one. Boniface, through his marriage, was supported by many of the Greeks. He declared that Baldwin was more perjured than the Greeks. He gave to his wife's eldest son the name and the imperial ornaments of the Emperor. The Marshal shows his estimate of the danger by the statement that if God had not taken pity on them they would have lost all that they had gained. The rival leaders, each with an army behind him, were on the verge of war. Baldwin remained firm, and marched towards Salonica. Boniface, with his own followers, and with nearly all the German Crusaders, went on their way back, apparently towards Constantinople. The latter reached and entered Didymotica on the Maritza, and a day's journey south of Adrianople. The Greeks submitted, and indeed the inhabitants of the country flocked in wherever he passed with offers of support. Boniface pushed on to and besieged Adrianople, in which Baldwin had left a garrison. The Crusader in command immediately sent messengers, who rode day and night, to the capital, to inform Dandolo of the rupture, and that Boniface, after having occupied Didymotica, one of the strongest forts in Romania, was supported by the Greeks, and was now laying siege to Adrianople.

Boniface makes a bargain with the Venetians.

Boniface then played a bold stroke to detach the Venetians from the side of Baldwin. In the beginning of August he made a bargain with their representatives in Adrianople, by which he was to receive 1,000 marks and lands in the west of the Balkan peninsula, which produced annually 10,000 golden aspers, and which he was to hold in fee from the republic and not from the Emperor. In return Boniface sold to the Venetians his rights over Crete, his claim to 100,000 golden aspers due from the Empire on account of Alexis the Fourth, his late pupil, and the rights over the fiefs with which Manuel had invested Reynier in Salonica. As the Venetians, in virtue of the agreement for the division of the Empire, were under no obligation to do homage for the territory which they received in Romania, Boniface, by this agreement, withdrew himself from vassalage to Baldwin. The trick was worthy of

Boniface, and it entirely succeeded in detaching Dandolo from the side of Baldwin.[1]

Meantime Baldwin had marched on Salonica. The intervening towns and fortresses had surrendered to him, and Salonica itself—then, as Villehardouin says, one of the best and richest cities of Christendom—surrendered on condition of retaining the privileges the city had enjoyed under the Greek Emperors.

Dandolo in Constantinople was still master of the situation, and appears to have had powers which made him something like a dictator. After taking counsel with the chief barons he sent Villehardouin, who is careful to inform us on several occasions that he had great influence with Boniface, to Adrianople. When he approached that city, Boniface, with the chiefs of his army, met him. In the interview the Marshal reproached the Marquis with having attacked the territory of the Emperor, and especially with having laid siege to Adrianople without having submitted his grievances to Dandolo. Boniface laid all the blame on the Emperor, but at length agreed to a truce. Boniface was to retire from Adrianople to Didymotica and place his case in the hands of Dandolo, Count Louis of Blois, Conon de Bethune, and the Marshal. Boniface withdrew to Didymotica, where his wife had remained, and the Marshal returned to Constantinople. The next object was to obtain the consent of the Emperor to place his case also in the hands of Dandolo. Messengers were sent to inform Baldwin of what had taken place. The Emperor in the meantime had heard of the siege laid to Adrianople by Boniface, and had hastened to its relief. He was, however, in considerable difficulties. Then, as now, the neighbourhood of Salonica was highly feverish. Some of his best followers had died, and many more were disabled with fever. Hence the army which followed him was weak and almost unfit for service. While he was on his way to the relief of Adrianople the messengers from Dandolo met him and formally requested him to submit the matters in difficulty

Proposals for arbitration.

---

[1] *Refutatio Cretæ*, Aug. 12 ; Taf. et Thorn. c. xxiii. p. 512 ; Phrantzer, 106.

with Boniface to the four arbitrators already mentioned, adding the distinct threat that they would on no account allow a resort to force between him and his late chief. The Emperor was irritated and angry. He consulted his council, in which, says the Marshal, who is throughout the partisan of Boniface, there were many who had helped to cause the broil. Many hard words — *grosses paroles* — were used. The Emperor made a compromise. His army was too weak to resist Boniface with his Greek allies. He dared not openly break with Dandolo, who was master of the capital, but he would not consent, until he knew the situation better, to place himself in the hands of the self-constituted tribunal. He replied that he would not pledge himself to submit the difficulty, but he would proceed at once to his capital, and in the meantime would promise not to attack Boniface.

Arbitration accepted.

On his arrival in Constantinople Baldwin recognised before the fourth day that the course proposed was the best which under the circumstances he could adopt. Boniface was sent for, and he also, after some hesitation, consented to come to the capital. On his arrival the arbitrators decided that the Emperor was wrong. Salonica was to be given to Boniface, and as a pledge that this should be done the Marshal was ordered to take possession of Didymotica, and to hold it until he should be assured that Boniface was safely installed in Salonica. This decision was carried out, and the principality or kingdom of Salonica was surrendered to Boniface, Marquis of Montferrat.

Death of three leaders of expedition.

While the first of the grave internal differences of the Crusaders was thus brought temporarily to an end, others of an equally serious character, which it is beyond my purpose to describe, presented themselves. Innocent's anticipation of misfortune was soon justified by events. There was, as he had foreseen, little hope of aid in the crusade from the conquerors of an Empire which they were not able to defend. Within eighteen months of the capture of the city three of the principal actors and a crowd of those only second to them in rank had died, and most of them by violent deaths. We have already seen that Baldwin fell into the hands of his enemies

and was succeeded by his brother. Dandolo ended his long
life in June 1205, and lies buried in or near the Great Church
of the Divine Wisdom.[1] Two years afterwards Boniface, who
had continued to be of doubtful loyalty until he appears to
have been contented by the marriage of his daughter to the
new Emperor Henry, met with a violent death. He was
caught in a defile in the Rhodope Mountains by the Bulgarians, and was mortally wounded.

The years that followed the Conquest were of wild disorder
and confusion. The government of the country was a task
to which the Crusaders were unequal. The attempt to rule
the ancient Empire under the forms of the Western feudal
system utterly broke down. The land was divided into fiefs
amongst the barons and knights, but the division caused much
disaffection and wrangling. Few were satisfied in the general
scramble which followed. In spite of an attempt to decide
differences by lot, the rule was that each should keep what he
could take. Western titles and dignities were introduced,
and we read in the Empire of the New Rome for the first
and last time of grand constables, seneschals, cup-bearers,
marshals, grand butlers, masters of the stables, and the like.
The Crusaders knew their own fanciful law of honour, but
despised the ordinary law by which mortals are governed. The
assize of Jerusalem became law for the Empire, though an
attempt was made to preserve a portion at least of the old
Roman administration, including the application of the Roman
law of Justinian as preserved in his capital. There was,
however, little chance that the new Western system of organisation could work harmoniously with the ancient Roman
administration which had lasted in Romania. Such chance as
there might otherwise have been was destroyed by forces outside the Empire. The same causes which had weakened the
dominion of the Byzantine rulers began to operate against

Disorder throughout Empire.

---

[1] A slab in the women's gallery, inscribed ' Henrico Dandolo,' commemorates
him. This, after having long been forgotten, was discovered a few years ago,
and though some of the archæologists of Constantinople whose opinions are
entitled to respect believe it to be comparatively modern, I see no reason to doubt
that it was placed in its present position shortly after Dandolo's death.

the Crusaders, and rendered them so feeble that instead of
being able, as they had fondly believed, to use the strength of
Romania against the Saracens, they had to implore aid from
the West to enable them to hold what they had conquered.

The deposed Emperor, Alexis the Third, and Alexis the
Fifth or Mourtzouphlos, were, at the time of the occupation,
still at large. The latter was captured by the Latins at
Mosynopolis, was brought to Constantinople, and was thrown
from the column of Theodosios. Alexis the Third was captured
and sent to Boniface, who held him as a prisoner, and gave to
Philip the satisfaction of stating how he should be disposed of.

The Moslems were at first greatly alarmed at the capture
of the city which to them was still the world's capital, was
still Rome. In their first alarm even Malek-Adel hastened
to conclude a truce of six years with Cardinals Peter Capuano
and Soffred ; but he and his so-called religionists soon recovered from the shock of the Conquest. Constantinople had
drawn away Crusaders from Palestine instead of adding to
their number. The Western soldiers, including even many
of the Templars, took the opportunity of leaving Syria in
order to share in the wealth which was offered them in
Constantinople. The natural result followed. The truce was
broken, and Islamism soon came into possession of territory
which had been held for many years by the Christians.
Though Innocent profoundly regretted this result, he was
forced to acquiesce in it, and even to authorise Baldwin to
retain the Crusaders in Constantinople whom he had previously
ordered to leave for the Holy Land. In the spring of 1205
the new Emperor was attacked by Greeks, Bulgarians, and
Comans, and it was in one of these attacks that the latter
succeeded in luring a considerable body of Crusaders into
an ambuscade, where they killed three hundred knights, captured the Emperor, and took him prisoner to Tirnova. It was
at this very time that the great body of Venetians, amounting
to 7,000, left Constantinople. The Crusaders were obliged to
withdraw to the capital, and nearly the whole of the country
was abandoned to the enemy. Still less success awaited them
in Asia Minor, where the Greeks were able to hold their own

after the first surprise caused by the capture of the capital, and where the invaders found themselves glad, in 1206, to make a truce with Theodore Lascaris. The story of the following years is one of struggle with the people whom they had conquered, of reckless disregard of their rights, of raids over the country in search of plunder, of attacks from the Bulgarians and Comans, and of almost incessant warfare until, sixty years after the Conquest the Greeks again obtained possession of the capital, and the Latin Empire of the East came to an ignominious end.

Venice obtained the richest rewards and the fullest pay-ment for her share in the conquest of Constantinople. Her acquisition of territory and of commerce made her for a time the undisputed mistress of the Mediterranean. Dandolo had stipulated that she should receive three out of the eight por-tions into which it had been agreed that Romania should be divided. He appears to have been allowed to take his choice of the portions of territory which were to be allotted as the share of the Republic. He naturally chose lands adjacent to those already possessed by Venice on the Adriatic, and such ports, islands, or sea-boards as she could readily defend with her fleet. Dandolo retained the rank which had already been given him of *Despot*, and was allowed to wear the imperial buskins. In addition, he took the curious title of lord of one-quarter and a half of the Roman Empire.[1]

The gains of Venice.

On the death of Dandolo his successor obtained a conces-sion from the Emperor authorising any Venetian citizen or ally to take possession of any of the islands in the Ægean or places on its coasts which were not already occupied by the Republic, and to hold it for him and his heirs. The granting of this concession was followed by a series of buc-caneering expeditions, which speedily captured and occupied a number of important positions. Gallipoli, on the Dardanelles, was seized by Marc Dandolo and another prominent citizen, and with the Thracian Chersonese was erected into a duchy.

---

[1] 'Henricus Dandolus, D. G. Venetiarum, Dalmatiæ atque Croatiæ dux, do-minus quartæ partis et dimidiæ totius imperii romani.'—*Vite de' Duchi di Venez*, in Muratori.

Another band, under Sanuto, occupied Naxos, Paros, and other isles, which were held by him and his descendants for four centuries. Chios was occupied by the great chiefs, Justiniani and Michaeli. A part of Eubœa and the Cyclades, the islands of Lemnos and Zante, were captured by others. The Republic itself took possession of Corfu. The great power of Venice over the Adriatic, the Ægean, and especially over the islands mentioned, and over a portion of the Morea, dates from the Latin Conquest—a power which was used on the whole well and wisely, which introduced or continued fairly good government, and which has left traces in well-constructed roads and fortresses in every place I have mentioned. But, as was natural, the results of the Latin Conquest were more markedly visible in Venice herself than in any of the possessions which she obtained. Her marts were filled with merchandise. Her ships crowded the great canals and her harbour with the spoils of Asia and the products of the Levant. Her architecture reproduced and improved upon that of Constantinople. The spoils of the New Rome were her proudest ornaments. Her wealth rapidly increased. The magnificence of the New Rome was transferred to Venice, which was during the fourteenth and fifteenth centuries the most splendid of Christian cities.

The Venetians continued to be opposed to the designs of Innocent, and years afterwards were reproached by him for sending wood, arms, and other munitions of war [1] to the Saracens in Alexandria. At a later period Innocent reproached them for mocking the Holy See, and injuring the cause in the Holy Land by inducing pilgrims who were able to fight to go to Crete and assist the Republic instead of combating the Saracens. In the next crusade, which was also due to the indomitable energy of the same pontiff, the Venetians were as far as possible excluded from all participation in it. Innocent named Ancona and Brindisi as the ports of embarkation for *Outre-mer*.

Beneficial results of the Con-   It was impossible that an event so important as the conquest of the city could have been without beneficial results

---

[1] *Inno. Ep.* xii. 142.

to Western Europe. Against the destruction of so much quest to Western Europe. that is valuable we may set off a knowledge of the comforts of a civilised and comparatively luxurious life conveyed to the West by men who, as we gather from all contemporary accounts, had been profoundly affected by the signs of wealth with which they were surrounded. Many small but valuable advances in Western civilisation are due to the Conquest. Silk weaving had been better understood in Constantinople than in any Western city, but Venice was soon able to rival her ancient enemy. Various seeds and plants found their way to the West. The diversion of the trade of Constantinople from the Bosphorus to the Adriatic or into overland routes probably benefited and helped to develop the civilisation of Western Europe. The commerce of the Empire passed into the hands of foreigners and rivals, and of these Venice naturally obtained the largest share. The valuable products of Central Asia which found their way into the ports of the Azoff and the Euxine, and which had been reserved jealously by the citizens of Constantinople for themselves, even at the time when the Emperors were granting capitulations for trade in every other part of the Empire, all these now went to Venice. Most of this trade was carried on by sea ; but the dangers which beset maritime commerce now that the shadow of the *pax Romana* had passed away caused a considerable portion of the valuable and less bulky products of India and Central Asia to be taken up the Indus, thence by camels to the Caspian, and then partly overland and partly by rivers to Venice or other European states. The great bulk of the trade between Asia and Europe was diverted from the Bosphorus into the Adriatic. Venetian ships for a time replaced in the Black Sea not only those of Constantinople but even those of Genoa. The Tartar races in the Euxine as well as the Saracens in Egypt and Syria traded almost exclusively with the citizens of Venice.

Innocent continued to condemn the conduct of the Cru- Evil results of the Conquest. saders and the Venetians in terms which show that they are the expression of his deliberately formed opinion and that of the great churchmen by whom he was surrounded. We have

seen that at times his language is that of profound indignation
at the iniquities which have been committed ; at other times
it is that of expostulation and of calm reasoning. But
throughout the many letters in which he addresses the actors
in this huge *fiasco* or alludes to their conduct, the sentiment
most predominant is one of sadness that the Crusaders should
have abandoned the object for which they were brought together. His letters leave the impression that he never ceased
to regret the failure of the crusade, which had been so carefully organised and from which so much might reasonably
have been expected. He appears on many occasions to feel
that it is impossible to make those whom he addresses understand what is the greatness of the opportunity which they
had missed. In the comprehension of the Eastern Question
of his day and of what statesmanship required for the interests
of Europe and of civilisation, he seems to stand at the
opening of the thirteenth century head and shoulders above
all other kings or potentates. The tone of his letters, their
gloom, when speaking of the prospects of Romania, of Asia
Minor, and of Syria, almost appear as if he alone in his generation foresaw how disastrous the conquest of the imperial
city would be ; as if he alone recognised that it was the
interest of Europe to make a supreme effort to strike a blow
at Mahometanism, which should make its further advance
upon Christian territory impossible. He tried and, no doubt,
to a certain extent succeeded in finding consolation in the
union of the Churches, which he fondly hoped was to be
brought about by the Conquest ; and though, as we have seen,
he recognised that the manner of the Conquest had placed a
great obstacle in the way of union, he yet hoped that the
'loathing' felt by the Greeks towards the Latins would in
time be softened down or entirely removed. He hoped that
the conquest of the city might still be of use in reducing
Jerusalem under Christian rule. He believed that its capture
during Easter week might possibly be regarded as a token
that Christ intended to make use of the wicked act of the
Crusaders by leading to a new entry into the Holy City, and
that the Greeks had been justly punished for their refusal to

help the Crusaders and for their toleration of a mosque within their city. In these facts he found consolation. The existence of this consolation and of this rejoicing in the union which so many pontiffs had laboured fruitlessly to effect brings out into stronger relief the intensity of his conviction that the destruction of the rival Empire was a blunder and a crime. He was profoundly sad at the failure of his expedition, at the conquest of an Empire whose preservation would absorb all the force of Christendom, and at the necessary diversion of Christian troops from Palestine.

We who can be wise after the event can see even more distinctly than Innocent how disastrous the conquest of Constantinople had been. The city had spent its strength in fighting against the hordes of Asia. Her outposts in Asia Minor had been carried by successive waves of barbarian invasion from the great plains of Central Asia. These waves had come flowing on multitudinously and overwhelmingly during a century and a half, pushed by the mighty movement of a Tartar emigration westward. Her powers had been exhausted in thus defending the first lines of Europe against a host whose deficiencies were immediately supplied by newcomers. We have seen in our recent small war in the Soudan what is the force which the spring-tide of fanaticism may supply to a horde of barbarians. The Seljukian Turks and the other Mahometan tribes against which the strength of the New Rome had been spent were still drunk with the new wine of their conversion to Islam, and fought with the same confidence of victory, recklessness of life, and even desire for death, with which the half-naked and ill-armed followers of an African Mahdi threw themselves on English bayonets. The legions of the New Rome withstood the rush of the Asiatic fanatics as steadily as did our own countrymen those of Africa. Again and again they succeeded in inflicting what was apparently a crushing defeat on the Mahometan armies. But the battle had to be fought again after the lapse of a few years, when new fanatics had come to take the place of those who had fallen. The flow of savage or barbarian hordes had, during the two centuries which preceded the disaster of 1204, been as constant on the north of the Black Sea as it had been on the south. Bulgarians, Comans, Pat-chinaks, Uzes, and other non-Christian peoples had attacked the imperial city in the rear while she was defending European civilisation in Asia Minor. The Sicilian expedition and internal troubles, arising partly from dynastic rivalries, partly from the weakness which had come upon her owing to Asiatic influences, and especially to the weakening of the despotic form of government before the oligarchical had become suffi-ciently strong to take its place, had lessened her strength, so that she was not able to offer the resistance which she had done two centuries earlier. But she gained breathing time from the divisions of the Seljukian Turks and from her victories over the Bulgarians and the Comans, and there appears good reason to believe that had she not been destroyed by the people of the West and her organisation put an end to during a period of sixty years, she would have been able at a later period to have made a stouter, and probably a suc-cessful, resistance to the Ottoman Turks. That this new body of Mahometan invaders was able a century and a half later to occupy several important positions in what they called as their descendants still call it, Roumelia, or the territory of Rome, and that two centuries and a half later they were able to capture the New Rome itself, was due to the fatal blow which had been inflicted by Philip of Swabia, by Boniface of Montferrat, and by Henry Dandolo.

That blow had been struck at the moment when the resources of the Empire had been expended. We ought not, however, to forget that its strength had been spent in stemming the torrent of barbarism, in fighting the battle of Europe against Asia, of Christianity against Moslemism. The Empire had maintained this struggle not altogether single-handed, for the efforts of the Crusaders had been on behalf of the same cause. But the Saracens were the special object of their attack, and the fact that the deliverance of the Holy Land was the peculiar aim set before them prevented anything like hearty co-operation with the Empire in attacking the Turks, even had there not been other reasons which made such co-operation impossible. Thus the great brunt of the struggle fell upon the Empire alone, and, in spite of the efforts of rulers like Manuel to persuade the western nations to come to their aid, Latin and German Europe preferred to fight Islam in its own way rather than to make common cause against the common enemy. The traditional feeling in the West against those who recognised the sway of the emperor of the New Rome has affected western historians of this period of Constantinopolitan history. As the descendants of peoples who acknowledged the rule of the Latin Church we have taken our ideas and our prejudices from our fathers, and are in this sense all of us the sons of the crusaders. Western Europe has been only too ready to find evidence of the corruption and the effeminacy of the eastern capital, to recognise that Asiatic influences had lessened the vigour which had characterised its government during the centuries preceding the Crusades, and to regret that its Church had less power in arousing enthusiasm than had the sister Church of our fathers. Hence it is that justice has not been done to the unceasing struggle of a century and a half previous to 1204, made by the Greek-speaking Roman empire and by the Christians of Armenia and Georgia. The facts that have been remembered are that the Eastern Church had refused to accept the supremacy of the Pope ; that Constantinople was taken by the crusaders ; that her population was powerless to prevent the capture of the city in 1453 by the Ottoman Turks. The facts that are forgotten are that if the Turks were unable to find a footing in Europe until 150 years after 1204 it was because the Eastern Empire had made so gallant a resistance during a like period before 1204 ; that she received a fatal blow from the huge expedition called the Fourth Crusade, but that, recovering for a while from this blow, she was yet able unaided to prolong the struggle long enough to pour forth a stream of learning and literature over the West ; and that the time gained while she kept back the Turks greatly diminished their strength, delayed their arrival in Europe, and enabled the West to grow strong enough to resist the Ottoman Turks when, two centuries after they had made good their hold upon Europe, they attained the period of their greatest strength, barely more than two centuries ago. That John Sobieski was able to drive back the Turks who were besieging Vienna in 1683 was due to the fact that the Eastern Empire had sacrificed itself as the vanguard of Europe.

Nor must it be forgotten that the resistance of the Empire had had a great effect upon the Seljukian Turks. The terrible blows inflicted on them had diminished their strength. They had already begun to show signs of weakness. During the latter years of the century Chengiz Khan, the great leader of a Tartar tribe which had adopted the name of Mongol,[1] had commenced his terrible career, and the attention of the Turks was in 1204 already turned away from the Empire to that of the more serious danger which threatened them in their rear. The capture of Constantinople by the western crusaders enabled the Turks to survive that danger. Had the Empire not been destroyed there is good reason to believe that it would have shortly recovered its strength, have continued its struggle, and that the Turks, with Chengiz Khan on one side and the imperial troops on the other, would have been annihilated.

The continual attacks of the Seljuks, while they had weakened the Empire, yet enable us to see how great had been its strength. The marches of Pizarro in the New World, of the Ten Thousand of Alexander, and at this very time of Chengiz Khan into China and subsequently into Transoxiana, were all easy, since they were through states which had become demoralised. No such demoralisation existed, and consequently no such march was possible under the rule of the New Rome. The Turks had to fight their way inch by inch, to hold what they captured against continual harassment, and, as I have so often repeated, were only able to maintain a settlement in Asia Minor because their numbers were continually recruited by fresh bands of immigrants into the country they had captured.

---

[1] The soldiers of Chengiz Khan repudiated the name Tartars as that of a people they had conquered, and called themselves Mongols. Notwithstanding the repudiation they were of Tartar origin. – Osborn's *Islam under the Khalifs of Baghdad*, 372.

The results of the Fourth Crusade upon European civilisation were altogether disastrous. The light of Greek civilisation, which Byzantium had kept burning for nearly nine centuries after Constantine had chosen it as his capital, was suddenly extinguished. The hardness, the narrowness and the Hebraicism of western civilisation were left to develope themselves with little admixture from the joyousness and the beauty of Greek life. Everyone knows that the Turkish conquest of Constantinople dispersed throughout the West a knowledge of Greek literature, and that such knowledge contributed largely to the bringing about of the Reformation and of modern ways of thought. One cannot but regret that the knowledge of Greek literature was so dearly bought. If the dispersion of a few Greeks, members of a conquered and therefore despised race, but yet carrying their precious manuscripts and knowledge among hostile peoples, could produce so important a result, what effect might not reasonably have been hoped for if the great crime against which Innocent protested had not been committed? Western Europe saw the sparks of learning dispersed among its people. The light which had been continuously burning in a never forgotten and, among the literary class, a scarcely changed language, had been put out. The crime of the Fourth Crusade handed over Constantinople and the Balkan peninsula to six centuries of barbarism, and rendered futile the attempts of Innocent and subsequent statesmen to recover Syria and Asia Minor to Christendom and civilisation. If we would understand the full significance of the Latin conquest of Constantinople, we must try to realise what might now be the civilisation of Western Europe if the Romania of six centuries ago had not been destroyed. One may picture not only the Black Sea, the Bosphorus, and the Marmora surrounded by progressive and civilised nations, but even the eastern and southern shores of the Mediterranean given back again to good government and a religion which is not a barrier to civilisation.

Errata

Page 35, line 13, *after* the first emperor *add* of note.

,, 90, ,, 3, *for* Alexis Angelos *read* Isaac Angelos.

INDEX.

—◦✦◦—

with Isaac's troops, 125 ; his death, 126
Fulk preaches the fourth crusade, 228

GALATÀ, derivation of the name, 178 *note* ; occupied by the crusaders, 301 ; confused with Pera, 319 *note*
Genoese, treaties of Manuel I. with the, 164
George, king of Georgia, wars against the Turks, 45
Georgia, conquest of, by Alparslan, 26
Gibbon, error of, as to the meeting-place of the first Nicene Council, 36 *note*
Godfrey de Bouillon, crusade of, 35
Greek Christians, character of their regard for relics, 364
Greek language, 3, 141, 388 *note*
Greeks, municipal spirit of the, 4 ; its influence on the duration of the Empire, 5 ; their mercantile tendencies, 9 ; their theory of government, *ib.*
Gregory VII., Pope, his appeals on behalf of the Eastern emperor, 32
Gyrolemna, the camping-ground of the Crusaders, 303, 304

HAGIA Sophia, 183, 352 ; plundered by the crusaders, 353
Hagiochristophorides, a creature of Andronicos I., 82, 84 ; killed by Isaac Angelos, 85
Henry VI. of Germany, crusade of, 130
Henry of Sicily claims imperial territory, 139
Hippodrome, the, 185
Hopf, Charles, historical collection of, 265
Huns, the, 51 ; attack the Empire, 52

ICONIUM, origin of the Sultans of, 30 ; recovered by Manuel I., 45 ; captured by Frederic Barbarossa, 48, 125
Innocent III., Pope, endeavours to impose Roman authority on the Eastern Church, 131 ; character

of, 223 ; his zeal for the deliverance of the Holy Land, 225 ; appeals to Alexis III., 226; agrees conditionally to the contract between the crusaders and the Venetians, 235 ; declines to aid Alexis IV., 274, 277 ; excommunicates the Venetians, 284 ; grants a conditional absolution to the crusading army, *ib.* ; appeals to the army, 285 ; condemns the expedition to Constantinople, 287 ; his indignation at the first attack of Constantinople, 379 ; replies to the Emperor Baldwin's letter, 381 ; denounces the conduct of the conquerors, 382 ; his anger against the Venetians, 383 ; reprimands Cardinal Peter Capuano, 385 ; reproaches Boniface, 386 ; asks the Russians to submit to the Roman See, 387 ; tone of his letters relative to the Conquest, 397
Iran, the term, 15 *note*
Isaac, a pretender, 99
Isaac Comnenos Sebastocrator in possession of Cyprus, 82, 89; murder of his sureties by Andronicos I., 82 ; refuses submission to Isaac II., 95; imprisoned by Richard I., 96, 129 ; attempts to obtain the imperial throne, 107 ; his offences against the English king, 128
Isaac II. makes an alliance with Saladin, 46, 125 ; his war with the Wallachs, 58, 91 ; defends Nicæa against Andronicos I., 81 ; supposed prediction of a soothsayer concerning him, 84 ; kills Hagiochristophorides, 85 ; proclaimed emperor by the people, *ib.* ; yields Andronicos to popular fury, 88 ; his character, *ib.*, 100 ; his difficulties with the Sicilians, 90 ; his conversation with his prisoner Count Baldwin, *ib.* ; defeat of his army by the Wallachs, 91 ; quells the revolt of Branas, 92 ; despatches an expedition to Cyprus against Isaac Comnenos, 96 ; marches against the revolted Wallachs and Bulgarians, *ib.*, 101 ; attempts upon the throne during his reign, 97 : his misgovernment, 100 ; deposed and imprisoned by his brother Alexis, 101 ; his treaties with the

session of Nicæa, 33 ; reach the
Marmora, *ib.* ; their successes
attract the attention of Pope
Gregory VII., 34 ; their struggles
with the crusaders, 36, 43 ; renewal of their numbers after defeat, 40 ; defeat the Emperor
Manuel, 45, 64 ; make a further
division of their empire, 47 ;
effects of their invasion on the
condition of the Empire, 48 ;
their wars with Alexis III., 108 ;
their sultans often the sons of
Christian slaves, 110 *note* ; stu-
pendous character of their conflict
with the Empire, 172

UZES, the, a Turkish people, 156

VARANGIANS, *see* Warings
Vaux, Abbot of, forbids the attack
upon Zara, 255
Venice, reproduction of Byzantine
life in, 11 ; helps the Empire
against Robert Wiscard, 132,
161 ; commerce of, with the Empire, 160 ; Venetians make common cause with the Empire, 161 ;
extraordinary commercial privilege granted them by Alexis I.,
162 ; expelled by John Comnenos,
ib. ; policy of Manuel I. towards
them, 163 ; jealous of other
Latin colonists, 167 ; makes war
against the Empire, *ib.* ; growth
of her hostility to Constantinople, 169, 232 ; chosen as the
port of departure of the fourth
crusade, 231 ; her contract with
the crusaders, 234 ; the crusaders
in, 241 ; proposes the attack of
Zara, 244 ; joins the crusade, 250 ;
concludes a treaty with Egypt,
263 ; excommunicated by Innocent III., 284 ; her fleet attacks
Constantinople, 305 ; charged
with taking an undue share of
spoil, 360 ; purchases the rights

of Boniface, 390 ; her gains by
the conquest of Constantinople,
395
Vermilion, the imperial colour, 330
note
Villehardouin, his account of the
fourth crusade, 242, 244 ; his
interview with Isaac II., 313

WALLACHS, the, 57 ; their successes against the Empire, 58,
91 ; establish with the Bulgarians
a Wallachio-Bulgarian state, 59 ;
revolt against Isaac II., 91, 96 ;
give trouble to Alexis III., 104
Warings or Varangians, connection
of, with England, 149 ; successive treaties made with them by
the Empire, 150 ; furnish a body-
guard for the emperor, 152 ;
their weapon, 153 ; their respect
for women, 154 ; fidelity of the
guard, 155
William I. of Sicily, his war
against the Empire, 134
William II. of Sicily makes war on
the Empire, 135
William of Tyre, his account of the
Turks, 16 *note* ; preaches the
third crusade, 123
Wiscard, Robert, attacks the Empire, 34, 133, 161
Woman, social position of, in Constantinople, 201

ZARA, attack of, proposed by the
Venetians to the crusaders, 244 ;
offer of its citizens to surrender
withdrawn, 254 ; captured, 255 ;
explanations of the expedition to,
given by contemporary writers,
260 ; destroyed by the Venetians, 290 ; convention of, submitted to the crusading army,
291
Zemiskes, John, defeats Swendoslav, 151

A

Classified Catalogue

OF WORKS

IN

GENERAL LITERATURE

PUBLISHED BY

LONGMANS, GREEN, & CO.

39 PATERNOSTER ROW, LONDON, E.C

NEW YORK: 15 EAST 16TH STREET.

1894.

MESSRS. LONGMANS, GREEN, & CO.

Issue the undermentioned Lists of their Publications, which may be had post free on application :—

1. MONTHLY LIST OF NEW WORKS AND NEW EDITIONS.
2. QUARTERLY LIST OF ANNOUNCEMENTS AND NEW WORKS.
3. NOTES ON BOOKS; BEING AN ANALYSIS OF THE WORKS PUBLISHED DURING EACH QUARTER.
4. CATALOGUE OF SCIENTIFIC WORKS.
5. CATALOGUE OF MEDICAL AND SURGICAL WORKS.
6. CATALOGUE OF SCHOOL BOOKS AND EDUCATIONAL WORKS.
7. CATALOGUE OF BOOKS FOR ELEMENTARY SCHOOLS AND PUPIL TEACHERS.
8. CATALOGUE OF THEOLOGICAL WORKS BY DIVINES AND MEMBERS OF THE CHURCH OF ENGLAND.
9. CATALOGUE OF WORKS IN GENERAL LITERATURE.

PRÆTERITUS · FUTURUS · TELLE · EST · LA · VIE

INDEX OF AUTHORS.

MESSRS. LONGMANS & CO.'S STANDARD AND GENERAL WORKS.

CONTENTS.

History, Politics, Polity, and Political Memoirs.

Abbott.—A HISTORY OF GREECE. By EVELYN ABBOTT, M.A., LL.D.
Part I.—From the Earliest Times to the Ionian Revolt. Crown 8vo., 10s. 6d.
Part II.—500-445 B.C. Crown 8vo., 10s. 6d

Acland and Ransome.—A HANDBOOK IN OUTLINE OF THE POLITICAL HISTORY OF ENGLAND TO 1890. Chronologically Arranged. By the Right Hon. A. H. DYKE ACLAND, M.P., and CYRIL RANSOME, M.A. Crown 8vo., 6s.

ANNUAL REGISTER, (THE). A Review of Public Events at Home and Abroad, for the year 1892. 8vo., 18s.

Volumes of the ANNUAL REGISTER for the years 1863-1891 can still be had. 18s. each.

Armstrong.—ELIZABETH FARNESE; The Termagant of Spain. By EDWARD ARMSTRONG, M.A., Fellow of Queen's College, Oxford. 8vo., 16s.

Arnold.—Works by T. ARNOLD, D.D., formerly Head Master of Rugby School.

INTRODUCTORY LECTURES ON MODERN HISTORY. 8vo., 7s. 6d.

MISCELLANEOUS WORKS. 8vo., 7s. 6d.

Bagwell.—IRELAND UNDER THE TUDORS. By RICHARD BAGWELL, LL.D. (3 vols.) Vols. I. and II. From the first invasion of the Northmen to the year 1578. 8vo., 32s. Vol. III. 1578-1603. 8vo. 18s.

Ball.—HISTORICAL REVIEW OF THE LEGISLATIVE SYSTEMS OPERATIVE IN IRELAND, from the Invasion of Henry the Second to the Union (1172-1800). By the Rt. Hon. J. T. BALL. 8vo., 6s.

Besant.—THE HISTORY OF LONDON. With 74 Illustrations. Crown 8vo., 1s. 9d. Or bound as a School Prize Book, 2s. 6d. *Although this book is primarily intended for a School Reading Book it is also suitable for general use.*

Buckle.—HISTORY OF CIVILISATION IN ENGLAND AND FRANCE, SPAIN AND SCOTLAND. By HENRY THOMAS BUCKLE. 3 vols. Crown 8vo., 24s.

Chesney.—INDIAN POLITY: a View of the System of Administration in India. By Lieut.-General Sir GEORGE CHESNEY. New Edition, Revised and Enlarged. [*In the Press.*

Crump.—A SHORT ENQUIRY INTO THE FORMATION OF POLITICAL OPINION, from the reign of the Great Families to the advent of Democracy. By ARTHUR CRUMP. 8vo., 7s. 6d.

De Tocqueville.—DEMOCRACY IN AMERICA. By ALEXIS DE TOCQUEVILLE. 2 vols. Crown 8vo., 16s.

Fitzpatrick.—SECRET SERVICE UNDER PITT. By W. J. FITZPATRICK, F.S.A., Author of 'Correspondence of Daniel O'Connell'. 8vo., 7s. 6d.

Freeman.—THE HISTORICAL GEOGRAPHY OF EUROPE. By EDWARD A. FREEMAN. D.C.L., LL.D. With 65 Maps. 2 vols. 8vo., 31s. 6d.

History, Politics, Polity, and Political Memoirs—*continued.*

Froude.—Works by JAMES A. FROUDE, Regius Professor of Modern History in the University of Oxford.

THE HISTORY OF ENGLAND, from the Fall of Wolsey to the Defeat of the Spanish Armada.

Popular Edition. 12 vols. Crown 8vo., 3s. 6d. each.

Silver Library Edition. 12 vols. Crown 8vo. 3s. 6d. each.

THE DIVORCE OF CATHERINE OF ARAGON: the Story as told by the Imperial Ambassadors resident at the Court of Henry VIII. *In usum Laicorum.* Crown 8vo., 6s.

THE SPANISH STORY OF THE ARMADA, and other Essays, Historical and Descriptive. Crown 8vo., 6s.

THE ENGLISH IN IRELAND IN THE EIGHTEENTH CENTURY. 3 vols. Crown 8vo., 18s.

SHORT STUDIES ON GREAT SUBJECTS. 4 vols. Crown 8vo., 3s. 6d. each.

CÆSAR: a Sketch. Crown 8vo., 3s. 6d.

Gardiner.—Works by SAMUEL RAWSON GARDINER, M.A., Hon. LL.D., Edinburgh, Fellow of Merton College, Oxford.

HISTORY OF ENGLAND, from the Accession of James I. to the Outbreak of the Civil War, 1603-1642. 10 vols. Crown 8vo., 6s. each.

A HISTORY OF THE GREAT CIVIL WAR, 1642-1649. 4 vols. Crown 8vo., 6s. each

THE STUDENT'S HISTORY OF ENGLAND. With 378 Illustrations. Crown 8vo., 12s.

Also in Three Volumes.

Vol. I. B.C. 55—A.D. 1509. With 173 Illustrations. Crown 8vo. 4s.
Vol. II. 1509-1689. With 96 Illustrations. Crown 8vo. 4s.
Vol. III. 1689-1885. With 109 Illustrations. Crown 8vo. 4s.

Granville.—THE LETTERS OF HARRIET COUNTESS GRANVILLE, 1810-1845. Edited by her Son, the Hon. F. LEVESON GOWER. 2 vols., 8vo.

Greville.—A JOURNAL OF THE REIGNS OF KING GEORGE IV., KING WILLIAM IV., AND QUEEN VICTORIA. By CHARLES C. F. GREVILLE, formerly Clerk of the Council. 8 vols. Crown 8vo., 6s. each.

Hart—PRACTICAL ESSAYS IN AMERICAN GOVERNMENT. By ALBERT BUSHNELL HART, Ph.D. &c. Editor of 'Epochs of American History,' &c., &c. Crown 8vo. 6s.

Hearn.—THE GOVERNMENT OF ENGLAND: its Structure and its Development. By W. EDWARD HEARN. 8vo., 16s.

Historic Towns.—Edited by E. A. FREEMAN, D.C.L., and Rev. WILLIAM HUNT, M.A. With Maps and Plans. Crown 8vo., 3s. 6d. each.

BRISTOL. By the Rev. W. HUNT.
CARLISLE. By MANDELL CREIGHTON, D.D., Bishop of Peterborough.
CINQUE PORTS. By MONTAGU BURROWS.
COLCHESTER. By Rev. E. L. CUTTS.
EXETER. By E. A. FREEMAN.
LONDON. By Rev. W. J. LOFTIE.
OXFORD. By Rev. C. W. BOASE.
WINCHESTER. By Rev. G. W. KITCHIN, D.D.
YORK. By Rev. JAMES RAINE.
NEW YORK. By THEODORE ROOSEVELT.
BOSTON (U.S.) By HENRY CABOT LODGE.

Horley.—SEFTON: A DESCRIPTIVE AND HISTORICAL ACCOUNT. Comprising the Collected Notes and Researches of the late Rev. ENGELBERT HORLEY, M.A., Rector 1871-1883. By W. D. CARÖE, M.A., and E. J. A. GORDON. With 17 Plates and 32 Illustrations in the Text. Royal 8vo., 31s. 6d.

Joyce.—A SHORT HISTORY OF IRELAND, from the Earliest Times to 1608. By P. W. JOYCE, LL.D. Crown 8vo., 10s. 6d.

Lang.—ST. ANDREWS. By ANDREW LANG. With 8 Plates and 24 Illustrations in the Text by T. HODGE. 8vo., 15s. net.

Lecky.—Works by WILLIAM EDWARD HARTPOLE LECKY.

HISTORY OF ENGLAND IN THE EIGHTEENTH CENTURY.

Library Edition. 8 vols. 8vo., £7 4s.
Cabinet Edition. ENGLAND. 7 vols. Crown 8vo., 6s. each. IRELAND. 5 vols. Crown 8vo., 6s. each.

HISTORY OF EUROPEAN MORALS FROM AUGUSTUS TO CHARLEMAGNE. 2 vols. Crown 8vo., 16s.

HISTORY OF THE RISE AND INFLUENCE OF THE SPIRIT OF RATIONALISM IN EUROPE. 2 vols. Crown 8vo., 16s.

THE EMPIRE: its Value and its Growth. An Inaugural Address delivered at the Imperial Institute, November 20, 1893, under the Presidency of H.R.H. the Prince of Wales. Crown 8vo. 1s. 6d.

History, Politics, Polity, and Political Memoirs—*continued.*

Macaulay.—Works by Lord Macaulay.

Complete Works of Lord Macaulay.

Cabinet Edition. 16 vols. Post 8vo., £4 16.
Library Edition. 8 vols. 8vo., £5 5s.

History of England from the Accession of James the Second.

Popular Edition. 2 vols. Cr. 8vo., 5s.
Student's Edition. 2 vols. Cr. 8vo., 12s.
People's Edition. 4 vols. Cr. 8vo., 16s.
Cabinet Edition. 8 vols. Post 8vo., 48s.
Library Edition. 5 vols. 8vo., £4.

Critical and Historical Essays, with Lays of Ancient Rome, in 1 volume.

Popular Edition. Crown 8vo., 2s. 6d.
Authorised Edition. Crown 8vo., 2s. 6d., or 3s. 6d., gilt edges.
Silver Library Edition. Cr. 8vo., 3s. 6d.

Critical and Historical Essays.

Student's Edition. 1 volume. Cr. 8vo., 6s.
People's Edition. 2 vols. Cr. 8vo., 8s.
Trevelyan Edition. 2 vols. Cr. 8vo., 9s.
Cabinet Edition. 4 vols. Post 8vo., 24s.
Library Edition. 3 vols. 8vo., 36s.

Essays which may be had separately price 6d. each sewed, 1s. each cloth.

Addison and Walpole.
Frederick the Great.
Croker's Boswell's Johnson.
Hallam's Constitutional History.
Warren Hastings. (3d. sewed, 6d. cloth).
The Earl of Chatham (Two Essays).
Ranke and Gladstone.
Milton and Machiavelli.
Lord Bacon.
Lord Clive.
Lord Byron, and The Comic Dramatists of the Restoration.

Speeches. Crown 8vo., 3s. 6d.

Miscellaneous Writings

People's Edition. 1 vol. Crown 8vo., 4s. 6d.
Library Edition. 2 vols. 8vo., 21s.

Miscellaneous Writings and Speeches.

Popular Edition. Crown 8vo., 2s. 6d.
Student's Edition. Crown 8vo., 6s.
Cabinet Edition. Including Indian Penal Code, Lays of Ancient Rome, and Miscellaneous Poems. 4 vols. Post 8vo., 24s.

Selections from the Writings of Lord Macaulay. Edited, with Occasional Notes, by the Right Hon. Sir G. O. Trevelyan, Bart. Crown 8vo., 6s.

May.—The Constitutional History of England since the Accession of George III. 1760-1870. By Sir Thomas Erskine May, K.C.B. (Lord Farnborough). 3 vols. Crown 8vo., 18s.

Merivale.—Works by the Very Rev. Charles Merivale, Dean of Ely.

History of the Romans under the Empire.
Cabinet Edition. 8 vols. Cr. 8vo., 48s.
Silver Library Edition. 8 vols. Crown 8vo., 3s. 6d. each.

The Fall of the Roman Republic: a Short History of the Last Century of the Commonwealth. 12mo., 7s. 6d.

O'Brien.—Irish Ideas. Reprinted Addresses. By William O'Brien, M.P. Cr. 8vo. 2s. 6d.

Parkes.—Fifty Years in the Making of Australian History. By Sir Henry Parkes, G.C.M.G. With 2 Portraits (1854 and 1892). 2 vols. vo., 32s.

Prendergast.—Ireland from the Restoration to the Revolution, 1660-1690. By John P. Prendergast, Author of 'The Cromwellian Settlement in Ireland'. 8vo., 5s.

Round.—Geoffrey de Mandeville: a Study of the Anarchy. By J. H. Round, M.A. 8vo., 16s.

Seebohm.—The English Village Community Examined in its Relations to the Manorial and Tribal Systems, &c. By Frederic Seebohm. With 13 Maps and Plates. 8vo., 16s.

Sheppard.—Memorials of St. James's Palace. By the Rev. Edgar Sheppard, M.A., SubDean of the Chapel Royal. With Illustrations. [*In the Press.*

Smith.—Carthage and the Carthaginians. By R. Bosworth Smith, M.A., Assistant Master in Harrow School. With Maps, Plans, &c. Crown 8vo., 3s. 6d.

Stephens.—Parochial Self-Government in Rural Districts: Argument and Plan. By Henry C. Stephens, M.P. 4to., 12s. 6d. Popular Edition, crown 8vo, 1s.

Stephens.—A History of the French Revolution. By H. Morse Stephens, Balliol College, Oxford. 3 vols. 8vo. Vols. I. and II. 18s. each.

Stubbs.—History of the University of Dublin, from its Foundation to the End of the Eighteenth Century. By J. W. Stubbs. 8vo., 12s. 6d.

History, Politics, Polity, and Political Memoirs—*continued.*

Sutherland.—The History of Australia and New Zealand, from 1606 to 1890. By Alexander Sutherland, M.A., and George Sutherland, M.A. Crown 8vo., 2s. 6d.

Thompson.—Politics in a Democracy: an Essay. By Daniel Greenleaf Thompson. Crown 8vo., 5s.

Todd.—Parliamentary Government in the British Colonies. By Alpheus Todd, LL.D. 8vo.

Tupper.—Our Indian Protectorate: an Introduction to the Study of the Relations between the British Government and its Indian Feudatories. By Charles Lewis Tupper, Indian Civil Service. 8vo., 16s.

Wakeman and Hassall.—Essays Introductory to the Study of English Constitutional History. By Resident Members of the University of Oxford. Edited by Henry Offley Wakeman, M.A., and Arthur Hassall, M.A. Crown 8vo., 6s.

Walpole.—Works by Spencer Walpole.

History of England from the Conclusion of the Great War in 1815 to 1858. 6 vols. Crown 8vo., 6s. each.

The Land of Home Rule: being an Account of the History and Institutions of the Isle of Man. Crown 8vo., 6s.

Wylie.—History of England under Henry IV. By James Hamilton Wylie, M.A., one of H. M. Inspectors of Schools. 3 vols. Vol. I., 1399-1404. Crown 8vo., 10s. 6d. Vol. II. Vol. III. [*In preparation.*

Biography, Personal Memoirs, &c.

Armstrong.—The Life and Letters of Edmund J. Armstrong. Edited by G. F. Armstrong. Fcp. 8vo., 7s. 6d.

Bacon.—The Letters and Life of Francis Bacon, including all his Occasional Works. Edited by James Spedding. 7 vols. 8vo., £4 4s.

Bagehot.—Biographical Studies. By Walter Bagehot. 8vo., 12s.

Boyd.—Twenty-five Years of St Andrews, 1865-1890. By A. K. H. Boyd, D.D., LL.D., Author of 'Recreations of a Country Parson,' &c. 2 vols. 8vo. Vol. I. 12s. Vol. II. 15s.

Carlyle.—Thomas Carlyle: a History of his Life. By J. A. Froude. 1795-1835. 2 vols. Crown 8vo., 7s. 1834-1881. 2 vols. Crown 8vo., 7s.

Fabert.—Abraham Fabert: Governor of Sedan and Marshal of France. His Life and Times, 1599-1662. By George Hooper, Author of 'Waterloo,' 'Wellington,' &c. With a Portrait. 8vo., 10s. 6d.

Fox.—The Early History of Charles James Fox. By the Right Hon. Sir G. O. Trevelyan, Bart.
Library Edition. 8vo., 18s.
Cabinet Edition. Crown 8vo., 6s.

Hamilton.—Life of Sir William Hamilton. By R. P. Graves. 3 vols. 15s. each.
Addendum to the Life of Sir Wm. Rowan Hamilton, LL.D., D.C.L. 8vo., 6d. sewed.

Hassall.—The Narrative of a Busy Life: an Autobiography. By Arthur Hill Hassall, M.D. 8vo., 5s.

Havelock.—Memoirs of Sir Henry Havelock, K.C.B. By John Clark Marshman. Crown 8vo., 3s. 6d.

Macaulay.—The Life and Letters of Lord Macaulay. By the Right Hon. Sir G. O. Trevelyan, Bart.
Popular Edition. 1 volume. Cr. 8vo., 2s. 6d.
Student's Edition. 1 volume. Cr. 8vo., 6s.
Cabinet Edition. 2 vols. Post 8vo., 12s.
Library Edition. 2 vols. 8vo., 36s.

Marbot.—The Memoirs of the Baron de Marbot. Translated from the French by Arthur John Butler, M.A. Crown 8vo., 7s. 6d.

Montrose.—Deeds of Montrose: The Memoirs of James, Marquis of Montrose, 1639-1650. By the Rev. George Wishart, D.D., (Bishop of Edinburgh, 1662-1671). Translated, with Introduction, Notes, &c., and the original Latin (Part II. now first published), by the Rev. Alexander Murdoch, F.S.A., (Scot.) Canon of St. Mary's Cathedral, Edinburgh, Editor and Translator of the Grameid MS. and H. F. Moreland Simpson, M.A. (Cantab.) F.S.A. (Scot.) Fettes College. 4to., 36s. net.

Seebohm.—The Oxford Reformers—John Colet, Erasmus and Thomas More: a History of their Fellow-Work. By Frederic Seebohm. 8vo., 14s.

Biography, Personal Memoirs, &c.—*continued.*

Shakespeare.—OUTLINES OF THE LIFE OF SHAKESPEARE. By J. O. HALLIWELL-PHILLIPPS. With numerous Illustrations and Fac-similes. 2 vols. Royal 8vo., £1 1s.

Shakespeare's TRUE LIFE. By JAMES WALTER. With 500 Illustrations by GERALD E. MOIRA. Imp. 8vo., 21s.

Sherbrooke.—LIFE AND LETTERS OF THE RIGHT HON. ROBERT LOWE, VISCOUNT SHERBROOKE, G.C.B., together with a Memoir of his Kinsman, Sir JOHN COAPE SHERBROOKE, G.C.B. By A. PATCHETT MARTIN. With 5 Portraits. 2 vols. 8vo., 36s.

Stephen.—ESSAYS IN ECCLESIASTICAL BIOGRAPHY. By Sir JAMES STEPHEN. Crown 8vo., 7s. 6d.

Verney.—MEMOIRS OF THE VERNEY FAMILY DURING THE CIVIL WAR. Compiled from the Letters and Illustrated by the Portraits at Claydon House, Bucks. By FRANCES PARTHENOPE VERNEY. With a Preface by S. R. GARDINER, M.A., LL.D. With 38 Portraits, Woodcuts and Fac-simile. 2 vols. Royal 8vo., 42s.

Wagner.—WAGNER AS I KNEW HIM. By FERDINAND PRAEGER. Crown 8vo., 7s. 6d.

Walford.—TWELVE ENGLISH AUTHORESSES. By L. B. WALFORD, Author of ' Mischief of Monica,' &c. With Portrait of Hannah More. Crown 8vo., 4s. 6d.

Wellington.—LIFE OF THE DUKE OF WELLINGTON. By the Rev. G. R. GLEIG, M.A. Crown 8vo., 3s. 6d.

Wordsworth. — Works by CHARLES WORDSWORTH, D.C.L., late Bishop of St. Andrews.

ANNALS OF MY EARLY LIFE, 1806-1846. 8vo., 15s.

ANNALS OF MY LIFE, 1847-1856. 8vo., 10s. 6d.

Travel and Adventure, the Colonies, &c.

Arnold.—SEAS AND LANDS. By Sir EDWIN ARNOLD, K.C.I.E., Author of ' The Light of the World,' &c. Reprinted letters from the ' Daily Telegraph '. With 71 Illustrations. Crown 8vo., 7s. 6d.

AUSTRALIA AS IT IS, or, Facts and Features, Sketches and Incidents of Australia and Australian Life, with Notices of New Zealand. By A CLERGYMAN, thirteen years resident in the interior of New South Wales. Crown 8vo., 5s.

Baker.—Works by Sir SAMUEL WHITE BAKER.

EIGHT YEARS IN CEYLON. With 6 Illustrations. Crown 8vo., 3s. 6d.

THE RIFLE AND THE HOUND IN CEYLON. 6 Illustrations. Crown 8vo., 3s. 6d.

Bent.—Works by J. THEODORE BENT, F.S.A., F.R.G.S.

THE RUINED CITIES OF MASHONALAND: being a Record of Excavation and Exploration in 1891. With a Chapter on the Orientation and Mensuration of the Temples. By R. M. W. SWAN. With Map, 13 Plates, and 104 Illustrations in the Text. Crown 8vo., 7s. 6d.

THE SACRED CITY OF THE ETHIOPIANS: being a Record of Travel and Research in Abyssinia in 1893. With 8 Plates and 65 Illustrations in the Text. 8vo., 18s.

Brassey.—Works by the late LADY BRASSEY.

THE LAST VOYAGE TO INDIA AND AUSTRALIA IN THE ' SUNBEAM.' With Charts and Maps, and 40 Illustrations in Monotone, and nearly 200 Illustrations in the Text. 8vo., 21s.

A VOYAGE IN THE ' SUNBEAM '; OUR HOME ON THE OCEAN FOR ELEVEN MONTHS.
Library Edition. With 8 Maps and Charts, and 118 Illustrations. 8vo. 21s.
Cabinet Edition. With Map and 66 Illustrations. Crown 8vo., 7s. 6d.
Silver Library Edition. With 66 Illustrations. Crown 8vo., 3s. 6d.
Popular Edition. With 60 Illustrations. 4to., 6d. sewed, 1s. cloth.
School Edition. With 37 Illustrations. Fcp., 2s. cloth, or 3s. white parchment.
SUNSHINE AND STORM IN THE EAST.
Library Edition. With 2 Maps and 141 Illustrations. 8vo., 21s.
Cabinet Edition. With 2 Maps and 114 Illustrations. Crown 8vo., 7s. 6d.
Popular Edition. With 103 Illustrations. 4to., 6d. sewed, 1s. cloth.
IN THE TRADES, THE TROPICS, AND THE ' ROARING FORTIES '.
Cabinet Edition. With Map and 220 Illustrations. Crown 8vo., 7s. 6d.
Popular Edition. With 183 Illustrations. 4to., 6d. sewed, 1s. cloth.
THREE VOYAGES IN THE ' SUNBEAM '.
Popular Edition. With 346 Illustrations. 4to., 2s. 6d.

Travel and Adventure, the Colonies, &c.—*continued.*

Curzon.—PERSIA AND THE PERSIAN QUESTION. With 9 Maps, 96 Illustrations, Appendices, and an Index. By the Hon. GEORGE N. CURZON, M.P., late Fellow of All Souls College, Oxford. 2 vols. 8vo., 42s.

Froude.—Works by JAMES A. FROUDE.

OCEANA : or England and her Colonies. With 9 Illustrations. Crown 8vo., 2s. boards, 2s. 6d. cloth.

THE ENGLISH IN THE WEST INDIES: or, the Bow of Ulysses. With 9 Illustrations. Crown 8vo., 2s. boards, 2s. 6d. cloth.

Howard.—LIFE WITH TRANS-SIBERIAN SAVAGES. By B. DOUGLAS HOWARD, M.A. Crown 8vo., 6s.

Howitt.—VISITS TO REMARKABLE PLACES. Old Halls, Battle-Fields, Scenes, illustrative of Striking Passages in English History and Poetry. By WILLIAM HOWITT. With 80 Illustrations. Crown 8vo., 3s. 6d.

Knight.—Works by E. F. KNIGHT, author of the Cruise of the ' Falcon '.

THE CRUISE OF THE ' ALERTE ': the narrative of a Search for Treasure on the Desert Island of Trinidad. With 2 Maps and 23 Illustrations. Crown 8vo., 3s. 6d.

WHERE THREE EMPIRES MEET: a Narrative of Recent Travel in Kashmir, Western Tibet, Baltistan, Ladak, Gilgit, and the adjoining Countries. With a Map and 54 Illustrations. Cr. 8vo., 7s. 6d.

Lees and Clutterbuck.—B. C. 1887 : A RAMBLE IN BRITISH COLUMBIA. By J. A. LEES and W. J. CLUTTERBUCK, Authors of ' Three in Norway '. With Map and 75 Illustrations. Crown 8vo., 3s. 6d.

Nansen.—Works by Dr. FRIDTJOF NANSEN.

THE FIRST CROSSING OF GREENLAND. With numerous Illustrations and a Map. Crown 8vo., 7s. 6d.

ESKIMO LIFE. Translated by WILLIAM ARCHER. With 31 Illustrations. 8vo., 16s.

Peary.—MY ARCTIC JOURNAL : a Year among Ice-Fields and Eskimos. By JOSEPHINE DIEBITSCH-PEARY. With an Account of the Great White Journey across Greenland. By ROBERT E. PEARY, Civil Engineer, U.S. Navy. With 19 Plates, 3 Sketch Maps, and 44 Illustrations in the Text. 8vo., 12s.

Pratt.—TO THE SNOWS OF TIBET THROUGH CHINA. By A. E. PRATT, F.R.G.S. With 33 Illustrations and a Map. 8vo., 18s.

Riley.—ATHOS : or, the Mountain of the Monks. By ATHELSTAN RILEY, M.A. With Map and 29 Illustrations. 8vo., 21s.

Rockhill.—THE LAND OF THE LAMAS : Notes of a Journey through China, Mongolia, and Tibet. By WILLIAM WOODVILLE ROCKHILL. With 2 Maps and 61 Illustrations. 8vo., 15s.

Stephens.—MADOC : An Essay on the Discovery of America, by MADOC AP OWEN GWYNEDD, in the Twelfth Century. By THOMAS STEPHENS. Edited by LLYWARCH REYNOLDS, B.A. Oxon. 8vo., 7s. 6d.

THREE IN NORWAY. By Two of Them. With a Map and 59 Illustrations. Crown 8vo., 2s. boards, 2s. 6d. cloth.

Von Höhnel.—DISCOVERY OF LAKES RUDOLF and STEFANIE : A Narrative of Count SAMUEL TELEKI's Exploring and Hunting Expedition in Eastern Equatorial Africa in 1887 and 1888. By Lieutenant LUDWIG VON HÖHNEL. Translated by NANCY BELL (N. D'Anvers). With 179 Illustrations and 5 Coloured Maps. 2 vols. 8vo., 42s.

Whishaw.—OUT OF DOORS IN TSARLAND : a Record of the Seeings and Doings of a Wanderer in Russia. By FRED. J.WHISHAW. Crown 8vo., 7s. 6d.

Wolff.—Works by HENRY W. WOLFF.

RAMBLES IN THE BLACK FOREST. Crown 8vo., 7s. 6d.

THE WATERING PLACES OF THE VOSGES. Crown 8vo., 4s. 6d.

THE COUNTRY OF THE VOSGES. With a Map. 8vo., 12s.

Sport and Pastime.

Campbell-Walker.—THE CORRECT CARD : or, How to Play at Whist; a Whist Catechism. By Major A. CAMPBELL-WALKER, F.R.G.S. Fcp. 8vo., 2s. 6d.

DEAD SHOT (THE) : or, Sportsman's Complete Guide. Being a Treatise on the Use of the Gun, with Rudimentary and Finishing Lessons on the Art of Shooting Game of all kinds, also Game Driving, Wild-Fowl and Pigeon Shooting, Dog Breaking, etc. By MARKSMAN. Crown 8vo., 10s. 6d.

Sport and Pastime—*continued.*
THE BADMINTON LIBRARY.
Edited by the DUKE of BEAUFORT, K.G., assisted by ALFRED E. T. WATSON.

ATHLETICS AND FOOTBALL. By MONTAGUE SHEARMAN. With 51 Illustrations. Crown 8vo., 10s. 6d.

BIG GAME SHOOTING. By C. PHILLIPPS-WOLLEY, F. C. SELOUS, W. G. LITTLEDALE, Colonel PERCY, FRED. JACKSON, Major H. PERCY, W. C. OSWELL, Sir HENRY POTTINGER, Bart., and the EARL OF KILMOREY. With Contributions by other Writers. With Illustrations by CHARLES WHYMPER and others. 2 vols. Crown 8vo., 10s. 6d. each. [*In the press.*

BOATING. By W. B. WOODGATE. With an Introduction by the Rev. ED-MOND WARRE, D.D., and a Chapter on 'Rowing at Eton,' by R. HARVEY MASON. With 49 Illustrations. Cr. 8vo., 10s. 6d.

COURSING AND FALCONRY. By HARDING COX and the Hon. GERALD LASCELLES. With 76 Illustrations. Cr. 8vo., 10s. 6d.

CRICKET. By A. G. STEEL and the Hon. R. H. LYTTELTON. With Contributions by ANDREW LANG, R. A. H. MITCHELL, W. G. GRACE, and F. GALE. With 64 Illustrations. Crown 8vo., 10s. 6d.

CYCLING. By VISCOUNT BURY (Earl of Albemarle), K.C.M.G., and G. LACY HILLIER. With 89 Illustrations. Crown 8vo., 10s. 6d.

DRIVING. By the DUKE OF BEAUFORT. With 65 Illustrations. Crown 8vo., 10s. 6d.

FENCING. BOXING, AND WREST-LING. By WALTER H. POLLOCK, F. C. GROVE, C. PREVOST, E. B. MITCHELL, and WALTER ARMSTRONG. With 42 Illustrations. Crown 8vo., 10s. 6d.

FISHING. By H. CHOLMONDELEY-PENNELL. With Contributions by the MARQUIS OF EXETER, HENRY R. FRANCIS, Major JOHN P. TRAHERNE, FREDERIC M. HALFORD, G. CHRISTOPHER DAVIES, R. B. MARSTON, &c.

Vol. I. Salmon, Trout, and. Grayling. With 158 Illustrations. Crown 8vo., 10s. 6d.

Vol. II. Pike and other Coarse Fish. With 133 Illustrations. Crown 8vo., 10s. 6d.

GOLF. By HORACE G. HUTCHINSON, the Rt. Hon. A. J. BALFOUR, M.P., Sir W. G. SIMPSON, Bart., LORD WELLWOOD, H. S. C. EVERARD, ANDREW LANG, and other Writers. With 89 Illustrations. Crown 8vo., 10s. 6d.

HUNTING. By the DUKE OF BEAU-FORT, K.G., and MOWBRAY MORRIS. With Contributions by the EARL OF SUFFOLK AND BERKSHIRE, Rev. E. W. L. DAVIES, DIGBY COLLINS, and ALFRED E. T. WATSON. With 53 Illustrations. Crown 8vo., 10s. 6d.

MOUNTAINEERING. By C. T. DENT, Sir F. POLLOCK, Bart., W. M. CONWAY, DOUGLAS FRESHFIELD, C. E. MATHEWS, C. PILKINGTON, and other Writers. With 108 Illustrations. Crown 8vo., 10s. 6d.

RACING AND STEEPLE-CHAS-ING. By the EARL OF SUFFOLK AND BERKSHIRE and W. G. CRAVEN. With a Contribution by the Hon. F. LAWLEY. *Steeple-chasing :* By ARTHUR COVENTRY and ALFRED E. T. WATSON. With 58 Illustrations. Crown 8vo., 10s. 6d.

RIDING AND POLO. By Captain ROBERT WEIR, J. MORAY BROWN, the DUKE OF BEAUFORT, K.G., the EARL OF SUFFOLK AND BERKSHIRE, &c. With 59 Illustrations. Crown 8vo., 10s. 6d.

SHOOTING. By Lord WALSINGHAM and Sir RALPH PAYNE-GALLWEY, Bart. With Contributions by Lord LOVAT, Lord CHARLES LENNOX KERR, the Hon. G. LASCELLES, and A. J. STUART-WORTLEY.

Vol. I. Field and Covert. With 105 Illustrations. Crown 8vo., 10s. 6d.

Vol. II. Moor and Marsh. With 65 Illustrations. Crown 8vo., 10s. 6d.

SKATING, CURLING, TOBOGGAN-ING, AND OTHER ICE SPORTS. By J. M. HEATHCOTE, C. G. TEBBUTT, T. MAXWELL WITHAM, the Rev. JOHN KERR, ORMOND HAKE, and Colonel BUCK. With 284 Illustrations. Crown 8vo., 10s. 6d.

SWIMMING. By ARCHIBALD SINCLAIR and WILLIAM HENRY, Hon. Secs. of the Life Saving Society. With 119 Illustrations. Crown 8vo., 10s. 6d.

TENNIS, LAWN TENNIS, RACKETS AND FIVES. By J. M. and C. G. HEATHCOTE, E. O. PLEYDELL-BOUVERIE and A. C. AINGER. With Contributions by the Hon. A. LYTTELTON, W. C. MARSHALL, Miss L. DOD, H. W. W. WILBERFORCE, H. F. LAWFORD, &c. With 79 Illustrations. Cr. 8vo., 10s. 6d.

YACHTING. By the EARL OF PEM-BROKE, the MARQUIS OF DUFFERIN AND AVA, the EARL OF ONSLOW, LORD BRASSEY, Lieut.-Col. BUCKNILL, LEWIS HERRESHOFF, G. L. WATSON, E. F. KNIGHT, Rev. G. L. BLAKE, R.N., and G. C. DAVIES. With Illustrations by R. T. PRITCHETT, and from Photographs. 2 vols. [*In the press.*

Sport and Pastime—*continued*.

FUR AND FEATHER SERIES.

Edited by A. E. T. WATSON.

THE PARTRIDGE.   Natural History, by the Rev. H. A. MACPHERSON; Shooting, by A. J. STUART-WORTLEY; Cookery, by GEORGE SAINTSBURY.   With 11 full-page Illustrations and Vignette by A. THORBURN, A. J. STUART-WORTLEY, and C. WHYMPER, and 15 Diagrams in the Text by A. J. STUART-WORTLEY. Crown 8vo., 5s.

THE GROUSE.   By A. J. STUART-WORTLEY, the Rev. H. A. MACPHERSON, and GEORGE SAINTSBURY.   [*In preparation.*

THE PHEASANT.   By A. J. STUART-WORTLEY, the Rev. H. A. MACPHERSON, and A. J. INNES SHAND.   [*In preparation.*

THE HARE AND THE RABBIT.   By the Hon. GERALD LASCELLES, etc.
[*In preparation.*

WILDFOWL.   By the Hon. JOHN SCOTT-MONTAGU, M.P., etc.   Illustrated by A. J. STUART - WORTLEY, A. THORBURN, and others.   [*In preparation.*

Falkener.—GAMES, ANCIENT AND ORIENTAL, AND HOW TO PLAY THEM. By EDWARD FALKENER.   With numerous Photographs, Diagrams, &c.   8vo., 21s.

Ford.—THE THEORY AND PRACTICE OF ARCHERY.   By HORACE FORD.   New Edition, thoroughly Revised and Re-written by W. BUTT, M.A.   With a Preface by C. J. LONGMAN, M.A.   8vo., 14s.

Francis.—A BOOK ON ANGLING : or, Treatise on the Art of Fishing in every Branch; including full Illustrated List of Salmon Flies.   By FRANCIS FRANCIS.   With Portrait and Coloured Plates.   Crown 8vo., 15s.

Hawker.—THE DIARY OF COLONEL PETER HAWKER, Author of 'Instructions to Young Sportsmen.'   With an Introduction by Sir RALPH PAYNE-GALLWEY, Bart.   2 vols. 8vo., 32s.

Hopkins.—FISHING REMINISCENCES.   By Major F. P. HOPKINS.   With Illustrations. Crown 8vo., 6s. 6d.

Lang.—ANGLING SKETCHES.   By ANDREW LANG.   With 20 Illustrations by W. G. BURN MURDOCH.   Crown 8vo., 7s. 6d.

Longman. — CHESS OPENINGS.   By FREDERICK W. LONGMAN.   Fcp. 8vo., 2s. 6d.

Payne-Gallwey.—Works by Sir RALPH PAYNE-GALLWEY, Bart.

LETTERS TO YOUNG SHOOTERS (First Series).   On the Choice and use of a Gun. With Illustrations.   Crown 8vo., 7s. 6d.

LETTERS TO YOUNG SHOOTERS. (Second Series).   On the Production, Preservation, and Killing of Game.   With Directions in Shooting Wood-Pigeons and Breaking-in Retrievers.   With a Portrait of the Author, and 103 Illustrations.   Crown 8vo., 12s. 6d.

Pole.—THE THEORY OF THE MODERN SCIENTIFIC GAME OF WHIST.   By W. POLE, F.R.S.   Fcp. 8vo., 2s. 6d.

Proctor.—Works by RICHARD A. PROCTOR. HOW TO PLAY WHIST: WITH THE LAWS AND ETIQUETTE OF WHIST. Cr. 8vo., 3s. 6d. HOME WHIST: an Easy Guide to Correct Play.   16mo., 1s.

Ronalds.—THE FLY-FISHER'S ENTOMOLOGY.   By ALFRED RONALDS.   With coloured Representations of the Natural and Artificial Insect.   With 20 coloured Plates.   8vo., 14s.

Wilcocks.—THE SEA FISHERMAN : Comprising the Chief Methods of Hook and Line Fishing in the British and other Seas, and Remarks on Nets, Boats, and Boating.   By J. C. WILCOCKS.   Illustrated.   Cr 8vo., 6s.

Mental, Moral, and Political Philosophy.

LOGIC, RHETORIC, PSYCHOLOGY, ETC.

Abbott.—THE ELEMENTS OF LOGIC.   By T. K. ABBOTT, B.D.   12mo., 3s.

Aristotle.—Works by.
THE POLITICS: G. Bekker's Greek Text of Books I., III., IV. (VII.), with an English Translation by W. E. BOLLAND, M.A.; and short Introductory Essays by A. LANG, M.A.   Crown 8vo., 7s. 6d.

Aristotle.—Works by—*continued*.
THE POLITICS: Introductory Essays. By ANDREW LANG (from Bolland and Lang's 'Politics').   Crown 8vo., 2s. 6d.

THE ETHICS: Greek Text, Illustrated with Essay and Notes.   By Sir ALEXANDER GRANT, Bart.   2 vols.   8vo., 32s.

Mental, Moral and Political Philosophy—*continued.*

Aristotle.—Works by—*continued.*

THE NICOMACHEAN ETHICS: Newly Translated into English. By ROBERT WILLIAMS. Crown 8vo., 7s. 6d.

AN INTRODUCTION TO ARISTOTLE'S ETHICS. Books I.-IV. (Book X. c. vi.-ix. in an Appendix). With a continuous Analysis and Notes. Intended for the use of Beginners and Junior Students. By the Rev. EDWARD MOORE, D.D., Principal of St. Edmund Hall, and late Fellow and Tutor of Queen's College, Oxford. Crown 8vo. 10s. 6d.

Bacon.—Works by FRANCIS BACON.

COMPLETE WORKS. Edited by R. L. ELLIS, JAMES SPEDDING and D. D. HEATH. 7 vols. 8vo., £3 13s. 6d.

LETTERS AND LIFE, including all his occasional Works. Edited by JAMES SPEDDING. 7 vols. 8vo., £4 4s.

THE ESSAYS: with Annotations. By RICHARD WHATELY, D.D. 8vo., 10s. 6d.

Bain.—Works by ALEXANDER BAIN, LL.D.

MENTAL SCIENCE. Crown 8vo. 6s. 6d.

MORAL SCIENCE. Crown 8vo., 4s. 6d.

The two works as above can be had in one volume, price 10s. 6d.

SENSES AND THE INTELLECT. 8vo., 15s.

EMOTIONS AND THE WILL. 8vo., 15s.

LOGIC, DEDUCTIVE AND INDUCTIVE. Part I. 4s. Part II. 6s. 6d.

PRACTICAL ESSAYS. Crown 8vo., 3s.

Bray.—Works by CHARLES BRAY.

THE PHILOSOPHY OF NECESSITY: or Law in Mind as in Matter. Cr. 8vo,, 5s.

THE EDUCATION OF THE FEELINGS: a Moral System for Schools. Cr. 8vo., 2s. 6d.

Bray.—ELEMENTS OF MORALITY, in Easy Lessons for Home and School Teaching. By Mrs. CHARLES BRAY. Cr. 8vo., 1s. 6d.

Crozier.—CIVILISATION AND PROGRESS. By JOHN BEATTIE CROZIER, M.D. With New Preface. More fully explaining the nature of the New Organon used in the solution of its problems. 8vo., 14s.

Davidson.—THE LOGIC OF DEFINITION, Explained and Applied. By WILLIAM L. DAVIDSON, M.A. Crown 8vo., 6s.

Green.—THE WORKS OF THOMAS HILL GREEN. Edited by R. L. NETTLESHIP. Vols. I. and II. Philosophical Works. 8vo., 16s. each. Vol. III. Miscellanies. With Index to the three Volumes, and Memoir. 8vo., 21s.

Hearn.—THE ARYAN HOUSEHOLD : its Structure and its Development. An Introduction to Comparative Jurisprudence. By W. EDWARD HEARN. 8vo., 16s.

Hodgson.—Works by SHADWORTH H. HODGSON.

TIME AND SPACE: a Metaphysical Essay. 8vo., 16s.

THE THEORY OF PRACTICE : an Ethical Inquiry. 2 vols. 8vo., 24s.

THE PHILOSOPHY OF REFLECTION. 2 vols. 8vo., 21s.

Hume.—THE PHILOSOPHICAL WORKS OF DAVID HUME. Edited by T. H. GREEN and T. H. GROSE. 4 vols. 8vo., 56s. Or separately, Essays. 2 vols. 28s. Treatise of Human Nature. 2 vols. 28s.

Johnstone.—A SHORT INTRODUCTION TO the STUDY of LOGIC. By LAURENCE JOHNSTONE. With Questions. Cr. 8vo., 2s. 6d.

Jones.—AN INTRODUCTION TO GENERAL LOGIC. By E. E. CONSTANCE JONES. Cr. 8vo., 4s. 6d.

Justinian.—THE INSTITUTES OF JUSTINIAN : Latin Text, chiefly that of Huschke, with English Introduction, Translation, Notes, and Summary. By THOMAS C. SANDARS, M.A. 8vo., 18s.

Kant.—Works by IMMANUEL KANT.

CRITIQUE OF PRACTICAL REASON, AND OTHER WORKS ON THE THEORY OF ETHICS. Translated by T. K. ABBOTT, B.D. With Memoir. 8vo., 12s. 6d.

INTRODUCTION TO LOGIC, AND HIS ESSAY ON THE MISTAKEN SUBTILTY OF THE FOUR FIGURES. Translated by T. K. ABBOTT. 8vo., 6s.

Killick.—HANDBOOK TO MILL'S SYSTEM OF LOGIC. By Rev. A. H. KILLICK, M.A. Crown 8vo., 3s. 6d.

Ladd.—Works by G. T. LADD.

ELEMENTS OF PHYSIOLOGICAL PSYCHOLOGY. 8vo., 21s.

OUTLINES OF PHYSIOLOGICAL PSYCHOLOGY. A Text-book of Mental Science for Academies and Colleges. 8vo., 12s.

Lewes.—THE HISTORY OF PHILOSOPHY, from Thales to Comte. By GEORGE HENRY LEWES. 2 vols. 8vo., 32s.

Max Müller.—Works by F. MAX MÜLLER.

THE SCIENCE OF THOUGHT. 8vo., 21s.

THREE INTRODUCTORY LECTURES ON THE SCIENCE OF THOUGHT. 8vo., 2s. 6d.

Mental, Moral and Political Philosophy—*continued.*

Mill.—ANALYSIS OF THE PHENOMENA OF THE HUMAN MIND. By JAMES MILL. 2 vols. 8vo., 28s.

Mill.—Works by JOHN STUART MILL.
A SYSTEM OF LOGIC. Crown 8vo., 3s. 6d.
ON LIBERTY. Crown 8vo., 1s. 4d.
ON REPRESENTATIVE GOVERNMENT. Crown 8vo., 2s.
UTILITARIANISM. 8vo., 5s.
EXAMINATION OF SIR WILLIAM HAMILTON'S PHILOSOPHY. 8vo., 16s.
NATURE, THE UTILITY OF RELIGION, AND THEISM. Three Essays. 8vo., 5s.

Monck.—INTRODUCTION TO LOGIC. By W. H. S. MONCK. Crown 8vo., 5s.

Ribot.—THE PSYCHOLOGY OF ATTENTION. By TH. RIBOT. Crown 8vo., 3s.

Sidgwick.—DISTINCTION: and the Criticism of Belief. By ALFRED SIDGWICK. Crown 8vo., 6s.

Stock.—DEDUCTIVE LOGIC. By ST. GEORGE STOCK. Fcp. 8vo., 3s. 6d.

Sully.—Works by JAMES SULLY.
THE HUMAN MIND: a Text-book of Psychology. 2 vols. 8vo., 21s.
OUTLINES OF PSYCHOLOGY. 8vo., 9s.
THE TEACHER'S HANDBOCK OF PSYCHOLOGY. Crown 8vo., 5s.

Swinburne.—PICTURE LOGIC: an Attempt to Popularise the Science of Reasoning. By ALFRED JAMES SWINBURNE, M.A. With 23 Woodcuts. Post 8vo., 5s.

Thompson.—Works by DANIEL GREENLEAF THOMPSON.
THE PROBLEM OF EVIL: an Introduction to the Practical Sciences. 8vo., 10s. 6d.
A SYSTEM OF PSYCHOLOGY. 2 vols. 8vo., 36s.
THE RELIGIOUS SENTIMENTS OF THE HUMAN MIND. 8vo., 7s. 6d.
SOCIAL PROGRESS: an Essay. 8vo., 7s. 6d.
THE PHILOSOPHY OF FICTION IN LITERATURE: an Essay. Crown 8vo., 6s.

Thomson.—OUTLINES OF THE NECESSARY LAWS OF THOUGHT: a Treatise on Pure and Applied Logic. By WILLIAM THOMSON, D.D., formerly Lord Archbishop of York. Post 8vo., 6s.

Webb.—THE VEIL OF ISIS: a Series of Essays on Idealism. By T. E. WEBB. 8vo., 10s. 6d.

Whately.—Works by R. WHATELY, D.D.
BACON'S ESSAYS. With Annotation. By R. WHATELY. 8vo. 10s. 6d.

ELEMENTS OF LOGIC. Cr. 8vo., 4s. 6d.

ELEMENTS OF RHETORIC. Crown 8vo., 4s. 6d.

LESSONS ON REASONING. Fcp. 8vo., 1s. 6d.

Zeller.—Works by Dr. EDWARD ZELLER, Professor in the University of Berlin.

HISTORY OF ECLECTICISM IN GREEK PHILOSOPHY. Translated by SARAH F. ALLEYNE. Crown 8vo., 10s. 6d.

THE STOICS, EPICUREANS, AND SCEPTICS. Translated by the Rev. O. J. REICHEL, M.A. Crown 8vo., 15s.

OUTLINES OF THE HISTORY OF GREEK PHILOSOPHY. Translated by SARAH F. ALLEYNE and EVELYN ABBOTT. Crown 8vo., 10s. 6d.

PLATO AND THE OLDER ACADEMY. Translated by SARAH F. ALLEYNE and ALFRED GOODWIN, B.A. Crown 8vo., 18s.

SOCRATES AND THE SOCRATIC SCHOOLS. Translated by the Rev. O. J. REICHEL, M.A. Crown 8vo., 10s. 6d.

THE PRE-SOCRATIC SCHOOLS: a History of Greek Philosophy from the Earliest Period to the time of Socrates. Translated by SARAH F. ALLEYNE. 2 vols. Crown 8vo., 30s.

MANUALS OF CATHOLIC PHILOSOPHY.
(Stonyhurst Series).

A MANUAL OF POLITICAL ECONOMY. By C. S. DEVAS, M.A. Crown 8vo., 6s. 6d.

FIRST PRINCIPLES OF KNOWLEDGE. By JOHN RICKABY, S.J. Crown 8vo., 5s.

GENERAL METAPHYSICS. By JOHN RICKABY, S.J. Crown 8vo., 5s.

LOGIC. By RICHARD F. CLARKE, S.J. Crown 8vo., 5s.

MORAL PHILOSOPHY (ETHICS AND NATURAL LAW. By JOSEPH RICKABY, S.J. Crown 8vo., 5s.

NATURAL THEOLOGY. By BERNARD BOEDDER, S.J. Crown 8vo., 6s. 6d.

PSYCHOLOGY. By MICHAEL MAHER, S.J. Crown 8vo., 6s. 6d.

History and Science of Language, &c.

Davidson. — LEADING AND IMPORTANT ENGLISH WORDS: Explained and Exemplified. By WILLIAM L. DAVIDSON, M.A. Fcp. 8vo., 3s. 6d.

Farrar. — LANGUAGE AND LANGUAGES : By F. W. FARRAR, D.D., F.R.S. Crown 8vo., 6s.

Graham.—ENGLISH SYNONYMS, Classified and Explained : with Practical Exercises. By G. F. GRAHAM. Fcp. 8vo., 6s.

Max Müller.—Works by F. MAX MÜLLER. SELECTED ESSAYS ON LANGUAGE, MYTHOLOGY, AND RELIGION. 2 vols. Crown 8vo., 16s.

THE SCIENCE OF LANGUAGE, Founded on Lectures delivered at the Royal Institution in 1861 and 1863. 2 vols. Crown 8vo., 21s.

BIOGRAPHIES OF WORDS, AND THE HOME OF THE ARYAS. Crown 8vo., 7s. 6d.

Max Müller.—Works by F. MAX MÜLLER —*continued.*

THREE LECTURES ON THE SCIENCE OF LANGUAGE, AND ITS PLACE IN GENERAL EDUCATION, delivered at Oxford, 1889. Crown 8vo., 3s.

Roget.—THESAURUS OF ENGLISH WORDS AND PHRASES. Classified and Arranged so as to Facilitate the Expression of Ideas and assist in Literary Composition. By PETER MARK ROGET, M.D., F.R.S. Recomposed throughout, enlarged and improved, partly from the Author's Notes, and with a full Index, by the Author's Son, JOHN LEWIS ROGET. Crown 8vo. 10s. 6d.

Whately.—ENGLISH SYNONYMS. By E. JANE WHATELY. Fcp. 8vo., 3s.

Political Economy and Economics.

Ashley.—ENGLISH ECONOMIC HISTORY AND THEORY. By W. J. ASHLEY, M.A. Crown 8vo., Part I., 5s. Part II. 10s. 6d.

Bagehot.—ECONOMIC STUDIES. By WALTER BAGEHOT. 8vo., 10s. 6d.

Barnett.—PRACTICABLE SOCIALISM : Essays on Social Reform. By the Rev. S. A. and Mrs. BARNETT.

Brassey.—PAPERS AND ADDRESSES ON WORK AND WAGES. By Lord BRASSEY.

Crump.—AN INVESTIGATION INTO THE CAUSES OF THE GREAT FALL IN PRICES which took place coincidently with the Demonetisation of Silver by Germany. By ARTHUR CRUMP. 8vo., 6s.

Devas.—A MANUAL OF POLITICAL ECONOMY. By C. S. DEVAS, M.A. Crown 8vo., 6s. 6d. (*Manuals of Catholic Philosophy.*)

Dowell.—A HISTORY OF TAXATION AND TAXES IN ENGLAND, from the Earliest Times to the Year 1885. By STEPHEN DOWELL, (4 vols. 8vo.) Vols. I. and II. The History of Taxation, 21s. Vols. III. and IV. The History of Taxes, 21s.

Jordan.—THE STANDARD OF VALUE. By WILLIAM LEIGHTON JORDAN. 8vo., 6s.

Leslie.—ESSAYS IN POLITICAL ECONOMY. By T. E. CLIFFE LESLIE. 8vo., 10s. 6d.

Macleod.—Works by HENRY DUNNING MACLEOD, M.A. THE ELEMENTS OF BANKING. Crown 8vo., 3s. 6d. THE THEORY AND PRACTICE OF BANKING. Vol. I. 8vo., 12s. Vol. II. 14s. THE THEORY OF CREDIT. 8vo. Vol. I. 10s. net. Vol. II., Part I., 4s. 6d. Vol. II. Part II., 10s. 6d.

Meath.—PROSPERITY OR PAUPERISM ? Physical, Industrial, and Technical Training. By the EARL OP MEATH. 8vo., 5s.

Mill.—POLITICAL ECONOMY. By JOHN STUART MILL. Silver Library Edition. Crown 8vo., 3s. 6d. Library Edition. 2 vols. 8vo., 30s.

Shirres.—AN ANALYSIS OF THE IDEAS OF ECONOMICS. By L. P. SHIRRES, B.A., sometime Finance Under-Secretary of the Government of Bengal. Crown 8vo., 6s.

Symes.—POLITICAL ECONOMY : a Short Text-book of Political Economy. With Problems for Solution, and Hints for Supplementary Reading. By Professor J. E. SYMES, M.A., of University College, Nottingham. Crown 8vo., 2s. 6d.

Toynbee.—LECTURES ON THE INDUSTRIAL REVOLUTION OF THE 18th CENTURY IN ENGLAND. By ARNOLD TOYNBEE. 8vo., 10s. 6d.

Wilson. — Works by A. J. WILSON. Chiefly reprinted from *The Investors' Review.* PRACTICAL HINTS TO SMALL INVESTORS. Crown 8vo., 1s. PLAIN ADVICE ABOUT LIFE INSURANCE. Crown 8vo., 1s.

Wolff.—PEOPLE'S BANKS : a Record of Social and Economic Success. By HENRY W. WOLFF. 8vo., 7s. 6d.

Evolution, Anthropology, &c.

Clodd.—THE STORY OF CREATION: a Plain Account of Evolution. By EDWARD CLODD. With 77 Illustrations. Crown 8vo., 3s. 6d.

Huth.—THE MARRIAGE OF NEAR KIN, considered with Respect to the Law of Nations, the Result of Experience, and the Teachings of Biology. By ALFRED HENRY HUTH. Royal 8vo., 7s. 6d.

Lang.—CUSTOM AND MYTH: Studies of Early Usage and Belief. By ANDREW LANG, M.A. With 15 Illustrations. Crown 8vo., 3s. 6d.

Lubbock.—THE ORIGIN OF CIVILISATION and the Primitive Condition of Man. By Sir J. LUBBOCK, Bart., M.P. With 5 Plates and 20 Illustrations in the Text. 8vo., 18s.

Romanes. — Works by GEORGE JOHN ROMANES, M.A., LL.D., F.R.S.

DARWIN, AND AFTER DARWIN: an Exposition of the Darwinian Theory, and a Discussion on Post-Darwinian Questions. Part I. The Darwinian Theory. With Portrait of Darwin and 125 Illustrations. Crown 8vo., 10s. 6d.

AN EXAMINATION OF WEISMANNISM. Crown 8vo., 6s.

Classical Literature and Translations, &c.

Abbott.—HELLENICA. A Collection of Essays on Greek Poetry, Philosophy, History, and Religion. Edited by EVELYN ABBOTT, M.A., LL.D. 8vo., 16s.

Æschylus.—EUMENIDES OF ÆSCHYLUS. With Metrical English Translation. By J. F. DAVIES. 8vo., 7s.

Aristophanes. — THE ACHARNIANS OF ARISTOPHANES, translated into English Verse. By R. Y. TYRRELL. Crown 8vo., 1s.

Becker.—Works by Professor BECKER.

GALLUS: or, Roman Scenes in the Time of Augustus. Illustrated. Post 8vo., 7s. 6d.

CHARICLES: or, Illustrations of the Private Life of the Ancient Greeks. Illustrated. Post 8vo., 7s. 6d.

Cicero.—CICERO'S CORRESPONDENCE. By R. Y. TYRRELL. Vols. I., II., III., 8vo., each 12s.

Clerke.—FAMILIAR STUDIES IN HOMER. By AGNES M. CLERKE. Crown 8vo., 7s. 6d.

Farnell.—GREEK LYRIC POETRY: a Complete Collection of the Surviving Passages from the Greek Song-Writting. Arranged with Prefatory Articles, Introductory Matter and Commentary. By GEORGE S. FARNELL, M.A. With 5 Plates. 8vo., 16s.

Harrison.—MYTHS OF THE ODYSSEY IN ART AND LITERATURE. By JANE E. HARRISON. Illustrated with Outline Drawings. 8vo., 18s.

Lang.—HOMER AND THE EPIC. By ANDREW LANG. Crown 8vo., 9s. net.

Mackail.—SELECT EPIGRAMS FROM THE GREEK ANTHOLOGY. By J. W. MACKAIL, Fellow of Balliol College, Oxford. Edited with a Revised Text, Introduction, Translation, and Notes. 8vo., 16s.

Plato.—PARMENIDES OF PLATO, Text, with Introduction, Analysis, &c. By T. MAGUIRE. 8vo., 7s. 6d.

Rich.—A DICTIONARY OF ROMAN AND GREEK ANTIQUITIES. By A. RICH, B.A. With 2000 Woodcuts. Crown 8vo., 7s. 6d.

Sophocles.—Translated into English Verse. By ROBERT WHITELAW, M.A., Assistant Master in Rugby School; late Fellow of Trinity College, Cambridge. Crown 8vo., 8s. 6d.

Tyrrell.—TRANSLATIONS INTO GREEK AND LATIN VERSE. Edited by R. Y. TYRRELL. 8vo., 6s.

Virgil.—THE ÆNEID OF VIRGIL. Translated into English Verse by JOHN CONINGTON. Crown 8vo., 6s.

THE POEMS OF VIRGIL. Translated into English Prose by JOHN CONINGTON. Crown 8vo., 6s.

THE ÆNEID OF VIRGIL, freely translated into English Blank Verse. By W. J. THORNHILL. Crown 8vo., 7s. 6d.

THE ÆNEID OF VIRGIL. Books I. to VI. Translated into English Verse by JAMES RHOADES. Crown 8vo., 5s.

Wilkins.—THE GROWTH OF THE HOMERIC POEMS. By G. WILKINS. 8vo., 6s.

Poetry and the Drama.

Allingham.—Works by WILLIAM ALLINGHAM.

IRISH SONGS AND POEMS. With Frontispiece of the Waterfall of Asaroe. Fcp. 8vo., 6s.

LAURENCE BLOOMFIELD. With Portrait of the Author. Fcp. 8vo., 3s. 6d.

FLOWER PIECES; DAY AND NIGHT SONGS; BALLADS. With 2 Designs by D. G. ROSSETTI. Fcp. 8vo., 6s.; large paper edition, 12s.

LIFE AND PHANTASY : with Frontispiece by Sir J. E. MILLAIS, Bart., and Design by ARTHUR HUGHES. Fcp. 8vo., 6s.; large paper edition, 12s.

THOUGHT AND WORD, AND ASHBY MANOR : a Play. With Portrait of the Author (1865), and four Theatrical Scenes drawn by Mr. Allingham. Fcp. 8vo., 6s.; large paper edition, 12s.

BLACKBERRIES. Imperial 16mo., 6s.

Sets of the above 6 vols. may be had in uniform Half-parchment binding, price 30s.

Armstrong.—Works by G. F. SAVAGE-ARMSTRONG.

POEMS : Lyrical and Dramatic. Fcp. 8vo., 6s.

KING SAUL. (The Tragedy of Israel, Part I.) Fcp. 8vo., 5s.

KING DAVID. (The Tragedy of Israel, Part II.) Fcp. 8vo., 6s.

KING SOLOMON. (The Tragedy of Israel, Part III.) Fcp. 8vo., 6s.

UGONE : a Tragedy. Fcp. 8vo., 6s.

A GARLAND FROM GREECE : Poems. Fcp. 8vo., 7s. 6d.

STORIES OF WICKLOW : Poems. Fcp. 8vo., 7s. 6d.

MEPHISTOPHELES IN BROADCLOTH : a Satire. Fcp. 8vo., 4s.

ONE IN THE INFINITE : a Poem. Crown 8vo., 7s. 6d.

Armstrong.—THE POETICAL WORKS OF EDMUND J. ARMSTRONG. Fcp. 8vo., 5s.

Arnold.—Works by Sir EDWIN ARNOLD, K.C.I.E., Author of ' The Light of Asia,' &c.

THE LIGHT OF THE WORLD : or the Great Consummation. A Poem. Crown 8vo., 7s. 6d. net.

Presentation Edition. With 14 Illustrations by W. HOLMAN HUNT, 4to., 20s. net.

POTIPHAR'S WIFE, and other Poems. Crown 8vo., 5s. net.

ADZUMA : or the Japanese Wife. A Play. Crown 8vo., 6s. 6d. net.

Barrow.—THE SEVEN CITIES OF THE DEAD, and other Poems. By Sir JOHN CROKER BARROW, Bart. Fcp. 8vo., 5s.

Bell.—Works by Mrs. HUGH BELL.

CHAMBER COMEDIES : a Collection of Plays and Monologues for the Drawing Room. Crown 8vo., 6s.

NURSERY COMEDIES : Twelve Tiny Plays for Children. Fcp. 8vo., 1s. 6d.

Björnsen.—PASTOR SANG : A PLAY. By BJÖRNSTJERNE BJÖRNSEN. Translated by WILLIAM WILSON. Crown 8vo., 5s.

Dante.—LA COMMEDIA DI DANTE. A New Text, carefully Revised with the aid of the most recent Editions and Collations. Small 8vo., 6s.

Goethe.

FAUST, Part I., the German Text, with Introduction and Notes. By ALBERT M. SELSS, Ph.D., M.A. Crown 8vo., 5s.

FAUST. Translated, with Notes. By T. E. WEBB. 8vo., 12s. 6d.

FAUST. The First Part. A New Translation, chiefly in Blank Verse; with Introduction and Notes. By JAMES ADEY BIRDS. Crown 8vo., 6s.

FAUST. The Second Part. A New Translation in Verse. By JAMES ADEY BIRDS. Crown 8vo., 6s.

Ingelow.—Works by JEAN INGELOW.

POETICAL WORKS. 2 vols. Fcp. 8vo., 12s.

LYRICAL AND OTHER POEMS. Selected from the Writings of JEAN INGELOW. Fcp. 8vo., 2s. 6d. cloth plain, 3s. cloth gilt.

Lang.—Works by ANDREW LANG.

GRASS OF PARNASSUS. Fcp. 8vo., 2s. 6d. net.

BALLADS OF BOOKS. Edited by ANDREW LANG. Fcp. 8vo., 6s.

THE BLUE POETRY BOOK. Edited by ANDREW LANG. With 12 Plates and 88 Illustrations in the Text by H. J. FORD and LANCELOT SPEED. Crown 8vo., 6s.

Special Edition, printed on India paper. With Notes, but without Illustrations. Crown 8vo., 7s. 6d.

Lecky.—POEMS. By W. E. H. LECKY. Fcp. 8vo., 5s.

Leyton.—Works by FRANK LEYTON.

THE SHADOWS OF THE LAKE, and other Poems. Crown 8vo., 7s. 6d. Cheap Edition. Crown 8vo., 3s. 6d.

SKELETON LEAVES : Poems. Crown 8vo. 6s.

Poetry and the Drama—*continued.*

Lytton.—Works by THE EARL OF LYTTON (OWEN MEREDITH).

MARAH. Fcp. 8vo., 6s. 6d.

KING POPPY: a Fantasia. With 1 Plate and Design on Title-Page by ED. BURNE-JONES, A.R.A. Crown 8vo., 10s. 6d.

THE WANDERER. Crown 8vo., 10s. 6d.

LUCILE. Crown 8vo., 10s. 6d.

SELECTIONS FROM POETICAL WORKS. Crown 8vo., 10s. 6d.

Macaulay.—LAYS OF ANCIENT ROME, &c. By Lord MACAULAY.

Illustrated by G. SCHARF. Fcp. 4to., 10s. 6d.

————————————— Bijou Edition. 18mo., 2s. 6d. gilt top.

————————————— Popular Edition. Fcp. 4to., 6d. sewed, 1s. cloth.

Illustrated by J. R. WEGUELIN. Crown 8vo , 3s. 6d.

Annotated Edition. Fcp. 8vo., 1s. sewed, 1s. 6d. cloth.

Nesbit.—LAYS AND LEGENDS. By E. NESBIT (Mrs. HUBERT BLAND). First Series. Crown 8vo., 3s. 6d. Second Series. With Portrait. Crown 8vo., 5s.

Piatt.—AN ENCHANTED CASTLE, AND OTHER POEMS: Pictures, Portraits, and People in Ireland. By SARAH PIATT Crown 8vo. 3s. 6d.

Piatt.—WORKS BY JOHN JAMES PIATT.

IDYLS AND LYRICS OF THE OHIO VALLEY. Crown 8vo., 5s.

LITTLE NEW WORLD IDYLS. Cr. 8vo. 5s.

Rhoades.—TERESA AND OTHER POEMS. By JAMES RHOADES. Crown 8vo., 3s. 6d.

Riley.—Works by JAMES WHITCOMB RILEY.

OLD FASHIONED ROSES: Poems. 12mo., 5s.

POEMS: Here at Home. Fcp. 8vo., 6s. *net.*

Roberts.—SONGS OF THE COMMON DAY AND AVE! An Ode for the Shelley Centenary. By CHARLES G. D. ROBERTS. Cr. 8vo., 3s. 6d.

Shakespeare. — BOWDLER'S FAMILY SHAKESPEARE. With 36 Woodcuts. 1 vol. 8vo., 14s. Or in 6 vols. Fcp. 8vo., 21s.

THE SHAKESPEARE BIRTHDAY BOOK. By MARY F. DUNBAR. 32mo., 1s. 6d. Drawing Room Edition, with Photographs. Fcp. 8vo., 10s. 6d.

Stevenson. — A CHILD'S GARDEN OF Verses. By ROBERT LOUIS STEVENSON. Small Fcp. 8vo., 5s.

Works of Fiction, Humour, &c.

ATELIER (THE) DU LYS: or, an Art Student in the Reign of Terror. Crown 8vo., 2s. 6d.

BY THE SAME AUTHOR.

MADEMOISELLE MORI : a Tale of Modern Rome. Crown 8vo., 2s. 6d.

THAT CHILD. With Illustrations by GORDON BROWNE. Crown 8vo., 2s. 6d.

UNDER A CLOUD. Crown 8vo., 2s. 6d.

THE FIDDLER OF LUGAU. With Illustrations by W. RALSTON, Crown 8vo., 2s. 6d.

A CHILD OF THE REVOLUTION. With Illustrations by C. J. STANILAND. Crown 8vo., 2s. 6d.

HESTER'S VENTURE. Cr. 8vo., 2s. 6d.

IN THE OLDEN TIME: a Tale of the Peasant War in Germany. Cr.8vo.,2s.6d.

THE YOUNGER SISTER. Crown 8vo., 2s. 6d.

Anstey.—Works by F. ANSTEY, Author of ' Vice Versa '.

THE BLACK POODLE, and other Stories. Crown 8vo., 2s. boards, 2s. 6d. cloth.

VOCES POPULI. Reprinted from ' Punch '. First Series. With 20 Illust. by J. BERNARD PARTRIDGE. Fcp. 4to., 5s. Second Series. With 25 Illust. by J. BERNARD PARTRIDGE. Fcp. 4to., 6s.

THE TRAVELLING COMPANIONS. Reprinted from ' Punch '. With 25 Illust. by J. BERNARD PARTRIDGE. Post 4to., 5s.

THE MAN FROM BLANKLEY'S : a Story in Scenes, and other Sketches. With 24 Illustrations by J. BERNARD PARTRIDGE. Fcp. 4to., 6s.

Baker.—BY THE WESTERN SEA. By JAMES BAKER, Author of ' John Westacott '. Crown 8vo., 3s. 6d.

Works of Fiction, Humour, &c.—*continued.*

Beaconsfield.—Works by the Earl of BEACONSFIELD.

NOVELS AND TALES. Cheap Edition. Complete in 11 vols. Cr. 8vo., 1s. 6d. each.

Vivian Grey.	Henrietta Temple.
The Young Duke, &c.	Venetia. Tancred.
Alroy, Ixion, &c.	Coningsby. Sybil.
Contarini Fleming,&c.	Lothair. Endymion.

NOVELS AND TALES. The Hughenden Edition. With 2 Portraits and 11 Vignettes. 11 vols. Crown 8vo., 42s.

Comyn.—ATHERSTONE PRIORY: a Tale. By L. N. COMYN. Crown 8vo., 2s. 6d.

Deland.—Works by MARGARET DELAND, Author of 'John Ward'.

THE STORY OF A CHILD. Cr. 8vo., 5s.

MR. TOMMY DOVE, and other Stories Crown 8vo. 6s.

Dougall.—Works by L. DOUGALL.

BEGGARS ALL Crown 8vo., 3s. 6d.

WHAT NECESSITY KNOWS. 3 vols. Crown 8vo., 25s. 6d.

Doyle.—Works by A. CONAN DOYLE.

MICAH CLARKE: A Tale of Monmouth's Rebellion. With Frontispiece and Vignette. Cr. 8vo., 3s. 6d.

THE CAPTAIN OF THE POLESTAR, and other Tales. Cr. 8vo., 3s. 6d.

THE REFUGEES: A Tale of Two Continents. Cr. 8vo., 6s.

Farrar.—DARKNESS AND DAWN: or, Scenes in the Days of Nero. An Historic Tale. By Archdeacon FARRAR. Cr. 8vo., 7s. 6d.

Froude.—THE TWO CHIEFS OF DUNBOY: an Irish Romance of the Last Century. by J. A. FROUDE. Cr. 8vo., 3s. 6d.

Haggard.—Works by H. RIDER HAGGARD.

SHE. With 32 Illustrations by M. GREIFFENHAGEN and C. H. M. KERR. Cr. 8vo., 3s. 6d.

ALLAN QUATERMAIN. With 31 Illustrations by C. H. M. KERR. Cr. 8vo., 3s. 6d.

MAIWA'S REVENGE: or, The War of the Little Hand. Cr. 8vo., 1s. boards, 1s. 6d. cloth.

Haggard.—Works by H. RIDER HAGGARD.—*continued.*

COLONEL QUARITCH, V.C. Cr. 8vo. 3s. 6d.

CLEOPATRA. With 29 Full-page Illustrations by M. GREIFFENHAGEN and R. CATON WOODVILLE. Crown 8vo., 3s. 6d.

BEATRICE. Cr. 8vo., 3s. 6d.

ERIC BRIGHTEYES. With 17 Plates and 34 Illustrations in the Text by LANCELOT SPEED. Cr. 8vo., 3s. 6d.

NADA THE LILY. With 23 Illustrations by C. H. M. KERR. Cr. 8vo., 6s.

MONTEZUMA'S DAUGHTER. With 24 Illustrations by M. GREIFFENHAGEN. Crown 8vo., 6s.

Haggard and Lang.—THE WORLD'S DESIRE. By H. RIDER HAGGARD and ANDREW LANG. Cr. 8vo. 6s.

Harte.—IN THE CARQUINEZ WOODS and other stories. By BRET HARTE. Cr. 8vo., 3s. 6d.

KEITH DERAMORE: a Novel. By the Author of 'Miss Molly'. Cr. 8vo., 6s.

Lyall.—THE AUTOBIOGRAPHY OF A SLANDER. By EDNA LYALL, Author of 'Donovan,' &c. Fcp. 8vo., 1s. sewed.

Presentation Edition. With 20 Illustrations by LANCELOT SPEED. Crown 8vo., 5s.

Melville.—Works by G. J. WHYTE MELVILLE.

The Gladiators.	Holmby House.
The Interpreter.	Kate Coventry.
Good for Nothing.	Digby Grand.
The Queen's Maries.	General Bounce.

Cr. 8vo., 1s. 6d. each.

Oliphant.—Works by Mrs. OLIPHANT.

MADAM. Cr. 8vo., 1s. 6d.

IN TRUST. Cr. 8vo., 1s. 6d.

Parr.—CAN THIS BE LOVE? By Mrs. PARR, Author of 'Dorothy Fox'. Crown 8vo. 6s.

Works of Fiction, Humour, &c.—*continued.*

Payn.—Works by JAMES PAYN.

THE LUCK OF THE DARRELLS. Cr. 8vo., 1s. 6d.

THICKER THAN WATER. Cr. 8vo., 1s. 6d.

Phillipps-Wolley.—SNAP: a Legend of the Lone Mountain. By C. PHILLIPPS-WOLLEY. With 13 Illustrations by H. G. WILLINK. Cr. 8vo., 3s. 6d.

Robertson.—THE KIDNAPPED SQUATTER, and other Australian Tales. By. A. ROBERTSON. Cr. 8vo., 6s.

Sewell.—Works by ELIZABETH M. SEWELL.

A Glimpse of the World.	Amy Herbert.
Laneton Parsonage.	Cleve Hall.
Margaret Percival.	Gertrude.
Katharine Ashton.	Home Life.
The Earl's Daughter.	After Life.
The Experience of Life.	Ursula. Ivors.

Cr. 8vo., 1s. 6d. each cloth plain. 2s. 6d. each cloth extra, gilt edges.

Stevenson.—Works by ROBERT LOUIS STEVENSON.

STRANGE CASE OF DR. JEKYLL AND MR. HYDE. Fcp. 8vo., 1s. sewed. 1s. 6d. cloth.

THE DYNAMITER. Fcp. 8vo., 1s. sewed, 1s. 6d. cloth.

Stevenson and Osbourne.—THE WRONG BOX. By ROBERT LOUIS STEVENSON and LLOYD OSBOURNE. Cr. 8vo., 3s. 6d.

Sturgis.—AFTER TWENTY YEARS, and other Stories. By JULIAN STURGIS. Cr. 8vo., 6s.

Suttner.—LAY DOWN YOUR ARMS (*Die Waffen Nieder*): The Autobiography of Martha Tilling. By BERTHA VON SUTTNER. Translated by T. HOLMES. Cr. 8vo., 7s. 6d.

Thompson.—A MORAL DILEMMA: a Novel. By ANNIE THOMPSON. Crown 8vo., 6s.

Tirebuck.—Works by WILLIAM TIREBUCK.

DORRIE. Crown 8vo. 6s.

SWEETHEART GWEN. Crown 8vo., 6s.

Trollope.—Works by ANTHONY TROLLOPE.

THE WARDEN. Cr. 8vo., 1s. 6d.

BARCHESTER TOWERS. Cr. 8vo., 1s. 6d.

Walford.—Works by L. B. WALFORD, Author of ' Mr. Smith '.

THE MISCHIEF OF MONICA: a Novel. Cr. 8vo., 2s. 6d.

THE ONE GOOD GUEST: a Story. Cr. 8vo., 2s. 6d.

West.—HALF-HOURS WITH THE MILLIONAIRES: Showing how much harder it is to spend a million than to make it. Edited by B. B. WEST. Cr. 8vo., 6s.

Weyman.—Works by STANLEY J. WEYMAN.

THE HOUSE OF THE WOLF: a Romance. Cr. 8vo., 3s. 6d.

A GENTLEMAN OF FRANCE. 3 vols. Cr. 8vo. 25s. 6d.

Popular Science (Natural History, &c.).

Butler.—OUR HOUSEHOLD INSECTS. An Account of the Insect-Pests found in Dwelling-Houses. By EDWARD A. BUTLER, B.A., B.Sc. (Lond.). With 113 Illustrations. Crown 8vo., 6s.

Furneaux.—THE OUTDOOR WORLD; or The Young Collector's Handbook. By W. FURNEAUX, F.R.G.S. With 18 Plates, 16 of which are coloured, and 549 Illustrations in the Text. Crown 8vo., 7s. 6d.

Hartwig.—Works by Dr. GEORGE HARTWIG.

THE SEA AND ITS LIVING WONDERS. With 12 Plates and 303 Woodcuts. 8vo., 7s. net.

THE TROPICAL WORLD. With 8 Plates and 172 Woodcuts. 8vo., 7s. net.

THE POLAR WORLD. With 3 Maps, 8 Plates and 85 Woodcuts. 8vo., 7s. net.

Popular Science (Natural History, &c.)—*continued.*

Hartwig.—Works by Dr. George Hartwig—*continued.*

THE SUBTERRANEAN WORLD. With 3
Maps and 80 Woodcuts. 8vo., 7*s.* net.

THE AERIAL WORLD. With Map, 8
Plates and 60 Woodcuts. 8vo., 7*s.* net.

HEROES OF THE POLAR WORLD. 19
Illustrations. Cr. 8vo., 2*s.*

WONDERS OF THE TROPICAL FORESTS.
40 Illustrations. Cr. 8vo., 2*s.*

WORKERS UNDER THE GROUND. 29
Illustrations. Cr. 8vo., 2*s.*

MARVELS OVER OUR HEADS. 29 Illustrations. Cr. 8vo., 2*s.*

SEA MONSTERS AND SEA BIRDS. 75
Illustrations. Cr. 8vo., 2*s.* 6*d.*

DENIZENS OF THE DEEP. 117 Illustrations. Cr. 8vo., 2*s.* 6*d.*

VOLCANOES AND EARTHQUAKES. 30
Illustrations. Cr. 8vo., 2*s.* 6*d.*

WILD ANIMALS OF THE TROPICS. 66
Illustrations. Cr. 8vo., 3*s.* 6*d.*

Helmholtz. — POPULAR LECTURES ON
SCIENTIFIC SUBJECTS. By HERMANN VON
HELMHOLTZ. With 68 Woodcuts. 2 vols.
Cr. 8vo., 3*s.* 6*d.* each.

Lydekker.—PHASES OF ANIMAL LIFE,
PAST AND PRESENT. By. R. LYDEKKER,
B.A. With 82 Illustrations. Cr. 8vo., 6*s.*

Proctor.—Works by RICHARD A. PROCTOR.

LIGHT SCIENCE FOR LEISURE HOURS.
Familiar Essays on Scientific Subjects. 3
vols. Cr. 8vo., 5*s.* each.

CHANCE AND LUCK: a Discussion of
the Laws of Luck, Coincidence, Wagers,
Lotteries and the Fallacies of Gambling,
&c. Cr. 8vo., 2*s.* boards. 2*s.* 6*d.* cloth.

ROUGH WAYS MADE SMOOTH. Familiar
Essays on Scientific Subjects. Cr. 8vo., 5*s.*
Silver Library Edition. Cr. 8vo., 3*s.* 6*d.*

PLEASANT WAYS IN SCIENCE. Cr. 8vo., 5*s.*
Silver Library Edition. Cr. 8vo., 3*s.* 6*d.*

THE GREAT PYRAMID, OBSERVATORY,
TOMB AND TEMPLE. With Illustrations.
Cr. 8vo., 5*s.*

NATURE STUDIES. By R. A. PROCTOR,
GRANT ALLEN, A. WILSON, T. FOSTER
and E. CLODD. Cr. 8vo., 5*s.* Silver
Library Edition. Crown 8vo., 3*s.* 6*d.*

Proctor.—Works by RICHARD A. PROCTOR.
—*continued.*

LEISURE READINGS. By R. A. PROC-
TOR, E. CLODD, A. WILSON, T. FOSTER
and A. C. RANYARD. Cr. 8vo., 5*s.*

Stanley.—A FAMILIAR HISTORY OF BIRDS.
By E. STANLEY, D.D., formerly Bishop of
Norwich. With Illustrations. Cr. 8vo.,
3*s.* 6*d.*

Wood.—Works by the Rev. J. G. WOOD.

HOMES WITHOUT HANDS: a Description
of the Habitation of Animals, classed
according to the Principle of Construction. With 140 Illustrations. 8vo., 7*s.*,
net.

INSECTS AT HOME: a Popular Account
of British Insects, their Structure, Habits
and Transformations. With 700 Illustrations. 8vo., 7*s.* net.

INSECTS ABROAD: a Popular Account
of Foreign Insects, their Structure, Habits
and Transformations. With 600 Illustrations. 8vo., 7*s.* net.

BIBLE ANIMALS: a Description of every
Living Creatures mentioned in the Scrip-
tures. With 112 Illustrations. 8vo., 7*s.*
net.

PETLAND REVISITED. With 33 Illustrations. Cr. 8vo., 3*s.* 6*d.*

OUT OF DOORS; a Selection of Original
Articles on Practical Natural History.
With 11 Illustrations. Cr. 8vo., 3*s.* 6*d.*

STRANGE DWELLINGS: a Description of
the Habitations of Animals, abridged from
' Homes without Hands '. With 60 Illustrations. Cr. 8vo., 3*s.* 6*d.*

BIRD LIFE OF THE BIBLE. 32 Illustrations. Cr. 8vo., 3*s.* 6*d.*

WONDERFUL NESTS. 30 Illustrations.
Cr. 8vo., 3*s.* 6*d.*

HOMES UNDER THE GROUND. 28 Illustrations. Cr. 8vo., 3*s.* 6*d.*

WILD ANIMALS OF THE BIBLE. 29
Illustrations. Cr. 8vo., 3*s.* 6*d.*

DOMESTIC ANIMALS OF THE BIBLE. 23
Illustrations. Cr. 8vo., 3*s.* 6*d.*

THE BRANCH BUILDERS. 28 Illustrations. Cr. 8vo., 2*s.* 6*d.*

SOCIAL HABITATIONS AND PARASITIC
NESTS. 18 Illustrations. Cr. 8vo., 2*s.*

Works of Reference.

Maunder's (Samuel) Treasuries.

BIOGRAPHICAL TREASURY. With Supplement brought down to 1889. By Rev. JAMES WOOD. Fcp. 8vo., 6s.

TREASURY OF NATURAL HISTORY: or, Popular Dictionary of Zoology. With 900 Woodcuts. Fcp. 8vo., 6s.

TREASURY OF GEOGRAPHY, Physical, Historical, Descriptive, and Political. With 7 Maps and 16 Plates. Fcp. 8vo., 6s.

THE TREASURY OF BIBLE KNOWLEDGE. By the Rev. J. AYRE, M.A. With 5 Maps, 15 Plates, and 300 Woodcuts. Fcp. 8vo., 6s.

HISTORICAL TREASURY: Outlines of Universal History, Separate Histories of all Nations. Fcp. 8vo., 6s.

TREASURY OF KNOWLEDGE AND LIBRARY OF REFERENCE. Comprising an English Dictionary and Grammar, Universal Gazeteer, Classical Dictionary, Chronology, Law Dictionary, &c. Fcp. 8vo.. 6s.

Maunder's (Samuel) Treasuries--*continued.*

SCIENTIFIC AND LITERARY TREASURY. Fcp. 8vo., 6s.

THE TREASURY OF BOTANY. Edited by J. LINDLEY, F.R.S., and T. MOORE, F.L.S. With 274 Woodcuts and 20 Steel Plates. 2 vols. Fcp. 8vo., 12s.

Roget.—THESAURUS OF ENGLISH WORDS AND PHRASES. Classified and Arranged so as to Facilitate the Expression of Ideas and assist in Literary Composition. By PETER MARK ROGET, M.D., F.R.S. Recomposed throughout, enlarged and improved, partly from the Author's Notes, and with a full Index, by the Author's Son, JOHN LEWIS ROGET. Crown 8vo., 10s. 6d.

Willich.—POPULAR TABLES for giving information for ascertaining the value of Lifehold, Leasehold, and Church Property, the Public Funds, &c. By CHARLES M. WILLICH. Edited by H. BENCE JONES. Crown 8vo., 10s. 6d.

Children's Books.

Crake.—Works by Rev. A. D. CRAKE.

EDWY THE FAIR ; or, The First Chronicle of Æscendune. Crown 8vo., 2s. 6d.

ALFGAR THE DANE : or, the Second Chronicle of Æscendune. Cr. 8vo. 2s. 6d.

THE RIVAL HEIRS : being the Third and Last Chronicle of Æscendune. Cr. 8vo., 2s. 6d.

THE HOUSE OF WALDERNE. A Tale of the Cloister and the Forest in the Days of the Barons' Wars. Crown 8vo., 2s. 6d.

BRIAN FITZ-COUNT. A Story of Wallingford Castle and Dorchester Abbey. Cr. 8vo., 2s. 6d.

Ingelow.—VERY YOUNG, and QUITE ANOTHER STORY. Two Stories. By JEAN INGELOW. Crown 8vo., 2s. 6d.

Lang.—Works edited by ANDREW LANG.

THE BLUE FAIRY BOOK. With 8 Plates and 130 Illustrations in the Text by H. J. FORD and G. P. JACOMB HOOD. Crown 8vo., 6s.

THE RED FAIRY BOOK. With 4 Plates and 96 Illustrations in the Text by H. J. FORD and LANCELOT SPEED. Crown 8vo., 6s.

Lang.—Works edited by ANDREW LANG. —*continued.*

THE GREEN FAIRY BOOK. With 11 Plates and 88 Illustrations in the Text by H. J. FORD and L. BOGLE. Crown 8vo., 6s.

THE BLUE POETRY BOOK. With 12 Plates and 88 Illustrations in the Text by H. J. FORD and LANCELOT SPEED. Cr. 8vo., 6s.

THE BLUE POETRY BOOK. School Edition, without Illustrations. Fcp. 8vo., 2s. 6d.

THE TRUE STORY BOOK. With 8 Plates and 58 Illustrations in the Text, by H. J. FORD, LUCIEN DAVIS, C. H. M. KERR, LANCELOT SPEED, and LOCKHART BOGLE. Cr. 8vo., 6s.

Meade.—Works by L. T. MEADE.

DADDY'S BOY. With Illustrations. Crown 8vo., 3s. 6d.

DEB AND THE DUCHESS. With Illustrations by M. E. EDWARDS. Crown 8vo., 3s. 6d.

THE BERESFORD PRIZE. With Illustrations by M. E. EDWARDS. Crown 8vo., 5s.

Children's Books— *continued.*

Molesworth.—Works by Mrs. MOLES-WORTH.

SILVERTHORNS. Illustrated. Crown 8vo., 5s.

THE PALACE IN THE GARDEN. Illustrated. Crown 8vo., 5s.

THE THIRD MISS ST. QUENTIN. Crown 8vo., 2s. 6d.

NEIGHBOURS. Illustrated. Crown 8vo., 6s.

THE STORY OF A SPRING MORNING, &c. Illustrated. Crown 8vo., 2s. 6d.

Reader.—VOICES FROM FLOWER-LAND: a Birthday Book and Language of Flowers. By EMILY E. READER. Illustrated by ADA BROOKE. Royal 16mo., cloth, 2s. 6d.; vegetable vellum, 3s. 6d.

Stevenson.—Works by ROBERT LOUIS STEVENSON.

A CHILD'S GARDEN OF VERSES. Small Fcp. 8vo., 5s.

A CHILD'S GARLAND OF SONGS, Gathered from 'A Child's Garden of Verses'. Set to Music by C. VILLIERS STANFORD, Mus. Doc. 4to., 2s. sewed ; 3s. 6d., cloth gilt.

The Silver Library.

CROWN 8VO. 3s. 6d. EACH VOLUME.

Baker's (Sir S. W.) Eight Years in Ceylon. With 6 Illustrations. 3s. 6d.

Baker's (Sir S. W.) Rifle and Hound in Ceylon. With 6 Illustrations. 3s. 6d.

Baring-Gould's (Rev. S.) Curious Myths of the Middle Ages. 3s. 6d.

Baring-Gould's (Rev. S.) Origin and Development of Religious Belief. 2 vols. 3s. 6d. each.

Brassey's (Lady) A Voyage in the 'Sunbeam'. With 66 Illustrations. 3s. 6d.

Clodd's (E.) Story of Creation: a Plain Account of Evolution. With 77 Illustrations. 3s. 6d.

Conybeare (Rev. W. J.) and Howson's (Very Rev. J. S.) Life and Epistles of St. Paul. 46 Illustrations. 3s. 6d.

Dougall's (L.) Beggars All: a Novel. 3s. 6d.

Doyle's (A. Conan) Micah Clarke. A Tale of Monmouth's Rebellion. 3s. 6d.

Doyle's (A. Conan) The Captain of the Polestar, and other Tales. 3s. 6d.

Froude's (J. A.) Short Studies on Great Subjects. 4 vols. 3s. 6d. each.

Froude's (J. A.) Cæsar: a Sketch. 3s. 6d.

Froude's (J. A.) Thomas Carlyle: a History of his Life.
1795-1835. 2 vols. 7s.
1834-1881. 2 vols. 7s.

Froude's (J. A.) The Two Chiefs of Dunboy: an Irish Romance of the Last Century. 3s. 6d.

Froude's (J. A.) The History of England, from the Fall of Wolsey to the Defeat of the Spanish Armada. 12 vols. 3s. 6d. each.

Gleig's (Rev. G. R.) Life of the Duke of Wellington. With Portrait. 3s. 6d.

Haggard's (H. R.) She: A History of Adventure. 32 Illustrations. 3s. 6d.

Haggard's (H. R.) Allan Quatermain. With 20 Illustrations. 3s. 6d.

Haggard's (H. R.) Colonel Quaritch, V.C.: a Tale of Country Life. 3s. 6d.

Haggard's (H. R.) Cleopatra. With 29 Full-page Illustrations. 3s. 6d.

Haggard's (H. R.) Eric Brighteyes. With 51 Illustrations. 3s. 6d.

Haggard's (H. R.) Beatrice. 3s. 6d.

Harte's (Bret) In the Carquinez Woods and other Stories. 3s. 6d.

Helmholtz's (Hermann von) Popular Lectures on Scientific Subjects. With 68 Woodcuts. 2 vols. 3s. 6d. each.

Howitt's (W.) Visits to Remarkable Places. 80 Illustrations. 3s. 6d.

Jefferies' (R.) The Story of My Heart: My Autobiography. With Portrait. 3s. 6d.

Jefferies' (R.) Field and Hedgerow. Last Essays of. With Portrait. 3s. 6d.

Jefferies' (R.) Red Deer. With 17 Illustrations by J. CHARLTON and H. TUNALY. 3s. 6d.

Jefferies' (R.) Wood Magic: a Fable. With Frontispiece and Vignette by E. V. B. 3s. 6d.

Jefferies (R.) The Toilers of the Field. With Portrait from the Bust in Salisbury Cathedral. 3s. 6d.

Knight's (E. F.) The Cruise of the 'Alerte': the Narrative of a Search for Treasure on the Desert Island of Trinidad. With 2 Maps and 23 Illustrations. 3s. 6d.

Lang's (A.) Custom and Myth: Studies of Early Usage and Belief. 3s. 6d.

Lees (J. A.) and Clutterbuck's (W. J.) B. C. 1887, A Ramble in British Columbia. With Maps and 75 Illustrations. 3s. 6d.

Macaulay's (Lord) Essays and Lays of Ancient Rome. With Portrait and Illustration. 3s. 6d.

Macleod's (H. D.) The Elements of Banking. 3s. 6d.

The Silver .Library— *continued.*

Marshman's (J. C.) Memoirs of Sir Henry Havelock. 3s. 6d.

Max Müller's (F.) India, what can it teach us? 3s. 6d.

Max Müller's (F.) Introduction to the Science of Religion. 3s. 6d.

Merivale's (Dean) History of the Romans under the Empire. 8 vols. 3s. 6d. each.

Mill's (J. S.) Principles of Political Economy. 3s. 6d.

Mill's (J. S.) System of Logic. 3s. 6d.

Milner's (Geo.) Country Pleasures : the Chronicle of a Year chiefly in a Garden. 3s. 6d.

Newman's (Cardinal) Apologia Pro Vitâ Sua. 3s. 6d.

Newman's (Cardinal) Historical Sketches. 3 vols. 3s. 6d. each.

Newman's (Cardinal) Callista : a Tale of the Third Century. 3s. 6d.

Newman's (Cardinal) Loss and Gain : a Tale. 3s. 6d.

Newman's (Cardinal) Essays, Critical and Historical. 2 vols. 7s.

Newman's (Cardinal) An Essay on the Development of Christian Doctrine. 3s. 6d.

Newman's (Cardinal) The Arians of the Fourth Century. 3s. 6d.

Newman's (Cardinal) Verses on Various Occasions. 3s. 6d.

Newman's (Cardinal) The Present Position of Catholics in England. 3s. 6d.

Newman's (Cardinal) Parochial and Plain Sermons. 8 vols. 3s. 6d. each.

Newman's (Cardinal) Selection, adapted to the Seasons of the Ecclesiastical Year, from the ' Parochial and Plain Sermons '. 3s. 6d.

Newman's (Cardinal) Sermons bearing upon Subjects of the Day. 3s. 6d.

Newman's (Cardinal) Difficulties felt by Anglicans in Catholic Teaching Considered. 2 vols. 3s. 6d. each.

Newman's (Cardinal) The Idea of a University Defined and Illustrated. 3s. 6d.

Newman's (Cardinal) Biblical and Ecclesiastical Miracles. 3s. 6d.

Newman's (Cardinal) Discussions and Arguments on Various Subjects. 3s. 6d.

Newman's (Cardinal) Grammar of Assent. 3s. 6d.

Newman's (Cardinal) Fifteen Sermons Preached before the University of Oxford. 3s. 6d.

Newman's (Cardinal) Lectures on the Doctrine of Justification. 3s. 6d.

Newman's (Cardinal) Sermons on Various Occasions. 3s. 6d.

Newman's (Cardinal) The Via Media of the Anglican Church, illustrated in Lectures, &c. 2 vols. 3s. 6d. each.

Newman's (Cardinal) Discourses to Mixed Congregations. 3s. 6d.

Phillipps-Wolley's (C.) Snap : a Legend of the Lone Mountain. With 13 Illustrations. 3s. 6d.

Proctor's (R. A.) The Orbs Around Us : Essays on the Moon and Planets, Meteors and Comets, the Sun and Coloured Pairs of Suns. 3s. 6d.

Proctor's (R. A.) The Expanse of Heaven : Essays on the Wonders of the Firmament. 3s. 6d.

Proctor's (R. A.) Other Worlds than Ours. 3s. 6d.

Proctor's (R. A.) Rough Ways made Smooth. 3s. 6d.

Proctor's (R. A.) Pleasant Ways in Science. 3s. 6d.

Proctor's (R. A.) Myths and Marvels of Astronomy. 3s. 6d.

Proctor's (R. A.) Nature Studies. 3s. 6d.

Smith (R. Bosworth) Carthage and the Carthaginians. With Maps, Plans, &c. 3s. 6d.

Stanley's (Bishop) Familiar History of Birds. 160 Illustrations. 3s. 6d.

Stevenson (R. L.) and Osbourne's (Ll.) The Wrong Box. 3s. 6d.

Weyman's (Stanley J.) The House of the Wolf : a Romance. 3s. 6d.

Wood's (Rev. J. G.) Petland Revisited. With 33 Illustrations. 3s. 6d.

Wood's (Rev. J. G.) Strange Dwellings. With 60 Illustrations. 3s. 6d.

Wood's (Rev. J. G.) Out of Doors. 11 Illustrations. 3s. 6d.

Cookery, Domestic Management, etc.

Acton.—MODERN COOKERY. By ELIZA ACTON. With 150 Woodcuts. Fcp. 8vo., 4s. 6d.

Bull.—Works by THOMAS BULL, M.D.

HINTS TO MOTHERS ON THE MANAGEMENT OF THEIR HEALTH DURING THE PERIOD OF PREGNANCY. Fcp. 8vo., 1s. 6d.

THE MATERNAL MANAGEMENT OF CHILDREN IN HEALTH AND DISEASE. Fcp. 8vo., 1s. 6d.

De Salis.—Works by Mrs. DE SALIS.

CAKES AND CONFECTIONS À LA MODE. Fcp. 8vo., 1s. 6d.

DOGS ; A Manual for Amateurs. Fcp. 8vo.

DRESSED GAME AND POULTRY À LA MODE. Fcp. 8vo., 1s. 6d.

DRESSED VEGETABLES À LA MODE. Fcp. 8vo., 1s. 6d.

DRINKS À LA MODE. Fcp. 8vo., 1s. 6d.

ENTRÉES À LA MODE. Fcp. 8vo., 1s. 6d.

Cookery and Domestic Management—*continued.*

De Salis.—Works by Mrs. De Salis—*cont.*
FLORAL DECORATIONS. Suggestions and Descriptions. Fcp. 8vo., 1s. 6d.
NEW-LAID EGGS: Hints for Amateur Poultry Rearers. Fcp. 8vo., 1s. 6d.
OYSTERS À LA MODE. Fcp. 8vo., 1s. 6d.
PUDDINGS AND PASTRY À LA MODE. Fcp. 8vo., 1s. 6d.
SAVOURIES À LA MODE. Fcp. 8vo., 1s. 6d.
SOUPS AND DRESSED FISH À LA MODE. Fcp. 8vo., 1s. 6d.
SWEETS AND SUPPER DISHES À LA MODE. Fcp. 8vo., 1s. 6d.
TEMPTING DISHES FOR SMALL INCOMES. Fcp. 8vo., 1s. 6d.
WRINKLES AND NOTIONS FOR EVERY HOUSEHOLD. Crown 8vo., 1s. 6d.

Harrison.—COOKERY FOR BUSY LIVES AND SMALL INCOMES. By MARY HARRISON. Crown 8vo., 1s.

Lear.—MAIGRE COOKERY. By H. L. SIDNEY LEAR. 16mo., 2s.

Poole.--COOKERY FOR THE DIABETIC. By W. H. and Mrs. POOLE. With Preface by Dr. PAVY. Fcp. 8vo., 2s. 6d.

Walker.—A HANDBOOK FOR MOTHERS: being Simple Hints to Women on the Management of their Health during Pregnancy and Confinement, together with Plain Directions as to the Care of Infants. By JANE H. WALKER, L.R.C.P. and L.M., L.R.C.S. and M.D. (Brux). Crown 8vo., 2s. 6d.

Miscellaneous and Critical Works.

Allingham.—VARIETIES IN PROSE. By WILLIAM ALLINGHAM. 3 vols. Crown 8vo., 18s. (Vols. 1 and 2, Rambles, by PATRICIUS WALKER. Vol. 3, Irish Sketches, etc.)

Armstrong.—ESSAYS AND SKETCHES. By EDMUND J. ARMSTRONG. Fcp. 8vo., 5s.

Bagehot.—LITERARY STUDIES. By WALTER BAGEHOT. 2 vols. 8vo., 28s.

Baring-Gould.—CURIOUS MYTHS OF THE MIDDLE AGES. By Rev. S. BARING-GOULD. Crown 8vo., 3s. 6d.

Battye.—PICTURES IN PROSE OF NATURE, WILD SPORT, AND HUMBLE LIFE. By AUBYN TREVOR BATTYE, B.A.

Boyd ('A. K. H. B.').—Works by A. K. H. BOYD, D.D., LL.D.
AUTUMN HOLIDAYS OF A COUNTRY PARSON. Crown 8vo., 3s. 6d.
COMMONPLACE PHILOSOPHER. Crown 8vo., 3s. 6d.
CRITICAL ESSAYS OF A COUNTRY PARSON. Crown 8vo., 3s. 6d.
EAST COAST DAYS AND MEMORIES. Crown 8vo., 3s. 6d.
LANDSCAPES, CHURCHES AND MORALITIES. Crown 8vo., 3s. 6d.
LEISURE HOURS IN TOWN. Crown 8vo., 3s. 6d.
LESSONS OF MIDDLE AGE. Crown 8vo., 3s. 6d.
OUR LITTLE LIFE. Two Series. Cr. 8vo., 3s. 6d. each.
OUR HOMELY COMEDY: AND TRAGEDY Crown 8vo., 3s. 6d.
RECREATIONS OF A COUNTRY PARSON. Three Series. Crown 8vo., 3s. 6d. each. Also First Series. Popular Ed. 8vo., 6d.

Butler.—Works by SAMUEL BUTLER.
Op. 1. EREWHON. Cr. 8vo., 5s.
Op. 2. THE FAIR HAVEN. A Work in Defence of the Miraculous Element in our Lord's Ministry. Cr. 8vo., 7s. 6d.
Op. 3. LIFE AND HABIT. An Essay after a Completer View of Evolution. Cr. 8vo., 7s. 6d.
Op. 4. EVOLUTION, OLD AND NEW. Cr. 8vo., 10s. 6d.
Op. 5. UNCONSCIOUS MEMORY. Cr. 8vo., 7s. 6d.
Op. 6. ALPS AND SANCTUARIES OF PIEDMONT AND CANTON TICINO. Illustrated. Pott 4to., 10s. 6d.
Op. 7. SELECTIONS FROM OPS. 1-6. With Remarks on Mr. ROMANES' 'Mental Evolution in Animals'. Cr. 8vo., 7s. 6d.
Op. 8. LUCK, OR CUNNING, AS THE MAIN MEANS OF ORGANIC MODIFICATION? Cr. 8vo., 7s. 6d.
Op. 9. EX VOTO. An Account of the Sacro Monte or New Jerusalem at Varallo-Sesia. 10s. 6d.
HOLBEIN'S 'LA DANSE'. A Note on a Drawing called 'La Danse'. 3s.

Halliwell-Phillipps.—A CALENDAR OF THE HALLIWELL-PHILLIPPS' COLLECTION OF SHAKESPEAREAN RARITIES. Enlarged by ERNEST E. BAKER, F.S.A. 8vo., 10s. 6d.

Hodgson.—OUTCAST ESSAYS AND VERSE TRANSLATIONS. By H. SHADWORTH HODGSON. Crown 8vo., 8s. 6d.

Miscellaneous and Critical Works – *continued.*

Hullah.—Works by John Hullah, LL.D.

COURSE OF LECTURES ON THE HISTORY OF MODERN MUSIC. 8vo., 8s. 6d.

COURSE OF LECTURES ON THE TRANSITION PERIOD OF MUSICAL HISTORY. 8vo., 10s. 6d.

James.—MINING ROYALTIES: their Practical Operation and Effect. By Charles Ashworth James, of Lincoln's Inn, Barrister-at-Law. Fcp. 4to., 5s.

Jefferies.—Works by Richard Jefferies.

FIELD AND HEDGEROW: last Essays. With Portrait. Crown 8vo., 3s. 6d.

THE STORY OF MY HEART: my Autobiography. With Portrait and New Preface by C. J. Longman. Crown 8vo., 3s. 6d.

RED DEER. With 17 Illustrations by J. Charlton and H. Tunaly. Crown 8vo., 3s. 6d.

THE TOILERS OF THE FIELD. With Portrait from the Bust in Salisbury Cathedral. Crown 8vo., 3s. 6d.

WOOD MAGIC: a Fable. With Frontispiece and Vignette by E. V. B. Crown 8vo., 3s. 6d.

Jewsbury.—SELECTIONS FROM THE LETTERS OF GERALDINE ENDSOR JEWSBURY TO JANE WELSH CARLYLE. Edited by Mrs. Alexander Ireland. 8vo., 16s.

Johnson.—THE PATENTEE'S MANUAL: a Treatise on the Law and Practice of Letters Patent. By J. & J. H. Johnson, Patent Agents, &c. 8vo., 10s. 6d.

Lang.—Works by Andrew Lang.

LETTERS TO DEAD AUTHORS. Fcp. 8vo., 2s. 6d. net.

BOOKS AND BOOKMEN. With 2 Coloured Plates and 17 Illustrations. Fcp. 8vo., 2s. 6d. net.

OLD FRIENDS. Fcp. 8vo., 2s. 6d. net.

LETTERS ON LITERATURE. Fcp. 8vo., 2s. 6d. net.

Macfarren.—LECTURES ON HARMONY. By Sir George A. Macfarren. 8vo., 12s.

Max Müller.—Works by F. Max Müller.

HIBBERT LECTURES ON THE ORIGIN AND GROWTH OF RELIGION, as illustrated by the Religions of India. Crown 8vo., 7s. 6d.

INTRODUCTION TO THE SCIENCE OF RELIGION: Four Lectures delivered at the Royal Institution. Crown 8vo., 3s. 6d.

NATURAL RELIGION. The Gifford Lectures, 1888. Crown 8vo., 10s. 6d.

PHYSICAL RELIGION. The Gifford Lectures, 1890. Crown 8vo., 10s. 6d.

10,000/1/94.

Max Müller.—Works by F. Max Müller.—*continued.*

ANTHROPOLOGICAL RELIGION. The Gifford Lectures, 1891. Cr. 8vo., 10s. 6d.

THEOSOPHY OR PSYCHOLOGICAL RELIGION. The Gifford Lectures, 1892. Crown 8vo., 10s. 6d.

INDIA: WHAT CAN IT TEACH US? Cr. 8vo., 3s. 6d.

Mendelssohn.—THE LETTERS OF FELIX MENDELSSOHN. Translated by Lady Wallace. 2 vols. Cr. 8vo., 10s.

Milner.—Works by George Milner.

COUNTRY PLEASURES: the Chronicle of a Year chiefly in a Garden. Cr. 8vo., 3s. 6d.

STUDIES OF NATURE ON THE COAST OF ARRAN. With Illustrations by W. Noel Johnson.

Perring.—HARD KNOTS IN SHAKESPEARE. By Sir Philip Perring, Bart. 8vo., 7s. 6d.

Proctor.—Works by Richard A. Proctor.

STRENGTH AND HAPPINESS. With 9 Illustrations. Crown 8vo., 5s.

STRENGTH: How to get Strong and keep Strong, with Chapters on Rowing and Swimming, Fat, Age, and the Waist. With 9 Illustrations. Crown 8vo., 2s.

Richardson.—NATIONAL HEALTH. A Review of the Works of Sir Edwin Chadwick, K.C.B. By Sir B. W. Richardson, M.D. Cr., 4s. 6d.

Roget.—A HISTORY OF THE 'OLD WATER-COLOUR' SOCIETY (now the Royal Society of Painters in Water-Colours). By John Lewis Roget. 2 vols. Royal 8vo., 42s.

Rossetti.—A SHADOW OF DANTE: being an Essay towards studying Himself, his World and his Pilgrimage. By Maria Francesca Rossetti. With Illustrations and with designs on cover by Dante Gabriel Rossetti. Cr. 8vo., 10s. 6d.

Southey.—CORRESPONDENCE WITH CAROLINE BOWLES. By Robert Southey. Edited by E. Dowden. 8vo., 14s.

Wallaschek.—PRIMITIVE MUSIC: an Inquiry into the Origin and Development of Music, Songs, Instruments, Dances, and Pantomimes of Savage Races. By Richard Wallaschek. With Musical Examples. 8vo., 12s. 6d.

West.—WILLS, AND HOW NOT TO MAKE THEM. With a Selection of Leading Cases. By B. B. West, Author of "Half-Hours with the Millionaires". Fcp. 8vo., 2s. 6d.